VillageTowns

The Next Step

VillageTown: a town of villages, built on the foundation of a sustainable market economy that creates an enriched, vibrant urban culture to support the social pursuits of Conviviality, Citizenship, Artistic, Intellectual & Spiritual Growth

10,000 population	Socially & culturally enriched
500 acres total made up of:	No cars within the village walls
20 villages with public plazas	Citizen-owned market economy
Each with its own distinct character	Affordable, a complete community
A cosmopolitan town center	Self-sustaining for 7 generations
A walk-to industrial park	For all ages and all stages of life
300-acre outer greenbelt	Self-funded and self-regulating

Jackson House Publishing Company
Auckland New Zealand

ISBN 978-0-9582868-8-6

Disclaimer: Nothing in this book/document is a representation, commitment or offer. The ideas presented herein are presented for general information only. They are not intended as legal, financial, investment or real-estate advice and must not be relied on as such. They may serve as a starting point from which such documents may be developed as part of the process of moving forward from a good idea worth doing to a plan to be put in place.

The VillageTown Stewards and Company is established to promote the building of VillageTowns worldwide. For more information, contact the company at:

The VillageTown Stewards and Co.
Church Bay Estate
Waiheke Island, 1971, New Zealand
Web site: www.villageforum.com
E-mail: info@villageforum.com
US Telephone (520) 505 9000
NZ telephone: 021-113-1600

Introduction / Invitation

We live in a time of unprecedented material wealth, in which more people have access to more resources and treasures than ever before in the known history of humanity. More of us are educated, giving us entry to the world's repository of knowledge through global systems of person-to-person communication that are almost free. Technology offers us extraordinary new capability almost every week. The totality of broad-based democratic wealth – meaning wealth available to the average person in first-world countries – is greater than ever before in history. It's not perfect, but it is unprecedented and on an upward path.

Yet with all this, something seems to be missing, not working right. As our tools and toys become more sophisticated, our sense of place, community, and common locality seem to be growing ever more hollow and bland. Everything is beginning to feel like everything else; every place is beginning to look like everywhere else. Somehow we are not taking advantage of the freedom and riches offered by our civilization, and all the while people report anxiety or outright fear about their future and the future of their loved ones.

What's missing is true community – authentic community that has character, is enriched in more ways than material and enables us to enjoy a good life; indeed, we are hard pressed to even define what a good life means. So we started anew; we began by asking fundamental questions, such as *What is the purpose of building communities?* and *Why do we waste so much time, money and energy doing things we don't enjoy, don't love and really don't even need?*

These questions led us to a plan to enable people to build what we call a VillageTown. This book describes what a VillageTown is, and then goes on to lay out the path to go from a good idea worth doing to a real, built, 10,000 person *common locality*; a community consisting of 20 side-by-side villages in a 150-acre car-free urban core built around a town center, with a 50-acre, walk-to industrial park, all surrounded by a 300-acre Greenbelt.

It becomes interesting when we get to the details. What happens if instead of using a developer who keeps the profits, we set up an *organizing company* that is recast into an *operating company* whose profits are then owned by the VillageTown citizens? What construction savings do we realize if all 4,000 homes and workplaces are built at the same time? How can we use those savings to invest to provide for our needs and aspirations?

Why should we build communities? To enable people to enjoy a good life, understood as the social pursuits of conviviality, citizenship, and artistic, intellectual & spiritual growth. *What should we build to facilitate those pursuits?* To answer that takes a whole book – this book. As you read it, you will find it tells how we intend to enable you to define what is important to you; how we empower you to get there. If family is important, it shows how to create a place that supports family. If the arts are important to you, this book shows how to create (and fund) a culturally-enriched community that is never boring. All these pursuits are built upon a solid economic foundation, creating local markets to support small-to-medium enterprises, while combining purchasing power to enable the community and its privately owned businesses to achieve economies of scale. There are many details; we invite you to learn more: read on.

It's Different

If you have not heard about VillageTowns before, please approach the idea with an open mind. It's not what you think it will be. It's different. It is different because it is driven by common sense rather than what drives so much of life today.

It took about two decades of conversation, research, travel, photography, writing, public speaking and reality checking to assemble the very wide range of details – what Christopher Alexander calls *patterns* as in *A Pattern Language* – to come up with the concept for VillageTowns. A great deal of it was collected rather than thought up – the best ideas have been around a long time, but some of the best tools to get things done have been invented only recently. It's a pragmatic mix of what works. Effectiveness is the measure.

As an idea, it takes people as they are; it does not tell people how to live, what to believe or how to act. It does, however, create the framework for what is called a *Social Contract*. Unlike the 18th century view of that concept, in the founding of the VillageTown the social contract is a very real event. Literally, 8,000 adults (*citizens*) and to a lesser extent, their 2,000 children, build their individual futures simultaneously. Most will not know each other; they will have different outlooks, views, indeed may even speak different languages. Each village will share common values that attracted their founders in the first place, but the VillageTown is intended to have a diversity of villages to keep life interesting.

For economic reasons, the VillageTown has to kick-start fast – a local business requiring a critical mass of 10,000 people cannot wait five years for stages of homes to be occupied. People carrying a mortgage or paying rent cannot afford to wait years for completion of their new home. Thus, the move-in week (or month) for the VillageTown will resemble opening day at a large university – many people moving in and beginning to create a social, cultural and economic experience. Welcome to Campus Earth.

Unlike the university, however, the VillageTown is intended as a permanent, multi-generational, *complete community*. It is intended that it plan for seven generations. For people whose ancestors are a melting pot, the VillageTown offers the opportunity to put down roots, find security, and begin to enjoy a good life. Connection becomes important.

The social contract is an agreement among individuals and families. As set out in the definitions on page 14, the social contract is a founding document accepted by all buyers and residents as a condition of habitation. They agree to abide by common rules, as made from time to time by their elected representatives. They agree they will have obligations and duties to protect individuals, property, the social fabric of the community, and to provide for (and enhance) individual wellbeing and VillageTown commonwealth. Because the people of each VillageTown are different, the particulars of each social contract are different – the VillageTown concept provides the means and the framework for development, but the future citizens decide on the content – it's their life, not ours.

Perhaps one of the more significant differences has to do with money and the local economy. The VillageTown keeps the profits of its construction. There is no developer. Because market forces determine the price of all the homes (except the subsidized *parallel-market* homes), and because there is a huge savings when 4,000 homes are built at the same time using high-volume production systems, the profits from such a development are likely to be in the hundreds of millions of dollars ($, £, €, ¥, etc). The sponsors of the VillageTown, the VillageTown Stewards & Company, collect a 10% reinvestment premium to fund future VillageTown development, but then leave the remaining hundreds of millions in profits in what becomes the VillageTown Operating Company – a private corporation that is owned by the citizens of the VillageTown. This company is a hybrid. Using corporate and contract law, it provides local governance, and also operates as a tax-paying private corporation serving the interests of its stakeholders (VillageTown citizens).

Those profits are established as a *Legacy Fund* whose skilled managers are charged with the job of investing in the community and its private sector businesses, planning for seven generations (175 years). The fund not only loans to or invests in local businesses, but it provides high-level professional expertise usually available only to large corporations – it levels the playing field. The fund also enables the VillageTown to guarantee zero unemployment (by supporting *standby-jobs*) and zero poverty (by its inherent design). As citizens, you own the Legacy Fund and the VillageTown corporation – it's your money.

Parents of school-age children comment that the educational approach is exceptionally different and very attractive: no school campuses. Primary classrooms are on the village plazas, next to offices, shops, cafés and all the other activities of adults in the village. Students have a thousand role models; they participate in life and see the point of their subject matter. They dine at home or in the village cafés. Sport is on the greenbelt. For high school, there are three or four *colleges* in the Town Center – academic, vocational, arts and perhaps high-tech. The arts schools also have classrooms in the *Artist Guild Halls* that are on each village plaza to support the *Creative Class*. 25 artists in each guild, 20 guilds, assures the VillageTown a culturally enriched environment. Education becomes a core part of good citizenship.

For those approaching their elder years, the VillageTown provides security. No cars within the village walls means one may live in the village until death. Elder housing and settled work enables independent living; self-insured nursing care provides beds in facilities on the plazas so elders remain a part of the community even when severely infirm.

In addition to families, for those who are single, or young adults, elders, or the creative class, or for people who now find only big cities offer them a place, the VillageTown provides hospitable habitat. As a complete community, it offers a wide range of entertainment and employment. Its walk-to industrial park supports blue-collar work. Its cosmopolitan town center hosts white-collar office jobs. In each village, especially around each village plaza, it allows and supports work space for many small businesses, shops and private enterprise.

In short, a VillageTown is new; it's old; it's different; it's a better place to call home.

THE BIG PICTURE

The world faces many challenges that were unknown a century ago. Some are global in magnitude – related to pollution, wasteful consumption of limited resources, economic instability, decline in educational standards, alienation and unemployment among youth, a desperate future for elders, rising crime, substance abuse, sharp increases in cancer and new diseases as well as poorer health, concern for food and water supplies and much more.

If we examine these social, economic, environmental and medical problems, we find a common denominator: the human **Driving Home-Range**. The term *home-range* was coined in 1943 by Zoologist William H. Burt who mapped the outside boundary of an animal's movement during the course of its everyday activities. If we apply this same concept to the home-range of a community of human beings who adopted the American model of mobility – a unsustainable model developed after World War II to provide markets for the industrial winners of the war (General Motors, Standard Oil, Dupont, etc.) – we find the home-range of the average American is based on driving a car over 35 miles a day. For a 10,000-population community, this means over a quarter-million miles of driving every day. It also means people become separated, and this social separation creates many new problems. The problem is not cars and roads; rather it is how we use cars and roads.

If we were to design communities based on a **Walking Home-Range**, we would need to change nothing in terms of cars and roads, yet many problems listed in the first paragraph would go into remission. That idea forms the foundation of what we call the **VillageTown**.

And that's just part of it. There is more to the VillageTown than a walking home-range.

Somewhere along the way, we stopped calling people citizens, and began to call them consumers. We lost our sense of why we build communities in the first place. Economic justification evolved from the foundation to the reason for being. We now educate children to get a job, rather than become fully-formed adults. If instead, we ask why we *should* build communities, we find the best answer was written over 2,300 years ago. **Polis** is the Greek word for one of the oldest and most proven models of community, what today we call the city-state. Aristotle explained that when several villages come together to form a self-supporting local economy, the purpose of the polis is to enable its people to enjoy *a good life* understood as the social pursuits of **conviviality, citizenship, and artistic, intellectual & spiritual growth**. The polis' *human-scaled* walking-home-range opens up a world of possibilities.

We coined **VillageTown** as a new word derived from polis to describe an urban home-range of about half a mile square in which everything people require to meet their needs and aspirations is local: economic, convivial, educational/political, creative and spiritual pursuits. It is a **complete community**, a common locality that combines 21st-century technology with the principles of a good life that was the purpose of the ancient *Polis* city-state.

First, let's do the numbers:* To achieve critical mass, optimal VillageTown population is 10,000 persons on a 500-acre /*200 hectare* greenfield site. It consists of a 150-acre /*60h* urban core and a 50-acre /*20h* industrial park, surrounded by a 300-acre /*120h* greenbelt that provides access to real Nature and a buffer zone that prevents cross-boundary conflicts. Within the urban core, a central cosmopolitan town center is surrounded by twenty 500-person villages. Each village is different; each is designed by the people who will live there: a sub-community that shares a value-set that gives the village its look, feel and character. Each village has its own central plaza surrounded by cafés, shops, offices, classrooms, chapel and an artist guild hall.

Next, let's talk money: 75% of the homes will be at market price, 25% targeted for lower-priced **parallel markets** to ensure the VillageTown remains a complete community; for the full range of society, not solely the privileged or elite. Net profits from the project will be in the hundreds of millions. Instead of a developer extracting those millions, after a 10% reinvestment premium, net profits go to a VillageTown operating company owned by the VillageTown citizens. Why? It rewards the buyers for committing up front, and it's necessary if we want a self-supporting local economy. It's essential if we seek **commonwealth** to assure no unemployment, no poverty, and during global hard times, resilience and continued wealth.

What's it like living there? First, it's safe. There are no cars in the villages and no outbound commuters. Children learn autonomy and independence living in a community where they are known and protected, not needing to rely on parents to drive them around. It also means elders need not move away when they can no longer drive. This cultural link between old and young is restored, and parents get a helping hand from older folk.

It's more secure – economically and socially. With its commercial and industrial centers, it creates jobs and creates wealth. With 20 villages, people know and look out for each other; small communities have a natural low tolerance for crime. It provides for the young, for young adults starting out, for single persons, the elderly and the weak as well as for mainstream folk.

It's socially and culturally enriched. Each village is different; walking from one to another is like travelling from one country to another. Each plaza has a development-funded *artist guild hall* to attract the creative class that provides cultural enrichment. Great, local food is featured: the VillageTown contracts with surrounding farmers to grow its food. Children have hundreds of role models in each village; their classrooms are on the plazas: while learning the basics, they observe adults living lives. Socially, it balances public and private space to enable people to get along. Environmentally, it's fully sustainable.

In order to achieve critical mass, all construction must occur at once: target 12 months from ground breaking to ribbon cutting. It seeks all permits in 3 months: as a development with almost zero adverse impact - no commuters, no noise, no pollution, it pays its own way and adds hundreds of millions to the regional economy. In exchange it asks for cooperation.

There is a lot more to VillageTowns. If we have captured your attention, please read on...

---

* Note: When we cite numbers, sizes, quantities, costs and prices, please appreciate that these serve only as a starting point – an estimate. Actual numbers will vary, as each project will conform to circumstances.

TABLE OF CONTENTS

A large book with over 400 color photographs, *How to Build a VillageTown* introduces the idea of a different way to live. It shows what is possible and how it is possible.

Life Liberty Happiness is intended as a faster read to get a feeling for life in a VillageTown. It tells the story of the retired town planner for Blandville – *the town that could be anywhere.* Having been responsible for over 50 years of development that turned Blandville into the archetypal

suburban sprawl, he lost his driver license when someone crashed into his car. Unable to get around, he sells his home and arranges for a driver to take him to a retirement home. He has no choice as he resigns himself to an empty future where he will have little to do other than keep himself comfortably busy while he waits to die. As his driver transports him one last time along the wide boulevards of Blandville, he points out to the driver the hollowness of what he helped build since the 1950's... a place built not to serve its citizens, but to sell more cars.

They stop for lunch at a VillageTown and are invited to take a tour. As he walks from one village to another, he meets locals, each of whom tell their story of life in their village. Most of the stories are real, and some were written by guest authors including former Secretary of the Interior Stewart L. Udall, Corporate Anthropologist Michael Henderson, Evolution Biologist Elisabet Sahtouris and others.

How to use this book – take the next step

After becoming familiar with the ideas in the first two books – *How to Build a VillageTown* that introduces the ideas and *Life Liberty Happiness* describing the look and feel of VillageTown life – some readers will be ready to move on to the next step – doing it.

This book is written to help accomplish that. It is not the business plan, which is far more complicated and would not make a particularly interesting read for the general public. This book sets out the major elements, the path and milestones that will lead from good idea to ground breaking to ribbon-cutting day.

The first challenge faced in such a journey is understanding what a VillageTown is in the first place. There are two reasons for this:

1. It's a new concept. For people to work together on it, they need to understand it.

2. It's not what pundits think it is. What passes for normal in today's world includes many systems and ways of doing things that fail to deliver. The VillageTown concept is not about trying to repair systems that no longer work well; it is about implementing or creating integrated systems that do work. Many people focused on fixing failing systems tend to look at the VillageTown through that distorted lens. Because of those distortions, they hopelessly confuse both themselves and others. They don't get it.

The second challenge: it's a big job. Make no mistake about it, this is a billion-dollar, complex project that involves 4,000 homes, 20 car-free villages and an industrial park – all constructed in one or two years. If a person with no experience or track record loves the idea, and they decide they will build a VillageTown, the result likely will be shambles and the VillageTown concept unfairly damaged by their attempt. Thus roles are set out in this book. There is a place for people who love the idea; indeed, they play an essential role. But to do it right, it is essential to employ the best professionals money can buy and give them a formal structure and proper funding. That structure and those roles are also set out in this book.

How should you use this book? Read it with a highlighter pen and notebook by your side. Consider forming a circle of people to read and discuss it together. Use the internet and connect through the VillageForum.com web site. Don't accept everything in the book as gospel; it is a work in progress as it moves forward. Ask questions, put forth ideas.

Become involved. Perhaps you want to become a core participant or a VillageTown Steward, or you want to work for one of the organizing companies. Use email to contact us.

After reading this book, do not put it on the shelf. Loan it to someone else or leave it at a café with the words "Café Copy" on it. Don't let this book gather dust; keep it in front of people. If you can afford it buy more copies, give them away to key people. Spread the word.

IF YOU ARE...

In today's world, it is said that if you cannot explain your idea in three minutes (the *elevator speech*) people will not listen. This is a challenge when one seeks to explain the VillageTown concept. There are so many different aspects to it. For example, we found the idea of a $200-million Legacy Fund was thrilling an entrepreneur with a great but struggling company, but of no interest to the designer and teacher parents of a young family concerned about day-to-day life and opportunity for their children.

In *How to Build a VillageTown*, chapter 1 begins on page 46. Before that there are fourteen different introductions, depending on who you are. So here is a two-page summary:

Baby Boomer: You need a plan. Old age is coming on sooner than you think. Soon there will be more sellers than buyers; the value of your house, investments and pension may drop; not slightly, but precipitously. Plus, there will be too many of your peers looking for government support; something will break. You should have started planning ten years ago, but since you didn't, get busy now. The VillageTown offers you a plan. Get a preview on page 101.

Entrepreneur: You need a more supportive environment, access to investment, expertise and affordable facilities. You also need a life outside of work, one that is stimulating and supportive; and that gives you time with family and friends. See page 58 for more detail.

Creative Class: You are an artist, musician, writer, film-maker; perhaps an inventor, scientist, designer or scholar. Your passion is creating; even if does not pay well. In tribal societies such people were supported by the rest of the community. In modern society, it's an endless struggle; you spend more time trying to pay the bills than creating. The VillageTown needs you, and is prepared to invest significant capital to enable you to create. Turn to page 127.

Elder: There was a time when at your age you had respect, security and remained a vital part of life. The VillageTown restores that. No cars in the villages means you need not move away when they take your license away. Settled work and elder housing are provided. Nursing care is self-insured; it's local care so you can remain in your village. See page 121.

Parents of a Young Family: What's most important? Safety for your children? A quality and meaningful education for them? That they grow up well, learning independence and autonomy so they become happy, thriving, participating members of society? The VillageTown is safe; it has no cars within and because everyone works locally – no commuting away. Your children's classrooms are on the village plaza; they have a thousand role models. It's a complete community, not a sterile suburb or crazy city. Go to page 110.

Young Person Starting Out: You have finished school and are looking for your first job. The VillageTown had designed affordable housing specifically intended for young people under age 26. You buy and build equity for your future. Youth said they wanted their own youth zone, so they could party, dance in the streets, be louder without bothering older folk. Good idea. The VillageTown has a policy of zero unemployment. If you want to work, the Legacy Fund will help you find a job if you can't find one on your own. See page 115

Single person or childless couple: Suburbs are notoriously inhospitable to people who do not follow the path of coupling and child raising. Singles and childless couples find they are more comfortable in the cities. The VillageTown is a *complete community*. It provides for a diversity of life styles, including encouraging villages for people who choose alternative life styles, including not having children. Such villages within the VillageTown will probably be more active and cosmopolitan; trendy with more discretionary income. See page 119.

Elected Official or Government Policy Maker: The VillageTown starts with a clean sheet. It then seeks to ask all the questions – and find the best answers – before it puts a plan forward. It solves a host of problems that make governing so challenging. Environmentally, economically and socially, it removes the problems: no cars within, no outbound commuters or shoppers; clean energy, self-contained waste-management and water-handling; zero poverty, zero unemployment, low crime and little burden on the criminal justice system; better and lower-cost education, better and lower-cost care for the weak, infirm and elderly, better health and lower-cost health-care; an economic boost to the region without commensurate financial burden on the surrounding taxpayers, no cross-boundary conflicts thanks to the Greenbelt; a regional (or even national) visitor attraction with festivals and events year-round. And many more benefits that don't fit in one paragraph. See page 232.

Master Planner, Architect or Designer: You will either love it or hate it, depending on how comfortable you are with the extent to which VillageTowns are outside the town-planning box. You have an important role, but it's not your show. The VillageTown needs you to enable the people who will live there to create the sort of character and authenticity that only comes when those who live with the results are involved with its design. It's their future, not yours; your job helps them to provide for their needs and aspirations. Turn to page 203.

Wage Earner Priced out of the Market: A complete community is a challenge when it becomes desirable; high earners drive home prices into the stratosphere. To overcome this, the VillageTown creates *Parallel Markets* for homes. In short, it means that you can afford to live in the VillageTown even if your job pays limited income, such as a teacher, civil servant, low-skill or service worker. See page 64 and page 259 for more detail on this concept.

Nearby Farmer: A VillageTown is 10,000 people to be fed everyday. It contracts with farmers on a permanent basis to provide the full range of foods. By cutting out the middleman who can take as much as 80% of the retail price of food, the VillageTown can pay more, for which it seeks healthier, more flavorful food. The VillageTown also provides employment for your children who otherwise may not be able to afford to live near you. See page 87.

Investor/Developer: The funding basis of a VillageTown is very different. There are excellent opportunities, but they are not anything like conventional development. See page 197.

DEFINITIONS

Borrowing from Euclid, we find it useful to begin with a set of definitions. Some terms are commonly understood; others like *Village* and *Town* we use in a particular way. Some like *VillageTown* are new words, although *VillageTown* is based on the ancient concept of *Polis (City-State)*.

A Good Life: The VillageTown purpose statement – when several villages come together to become self-supporting, or nearly so (a strong local economy), the purpose for its continuance is to enable its citizens to enjoy *A Good Life* understood as the social pursuits *Conviviality, Citizenship and Artistic, Intellectual & Spiritual Growth*.

Home Range: A term used by zoologists to describe the territory an animal covers in its day-to-day routine. It is not a term used by planners, but it should be, because it makes a distinction between the day-to-day territory people cover to accomplish the mundane chores of daily life, and the wider range traversed for commerce, visiting and other non-routine personal travel.

Driving Home Range: The home range of people using cars. Example: modern suburbs.

Walking Home Range: The home range of people whose day-to-day destinations are within walking distance, and where cars are not permitted. In Western societies, if people change their home range from driving to walking, a host of problems facing society will vanish instantly.

Village: In our context, a village is a small, medium-density design of attached housing of 2-3 stories. 500 people is optimal; typically 200 homes. Each village is defined by its central plaza surrounded by high-activity commercial offices and mixed use above and behind. In local matters (only related to its villagers) the village can be self-governing as it sees fit. In most cases, the villages will have clearly defined boundaries and each will have a distinctive character.

VillageTown: An internally-self-governing town of villages based on a walking home range. To support a strong local economy and an enriched social & cultural environment, its optimal population is 10,000. Its villages are contiguous (side-by-side), all within walking distance, and each has its own theme (character as defined in design, sounds, sights & activities). See page 31.

Town Center: The cosmopolitan center of the VillageTown, with higher (3-4 story) buildings providing commercial offices, apartments, grand homes, a Traveller's Inn as well as the town square (large enough for the whole population to stand and see a speaker on a balcony). The square is surrounded by the VillageTown Hall, clock tower and other prominent public buildings.

Urban Core: The 150-acre (60h) medium-density, mixed-use VillageTown inhabited zone with (recommended) 20 villages and the central Town Center – surrounded by the Greenbelt.

Walk-to Industrial Park: The industrial zone of a VillageTown, outside the urban core, within the walking home range, but with transport linkages to motor vehicles, rail, boat, etc.

Greenbelt: A large (best if 60% or more of the VillageTown land) zone surrounding the urban core. Reserved for nature, trees, fields, outdoor sport, gardens, etc, it provides a buffer zone.

Social Contract: A founding document accepted by all as a condition of habitation; agreeing to abide by common rules, as made from time to time by their elected representatives, with corresponding obligations and duties to protect individuals, property, the social fabric of the community, and to provide for and enhance individual wellbeing and VillageTown commonwealth.

VillageTown Operating Company: A private corporation incorporated by the VillageTown Stewards & Co. as the *Organizing Company*. When the VillageTown is built and titles to homes pass, the organizing company is reorganized as an operating company. Ownership passes to the VillageTown citizens, including ownership of its cash and assets. It is a hybrid. Using corporate and contract law, it is the instrument by which the citizens of the VillageTown are self governing. It also runs for-profit, tax-paying businesses, intended to serve its stockholders, the citizens.

Reinvestment Premium: A 10% fee paid to the VillageTown Stewards & Co in lieu of profit-taking to provide a capital fund to start future VillageTowns worldwide.

Commonwealth: The overall wealth of the VillageTown based on private enterprise & markets.

Legacy Fund: The net profits derived from selling at market price the unrestricted homes and other buildings in the VillageTown. Expected to be in the hundreds of millions of dollars, this fund is owned by the VillageTown Operating Company and prudently managed to invest in or be loaned to private enterprises in the VillageTown in a manner that increases the commonwealth. Planning is for seven generations (175 years). The Fund also funds social & cultural benefits.

Telepresence: The convergence of internet, telecommunications, computers, audio/video and robotics, that enables a person to be in two places at the same time. Telepresence is the shift in technology that enables the VillageTown local economy to grow without the tyranny of distance.

Parallel Market Homes: A different approach to affordable housing where the target buyer's market is controlled instead of using price controls or a state-housing model of rental homes.

State of Society: A term that became popular in the 18th century as the hierarchical governing systems based on monarchy were challenged by western thinkers. In it people agree to a structure of governance to enable people to get along with each other while not limiting liberty.

Freedom: The ability of a person to do what they want, without restraint, until their exercise of freedom impinges on others. Freedom can be individual, meaning that one can cross the frontier into the wilderness and be free (subject to the restraints of Nature which govern survival).

Liberty: The total of all freedoms within the context of society. Liberty is a social word, and only makes sense when talking about individuals and organizations within society. See page 263.

Justice: We borrow Plato's definition of justice: *minding one's own business.* The VillageTown seeks to influence this first through better design. Soundproof walls make better neighbors. A careful design of public and private space better enables people to get along with each other.

Peace: Freedom from civil commotion and violence of a community. Peace is an active condition associated with quiet, often better attained by design. *Keeping the peace* is one role of the operating company. In the villages, keeping the peace is often done best by respected citizens.

Order: A state of society in which people live in a peaceful or harmonious condition. Order protects individuals, private and public property, the social fabric of the community, and provides for and enhances both individual wellbeing and the commonwealth of the VillageTown.

Security: *Order* tends to be social in focus. In contrast, *security* tends to refer to personal *freedoms-from* as in freedom from danger or fear, and freedom from poverty or financial cares. Security is well-founded confidence; it tends to be long-term. For children, security is adults providing for them in a way that enables healthy growth into adulthood. For workers, security is knowing that they will have work. For savers, it is knowing their savings & purchasing power are protected. For elders, security is confidence that the social contract promised to provide for them as they age and become weaker and infirm, will in fact deliver on its promise.

Environmental Sustainability: A subset of good citizenship. Sustainability is an overused term often driven by fear (we will run out of fuel, the earth will cook, we are facing economic collapse). In the VillageTown, sustainability means to embrace the principle of leaving the Earth in as good or better shape than it was left to us. The VillageTown seeks to accomplish this through design that treads lighter: need less; clutters less. The VillageTown accomplishes this through smarter planning and capital investment in truly sustainable closed-loop systems, not greenwash. See page 268.

Creative Class and Guild Halls: In order to provide for a culturally enriched environment, the VillageTown invests in facilities that attract both traditional creative people (musicians, actors, artists, film-makers, writers, etc) as well as the broader definition (scientists, engineers, inventors, designers, engineers, intellectuals, high-tech, etc.). Each village plaza gets its own Guild Hall that provides rent-free space for the guild members, and each member is provided rent-free housing that provides support on the principle that it is cheaper to save a dollar than to earn one.

Chapel, Church, Cathedral: Lacking a neutral common-tongue word for a sacred building of varying scale, the VillageTown uses the traditional western terms, without implying religious affiliation. Villages formed around a particular religion may request their church be designated for it, while non-religious villages will have their church for rites of passage, peace and sanctuary.

TEN ELEMENTS OF A VILLAGETOWN

1. **The VillageTown Purpose - *a Good Life:*** Create and sustain a self-supporting local economy that enables its citizens, youth and visitors to enjoy *a good life*, understood as the social pursuits of conviviality, citizenship, and artistic, intellectual & spiritual growth.

2. **Design – *A Walking Home-Range*:** Construct a compact, affordable, comprehensible and wonderful human-scaled community made of multiple villages within the larger common locality of a town. A town whose urban core is car-free and all day-to-day destinations are within a 10-minute walk. A town that is socially, culturally and economically enriched. A town that is sufficiently diverse, complex and authentic to provide a continually motivating, inspiring and worthwhile place to live. Discourage outbound commuting. Move destinations not people; proximity creates community.

3. **Policy: Sustainable Management of Resources**: Enable the community and people to provide for their economic, social, cultural and spiritual wellbeing while protecting and preserving the natural & physical environment for present and future generations. Use the budget to buy the best sustainable technology. Note that sustainable systems, architecture and design are the basis of good policy but not bragging points – building a wonderful community based on fear of catastrophe makes no sense. Plan for seven generations.

4. **Authenticity, Character and Beauty**: The most wonderful places in the world are shaped by the people who will live with the results, long after the hired experts move on to their next job. Beyond architecture's utilitarian purpose of protection from hazards and climate, well designed, built and cultivated spaces exist to provide connection, stimulation, production, contentment, hospitality and daily delight. Beauty, harmony, utility, efficiency, durability, authenticity, character and timelessness are all valuable attributes. These are best accomplished by enabling the people who will live there to shape the look, feel and function of their home and village to meet their needs and aspirations. Make reference to locality and history, but also create it.

5. **A Complete Community**: A community is complete only if it can be called home by all ages and stages of life, a wide range of incomes, education, occupations, skill levels, social and cultural backgrounds, outlooks and ways of life. In economies with a wide range of purchasing power, parallel markets for home ownership prevent gentrification without bureaucracies. In human-scaled complete communities there is no poverty, only the weaker and stronger, where all participate and the stronger help the weaker. In complete communities, there is no unemployment, for there is always work that can be found. Build and maintain such a place and call it a VillageTown.

6. **Diversity of Talent**: Seek out, identify, invite, foster, educate and train diverse talent that enriches the community in every way – business and economic, social, cultural and spiritual. Especially provide for the creative class that breathes life into a community; protect their ways of life, and preserve their platforms for creativity. In the education of the young, place classrooms in the center of each village, so children are exposed to the diversity of talent every day by witnessing adult role-models going about their business.

7. **Commonwealth**: Promote local, wealth-creating private enterprise with a framework of a local economy that is diverse, self-creating, self-informing, self-regulating, balanced, transformational, reciprocal, empowering, responsive, resilient and protective. Establish a community-owned operating company that benefits the VillageTown commonwealth through VillageTown-owned governance, for-profit businesses and non-profit services. Establish a bank and investment fund to support private enterprise and the community. Look not to national or global systems for the answers; they are too big and too vulnerable to manipulation by special-interests. Protect your food, homes, community, money and employment. Care for all your young, weak and elders. Work in harmony with national & global systems, but keep them out of your life and your purse. De-monetize daily life using design and capital investment to reduce or eliminate ongoing unnecessary personal and community costs. It's cheaper to save a dollar than earn one.

8. **Local food and drink**: Food and water are the basics of life. Know your farmers, know your food. Conviviality embraces food and drink; make it nourishing, healthy, flavorful and delightful. Control and protect your food and water sources. Grow for quality, not for yield. Put on festivals and celebrations around food and drink. In the public establishments on the plazas, go beyond the popular stimulants of sugar, alcohol, caffeine and other drugs; invent and serve drinks that are convivial but also good for you. Avoid food produced by organizations whose pecuniary interest is not aligned with your culinary interest.

9. **Liberty and governance**: Protect personal freedom and respect the values of dissimilar communities. Keep the peace, preserve civility, protect private property, care for the infirm, give a hand-up to the poor, support the family and protect the commonwealth. Govern locally using checks and balances. Regard and speak about your people as citizens, not consumers. Liberty and freedom are important. Cultivate free communities. Use design, such as soundproof walls, to shape behavior before resorting to rules to enforce conduct. Balance public and private space so people can find solitude within proximity. Limit rule-making to enabling people to get along, rather than telling people how to live.

10. **Invest in your life**: VillageTowns are not for everyone, nor are they intended to be. They are intended to be the ultimate tangible investment – investing in that which affects you, your family and friends, on a day-to-day basis, paying returns that can last for generations. If you love the idea, build your village; if not, pass it on to someone who will.

Our ancestors lived in times of slow change; we live in an era of fast change. We live in a time when the powers of the individual are being expanded beyond the imagination of our ancestors. While our ancestors had only eyes, we now have lenses that let us see the smallest and largest things in the universe. Where they had only feet, horses and sails, we now have cars and planes. When they had only books and teachers, we now have the Internet that increasingly is becoming the storehouse of the world's knowledge – even with translators, so we can read many languages. We have tools that extend the powers of our eyes, ears, touch and most importantly our brains. We now have the word *Telepresence* which means we can be in two or more places at the same time. A doctor in LA Medical Center can perform an operation in Africa, using robotic hands and video cameras that can see better than eyes – and students can watch the operation from the doctor's point of view.

However, while these powers are great and seductive, we also live in an era of increasing isolation – a problem because inherently we are social animals. Our cars separate us. Our homes separate us. While the Internet, cell phones and wireless technology enable long-distance connection, they are no replacement for face-to-face contact. This is especially the case with children and with elders. Children are now spending as much as eight hours a day interacting with electronic media instead of being outdoors, playing with their peers, or interacting with adults. Elders are becoming increasingly isolated as the complete community is being replaced by age-segregated housing: suburbs to raise children, cities for single adults and couples, retirement homes for old folks who can no longer drive.

Our governmental systems have become a force unto themselves, no longer serving the needs of people, or even understanding what those needs are. What in politics is called the left and the right seem to be more preoccupied with beating each other than understanding and solving the many and growing challenges facing our global civilization.

On the left, humanity is viewed more as a biological organism where the individual is a cell of the state; humanity matters more than the person. Increasingly life becomes more bureaucratic as the state regulates more and more of daily life. Done in the name of safety and for tax collection, ordinary citizens find their lives interfered with by the state.

On the right, the social order is under attack, as monied interests manipulate government systems for their own pecuniary and power interests, creating a majority of losers and a minority of winners who increasingly control the wealth and resources of nations. Common wealth is privatized; the public good is off the agenda. As these private corporations grow in power, they introduce a different form of control – engineering goods, services, even how and where we live to serve their pecuniary interest. Suburbs were invented to sell cars. Freeways weaken small towns, and big-box chains built near the freeways finish them off. While the corporate pundits argue the private sector is about choice, in fact, too often the power of such corporations eliminates choice.

Missing from both sides is what 18th-century philosophers called the Social Contract. The Social Contract finds a middle ground between the left and right. It starts with the individual and the family, who come together with other individuals and families to form communities. In forming communities, these individuals and families agree to cooperate; to specialize so that their quality of life can rise above the subsistence level. They agree to a set of rules so they can get along, and they agree on due process of law and consequences when someone breaks the rules. They agree to tax themselves to pay for services and goods that as a community they deem necessary or of value, but that would not be better provided by private enterprise. For Social Contracts to work, power must be distributed – a system of checks and balances so no single individual or group can do what they want without the consent of others. While idealistic philosophers dream of utopias where everything and everybody works in harmony, the Social Contract presumes some people will be corrupt, dishonest, greedy, lusting for power, or sociopathic.

Wealth is created when people can create surpluses. If a people must spend every hour of every waking day struggling to survive, they will have no time to free themselves. We now live in an era where what we call the first world has developed so much surplus wealth that the majority of citizens in a nation can (and do) work at wealth-converting (or even wealth-destroying), rather than wealth-creating, jobs. Wall Street at one time was the place where the nation's surplus cash was invested in start-up and growing industries that fostered wealth creation. Today, much of Wall Street money is a zero-sum game resembling a casino, while businesses and industry that need capital find it very difficult, or exceptionally costly, to access needed cash. The upshot is struggle at a time when we should be thriving.

How can we change this? The short answer is that we cannot do much as solo individuals or families, but we can accomplish a great deal if we establish a business plan and a Social Contract between a relatively small number of individuals and families.

The largest purchase most families will make in their life is the family home. If we take the *average*-priced home at $250,000, that is not a lot of purchasing power. If 200 families buy homes at the same time in the same location, their combined purchasing power is $50 million. If twenty groups of those 200 families buy homes the same way, their combined purchasing power is a billion dollars. If they earn an average family income (usually about 25% per year of the price of the home), that would suggest not only a capital investment of a billion dollars, but an income of about a quarter billion dollars a year. That is clout.

When brought together through a social contract, these buyers do not pool their money; instead they invest it at the same time – individually, but in parallel. They do so using conventional contract and corporate law. They set up conservative institutions like a bank, with the twist that as its customers, it is established so they become its owners – they keep its profits within their social contract. None of these are new ideas. They are merely tools, organized so that individuals and families can secure their needs and aspirations.

Humans are social beings. Even in nomadic times, humans lived in community. The human species is not equipped to survive solo, like the jaguar, but lives best in groups, like the lion.

When we use words like community, society and civilization, we acknowledge the social nature of humans. We cooperate. We specialize because we are more efficient and effective mastering specialties. We developed money as a more effective way to trade expertise.

However, the history of humanity also shows the negative tendency of dominance; one group of people controlling another. Whether it is slavery, a police state or the more benign wage-slave state, it is based on dividing people into winners and losers. As humanity moves from a brutish state to a more civilized one, liberty — freedom within society — becomes more established. Instead of brutes dominating by force, people give up their liberty for security. This is an unnecessary trade-off.

In the 17th and 18th centuries, especially in the West the concept of liberty became prominent in social and political philosophy and government. In those times, the fight for liberty was against oppressive governments.

Today, to secure liberty, we must look at a more subtle force — the over-engineered franchising of life. In the name of investor profits, large corporations manipulate the public and their elected & appointed representatives to make decisions that are profitable for their investors but not good for the rest of us.

In the 1970's civilization began to experience a historic shift. In the West, people began to shift from being producers to being consumers. In the Orient, what were mostly agricultural nations became producers. Technology began exponential growth; moving us away from centralized command-and-control hierarchies to virtual systems that reduce the *tyranny of distance*. The impact of this on the social values of liberty and security are profound, especially in the context of the Village Town.

This shift to consumerism has a deep effect on how people live. Roots are cut. People are no longer from anywhere. Often their identity, their thoughts, even their accent comes from media.

The traditional need of humans to cooperate is disrupted by this consumerism as we invented new ways of providing for our needs. Instead of traditional farming, we have factory farming, where million-dollar machines replace the extended family to grow food. Instead of harvesting and storing, we shop at supermarkets, buying packaged food, and eating at fast-food outlets. We no longer know our food or ourselves.

Where local folk used to entertain each other with home-made music — a social activity, we now are an isolated people walking down the street with ear buds listening to manufactured, purchased (or pirated) and copyrighted music.

While these advances in technology provide us with extraordinary new powers, and in many ways make life a lot easier, (and less back-breaking — we live longer as a result), the unanticipated negative side effects have created sociological and psychological damage.

It is harder to know who we are, and we are bombarded by media with life-style choices presented to us not because they are good for us, or will help us on our life journey, but because by adopting them, we buy something. *Emô, ergo sum.* We become the life we buy.

There is a cost to this. Living a consumer life, the heart suffers; it feels the loss — something deeply important is missing. Human nature yearns for community — for that social connection that gives the opportunity to explore and become who we are. This is not a new idea, the ancient Greeks had an inscription over the Temple at Delphi: γνῶθι σεαυτόν, which translates to *know thyself.*

To find a better way, don't look to the large institutions that dominate the globe. The freedom to find a better way exists. All the tools we need to do it are legal and accessible. It's up to us to take that freedom and use it.

IF YOU ARE READY TO BEGIN NOW...

This book goes into great detail about the aspects of a VillageTown and how it works. Most people want to learn a lot more before they are ready to proceed. This makes sense; creating your home within a VillageTown is a major life-step. But there are some people who get it, love it and are ready to go. This page is for those people.

It is important to understand however, that if you expect a modern consumer experience where you buy a packaged, pre-engineered product, it is time to unlearn that expectation. One element of the VillageTown is its character and authenticity. That must come from you and the ten thousand others who shape the future. We provide the framework, but within that framework, you create its life, character and personality.

How to begin? Get in touch. Contact the VillageTown Stewards through the web site. Follow our progress, or if you want to do more, volunteer and become involved. The process is laid out starting on page 160.

The major trigger will be to find the first stage of capital required to set up the Organizing Company and employ the professionals who will make it happen. Where is the first project? That depends on where the funds come from. As of this writing, there are four candidate areas: New Zealand, America, Europe and Australia – each has its attractions and limitations. Each has a different group of Stewards working on it.

The first project will begin when (a) the funds come, (b) the host jurisdiction and government show strong support – or if (c) an effective Village Coordinator steps forward and recruits about 200 home buyers ready to form their village. This latter approach has great power. If 200 families (about 500 people) come together and declare they are ready, to go, this represents substantial purchasing power. Purchasing power moves people. It attracts funding; it excites politicians. It calls the attention of the media. To learn more about this, turn to page 189.

You don't have to take on the volunteer coordinator role. If you prefer not to be in the limelight but make a quieter contribution, that's not only fine, but very helpful. The best thing you can do right now is to spread the word. Literally, spread the word *VillageTown*. It's a new idea. Direct people to the web site, to this book, the other two books, and build a wave of interest. Projects begin with a vision, and they grow as that vision is shared. There is an old saying in Oceania: *If we can conceive of a vision, can hold and sustain it, it can be achieved.* And another one says: *Energy flows where attention goes. To change experience, shift attention.*

One heads-up from the VillageTown Stewards, however. We only work with delightful people. Please check any angst and ego-crazy-making at the door; you can retrieve it again when you leave. Life is too short to waste it on energy-sapping drama when we are trying to get something done; especially something as enjoyable as creating a VillageTown.

Victor Papanek wrote: "**We all sense that something has gone terribly wrong with our communities.** Hamlets and cities, slums and suburbs all lack a sense of cohesion. Not only is there no center there – there is no there there. Cities, towns, villages and communities that were designed hundreds of years ago are obviously based upon some basic purpose of living that eludes the designers of our own time. Previous ages possessed one great advantage: a precise moral aim that gave meaning and direction to all planning and design... Builders knew precisely what they wanted.

What then is the purpose of contemporary planners? Earlier builders knew what they were doing because they followed the cultural imperatives of their society as their minds conceived them. Modern designers, whose purpose is the nourishing of public taste, have tried desperately hard – and with little success – to find out what that taste is. To help in this quandary, the designer uses research staffs and questionnaires, and what does he discover when at last his work is complete? That those for whom he has built move back to the old quarters of the city." *(continued page 24)*

Page 105 *The Green Imperative* by Victor Papapnek © 1995 ISBN 0-500-27846-6 Thames & Hudson (UK).

PART 1: A NEW FORM OF "HOME-RANGE"

Zoologists call it *Home-Range* – the territory a wolf pack (or any animal) covers each day to provide for their needs of food, security and play. The *human home-range* is similar. Starting at home, it is the territory people in a common locality cover in the typical day to accomplish the mundane chores of daily life – work, shopping, school, daycare, recreation, friends, church, dining out, social/sports events, driving the kids, fueling & maintaining the cars.

Starting after World War II, America passed and funded laws inventing a new form of *driving home-range* known as the suburb by separating day-to-day destinations. The intent was to boost the economy by creating a larger market for cars and car-supporting industries such as petroleum, steel and chemicals. Congress did it by funding the world's largest public works project: the Interstate Highway program. Separating destinations through zoning means the average American drives 35 miles a day. This may not sound like much, but for every 10,000-person common locality, it means over one-quarter-million miles of home-range driving every day – more in the suburbs. Much of the world adopted the new American system. The policy worked. Money flowed. The economy boomed for 50 years.

However, effect on people was not part of the policy's scope. It crushed the extended family, crippled natural support systems, and strewed pollution. While seemingly wealthier, people from all walks of life report life being less fulfilling. Life seems to have lost its flavor. We redefined citizens as consumers. In doing so, society lost its way; life lost its purpose.

Purpose: Why do we, and why should we, build communities?

Why do we build communities? To sell cars. Why should we build communities? To enable people to provide for their needs and aspirations. Let us examine this better reason:

Victor Papanek, a protégé of Frank Lloyd Wright, (see quote on page 22) points us in the right direction by suggesting that 2300 years ago Aristotle gave the best answer, writing that when several villages come together to become *self-supporting*, the purpose of their continuance as a **polis** (city-state) is to enable their citizens to enjoy *a good life*. Papanek says it is to enable people to enjoy the social pursuits of *conviviality, citizenship and artistic, intellectual & spiritual growth*.

Create a car-free, transport-free home-range within the existing infrastructure

As we examined this better reason to build communities, it became apparent that today's core problem is the car-scaled driving home-range. If we move all day-to-day destinations close together to make cars unnecessary, we remove the need, cost and burden of the car's machine-scaled infrastructure. Create a walking home-range and new opportunity abounds.

This is not a radical proposal to get rid of cars or shift to train transport. With their point-to-point efficiency and the certainty that technology will solve their fuel and pollution problems, cars, trucks and roads remain brilliant ways to keep business moving and to access

..."Until very recently there has been no such thing as a changing purpose in planning settlements. That old towns are charming and new ones are not is due to the fact that city planners of former times – of ancient Greece, of medieval city states, of the heart of Amsterdam, London, Paris or Vienna – did not pursue different aims as their age changed, but instinctively always worked toward the one unchanging purpose that has always made people desire to live in urban centers in all human communities. Aristotle said that men form communities not for justice, peace, defense or traffic, but for the sake of a good life. This good life has always meant the satisfaction of man's four basic social desires: *conviviality, citizenship, artistic & intellectual growth, spiritual development & fulfillment.*"

Page 105 continued from previous page - Victor Papapnek

destinations beyond the home-range. It simply proposes to disconnect car dependency from the home-range. The effect of this is to eliminate home-range spawned congestion, pollution, separation and alienation; and to enable the creation of a self-supporting economy where people enjoy a good life. Let us explore this idea of a *self-supporting* local economy.

A self-supporting local economy - the basis for a good life

In a global economy, self-supporting does not mean what it meant 2,000 years ago for the *polis*, (the city-state). But, as one explores this idea of bringing villages together to become self-supporting, its potential is great. It creates a local economy based on businesses that sell local to local (L2L) supported by a smaller sector of businesses that sell local to global (L2G). L2L businesses turn money within the community. They start with the basics like local food and then extend to a wide range of goods and services. L2G businesses bring cash in from the outside world and form the basis of self-supporting trade. The L2G business imports money and spends most of it locally, This creates *money-turn*, which has a *multiplier effect*. The measure of success is not perpetual growth in GDP, but attaining and sustaining a broad base of wealth and wellbeing for the *polis*, as it was with the city-state.

As Aristotle reminds us, however, the purpose of fostering this self-supporting local economy is not solely to create and sustain wealth. We do not live to work, rather we work to live; the measure is the extent to which people may enjoy a good life. Earning a living enables people to have fun, to enjoy life, to take care of people and their environment. Earning a living enables further growth: in creative expression, in thoughts of the mind and in the realms of spirit. Aristotle's polis provides the means to do all these things.

At a fundamental level, the polis economy is about moving from scarcity to abundance, from meanness to generosity. Money symbolizes wealth – at one time a word associated with well-being. Today, we are bombarded by hyper-ventilating media that defines wealth in a form that is unattainable by almost all – the mansion chocked full of luxuries on vast acres of land surrounded by high walls with security guards, the garage full of flash cars, the grand yacht and the private jet to fly to the private island or ski chalet in a trendy resort. While this may be the aspiration for a few who get there and the many who feel they have failed because they did not, as a useful definition of wealth, it flops.

The old term *commonwealth* is more useful, as it describes what happens when a critical mass of people live in the same place, and work in private enterprise that is contained within a single market economy. A market economy emerges when enough people in the same place are productive. They exert energy to make things or accomplish useful results. At the baseline, they meet their needs, but as they grow, they begin to create more wealth than is needed for subsistence. They find not all of their waking hours are needed to survive.

In the first-world countries, ordinary people have gone so far beyond mere survival that they appear fabulously wealthy compared to historical standards and expectations. The

Both of these are pedestrian streets with shops on both sides. Yet the one above is romantic. For its visitors it is a dream place to visit or stay. The other place, below, is commonplace; it could be anywhere – in Australia or Austria, North America or South Africa. It's not necessary to have mules to deliver suitcases from where the boats with travellers arrive, but it adds to the romance, and it's eminently practical when the streets are narrow.

It is interesting that even in the no-car shopping mall, one finds cars – in this case a new car that can be won by signing up for some contest. Malls are designed to extract the largest amount of money from a shopper in a three-hour time frame. They are single-minded in their focus and purpose. As such, they are hollow places that fail to feed the soul.

amount of time ordinary people have for other-than-survival activity is huge. However, instead of enjoying that luxury time, they find they are entangled in a complicated, consuming, transport-based system whose various parts perpetually wear out at great cost to everyone. This complicates life, trapping us in lives characterized by stress, aggravation and scarcity. A visitor from another planet would look at our systems and conclude we were slightly insane.

From these ideas and observations came research and from the findings, a direction

It is one thing to talk about such observations. It's quite another to figure out what to do about them. We asked: *how can we untangle this mess of muddle to pursue our needs and aspirations?*

Clutter: As we began to search for answers, we took a step back and examined every *thing* and every activity in modern life and asked *is this really necessary or just another contributor to entanglement?* So many things in life are invented, made and sold not to make life better, but because someone can make a profit by selling us clutter. We don't think a lot about it.

Wake up, look around: In our research we looked at where people live, where they work and what they do during the day and the evening – how they use time when they are not asleep. We asked them if they liked how they used their time, if they liked their surroundings.

Their first answers sounded as if they were coming out of a drugged-like state. Most people were too busy, too caught up and distracted to think much about it. They were worried about their job; if they had children, they were worried about the kids. In most cases, their home and neighborhood was not all they wanted, but it was what they could afford at the time: life as a compromise. Then we asked about their dreams and aspirations.

What makes life good?: When we shifted the subject to aspirations, to what they would have if by a miracle it could happen, there was an awakening effect in the conversation. Once they let go of the self-censoring denial, they would talk about what they loved – wonderful places they visited, the times of their lives when they felt they belonged, when life was good. Some older people told of tough times – London in the Blitz, small towns in the Great Depression. For others college was the high point, a time when they had a community of intellectual and artistic growth. Some folks mentioned early marriage, when money was scarce, but life was more alive. A consistent thread told of people sharing experience.

Enrich life: Next we explored what enriched the public experience, the alternative to filling homes with gadgets of distraction. We found the old town and village plazas – with their cafés, taverns, shops, stores, theaters, guild halls, meeting places and places of worship – created social attraction that beat sitting on the sofa watching TV or at the computer desk cruising the net.

Provide variety: We also learned variety is important. The most delightful place can become boring if it is the only place in town. The best examples had completely different feelings all within a few blocks: visit cities that have an Italian section next to a Chinatown next to an Arts District and so on. We saw that it works best to provide many different villages, all within

With the solo parent or both parents working, society monetizes the raising of children, placing them in child care and preschool where too often underpaid, overworked professionals substitute for parents and community. Children no longer learn independence and autonomy because society has come to accept a world where it is unsafe to let them roam the community at will. Cars can run them down; cruising predators may abduct or harm them. Adults drive away from their communities; there is no one to keep an eye out. In contrast, a VillageTown operates all day, every day, with no cars and with a low tolerance for crime. Children become a part of daily life, naturally looked after by adults and elders. It really does take the village to raise the child.

walking distance, with a larger walk-to town center for a more cosmopolitan experience.

Urban and Nature: It became apparent people need access to real Nature, not solely the tamed city park. Beyond the wall or hedgerow marking the urban-core boundary, people need a greenbelt with places to walk, play, engage in sports or exercise, garden, or sit and do nothing. Folks need fields of flowers to run through, equestrian trails, a cemetery, and groves of trees to enjoy simple peace and quiet. People need to experience Nature on her terms.

Build centers, public places: These simple decluttering changes of moving destinations and enriching the experience have profound effects on quality of life. In response to Papanek's writing about today's developments (*Not only is there no center there – there is no there there*), it is important to create many centers and many experiences that happen in those centers.

Ideologically neutral: We found a negative driver was ideology. Most intentional communities came with a political slant – some socialist, others libertarian. Avoid this. How to handle money – tax the rich to support the poor, or tax no one and let wealth creation trickle down – is a decision the citizens make if they particularly care. When the scale is right, when folks are neighbors, most help each other out naturally not ideologically.

Trust the wisdom of crowds: In *Wisdom of Crowds*, author James Surowiecki showed that disparate groups of people get it right more often than professionals. Professionals bring expertise, but when they are handed authority to decide how people will live, the outcome never seems to deliver on the promise. Their expertise is too narrowly defined. It's too much head and not enough heart. Sometimes they make decisions on the command of their pay-masters; decisions driven by pecuniary interest, not people's needs and aspirations. This is not to say that on their own the crowd will get it right. It's the difference between a lynch mob and a jury. In the jury, ordinary people get it right more often than professional judges, but only in a formal environment supported by a professional framework. From this we came up with a design framework to enable ordinary people to create wonderful places.

A new model for development: This latter lesson posed a challenge. The usual model is investor/developer driven, where the crowd – the future villagers – is not involved until all is built and ready for them to buy. For us to apply all these lessons we learned, we had to come up with a new model; in essence one that turns real-estate development upside down. We call it an *organizing company* – a company that organizes both the buyers and the project to build the community those buyers need and will love. It is a very different model.

A new word - *VillageTown*: It became clear this was a new form of community, one based on the ancient concept of the Polis, usually translated as City-State. In today's world of nations, a 10,000-population community with its own army and law is not relevant, but the core values of the polis suggested a new word, ***VillageTown***. The word was late in coming. In the first book, we did not have a word, writing instead *for now we leave it to the pundits*. Like the statue inside a block of marble being revealed, it took time for the beauty to emerge.

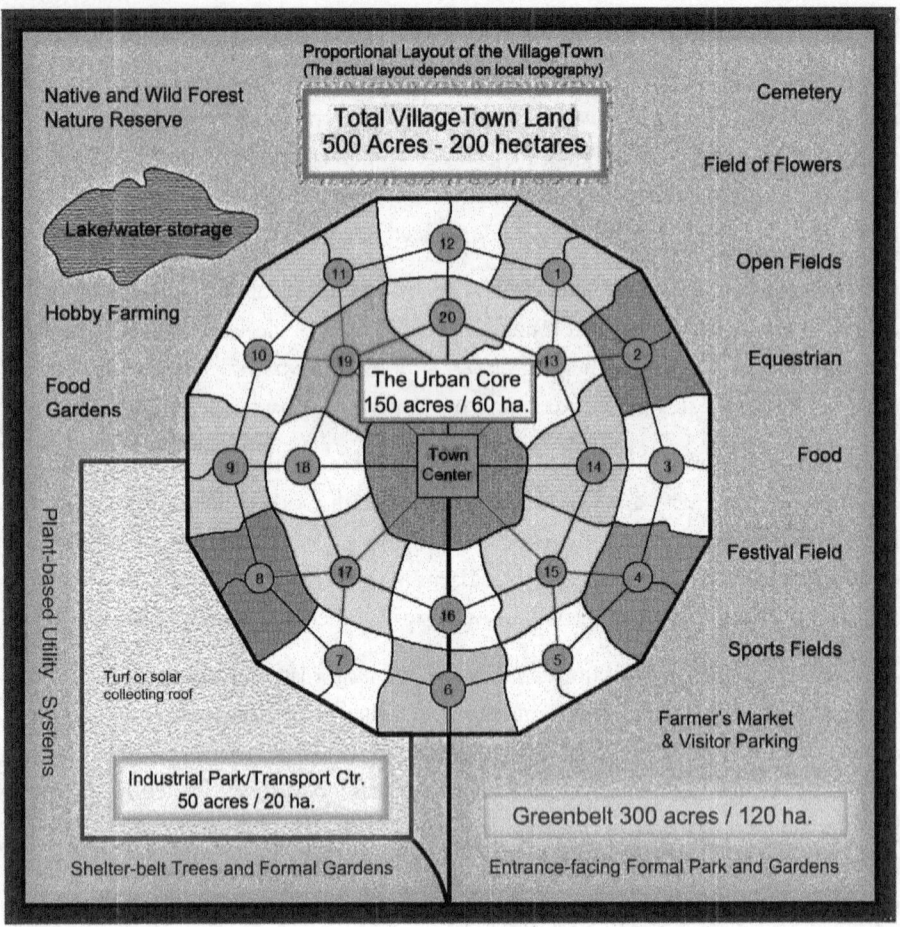

Proportional Layout of the VillageTown
(The actual layout depends on local topography)

Native and Wild Forest
Nature Reserve

Cemetery

**Total VillageTown Land
500 Acres - 200 hectares**

Field of Flowers

Lake/water storage

Open Fields

Hobby Farming

Equestrian

Food
Gardens

12 11 1 20 10 19 13 2 18 9 14 3 8 17 15 4 7 16 5 6

**The Urban Core
150 acres / 60 ha.**

Town Center

Food

Plant-based Utility Systems

Festival Field

Turf or solar
collecting roof

Sports Fields

Farmer's Market
& Visitor Parking

Industrial Park/Transport Ctr.
50 acres / 20 ha.

Greenbelt 300 acres / 120 ha.

Shelter-belt Trees and Formal Gardens

Entrance-facing Formal Park and Gardens

This diagram is intended to show the proportions of a theoretical VillageTown. The core includes a common locality of 20 side-by-side villages and the town center. Outside one finds the walk-to Industrial Park & Transport Center. Surrounding all, the Greenbelt gives villagers a true experience of Nature and at the same time prevents cross-boundary conflicts. This mitigates concerns from neighbors who will only see trees and parkland, and who will not suffer any commuter traffic.

Every VillageTown will be different, defined by the land, the law, the local conditions and the people who will live there. In this simple drawing, which presumes available greenfield land of about 500-acres (200h), the ideal proportions of urban space to greenbelt are laid out. It shows the villages connected by their primary roads. Each village has its public plaza in the middle. This urban core occupies about 150 acres (60h), the industrial/transport land about 50 acres (20h) and the greenbelt about 300 acres (120h).

In some places, the urban core will be smaller, because there are fewer or smaller homes, or larger, because the homes may be larger or have more inner courtyards or because there are more open-space pockets inside the urban core. These variables are determined by land availability, price and weather (colder climates tend to keep homes smaller/closer).

In brownfield locations (typically in a city where the prior land use is obsolete), the layout may be very different, and it may involve compromises to work with more constricted land. The same may apply in suburban locations where a collapsed new sprawl project leaves a partially completed site (roads in, no buildings) that can be adapted.

DEFINITION: VILLAGETOWN

In taking the next step toward transforming an idea worth doing into a place that 10,000 people call home, we begin by introducing a new word into the common tongue. The word is *VillageTown*. It is an idea about common locality that means something specific; for many to agree to build this special form of place, all must be talking about the same thing.

A VillageTown is a town made of villages, ideally about twenty side-by-side villages – each with its own special character, all set around a more cosmopolitan town center.

Villages are important because most people are inherently social; people need each other and enjoy the company of others. Most people do best in communities where they are known and know others. Villages work best with about 250-750 people: 500 on average which typically means about 200 homes.

Towns are important to achieve an economic critical mass and to serve as the counterpoint to over-familiarity in the village. Towns enable more social and cultural enrichment with many things happening – always the opportunity to meet someone new. For this reason, a town made of villages offers the best of both worlds: A *VillageTown*.

To be clear: a VillageTown is not a utopia (where everything and everyone works in harmony). Utopia is a lovely idea, but it's not how the human ego defines reality. Instead a VillageTown is based on the Jeffersonian principle of checks and balances, capable of preserving what works and fixing what fails. A VillageTown creates a framework upon and within which social order self-creates. It uses timeless patterns of design to reduce the friction points that tend to create conflict between people. VillageTowns can be rural market towns, brownfield developments or in some cases built on empty suburban land. They should have a walkable urban core, a walk-to industrial park and a walk-to greenbelt.

A VillageTown brings no ideological affiliation; it is not an *intentional community*. It is intended for all ages and stages of life; it seeks to be a *complete community*, a place for the full range of incomes, occupations, education and outlooks. Instead of ideology, the VillageTown tests by practicality – is it working? If it is not working, how do _we_ change it?

The VillageTown borrows two overarching statements. The first from Aristotle and Papanek and the second from the New Zealand Resource Management Act:

- **Purpose**: *to create and sustain a local economy that is self supporting to enable its citizens, youth and visitors to enjoy a good life, understood as the social pursuits of conviviality, citizenship, and artistic, intellectual & spiritual growth.*

- **Policy**: *to enable people and communities (villages) to provide for their economic, social, cultural and spiritual wellbeing while protecting and preserving the natural & physical environment, for the present & the foreseeable needs of seven generations.*

Experience: VillageTown

VillageTown life begins in the home - your home. When you wake up the in morning, the first thing you note is that it is quieter. There are no cars and trucks on the street. The walls are thick, so you do not hear your neighbors. The rooms are warm in winter, cool in summer because they were designed to work with sun and shade. Your home feels right.

Design: For the founders, the process of development is intended to encourage you to custom design your home to fit your tastes, because this is how character and authenticity are attained. Size is determined by need and budget – bigger homes will cost more. The level of interior finish is up to you and your budget. Unlike suburban homes where increasingly life is within – the video room, exercise room, and computer room, village life means many people will find they are out-and-about more often. Entertainment will be a close walk; more likely to be more social.

Design: The home becomes the place of family, sanctuary, and privacy. While not mandatory, flat rooftop gardens will be recommended for many homes – an open space to enable outdoor living that is private. Care will be taken in building placement to encourage exposure to sunlight in temperate climates, and shaded space in tropical ones. Rooftop gardens may have a partial sloped roof with solar panels facing the sun (connected to the VillageTown grid, rather than powering each house separately – it's more efficient). Note that you won't need a garage.

Design: Some homes will be simple rectangles, others may have inner courtyards, or even shared courtyards to provide that sense of the secret garden within. Most homes will be attached, as found in older urban design, but attached with soundproof walls.

In the morning your first decision may be about breakfast – where to eat. Will you eat at home - preparing fresh foods harvested nearby, or walk to the village plaza with its cafés offering the smells of fresh-baked bread and coffee? The tradition of affordable café life comes from old Europe but unlike the chain-imitations of a Starbucks, in the VillageTown café life is locally owed, locally operated and infused with character and authenticity.

Design: All streets will be pedestrian, but the front streets will be more formal than the rear. In some cases, the rear street may be a central paved footpath and then grass, plants or gardens along the buildings. Rear porches may encourage a smaller sense of neighborhood to evolve along these rear greenstreets – very different than the typical urban back alley that is home to trash cans and parked cars.

Design: The streets lead to the central plaza, one plaza per village, 21 in total including the larger Town Center. The plazas are the hubs, the places of activity, the stage upon which the public life of the community is performed. They are places where one meets without an appointment. Each plaza reflects the character of its people, each should be very different.

It's time for work. Where do you work? For some, work is an office or shop on the plaza. For others it may be an office on the ground floor at home – perhaps facing the street if it has visitors. White-collar jobs in larger businesses will be in the town center where four-story office buildings provide for larger businesses. Blue-collar workers walk in the other direction, toward the walk-to industrial park, where the VillageTown makes both goods it needs and goods that support trade that creates local wealth.

Design: Some homes on the busier streets may have small, low-traffic home offices or shops run by the residents of the building. Others will be purely residential, as their occupants walk to work on the plaza, in the downtown commercial district or the walk-to industrial park just outside the VillageTown walls.

Intent: In work, a VillageTown is intended as a productive society, rather than a consumer society. What this means is that the local economy is intended to be self-supporting within the context of the larger global economy – not that it will make everything that it needs, but it will engage in sufficient wealth-creating productivity to remain economically enriched. On a long term basis, as the American economy now is discovering, a consumer society cannot sustain itself.

It's time to take a break - again you have choices. Do you want to see people, or be alone? If you walk to the plaza to get a drink and snack, you will meet people. Young and old will be there; people you know and visitors who feel welcome. Some of the cafés will have long-tables, intentionally designed to encourage people to connect without an introduction. Alternatively, you may prefer time alone. You head in the opposite direction, toward the greenbelt. A well designed VillageTown will have quiet, less-travelled footpaths, walkways not intended for high traffic that head toward peaceful destinations.

Design: In well-designed VillageTowns, the walk from home should give one a choice of highly-trafficked, or lesser traveled. If one walks toward the plazas or town center, life will be active, vibrant, colorful and stimulating. If instead one walks toward the surrounding greenbelt, one heads toward quiet, tranquility and a connection with real nature (as opposed to the typical city park). Even the greenbelt will have more and less active parts – an equestrian or sports field will have a different feeling to it than a stand of tall trees or a field of flowers that extends far into the distance. If one is lucky the site will already have such trees and vegetation. If not, it will be planted, and may take a generation or two to grow to maturity.

For lunch, you may decide to walk home, and join your family in a meal – if you have school-aged children they may walk home as well. Or you may decide you want something different; instead of walking to your familiar village plaza, you go down to the more cosmopolitan town center or to another village that has a completely different feel.

Design: Just as each village is different, each plaza will have a different feel, a different character to it. The architecture will be different; the food and drink may be different. The people may speak another language and their mode of dress may reflect different values or even a different culture – especially the case in a VillageTown formed in a country that supports immigration such as New Zealand. The plazas are intended to be active places day and night. Children will abound, since the classrooms will be on the plazas giving them many role models of real life. For families with school-aged children, education will be more meaningful and safe. Old people (elders), will be everywhere, as a car-free village means they can remain, life-long.

After work you join your friends and family in search of entertainment or social activity. Or perhaps you go for an evening walk on the green streets or a run in the greenbelt. You find you are spending a lot less time watching TV or seeking internet entertainment. There is too much real-life happening outside your door; it is far more attractive.

Design: With an artist guild hall on each village plaza, the plazas host cultural activity as well as shops and services. Festivals, celebrations, local sports and markets will happen there and on the greenbelt. With a critical mass of 10,000 people and at least 1,000 visitors at any one time, there will be many things to do. This is the experience of a complete community.

THE ELUSIVE QUALITIES OF AUTHENTICITY AND CHARACTER

Windsor California is a showcase for New Urbanism, where in a dying agricultural town a developer/architect embraced a design philosophy of returning to the small-town scale before suburban sprawl. While better than the alternative, the qualities of authenticity and character unfortunately eluded the designers; it looks cartoon-like — especially the sameness of the windows, doors and outline details. In contrast, this ancient fishing village cum local holiday resort in Spain oozes character and authenticity. In part, it is the fact that the Cadaquez buildings show the personality of the people who not only had them built, but would then live or work in them. In front it is human-scaled, not a car-scaled street that forces people onto the margins.

COMMON LOCALITY – PARTICIPATE IN THE DESIGN OF YOUR VILLAGE

At one time, sociologists would speak about *common locality* in referring to a community of people who are defined by their local geography – what they called home. For most of human history, this was a walkable distance, and it usually involved a social core, called a hamlet, a village, a town or a neighborhood within a city. 20th-century government zoning and transport policy too often destroys common locality. The VillageTown restores it.

In communities of 250 to 750 persons who share common locality, people know each other. A community can be a college, a company, a tribe or a village. Within such a community, people tend to form smaller groups of friends – people with whom they share common interests. This population size of community tends to support a sense of belonging; it is easier to get to know people. Communities of 250-750 tend to come together when something goes wrong. If someone becomes ill or injured they will be looked after by friends and neighbors. If a family suffers a setback or death, others will look after the children or cook meals. If so minded, communities of that size do celebrations, rituals and festivals well. They make their own entertainment rather than watch professionals.

The core community in a VillageTown is the village, which on average will be home to about 500 people. It is expected that this will require about 200 homes, except in villages with a disproportionate number of single adults which may have more but smaller units. The ideal VillageTown will have twenty villages, plus the cosmopolitan Town Center.

By having multiple villages, one instantly creates diversity of people, culture and experience. When one's own village becomes too familiar, it is a short walk to another one. However, if each village is designed by professionals, they run the risk of having a certain artificial, cartoon quality to them. The commercial world has become good at imitation, at copying attractive archetypes, but in a way that never seems to capture the essence. What is missing is character and authenticity. In the photographs to the left, the difference between imitation and the real thing is evident.

These elusive qualities manifest more easily when each home, each workplace and each community reflects the individual and shared personality of the people who live there. These qualities are far more difficult to capture using a professional design team. The answer is obvious. Engage the individuals and groups in the design process.

This is done in a formal process called Dynamic Engagement, but it begins earlier when certain people are attracted to certain villages through something they share in common. It will be encapsulated in a word or a name for that village, perhaps a nationality, a passion or a particular demographic. An Italian village instantly conjures up a place with warm pastel plastered walls, opening upper-floor balconies with potted plants and vines, the smell of bread baking, a café bustling with people talking over food and drink, children everywhere, old people talking for hours on plaza benches, the tradition of the early evening stroll on the main streets. If the village is made up of new immigrants, it helps them make the adjustment – when one moves to a new land, one is instantly a foreigner and a familiar village helps them adjust. The next village over, however may have been called together by people in the film-making industry, producers, actors, set designers – such a village would have a completely different feel to it and could even be designed to function as a living set.

The clustering is self-selecting, but the challenge for the future villagers is to write that general look and feel in a design and an architectural code. This code governs the instruction to individual architects and artisans who create the public face of each private home and workplace. The setting of the central plaza is determined by the villagers – *how will the lamp posts look?* – a question influenced by the local artisans who hand make such ornaments. Where do the benches go? Should the plaza have a fountain or a bandstand or both? Should there be a low-walled area for children to skate, play with balls and enjoy themselves within sight of parents, but far enough away not to have balls knocking over coffee cups?

Low-walled play area in the plaza. Note how close to the café tables; yet it works.

The future villagers work within a budget, but they may decide to self- assess themselves a slightly higher mortgage to add amenities important to them. In a cold climate, they may elect to have a winter walk between the backs of the homes – a glassed-in foot path that enables them to walk to the plaza without snow or bitter cold air. Within the allowable rules of the zone, they determine where the secondary streets go, and place the scale model of their home where it will be built – perhaps meeting their next-door neighbor in the process.

In all of these small decisions that shape a community, the people who live with the results are encouraged by the support professionals to specify what is important to them. Ornament and detail create character. One village may decide they want hanging plants from the light posts with automatic drip feed. The time to decide that is at the beginning before the posts are ordered so that water pipes are installed. The youth village may want a design that enables them to dance in the streets late at night without disturbing other villages – a design that can be accommodated if it is set out at the beginning.

Of course, all of these extra details cost money. Where does it come from? The answer to that question begins in the next section.

Your Hundred-Million Dollar Legacy Fund

To get anything big done in today's world you need big money, and it always seems that someone else has it and they don't want to give it to you – except for the biggest purchase in most people's lives: buying a home. At that point, if you can show the bank that you will repay them with interest, they will loan you hundreds of thousands over a long period of time, up to thirty years. If you want to build a house, they will give you a construction loan and then convert it into a mortgage. They will loan it to you based on the market value, usually requiring you put up a down payment to give them comfort that you have a personal stake in paying them back.

If you build one home, and you are careful, that home will be worth about what it cost you to build. This is because you bought the land at retail, after it was subdivided, after someone else made the subdividing profits. It is because you paid retail for materials and labor, and there seemed to be a whole line of professionals and bureaucrats charging fees and percentages that add to the cost, but not to the value. In New Zealand, this is called *clipping the ticket*, and when one looks carefully, it is appalling how many times you'll get clipped.

If instead, you and 4,000 other buyers agreed to buy and build at the same time, you generate a *cost differential*, the difference between what it costs to build one home and what it costs when *economies of scale* kick in. That differential can be huge, adding up to hundreds of millions of dollars in savings on land-acquisition costs, materials bought at wholesale or even factory prices, and large tooling that saves far more on labor than the cost of the tools. Some, but not all, of this differential is invested in the VillageTown to lower cost of living, lower its environmental footprint, strengthen the economy and increase quality of life.

Obviously, it is not feasible for you and 4,000 other buyers to do this on your own. That is where the VillageTown organizing company comes in. The organizing company looks like a developer, except that it works for your collective interest rather than for its own pecuniary interest. It employs the best professionals money can buy, paid for their expertise with a salary and a success bonus dependent on the size of the *Legacy Fund* they leave to you. While potential start-up investors may try to claim the cost differential as profits, this should be resisted. It's your money, not theirs. It comes from your willingness to pre-identify, and as such it should be separated out from legitimate investor return on investment.

The Legacy Fund is what happens to the net cost differential. While it would be possible to rebate to each buyer their cost savings, this would be counterproductive. This would attract speculators who would buy the homes, then sell them for a large capital gain once built, thus defeating the point of the VillageTown. Instead a fund is established that is owned by the citizens as part of the VillageTown operating company. It is your reward; your money, not as an individual but as a community. The role of the VillageTown fund mangers

In the development business, the *market absorption rate* refers to the speed at which new homes are sold in a region. When the job market expands, people move from other places, needing a home; some buy in a new development, others buy or rent older homes while the seller moves up. The jobs drive the economy as people buy consumer goods, stimulating the shopping-mall business, big-box stores and franchised businesses which cater to the consumer. It becomes a formula for money-making which is why so many places begin to look like everywhere else.

is to assure it is managed well, to provide not only for now, but to plan for seven generations.

This large pool of capital creates options for the VillageTown. It becomes the empowerment tool that makes good things possible. It becomes the force that enables people to create and experience a much more enriched way of living – to provide for their needs and their aspirations. To use the current business slang *it's the game changer.*

We need to mention at this point, that this piece of the VillageTown puzzle only surfaced somewhat recently, yet it is clear that it may be one of its most important parts. Prior to the 2008 credit crash, no one had crunched the numbers to reveal the potential magnitude of the differential. When the VillageTown idea was evolving, the idea of pre-identifying the buyers came from the need for authenticity and character. In order for a place not to feel like what is sometimes called *cartoon architecture*, the homes and villages need to reflect the character of the people who live there. It is important that villagers pre-identify to set out the look, feel and function of their village, homes and workplaces.

However, after 2008 credit crash, the necessity for the villagers to self-select in advance became doubly important. It offers a completely new model for financing, and promises to turn real-estate development upside down. At a time when very little new development is taking place, pre-identifying becomes essential for the VillageTown to secure funding.

This power to act in concert is more likely for VillageTown buyers as a group than it is for a developer. The typical developer relies on regional market growth to sell what he builds. In the industry it is called the *market absorption rate;* it can take decades to sell a development. New regional jobs must be created to drive more regional new home sales. Not so with a VillageTown that attracts people who bring their work with them. This self-creating local economy creates its own market demand before construction begins.

The potential is awesome, especially if the regional market has a wide spread between cost and market value. If the total cost of high-volume construction, including amenities and overhead is $100 per square foot ($1,000 per m²) and the market price is double, the Legacy Fund could begin with hundreds of millions of dollars. The fund rules require it be invested for the common good – for current and future generations. The Fund can invest in local businesses to help them grow strong, while returning profits to the Fund. It can invest in the walk-to Industrial Park to attract more small to medium enterprises. It can enable small business to be on a more level playing field with big business and in doing so, the local economy will become self-supporting, self-growing and self-protecting. The Legacy Fund and its implications are discussed in more depth starting on page 141, but in thinking about its potential, consider how it might work with the idea of village themes. What if the organizing company were to do a global search to invite outstanding and desirable industries to move the whole business, including the staff? By having a village based on nationality, and targeting a particular country for invitations, the families will feel more comfortable making the move. Let's explore this idea in more depth:

Directions to find *a good life*, as found on a wall in Deya, Mallorca, Spain.

The VillageTown Administration combines non-profit services with tax-paying businesses

The VillageTown as a Corporation

As the world moves more toward corporatism, and as corporate law claims more power while government law weakens, it makes sense to use corporate law.

The VillageTown begins as an *Organizing Company* whose stock is held in trust by the VillageTown Stewards & Co. When the VillageTown is built, the Stewards relinquish the stock to recast it as an *Operating Company* and ownership and control move to the citizens of the VillageTown. It's not a cooperative; it is a corporation with all the privileges and power that corporations are being accorded by national & international law.

Typically, in new residential developments and planned communities, a private association is established to provide private governance for the community. There are laws (often restrictive) that regulate such private associations. Fees are assessed by the private association, to pay for services that often are also being funded (but not provided) through local property taxes or rates paid to the host jurisdiction. These associations tend to have limited scope and effectiveness because they lack clear distinctions between governance, administration, and judiciary functions, and because law restricts what they can do.

The VillageTown approaches the governance needs differently. It provides both private (community-owned) local governance and a private corporation established to serve the commercial and wellbeing interests of its stakeholders, the citizens of the VillageTown. On its local governance side it uses proven systems of checks and balances for local government.

Local VillageTown Governance

The most important document the VillageTown will draft is what may be called the *charter* by which governance is established and anchored in the title to each VillageTown property. It must be written in simple, unbreakable language, yet be framed to allow the VillageTown to evolve. This social contract promises to be legally sophisticated, and the organizing company should budget for the best legal minds in the country to get it right.

In simple terms, its governance uses a familiar tripartite structure with:

1. **Legislative** – An elected board of representatives who speak by resolution to make policy, adopt budgets, and vote fees that are the equivalent of property taxes/rates.
2. **Executive** – The administration that executes the policy and resolutions of the elected VillageTown Board. Its CEO or chief is an elected position, which functions both as a private corporate CEO and a private governance Mayor.
3. **Judicial** – The VillageTown Court that hears and decides on local matters. Its judges should have legal training to qualify them for election. In addition to this judicial function, two part-time appointed but then independent positions conduct the

business of the judicial to maintain checks & balances:

- **Prosecutor,** appointed by CEO, represents the VillageTown against the individual.
- **Ombudsman,** appointed by the Board, represents the individual against the group.

Crime Intolerance: A major problem in many local communities today is the failure of government in relation to petty and sometimes serious crime. It wasn't always this way. As VillageTown Stewards' Chairman Emeritus, Stewart L. Udall said: *In small towns like mine, you had very little crime and people were good neighbors. One of the great advantages, in my view, of small and middle-sized towns is that neighbors are concerned about their neighborhoods. Small communities are very intolerant of crime, and the neighbors looked after the kids as they carried on around town**. However, over time small and large communities suffer more crime. The governing powers they once held to prevent crime have been weakened and rendered less effective.

However, corporate and land law grant power that local governments lack – the power of dismissal and eviction. For it to be effective, the ultimate penalty that must be written in the VillageTown charter is the power to auction the home of a VillageTown citizen found to have breached the rules of the VillageTown, stripping the offender of their VillageTown citizenship and the right to live in the VillageTown. This power must be embedded in contract law, following due process. For this reason, the judicial function of private governance must be formal, structured, and in accordance with state and national law. In some states, this may be easy, but in others it may require the land be held in a form of leasehold to give the freeholder (the VillageTown) certain powers to make rules, collect fees and evict those found guilty of defined and major offences.

This power also is essential to protect parallel-real-estate homes, where the seller and buyer make a contract, and the VillageTown must step in when it becomes public knowledge that the buyer was not within the target market (in other words, they cheated). In such cases, the VillageTown prosecutor investigates, and brings charges before the court. If they find the buyer did cheat, they can order the home be resold to a qualified buyer or be subject to a public auction. This potential threat must be structured in a way to protect the long-term mortgage-securities holders, to assure them that any losses in the difference between the auction price and mortgage are not carried by them.

Non-Profit Services such as Public Utilities, Road Maintenance, etc.

The VillageTown runs its own water, sewage, solid-waste recycling, electric, tele-communications – including phone and broadband, and public services such as operating the nursing-care facilities and medical clinics. These services will enable the VillageTown to take advantage of the best technology to minimize negative externality and provide a closed-loop, sustainable management of such non-profit services. These services will be funded in part by annual fees, but also may benefit from proceeds earned by the Legacy Fund.

---

*   Cameo by Stewart Udall page 193, *Life Liberty Happiness*, 2009, Jackson House Publishing Company,

For Profit Businesses – VillageTown Subsidiaries

Wealth is created by industriousness, when people are productive. It is created when people are busy, engaged in business. Anthropologists tell us that in tribal societies, 80% of the community are engaged in productive work, and the remaining 20% are children.

A VillageTown defines itself as a community, but then uses the legal framework of the corporation to support the private enterprises of its citizens. Some of this support comes from the Legacy Fund investing in private businesses, and other support comes from VillageTown-owned businesses. The VillageTown itself is a private, tax-paying corporation as well as governance body that enables its people and villages to look after local matters.

Private Businesses

Probably run as subsidiary, tax-paying ventures, the VillageTown corporation runs ventures including the bank, the legacy fund, the rental cars, the food services, the buying club, and possibly the sewage and waste-management services if these produce profits through smart reuse of surplus material. Profits are paid to its parent corporation, the VillageTown, to reduce local taxation (fees, taxes or rates) and fund its non-profit services.

Combined Purchasing Power

The wholesale-buying group and the food-services group are businesses that combine villagers' purchasing power to lower costs and buy services that may not be available to individuals. For example, in some countries, one requires private medical insurance, but unless one is part of a company plan, the policy can cost more and offer less. The VillageTown can purchase group insurance for any or for all its citizens, thus securing a better price. It can tailor such a plan by operating its own preventative-care medical facilities, and it can self-insure on small claims. It can do the same with business insurance, liability insurance, home insurance and car insurance where it can either act as a wholesale buyer and retailer, or lower costs through a combined self-insurance/reinsurance plan. Additionally, the legacy fund can engage in joint ventures with local businesses, using its capital to bring several together under its umbrella so they may be more effective than working alone. This can enable them to compete with larger corporations.

Legal and Business Services

The VillageTown can also engage in collaborative business services, such as hiring lawyers with patent skills to support a cluster of inventors and entrepreneurs, or employing human-resource experts to enable small local businesses to have access to the same level of expertise as large companies. It also can hire litigation lawyers to create a level playing field for its small local businesses when they seek to do business in the predatory global economy. This is especially the case when chain stores and franchises seek to use their muscle to bankrupt local businesses to secure local control of markets.

To understand how we got here, it's important to understand the Depression and WW-II

Historical context - How we got here

For this section, we are grateful to VillageTown Stewards' Chairman Emeritus, Stewart Udall (1920-2010), former US Secretary of the Interior and a Congressman in 1956 when the USA adopted the Interstate Highway Program that paved America. He was an eyewitness to history. *There was no debate* he said. *It was the biggest mistake of the century.*

Over the past half century, humanity experimented with a radical new design of habitat based on expanding the *home-range* by separating destinations so people must drive – a new form of community that became known disparagingly as suburban sprawl as it consumed land and resources in a way that was bland at best, and ugly and toxic in too many places.

It began in America after the Second World War when a decision was made to build new communities to serve the political and pecuniary interests of governments and large corporations. The stated purpose was to forestall another Great Depression by creating a new market for cars and gasoline. Build highways, zone to create separations between destinations so driving is required, and developers will build suburbs. It's not sustainable, but for the first 50 years, it worked. Unfortunately, it worked by mortgaging future generations and gradually making every place look like everywhere else.

The men who voted to turn the successful war machine into the successful stimulant of the economy did so with honorable intentions. It was a more innocent time than today. Freshman Congressman Stewart Udall voted for the Interstate Highway Program, as did everyone else in Congress. As he explained 53 years later:

My early experience was the early years of the Great Depression, and I learned how people coped with a depression. Most people today don't realize the Depression lasted eleven years. We got out of the Depression when the Pearl Harbor attack occurred – when we realized we were in a global war and we had to convert our economy. They shut down all the automobile factories in Detroit and they converted them to making tanks; the bombers that I flew on were made in Detroit by one of the automobile companies. The United States had an abundance of oil and because we had technological knowledge, we built ships and tanks and airplanes and so on. After Pearl Harbor I volunteered for the Army Air Force. I saw the war from the air; I was a gunner on bombers flying out of Italy. We were going after oil, an area called Ploiesti in Romania. We bombed that several times trying to cut off their supplies, because oil was very important during the war.

The war gave us faith in oil and faith in technology. I am not negative about technology. But this country at that time, we thought technology would solve all of our problems. No reason to worry about technology because technology is growing. We see now that that was a huge mistake. In 1956, as a junior congressman of course, I had very little influence but I recall that Albert Gore Sr. from Tennessee, a Senator, was the sponsor of the Interstate Highway program.

The lead that won the Second World War for America was as much an additive in the gasoline as it was the lead in bullets. The toxic gasoline additive known as *tetraethyl lead* enabled US equipment to run higher compression engines, thus being able to do more with the same amount of fuel. It made American jeeps, trucks, tanks and planes go faster and further than the enemy's.

The patent for that additive was held by the Ethel Gasoline Company which was owned by Standard Oil (now Exxon), General Motors and Dupont. The men who ran those companies were friends of the policy makers of the time; indeed GM's Chairman Alfred P. Sloan spoke at President Eisenhower's funeral; Francis V. du Pont served under Eisenhower as the US Commissioner of the Bureau of Public Roads from 1953-55.

After the war, jeep production became car production, and the commercial aviation industry took over from long-distance rail. The captains of industry whose firms owned the Ethel Gasoline Company won the spoils when peace came; the new era of cars, oil, and chemicals began.

I did not participate in the debate, there were very few questions asked. I was amazed when I look back – there was never any discussion about whether we had enough petroleum or natural gas to adopt what I call a one-person-one-car transportation system. But we went ahead and did it. There was a kind of an aura that we have unlimited oil and this is a good idea. After I left my post in the Cabinet, in the early 1970s I was one of the first people that saw that this wasn't going to work. We've gone too far and we are going to have to have different priorities as far as transportation and oil are concerned.

It has been a fascinating period for someone who went to Congress when he was 34, and now I come out and I am advising my children that they are inheriting a different world. Their world is 'Think small, drive small, walk a lot, build transportation systems that encourage people to walk, break up your cities into smaller parts, and that's the way you are going to solve the problem that the United States has today"*

The approach America chose to forestall another depression was put forward by captains of industry (see the annotation about the patent on tetraethyl lead on the previous page). To create demand for these war-winning commodities, a new form of living had to be invented; this became known as the suburb. For perhaps the first time in history, a democracy reinvented itself where at its very core purpose, people's daily lives were reorganized to serve policy rather than policy serving people and communities.

To do this, the country had to destroy its existing urban housing stock – solid brick buildings that required weeks of bashing with the wrecker's ball because the cities were so well built. Strong blue-collar communities were destroyed by block-busting as cities turned into ghettos. They ripped up perfectly good urban rail lines and paved over high-quality arable land. The history was both shameful and squandering.

It did not happen overnight. The Servicemen's Readjustment Act of 1944 – commonly known as the GI Bill of Rights guaranteed war veterans home loans that enabled millions of U.S. military men to purchase their first homes with inexpensive mortgages. This too helped create the market for suburbs.

Gradually, policy makers realized that the construction of a multi-lane, limited access freeway extending out and around an older city would cause a building boom that depended on cars to get from home to daily destinations. In 1956, they committed America to that model, funding the largest public-works project in the history of mankind. It became the American way.

The plan achieved its goal. America kept itself out of a second Great Depression, became the pre-eminent super-power in the world, and as a happy side effect, saw its corporations grow to be some of the largest in the world. *What's good for General Motors is good for America* became a slogan of the new era.

---

*	Excerpted from a video taped interview 20 June 2009 available at www.villageforum.com. Stewart L. Udall passed away nine months later on 20 March 2010, age 90.

The big-box shopping mall now defines the character of almost every town in America

The one person - one car policy is firmly in place. Until it starts to run out of gas.

This ethos drove a building frenzy that continued all the way until the credit crash that struck in 2007. In the United States millions of homes were built that had no buyers. Malls spread, to the point where one could be thousands of miles apart, yet it all looked the same – the same franchises and chains, the same acres of parking and the same hollowness.

The problem was not only American, however. In Europe, the same thing happened, resulting in millions of unsold homes and apartments that blot the land. Even pristine countries like Switzerland find the same challenges with box stores covering the landscape. Everyone was doing it because credit was easy, and the formula made money for the developers and investors – until it all collapsed when it became apparent it was a nonsense.

In hindsight, it is clear that suburban sprawl produced a thicket of new problems and challenges so bad that leaders and industry cannot even agree on the magnitude or character of the problems, much less implement good solutions.

This tangle of seemingly unsolvable, aggravating and in some cases potentially catastrophic problems came about when business opened new markets by changing how people live. Everyday life became monetized. Driving became essential. The economy was built on what economists call *negative externality* – creating artificial wealth by externalizing the pollution of earth, water, air and our own bodies – someone else pays.

About 60 years later, when even its staunchest defenders had to admit unanticipated negative side effects were beginning to bite, the next generation began to question the foundation and presumptions upon which the great suburban experiment was built. There tended to be three responses that came from this:

- Denial/obfuscation – the favorite answer for those still benefiting
- Keep going in the same direction but try to fix what is broken
- Go back and ask the right question, find the best answer, start over again.

Most of the sustainability movement is focused on the second option, trying to fix broken systems – a challenge because the systems are purpose-built, but built for the wrong purpose. The adverse social effects tend not to be considered in their fixes. If we invent transport that runs on renewable resources we solve global warming and peak oil, but fail to address the effect of emptying out a community during the day.

In contrast, the VillageTown follows the third approach. We accept that new real-estate development will continue to be a part of global economic systems. Thus we went back to first principles to examine how real-estate development can be designed so it does not have negative side effects. We begin this examination by identifying the right questions to ask, starting with the most obvious: Why do human beings need communities? What is their purpose? Do today's communities serve those needs? If not, what would?

The Industrial Revolution

The Technology Revolution

TELEPRESENCE - THE SHIFT IN TECHNOLOGY

Every time there is a shift in technology, it affects how people live.

In the 19th century, the industrial revolution changed the size and price of tools. Factories required large numbers of people to run them, and they drew their workers from the small towns and villages in the countryside. Instead of buying shoes from the local cobbler, for example, shoes began to come from factories that made extensive use of large machinery.

This gradually caused small towns and villages to weaken. In the 20th century, when road transport exploded on the scene, the small towns and villages began to die off, especially when the limited access highways bypassed Main Street.

Beginning in the 1950's, as global shipping shifted from break-bulk to container ships, the industrial revolution began to shift from first-world to low-wage, low-regulation, developing countries. Manufacturing moved elsewhere because shipping goods by sea became very inexpensive. In first-world countries, especially the USA, the growth industry was in new malls and big-box stores on the edge of town selling products made overseas. These of course wiped out what remained of the small-town local economy.

In the 21st century, a new shift in technology is emerging. Initially called the computer revolution, then the internet and now electronic convergence of phone, TV, PC and robotics, the word that best encompasses the technology is *telepresence*. Not only can one have a face to face business meeting using systems like Cisco's telepresence (or Skype on the low-price end of the scale), but a doctor can participate in surgery using telepresence, or a scientist can explore the depths of the ocean from the comfort of an office on dry land. Telepresence opens up new ways for people to work, and therefore opens up new places where they can live. Telepresence allows millions to chose where they want to live based on quality of life rather than proximity to the office and markets. To borrow an Australian phrase, it vanquishes the tyranny of distance.

Telepresence is especially important in the VillageTown. Telepresence workers can select where to work based on quality of life, rather than proximity to the office, suppliers or competitors. While working at home has its drawbacks (isolation for one), working in a telepresence office in the VillageTown provides important social stimulation. For this reason, it is paramount that the VillageTown invest in the fastest broadband systems available on the market, and design its infrastructure to support future upgrades easily. Further, the VillageTown should reduce the cost of such systems to the absolute minimum. Make broadband as "free" as the public highways.

When the industry fails to understand what people need and love

In this photograph, the middle section is a failed subdivision, a weed-infested lot abandoned after the credit crunch of 2008. In the bottom and top of the photo, the consumer is offered choices of size, but with a blandness totally devoid of character or beauty. It makes money, but not life.

Architect Christopher Alexander wrote: "In the 20th century we have passed through a unique period, one in which architecture as a discipline has been in a state that is almost unimaginably bad. Sometimes I think of it as a mass psychosis of unprecedented dimension, in which the people of earth — in large numbers and in almost all contemporary societies — have created a form of architecture which is against life, insane, image-ridden, hollow. The ugliness which has been created in the cities of the world, and the banality and pretentiousness of many 20th century buildings, streets, and parking lots have overwhelmed the earth. Much of this construction is caused by developers, housing authorities, owners of hotels, motels, airport authorities. In this sense architects might be considered blameless, since in some degree the ugliness of what has been created is caused by new relations between time, money, labor, and materials, and by a set of conditions in which the real thing — authentic architecture that has deep feeling and true worth — is almost impossible."*

*   The Nature of Order- Book One Page 6 by Christopher Alexander: ISBN 0-9726529-1-4 © 2002

Understanding People's Needs & Aspirations

As of this writing, VillageTown is an idea not a built town. While it receives enthusiastic support, the test comes in moving from talk to action. At that point two questions are key:

- **Will it sell?** Will the critical mass of people for each village come forward?
- **Will it thrive?** Will the critical mass of businesses move to, or start in, the VillageTown?

There is no way to answer these questions except to begin a project. In part, a positive answer will depend on location. If a project begins in the US, Australia or Europe, its immigration policies mean it must draw upon the existing population plus its expat citizens wanting to return home. In smaller countries, such as New Zealand which has a much more open immigration policy, the market is world-wide where the VillageTown becomes a reverse brain drain as first-world refugees (successful people who feel their home country's systems are failing) apply to move.

Within the target country, location means choosing the right place. California would be more attractive than North Dakota, even though California is more expensive, regulated and populated. Sydney would be more attractive than the Atherton Tablelands above Cairns because the complete population of a VillageTown located near Cairns must move from somewhere else. In New Zealand, *best location* is about climate and access.

The first VillageTown will be the hardest. After it is built, people will be able to see it, experience it and feel more comfortable that it is real. This is why the first VillageTown will involve a gradual process of commitment. People will self-identify and if they qualify, they will select their particular village. Initially, they will do so with no financial commitment. Instead start-up funds for the initial stages of the project are secured externally. When those future villagers see *they are the project*, and they are confident it is real and true, the organizing company asks them to commit a good-faith deposit to show clear intent.

Why will they make such a profound life-changing decision? In answer, it is important to understand the difference between motivating people and enabling them to provide for their needs and aspirations. People are motivated to buy or rent a suburban home, or move to a retirement home when old, to provide for only the most fundamental and basic needs. They accept limitations as a compromise, because it is what is on offer. Most have little choice.

In contrast, the VillageTown opens up new possibilities for them. It offers them the ability to consider qualities of day-to-day life that may exist in their dreams, but never in their self-censoring adult world, where they have been indoctrinated to accept less. The VillageTown casts out that self-censoring; showing that it is possible to create and live in a community that enables people to provide for their needs and aspirations. It not only shows the possibility, it provides a track to get there. So next, let us consider the difference between what is generally on offer today, and what the VillageTown will offer...

There is a certain hollowness about the suburbs; empty during the weekday; chores on weekends.

Housing for tenants tends to be for folks passing through, for seniors it's for passing on – sad.

Motivation: Why people buy the homes in the suburbs

- **Location**: Within commuting distance of work, driving distance of shops.
- **Price**: Affordable mortgage within personal/family budget.
- **Eventual Capital Gains**: When mortgage is paid, it becomes the primary asset.
- **Control**: Home ownership allows more freedom of use, decoration, etc.
- **Tax deductions**: Interest & local taxes are deductible in some countries.
- **Identity**: Home ownership provides a sense of identity; pride of ownership.
- **Safety**: It feels safe, although "normal" includes alarms and every door locked.
- **Schools**: For parents, access to better schools can drive a purchase decision.
- **Stuff**: It provides a place to store cars & consumer goods that are part of modern life.
- **Easy**: It's there. It's what is on offer. It is what people do. Not many alternatives.

Motivation: Why people rent

- **Location**: Same as above
- **Money**: Not qualified to buy, can't afford to buy, or buying is too entangling
- **Distrust of the market**: Home ownership does not always mean capital gains.
- **Transient**: Moving on, getting a job elsewhere; selling a home can be hard.
- **Simplicity**: It's there. Sign papers, post a deposit, move in; sometimes furnished.
- **No Maintenance**: Someone else does the repairs.
- **Unencumbered life**: Works easier if one is single or has no dependent children.

Motivation: Why elders go to retirement homes

- **No driver license**; cannot get around easily.
- **Physically weaker;** need more support, including emergency response.
- **No alternatives**. Children can't help. They ask their parents to move there.
- **Loneliness:** it's what's on offer. It's how society houses its elders.

What's missing?

Notably absent from these answers provided to today's consumer, is any sense of what it is to be a social human being. Dominant in these lists is a focus on money – earning it and spending it. But also it suggests a sense of powerlessness – that there really is not a lot of choice when it comes to the search for home.

Why?

The people who will live in these places no longer have much of a say in what is built. Decisions are made by investors, developers, builders, and local-government officials. The driving force for the private sector is profit and this is often shaped by what fits the rules. *Why make life difficult for yourself?* one successful developer asked, when learning about the VillageTown concept. His view: build what is easy to get approved and easy to sell.

In a VillageTown different criteria apply to why people will buy; why some will stay for life. These aspirations create a stronger initial attraction. They foster deeply-rooted bonds that make their VillageTown more than just a place to stay while passing through. The reasons to buy homes in a VillageTown center on the creation of a different relationship – a different relationship to land, house, home, community and place.

- **Belonging:** You know your neighbors, they know you. You support each other and friendships grow more easily because of proximity. This occurs naturally, because of the car-free design where you walk everywhere.
- **Economic security:** You live in a self-supporting local economy that provides greater control over money, earnings & savings. You can generate wealth and you are more protected from instability in the global economy. Zero unemployment and no poverty.
- **Lower cost of living:** Combined purchasing power lowers cost of goods and services. This becomes increasingly important as the world moves into a era of higher inflation.
- **Commonwealth – the Legacy Fund:** Cost savings from building all at once stay in the community, potentially funding a pool of many millions of dollars to create a broad-based wealthy community for all people regardless of their personal earnings power.
- **Diverse Life-styles:** It's not the monoculture of the suburbs.
- **Family integrity:** The streets are safe; children are looked after by a thousand eyes. Elders abound; they are provided for and naturally help out. Parents work nearby. They can share child minding. This relieves the isolation-pressure on parents that crushes too many marriages, breaks families and emotionally scars children.
- **Teenage life:** The VillageTown offers teens a wide variety of activities that enable them to develop independence and autonomy in a safer, more secure environment. Their territory will expand from their own village to the many villages and the town center. They will have after-school job opportunities and cultural choices through the Guild Halls. Parents need not drive younger teens, and car crashes, the number one killer of older teens, will be less likely since driving is not a central component in VillageTown life.
- **Education:** The VillageTown offers the opportunity for outstanding education of children. It does take the village to raise the child. By keeping classrooms in the villages, children have many role models while studying.
- **Connection to land:** The land anchors people; place becomes part of person and family. For many the connection becomes permanent, a place to plant generational roots. The cemetery marks your generations.
- **It's yours:** You help define your village. You create home & community to provide what you need and love.
- **Special character:** The founders of each village will make history as they define its special character reflecting their needs, dreams and aspirations. Each village is different, adding variety to the town; making day-to-day life more interesting. Walking from one village to

another is like flying from country to country: a diverse, enriched cultural experience.

- **Conviviality:** The Villages plazas are places to enjoy others; no appointment needed; great food & drink. It's a fun, stimulating place to live.
- **Citizenship:** Taking care is an integral part of village and town life. It occurs on every level: looking after others, educating the young, caring for the land, protecting the natural and physical environment, or holding elected office to serve the community.
- **Artistic & intellectual activity:** By building the guild halls and attracting college & research groups, the villages become more stimulating places. It's colorful, vibrant, active, spontaneous, with lots of movement & rhythm.
- **Spiritual pursuit:** Provides for organized religions and for those on their own who seek the sacred & holy.
- **No Fear:** Villages do not tolerate crime. They hold the means to protect themselves. In a car-free place where people know each other, delinquency & crime cannot take root. People enjoy life more fully with less worry.
- **Health & medical:** Community-owned health care offers local control over medical care.
- **No cars:** Designed so all destinations are within walking distance and intended as a 24/7 community with no outbound commuters, the VillageTown removes over 6,000 cars from the road and cuts driving by over a quarter-million miles per day. This eliminates hassles, keeps the air, water and streets cleaner, and allows for a quieter, safer place to live. Also it reduces a family's cost of living by about 15% with no pain or inconvenience.
- **Many choices:** The variety of affordable housing choices is broad: private attached homes, small flats, rentals, college-type halls, extended-family housing, mansions, settled elder & infirmity housing, youth housing, etc.
- **Comprehensive life investment:** For the price of a home, you invest in a way of life that provides, protects and enables you to pursue the finer things in life. It is likely that your home will significantly appreciate in value as others see the benefits of living in a VillageTown. However, for most this will remain a potential asset, as one would have no good reason to move away. It is the ultimate tangible investment.

Discussion: Motivation vs Aspiration

These two lists on motivation and aspiration do not claim to be universally accurate or complete; that is not the point. They are not intended to provoke argument but to facilitate discussion. The difference between motivation and aspiration may be understood as the difference between compromise and visualization; the difference between accepting what is on offer and what happens when people come together to explore what is possible. To visualize what is possible, we need to shift the discussion to what attracts us. The first part of attraction relates to employment. People need to make a living, thus the VillageTown supports its local economy. People focus on balancing their cost of living so they then can begin to enjoy the social pursuits of a good life. But how does it look from the businesses perspective? What makes the VillageTown attractive to businesses?

The VillageTown seeks to attract small to medium enterprises (SME). It will avoid dominance by a large company (company towns can threaten long-term economic wellbeing) and avoid chains and franchises that leak money from commonwealth.

Why will the SME will move to the VillageTown?

- **Personal:** The decision-maker is looking for quality of life. If they have a family it is a good place to raise children, if they have aging parents, it is a good place to have them nearby. If they are single, it's a good place to meet people and to have fun. If they enjoy social or cultural stimulation, the VillageTown offers it. Life is more than business, and the VillageTown offers more.
- **The *Legacy Fund* creating a supportive business environment:** As discussed in more detail on page 37 and on page 141, the VillageTown begins with a capital fund derived from the saving differential in building all homes at once. It establishes a fund management group committed to preserving and growing the VillageTown commonwealth. In markets with high property values, this differential can add up to hundreds of millions of dollars. The concept of commonwealth includes both economic and social/cultural aspects. The business focus is both clear and on a local level it offers a very high level of support for VillageTown businesses. It invests in local businesses. It provides access to expertise that the typical SME could never afford. It combines purchasing power to lower costs and secure better services. It has the option of opening remote and international field offices to represent local products in other parts of the country and in other nations.
- **Staffing:** In a competitive marketplace, attracting the best people involves more than pay and perks. Just as the VillageTown offers a quality of life that attracts the decision-maker to move their business, those same qualities will enable that business to attract the best employees. The tangible and intangible benefits and advantages of the VillageTown will encourage the best candidates to choose a VillageTown job.
- **Parallel market housing:** The VillageTown intentionally creates parallel markets so that housing is affordable by the normal cross section of society, not only the rich. This includes homes for blue-collar industrial, office, and shop workers who otherwise may find they have a job, but can't afford to rent or buy.
- **Available facilities:** If the business needs industrial space, it is there. If it requires office space, workplaces, commercial property, or a home office, all is available, and thanks to the no-load-bearing design for interior walls, such work space can customized to requirements. In some cases, it will allow a small apartment above or behind the business to enable an entrepreneur to focus fully on the work of a start-up business, with a place to sleep until they can afford a proper home or apartment.
- **Affordable facilities:** Pricing decisions on commercial/industrial space are made by

the organizing company which may make strategic lease concessions to attract the right businesses that will strengthen the local economy. If the VillageTown starts with a large legacy fund, the fund managers may decide to retain ownership of some of the industrial or commercial business space, and offer long-term leases at low, or even dollar-a-year rates to permanently enable valuable businesses to remain competitive in a global economy. By lowering the rent on such property, the VillageTown earns less on its capital, but strengthens the commonwealth and assures the social diversity by retaining jobs for workers who choose a trade rather than a white-collar profession. This sort of strategic thinking is part of the VillageTown long-term brief.

- **Lower cost of doing business**: In negotiating staff wages and salaries, the ultimate driver is the cost of living. If the price of fuel doubles, the employees have to pay double or they cannot get to work. The VillageTown eliminates the cost of commuting. It lowers the cost of food, heating & cooling, consumer goods, entertainment, health care, education for the young, care for the elderly. Thus, the cost of making goods and providing services is lower in a VillageTown than in the normal competitive market – making it attractive to the SME.

- **Right location with right technology**: Choosing a location within two hours of an international airport is important to businesses that sell local-to-global. The VillageTown owns its local telecommunications company, thus it can buy wholesale global telecommunications services and offer them, including world-wide toll-free telephone calling and video conferencing, as part of the business support package. By doing this, location becomes virtual. All of this is made possible because of ultra-high-speed broadband, which now enables local-to-global business to effectively conduct business via *telepresence*. However, when a face-to-face meeting is required, or the overnight package must arrive, locating within two hours of the airport enables the business to be linked in. In some cases, two hours means by car or mass transport. However, there may be locations where it makes more sense for the VillageTown to invest in its own airport and commuter airline. Some locations may already be served by a commuter airline, but because it has a monopoly, it may not serve the VillageTown interests. In such cases, the VillageTown may elect to start its own commuter airline and subsidize tickets for VillageTown stakeholders & businesses.

- **Future opportunities**: To the extent that other VillageTowns are built in other locations, there should be an intrinsic connection that facilitates market entry as well as sourcing that which is not available locally -- a VillageTown cross-border reciprocity, both in doing business and in Legacy Fund investing.

Businesses will be attracted to the VillageTown because it understands and values the importance of thriving, independent businesses to keep its commonwealth healthy. It puts its money where its mouth is, both in initially attracting the businesses and in supporting their success in its long-term planning and provision of service.

To get a good sense of what a human-scaled town feels like, it's best to travel to Europe and visit the old central districts that, for the most part, still prohibit cars. This lovely town of Alcudia in Spain on the island of Mallorca has wider streets than the sometimes too-tight medieval streets of other old European towns. The pavement is of cut stone that stays clean because there is no traffic other than pedestrians and push carts. Note how the afternoon sunlight bounces off the lightly-tinted walls, making the street bright and welcoming, but not too hot.

Before cars changed the character of streets, what is today called mixed-use zoning was commonplace. Residences were above and behind commercial establishments for those who enjoy the buzz of the night life. The same will be true in the VillageTown. Microzoning means some parts will have mixed us, whereas other quieter streets will be strictly for residences – and the decisions on how this is laid out is made by the people who will live with the results.

PART 2: VILLAGETOWN FEATURES & ATTRACTIONS

This section is a required tutorial. Without reading this part of the book, it is most likely you will misunderstand certain key features – pieces of the puzzle – and therefore will not understand the full picture. The VillageTown is not only a different way of living; it's a different process to get there. While some elements are flexible, intended to fit the geography, the economy, and the individual needs of the future villagers, other aspects are non-negotiable because if they are transgressed, it's no longer a VillageTown. For example:

- Cars are not driven within the village walls. The VillageTown is a walking home range.
- Students will not be bussed to half empty regional schools – classrooms are on the plaza
- Buildings will be non-combustible and fire-proofed to avoid *design by fire truck*
- Most housing will be attached – wide and shallow to let in more sunlight
- You cannot bring in or start a franchise or chain that will weaken the local economy

However, there are other aspects that are negotiable or situational. For example:

- While 10,000-population is optimal, some sites may dictate smaller population numbers
- The town plaza zone may have higher buildings, even some commercial office buildings
- While we prefer not, there may be some workers in the region who commute inbound
- Brownfield sites may require compromises on the optimal design

Often in the question period after a public talk on VillageTowns, people will ask questions like *"will you allow people with profound intellectual disabilities?"* or the rather curious question *"will you allow rich people to live in the VillageTown?"* In answer, we reply by holding up an imaginary mirror, and ask them what they will allow: *"It's your village, not ours."* It takes a while for people to understand the freedom they have but don't use. The intent is to create a *complete community* in which each of the 20 villages decides for itself what is important.

We, the Stewards, create a framework, a set of boundary conditions that defines in general what a VillageTown is, but within that framework, we do our best to avoid injecting our values into what will be the villagers' community, not ours. The purpose of the boundary conditions is to give the model coherence. There are many other models, such as suburban developments, new urbanism, gated communities, apartment living, life-style farmlets, ecovillages, co-housing, transition towns, and theme communities like airparks or boatparks (where you can sleep next to your plane or boat). The VillageTown is not one of those models, it is its own model; it stands on its own merits.

Thus, in this next section, we discuss a few of the elements that make up the framework that defines a VillageTown. They are complementary; they fit together. If one is changed, the whole is altered. For coherence, we set these elements out following the format of local economy that enables conviviality, citizenship and artistic, intellectual & spiritual growth.

Conviviality

Citizenship

Artistic, Intellectual and Spiritual Growth

PRIME ATTRACTIONS OF THE VILLAGETOWN

What attracts people? Different people are attracted by different parts of the VillageTown. Some are concerned about money; others want to know what it will be like living there, what's it like raising children, growing old, or how creative and stimulating a place it will be. A single person has different priorities than a working family.

In this book, we focus on the early phase of the VillageTown, when it is a new idea. Explaining it is a challenge, because the audiences are so varied. The interests of a single person in their early 30's are very different than those of a family with school-aged children or a boomer approaching eldership. It's useful to follow the same structure as the purpose statement: the economic foundation upon which *a good life* is built and then the elements of a good life. For those focused on single issues such as environmental sustainability, we remind them that in a sane society (like a VillageTown), sustainability is a subset of good citizenship.

THE ECONOMY – A SELF SUPPORTING ECONOMIC FOUNDATION

Legacy fund - Hundreds of millions remain with the VillageTown to provide for its ongoing wellbeing. So many things become possible, if only a community has the money to pay for them. The VillageTown begins with an unprecedented legacy fund because (1) its buyers pre-identify and (2) the organization established to build their community keeps their cost savings in trust for them, passing them on when the property title passes. Depending on the market where the VillageTown is located, this legacy fund could begin with hundreds of millions of dollars to invest in businesses and resilient systems.

Buy-in - No matter how attractive a place is, if it is unaffordable except to an exclusive group, it can never be a *complete community*. The VillageTown offers a wide range of pricing options to make initial and on-going home prices affordable to the full range of buyers and renters. It does so without requiring a bureaucracy. The VillageTown is intended for all the socioeconomic classes one would find in a complete community. This includes high-school graduates seeking blue-collar jobs, essential workers in low-paying or fixed-salary jobs, artists, young first-time home buyers, single adults of all ages, elders, the disadvantaged & disabled, and other target groups that make up the rest of a complete community. It backs this intent with carefully crafted investing including parallel markets for housing. On the other end of the economic scale, the VillageTown provides the quality of life and the facilities to attract the successful and the wealthy who will bring or start the businesses that contribute to the robust local economy. Given its legacy fund, the VillageTown may invest in some of these entrepreneurial businesses. Housing options include the town-center zone, a place for four-story buildings with a larger footprint, not necessarily attached. A community needs its rich people just as much as it needs those who, through lack of skill or education or by choice, earn and own less. A complete community provides for the normal cross section of society as found in the host nation. Given the inherent desirability of a VillageTown some of this must be achieved by the creation of parallel housing markets.

Parallel Housing Markets - One of the most difficult challenges governments face is how to make homes affordable without creating segregated stigma-zones. Typically, they end up as state housing managed by a costly bureaucracy. The VillageTown approaches this from a different perspective. It creates *parallel markets*. It identifies a disadvantaged buying class and determines why they have difficulty competing in the open market. A teacher, for example, is in a fixed pay band; if the median teacher's salary is $50,000, the bank will loan on a $200,000 home. But if the VillageTown becomes desirable, that home could sell for $400,000, meaning the teacher has to commute or live in subsidized housing. In the parallel market, the VillageTown sells the teacher the $400,000 home for $200,000. It retains a partial interest in the home that requires when the teacher goes to sell, they can sell at any price, but only to a buyer in the target market – another teacher or a civil servant whose fixed pay band is the same. This guarantees a stock of affordable homes. Since market value is driven by what the bank will loan, the selling price is automatically inflation-adjusted. Of course, not all those eligible for parallel homes will participate in the plan, and they are under no compulsion to do so – some will prefer to pay more and benefit from potentially higher capital gains. The parallel markets exist to offer more choice; to assure that the community remains complete. Such a system may not always work perfectly, but should work better than what is on offer today. It uses market forces to regulate the prices, but creates parallel markets to maintain affordable housing. The details will be worked out by the organizing company when it implements the systems.

Own the bank - At one time the banking industry was conservative, allowing people who saved money to earn a modest interest on deposits so people who needed money to create wealth or fund a purchase over time could borrow money at a higher rate. The bank covered costs and made modest profits by the difference between the deposit and the loan interest. Usually those banks were locally owned, and the profits stayed in the community. Those banks are harder to find today. Instead, banks tend to be large institutions that drain down the wealth of a community, often siphoned off by Wall Street. The VillageTown begins with about 4,000 home buyers, the vast majority of whom will need construction loan/mortgages that, when combined, could easily add up to more than a billion dollars. Rather than give that away to outside financial institutions, the VillageTown starts its own bank (or legal equivalent), packages the mortgages into prime mortgage-backed securities*, and sells these to institutional buyers such as insurance or pension funds. The fees it collects from servicing the mortgages will support ongoing operation of a retail bank that is owned by the VillageTown. Since its ultimate stockholders are the citizens of the community, the bank understands its decisions must always be made to be in the best

---

* Please do not confuse *prime* mortgage-backed securities with the *sub-prime* instruments that almost crashed the global economic system. Prime means the use of conservative banking practices to assess and assure the borrowers can and will pay their mortgages.

interest of the people and communities of the VillageTown. Owning the bank gives the community more control over its money. It's your life, your money, your future.

Cost of living: investing in infrastructure - Because the VillageTown does not use a high-risk, developer business model (speculative investment that may return high profits), it is able to invest significant profits back into the VillageTown to lower the ongoing basic cost of living for the villagers. This can include its own power company, broadband & telecommunication services, for-profit managing of solid waste and sewage, health facilities, and a host of other services that otherwise leak community wealth.

Cost of living: investing in combined purchasing power - The VillageTown can operate a buying club that combines purchasing power. Using professional buyers with a brief both to negotiate the best wholesale prices, and to select better, longer-lasting and repairable products with least-waste packaging, it can lower the cost of buying, keeping, and disposal.

Cost of living: durable buildings - In some countries today, the durability standard for buildings is 50 years, meaning it is legal to build a home that will not last much longer than half a century. The VillageTown standard is to plan for seven generations, and to lower both the long-term cost and the on-going cost of maintenance. Further, as much as possible, the buildings will be designed to have no or minimal load-bearing internal walls, allowing internal walls and building use to change as needs change. The proposed design systems will encourage generous building size, while substantially lowering energy leakage.

In all of these cost-of-living areas, it follows the simple principle that *it's cheaper to save a dollar than earn one*. A saved dollar takes no time to earn and it is not taxed.

Monetizing and De-monetizing Life: The World Bank tells us that over one billion people in the world live on less than a dollar a day. While this statistic is shameful and a sad commentary on the inequities of human life, it also makes no sense if one lives in a monetized society. To live on less than a dollar a day means the necessities of life are not monetized.

When you hire a baby-sitter, that is a monetized transaction. If you buy an extra bed and families share *sleep-overs*, you have de-monetized child care. In many cases, by de-monetizing, the quality of the experience rises as well. When elders are looked after in their own community, they are less depressed because they are interacting with everyone, old and young. When good water is available at drinking fountains, the monetized cost of bottled water is removed - drink as much as you want, it's free, and there is no disposing of a bottle. If you grow food in your garden, you de-monetize the cost of food – you substitute unpaid, untaxed labor for money. Additionally, you may find gardening to be fulfilling, and the food varieties you select taste better and are healthier because they are not selected to endure supply-chain shipping.

Economically more secure - The local economy develops resilient systems to protect itself from predatory economic forces, focusing on wealth creation by developing local opportunity, using its skill base smartly and encouraging local spending. The industrial park assures that it can make products needed on an ongoing basis. Money turn keeps local dollars cycling multiple times within the community. Examples include food from local farms, self-insurance, and a VillageTown bank to stem money (wealth) leakage.

In ancient tribal cultures, before segregation of rich and poor became institutionalized by law, there was no such thing as poverty and unemployment. There were weak and strong members of the community, and as part of being human, people looked after each other. No matter how weak, however, adult members of the community participated and contributed to its productivity and wellbeing. This is a model worth remembering.

In small communities, people naturally tend to look after each other. Not everyone of course – some people are self-centered and uncaring – but usually enough people do care that a natural safety net emerges as part of the community. If one then adds to this a Legacy Fund – where the community starts its existence with hundreds of millions of dollars set aside for its long-term wellbeing, the concept of taking care rises to a higher level.

The organizing company's mission statement for Legacy Fund managers includes zero tolerance for economic poverty or unemployment. By *economic poverty* we mean people lacking resources to become productive in contrast to people suffering from alcoholism, drug abuse, mental illness, or other disabilities where poverty is a symptom rather than the cause.

No unemployment - The Legacy Fund invests in local businesses. Such investment should require the business create and maintain flexible standby jobs that can be kept in readiness and activated at any time that a VillageTown citizen loses their job and cannot find another. Some jobs will be in the private sector; others will be managed directly by the Legacy Fund and the VillageTown operating company. There is always some sort of low-skill product or service that can be made or provided that will generate wealth which can be used to pay wages. At all times, have these jobs on standby. Goal: zero unemployment at all times.

No economic poverty - This involves two different kinds of poverty: moving in and later on. Some people will be classified as poor when they move to the VillageTown, especially when it starts out. Other individuals and families run the risk of dropping into economic poverty some time in their lives, and the VillageTown needs to have a safety net to offer a *hand-up* rather than rely on the state to offer a handout. Goal: full productive participation.

Poverty at the onset - The VillageTown is not intended as an elitist gated community to isolate the comfortable class from the less well off. Rather it is intended as a complete community, with people from all walks of life. Some of these people will be classified as living below the poverty line, and it is important that the VillageTown do its part to help such people gain control over their lives and get off the welfare roles.

In founding a VillageTown, the organizing company should approach the government welfare agency to identify dependent clients who want to better themselves; to move off of welfare and move into the VillageTown. The organizing company would qualify such people to assure they were truly committed to breaking their poverty cycle and working their way into meaningful, productive work. For solo parents with young children, life in the village instantly relieves some pressures because the design of a VillageTown makes it inherently easier to look after children.

Particular villages within the VillageTown may consider making this hand-up part of their identity. They may elect to host an ongoing *hand-up home* for a family in poverty where they invite a needy family to move in, take the hand-up, become a productive member of the community and to move into a home of their own, creating an opening for the next family to begin the climb to dignity, autonomy and independence. Note that while these ideas are proposed on their own merit, they also make the VillageTown concept exceptionally attractive to government policy makers in offering an alternative to the status quo.

Poverty later on - Death of a loved one, divorce, debt and disability tend to be the major life-changers that can bring an individual's life crashing down, no matter how comfortably they were doing before. This can happen to anyone at any time, and without a supportive community, it can be especially hard to recover. Unlike unemployment, where the primary need is to get back to work to pay the bills, have something to do, and retain a sense of self worth, the need after a life-changing crash can also involve the need for housing.

In *Life Liberty Happiness* – a story about a visit to a VillageTown set somewhere in the future – the *Suvie Village* was designed by single people for people living solo. While most were there by choice, it did include a facility for the losers of divorce - the husband or wife who ends up moving out of the family home and who otherwise may end up in a life-crushing environment. Similar housing should be set aside for teens who would otherwise run away and end up on the streets. Such safety-net homes need not be large, expensive, or plush, but it is important that they are available. Further, it is important that they are part of the village, to enable those people to get back on their feet, thus avoiding a crash into poverty.

Damaged individuals - As noted above *economic poverty* does not include people who are classified as poor as a result of some form of damage, be it mental, emotional, addictive, or physical. It is the damage that makes it difficult for such individuals to become participating and productive members of society, and in the absence of support systems, this often results in a life of poverty.

While decisions about how to support damaged individuals is made at the village level by village founders, it is important that the organizing company press for appropriate planning from the onset. There may be villages established by compassionate people, perhaps sharing a common religious belief, who conduct outreach to help such people. The job of the organizing company and later the operating company is to assure that these people receive the care they require, in a way that does not cause fear for villagers.

The Bottom Line - Inherent in the structure of a 500-person community is the care taking that is part of being human. This happens naturally. To enhance this, purpose-built homes and an allocation from the Legacy Fund should ensure a strong safety net to help the weak.

No, you don't give up your car. You just give up the addiction

Moving to a Village Town does not mean you must sell your cars. The Village Town will have a covered parking garage in the transport center where you can buy or lease a parking space. If you deem it important, you can pay to have walls and a door to protect your car or fleet.

What you give up is a car-based, driving home-range – the need to use the car for day-to-day chores like driving to work, transporting the kids, shopping or going out for a night on the town. If you want to drive to the city, the car is there. If you want to do that archetypal drive in the countryside that the car ads show, it will be easier for you to get there and more fun than if you lived in the sprawling suburbs.

However, after a while many villagers will find that owning a car no longer makes sense. The insurance, depreciation, (and the parts that stop working through lack of use), eat away at their savings accounts while the car sits there gathering dust. Instead, the villager will find that when they need a car, it is easier and cheaper to rent one from the motorpool. Unlike renting from a national chain, motorpool rentals are Village Town owned, perhaps operated as a non-profit business exclusively for its Village Town citizens. If you need to rent a pickup truck to bring home the bargains from a day antique hunting in the countryside, it's yours for the day. If you want to rent the Rolls for an elegant night on the town, it will cost more but be fun. Many of the day-to-day cars may be hybrid or electric cars, or perhaps run on alternative fuels such as alcohol produced by the waste treatment center.

If a Village Town finds it has a need for regular outbound transport – say people going to the major airport for national or international travel, it may run its own non-profit shuttle van or if traffic to the airport is a problem, it may invest in its own commuter airline. This latter option is especially important if the current airline holds a monopoly; and charges exorbitant fares to subsidize other routes where competition is stiffer.

No Cars in the Local Transport Area

Cars are everywhere – what greets a visitor to a suburban home is not the front door, but the view of a paved driveway and double-wide garage. According to the US Energy Information Agency, approximately one third of the average US home is devoted to parking the cars. Cars dominate the streets; it's hard for those who live in new world countries to imagine what life is like without cars everywhere one looks. In many places the only time one has true silence, free from the background noise of the internal combustion engine is during a severe snow storm when all traffic stops for a brief while.

Ironically, the only familiar public place where cars are banned is the shopping mall, where pedestrian streets allow one to walk among stores free from cars driving by. Of course, such places are surrounded by acres of black pavement to park thousands of cars.

To truly experience the wonder of car-free local zones, travel to the historic towns of the old world. Designed before cars, the streets are narrow, intimate and delightful. They now are tourist attractions because of their character and beauty. The experience of pedestrian streets is magic. Streets need not be straight, because people can turn more easily than wheeled vehicles. Streets need not be wide because a walking person occupies one percent of the space of a car driving at 30 mph / 50kph.

In the list of car-free zone tangible benefits on the next page, it should be noted that not one addresses the big issues of the day, most notably the concern that burning fossil fuels contributes to global warming, and global degradation of the environment, or proposed solutions such as cap & trade in carbon credits. This is intentional. The reasons to ban cars can solidly stand on local quality-of-life issues. Within a local community, cars designed to be safe in a highway-speed crash are too big, too fast, too hard, and too expensive. They make absolutely no sense when one can walk to one's daily destinations within ten minutes.

For now, cars have the problem of the internal combustion engine, but like tobacco smoking, it is something civilization will not easily give up. Longer term, it is safe to presume that the polluting aspects of motor vehicles will be solved when the energy industry squeezes out the last accessible sources of fossil fuels and then moves on to renewables. However, if that happened tomorrow, it would not change the negative effect that cars have on the local community. Cars have their place, but it is not inside the village.

Design by Fire Truck: On Virginian op-ed writer Jim Bacon's site *baconsrebellion. com*, Bacon writes that many jurisdictions' road-width rules are prescriptive, dictated by the Fire Department/Marshall. This wrecks the human-scaled feeling of a traditional village street and has some bad side effects. Studies show wider streets result in speeding; more lives are lost through speeding cars killing children, cyclists, and pedestrians than are saved by big fire trucks. In a town with combustible buildings the argument is public safety, but sometimes the problem is the closed-mindedness of the official who must give

CAR-FREE ZONES OFFER TANGIBLE BENEFITS WITH NO NEGATIVES:

1. Homes cost less - no funds needed for driveways or garages
2. Workplaces cost less - no funds needed for off-street parking or large truck bays
3. Village costs less to build - no need for on-street parking or parking meters/enforcement
4. Village uses less land - roads narrower, no parking for businesses, no driveways/garages
5. Roads are cleaner - no dripping oil, no tire-tread marks
6. Roads last longer - less weight (and wear & tear) on the streets on a day-to-day basis
7. Roads are more attractive - paverstone roads easy to access, lift pavers - no patches
8. Buildings remain cleaner as the dust and grit from tires and diesel exhaust are eliminated
9. The air is cleaner with no tailpipe and fuel tank emissions, no tire and brake dust
10. Children, pets and elders safer - no risk of getting run down by a car
11. Elders need not leave when they lose their driver license - all is within walking distance
12. Destinations closer - All is in closer proximity because the village takes up less space
13. People live in a quieter environment, no cars passing by, especially when one is sleeping
14. No social pressure on status about what kind of car one drives
15. Dining alfresco (outside) along the street becomes far more enjoyable
16. Youth find other activities - society maintains a naturally higher level of non-supervision
17. People connect - when not cocooned in a steel & glass chamber, people connect better
18. Eliminates anonymous predatory behavior enabled by the car; fear is reduced
19. Safety issues for fuel storage are eliminated; gas & diesel kept only at the motorpool
20. Save money - no need to buy, finance, depreciate, insure, license, inspect, run, fix or fuel.

the approval. There are smarter ways to deal with the life-threatening hazard of structure fires. The most obvious are to build with four-hour fire-rated masonry materials that don't burn, provide strategically located fire-suppression hoses and equipment throughout the villages, and install sprinkler systems that automatically put out interior fires. This approach works when all the homes are built at the same time, and built to the same high standard. Sprinklers may seem expensive, but when measured against the cost of wider streets, turn-around areas for trucks and the blow-out scaling of design by fire truck, they are not.

When cars are great - Cars are marvelous tools when one must travel longer distances. Unlike mass transport, they go from departure point to destination directly, involve no waiting (except for traffic jams), and they carry more luggage and goods than one can reasonably carry on a bus or train. They can be fun and, love them or hate them, they are here.

Therefore, it needs to be made clear that the VillageTown is not anti-car. Any citizen who moves in is welcome to bring as many cars as they want, all of which they park in the secure, covered transport center where they may lease or own a carpark, or if they wish, even build their own walls and doors on their space. They can drive their car anywhere except inside the VillageTown walls. Over time, one may expect that most people will not bother, and will instead prefer to rent cars from the motorpool when they need them.

SOLVING REGIONAL CONGESTION: NO OUTBOUND COMMUTERS

The purpose of the VillageTown is to create a complete community that does not empty out during the weekday. The concept of a bedroom community (suburb) where people live in one place that they vacate during the day destroys any real sense of community. For people who live this way, they don't notice what is missing, but when they visit a place that is dynamic, thriving and happening all day and all evening, they wake up.

There will be people who will want the village life, but are employed in a job that cannot be moved, such as a specialist surgeon in a metropolitan hospital. While the VillageTown would love to accommodate such people, the organizing company must say *no* and actively discourage commuters working outside the VillageTown. For the most part, it can be expected that social pressures will discourage commuters from moving to the VillageTown. However, some potential host jurisdictions have special problems, most notably limited access where road upgrades are not feasible. In such cases, the host may require that the VillageTown prohibit daily outbound commuting. Under the terms of its founding documents, the VillageTown should have the power to do so.

For some workers and businesses, telepresence may offer a solution. If one's work is predominantly conducted on the phone and on-line, that work can be done anywhere. If one needs to be in the office to talk with others and to attend meetings, the latest telepresence technology may address that requirement. However, there are some jobs that cannot be moved to the VillageTown and this is where the VillageTown is not for everyone.

what does time mean to you?

This Italian plaza hosted a rolling dialogue for over an hour as people came up, and joined in the conversation while others left for home. Their commute is by foot or bike. It probably takes two minutes or less, but like their counterpart commuter stuck in traffic on the freeway, it took them half an hour to get home, only 28 minutes of it was spent in social interaction - *a good life*.

PURPOSE OF THE ECONOMY: TO ENABLE CITIZENS TO ENJOY A GOOD LIFE

A good life defined as: Conviviality, Citizenship, and Artistic, Intellectual & Spiritual Growth. The VillageTown invests in infrastructure that supports these social pursuits.

TIME:

More quality time - In a car-based society, an inordinate amount of time is wasted in cars – commuting of course, but also shopping, driving children and taking the car to be maintained, repaired, inspected, and cleaned. Even the typical daily bus / mass-transport commute yields low-quality time, although some try to make it more stimulating listening to podcasts or packing in more work on a laptop. In a human-scale VillageTown commuting may still take 30 minutes, but 28 minutes of that is stopping to chat with friends and acquaintances, the epitome of conviviality. In a suburban community, weekends demand time to mow lawns, wash cars, and perform other chores that rob quality time. By eliminating machine-time, villagers instantly get more free time. The VillageTown then supports a wide range of social and cultural opportunities to enable villagers to use their free time in a manner that is more interesting and fulfilling.

PLACE:

Plaza life - When its citizens do not commute by car or public transport to someplace else, the village plaza with its cafés, shops, offices, classrooms, and creative arts becomes

Café Life

Car-Free Streets

Greenbelt Activities

an active place. In good weather, the cafés spill out into the plaza with the morning-coffee crowd, mid-morning parents with babies & toddlers, lunchtime workers & plaza students, retired folks enjoying the company of others, the early-evening promenade, and the night-time dining and late partying. During the day, and for some late into the evening, offices are filled with workers, both on the ground and upper floors. In plaza workshops people make things. This includes special workshops for *settled work* where elders supplement their income making things they love but which could not be done when they were raising a family. From time to time, celebrations and festivals are held on the plazas; the seasonal events that make life special. In a VillageTown, villagers and visitors have a choice of twenty village plazas, plus the larger and more cosmopolitan central town square.

Streets and paths - Everything within a 10-minute walk means the primary streets (higher-activity shops and offices) allow both pedestrians and slow-speed pedalled or electric vehicles to get to where they need to go. In addition, however, the secondary streets and the walking paths for foot traffic allow one to take a two-hour, labyrinth-type of walk from one village to another. For the quiet walk after work or on a weekend, this allows a more private and slower experience and with 150 acres of urban-core land area there will be many variations for enjoyment and exercise.

All weather - Not every place has great weather all year long, but the VillageTown can allocate funds to invest in "outdoor" glass shelters that provide a respite from the off-season. If the winter is cold with rain or snow, some of the plazas may build an arboretum, a tropical glasshouse with trees, plants, moist air, and summer temperatures. Such a place would include paths to walk, tables to dine and places for children to play. In VillageTowns with extreme cold weather or many months of snow, a village may elect to pay for *winter-walks*, where the backs of homes are set close enough to connect their roofs with glass cover and sufficient heat from renewable sources to walk to the plaza in spring-like conditions, even if the land outside is locked in ice or snow.

Greenbelt / Real Nature - Surrounding the urban core, which is about people, a wide greenbelt provides more than a buffer zone to prevent cross-boundary conflicts. For the neighbors of the VillageTown it means that in their backyard they see trees and fields, not a new development. But for the villagers, it provides a connection that all humans need, but many know not. The Kaiser Family Foundation tells us children aged 8 to 18 today spend 7.5 hours a day indoors using electronic media. Doctors now write specific prescriptions for outdoor activity, as if this is a medical problem. Where land is available, the VillageTown seeks to include a greenbelt that gives a real experience of Nature, not an over-engineered playground in a town park. Using about 60% of the total land area, the Greenbelt will serve many functions including replanted (or preserved) recreational woods and Nature preserves, as well as formal and community-allocation food gardens, festival, sports, and equestrian fields, open fields and meadows, fields of flowers, and a cemetery.

CONVIVIALITY

Having covered the importance of the local economy in supporting a good life, we turn now to the details of a good life, beginning with the social pursuit of conviviality.

In discussing these aspects of a good life, the focus is not on how people have fun – that's something they can do without help from the Stewards – but in what facilities the VillageTown invests and how such facilities are designed to foster conviviality. This includes investing in plazas, sports fields, café space, theatres and entertainment halls.

Conviviality is often associated with food and drink. Food is also an important part of the economy, and as such, we cover the economic aspects of food in this section on conviviality. As usual history plays a helpful role in understanding how things have changed and what is lost when food serves pecuniary interest over culinary.

If you travel to the old world you will find a plaza in the middle of town where farmers and food producers (bakers, brewers, butchers, cheese makers) would bring their goods to sell. Having made their money for the week, they would buy needed goods for themselves, and then retire to the pub or tavern for a drink and a catch-up on the events of the week. This was the *single town-country economy*, where distance was dictated by how far a horse could carry a wagon of food to market and come home before dark. See page 162 for before/after photos of a 15th-century market square.

With the advent of portable refrigeration and motor vehicles, local distance was blown apart – creating the disconnected markets where farms sell world-wide and towns buy world-wide. Now that fuel prices are rising, the local town-country economy is beginning to look competitive once again. However, to restore what was lost, we need to do more than just grow the food nearby and deliver it to the VillageTown. We need to remove the motor vehicles from the streets and from the plazas, so people can walk freely, or sit outside and catch up with the news of the week without the noise and stink of cars, trucks and mopeds driving by.

Beyond the conviviality of food and drink, make a note to replace engineered fun with do-it-yourself fun. The adventure playground built by playground companies leaves little room for children's imagination. Sometimes less design is better. Provide space for children to invent their own ways to have fun. Do the same for grown-ups. For example, set aside land in the greenbelt where adult citizens can create obstacle courses to keep fit or re-enact periods of history. Create the space and then let people invent their own forms of conviviality.

The plaza is the place where you meet without an appointment

The Central Role of the Village Plazas and Town Center

In the mid 1990's, Claude Lewenz secured funding to conduct research on what has become the VillageTown idea. Instead of going to experts and books, he began by going to ordinary (and extraordinary) people and asking fundamental questions about needs and aspirations. Only after the research concluded, did he go to the books and experts to seek confirmation.

Perhaps the book that was most closely aligned was Christopher Alexander's *A Pattern Language*. In that book, pattern 61 calls for small, public squares, writing *"A town needs public squares; they are the largest, most public rooms, that the town has. But when they are too large, they look and feel deserted."* The pattern then goes on to provide a mathematical analysis of the right size.

However, while in that book, the public square or plaza is just one of 253 patterns, in the VillageTown research the plaza and the town center emerged as paramount. They are the core defining feature of public life. This is why each village will have its own plaza, and why the founding villages will take the time to define their character and qualities.

For the pursuits of conviviality and citizenship, there is no replacement for the plaza. It provides the public stage for the community. People walk to it for food and drink. They see friends or people with whom they wish to connect – no appointment is needed. They talk, sometimes standing, and other times invite each other to sit down, and order a cup of coffee or a snack.

A well-designed plaza has a place for young children to play. In the photo on the bottom of the opposite page, the small town of Soller, Mallorca designed its plaza with a raised flat play area around the central statue. The area is made of smooth stone, so roller skates and skateboards do not make loud noise, and it has walls to keep balls and skateboards from hitting the adults enjoying drinks and food under the umbrellas next to the walls. The walls also make a comfortable place for people to sit, and parents will keep an eye on their children while chatting with other parents.

As in the old towns, the ground floor around the plaza is generally commercial. Some are cafés and restaurants, others are shops and professional offices that serve the public. Upstairs, many are private residence for people who enjoy the entertainment of watching plaza life. These homes may have balconies with full-length opening windows, or even patios that extend out into the public area, providing weather protection below, while above providing a place for tables, chairs, potted plants, climbing vines and trees.

The town center square is larger, and often may appear deserted. Its purpose is to provide perspective for the grand buildings, and also an outdoor place where the whole town can stand for a public event, such as an important speech, joining in a festival of community song or a large seasonal open market.

Conviviality can be as simple as going for a walk with a friend. When the streets are for people, not cars, the whole character of conviviality changes – it becomes more friendly.

Café culture is as much about social interaction as it is about food. Even the design of the sitting area can affect conversation, as shown below, where the wide bar, open to the table in front opens up a connection that a square table alone makes more difficult.

Conviviality can be about sport, but like this Oxford tavern cricket game, it need not be formal

CONVIVIALITY – HAVING FUN AND ENJOYING OTHERS

Conviviality comes from the Latin words for *to come together* and *to live*. It is associated with feasting, celebration, and enjoying others' company. Conviviality includes café lifestyle, travellers' inns, parties, friendly sports events, or a pleasant stroll through the village streets. Go into almost any community designed before our present age, and you will find the tavern, the pub, the coffee house, or the inn that welcomes members of the public. Conviviality means different things to different people. It is important that the plan is to provide for a wide range of local, accessible convivial activities.

Conviviality includes:

Belonging - Human beings are social animals; they seek out the company of others, and they enjoy living in a social environment where not only are they known and know others, but where they have a sense of belonging. The design of the VillageTown fills this need for many – both in the size of each village and the way each village is originally created. Research and common knowledge shows that communities of 250 - 750 provide the right size to connect with others, thus the average village is projected at 500 people. The village creates an innate sense of belonging through its design. This is further reinforced in the planning stage because the Dynamic Engagement planning process is separate for each village. Future villagers sign up for a particular village based on the special character or theme that a volunteer village coordinator set out. The future villagers attracted to that village share that theme, thus immediately they have something in common. Then, during the Dynamic Engagement process, some of those villagers get to know each other in an especially important activity – the planning of the look and feel of their village. In this way, villagers share not only the place they live, but how they created it.

Know thy farmer: The joy of good local food - Food & drink are our most basic needs; they are often associated with conviviality. Traditionally, market towns provided the anchor for the surrounding farms; they were two parts of the same local economy. The VillageTown restores that relationship, giving the farmers choice. Today, farming is dominated by the middlemen: the supermarket and the fast-food-chain buyers; the farmers become price-takers, not price-setters. The middleman monopoly squeezes the farmers to grow more on the same land for less money; farms have become toxic-material sites growing for yield, not for flavor and nutrition. It makes good economic sense to include farmers in the VillageTown's local economy by contracting directly to the farmers to feed the VillageTown. The VillageTown buys more affordable, healthy (chemical-free), and flavorful food. Fresh, delicious, locally-grown materials provide the stock for culinary delight and a convivial society. The VillageTown earns a reputation for food people love.

Café Culture - In many cultures, eating with others in the café, the restaurant or the tavern, sometimes as planned, other times spontaneously, is the essence of conviviality. The plazas are built to encourage café life. The challenge with cafés and taverns comes with those who

This active town in Spain got their plaza right. Along the edges, it is surrounded with cafés that offer alfresco dining during good weather. Then in the middle, on this slightly sloped land, they built a beautiful stone platform made of smooth stone rather than harsh concrete or ugly asphalt. Inside the larger and smaller rings, children play on skateboards and bikes, and with balls. Parents sit on the raised edges. It provides just enough of a barrier that the children's activities do not upset the food and drink, but it allows everyone to share the same plaza.

Sitting Places: Benches on the plaza are perhaps one of the simplest ways to foster conviviality. No appointment is necessary. Walk over, sit, and enjoy. People will come by, a conversation will strike up and soon friends are doing what friends together do.

can't afford the daily cost of such food and drink, or who find they prefer food and drink not laced with caffeine, alcohol, or sugar. Much of the cost of café style dining is in the rent. Thus a Village may elect – adding about $4 a month to a mortgage – to pay for the cost to build the facility which it then rents to a proprietor for a dollar a year. The condition of keeping the lease is great food, drink, service, and ambiance at affordable prices. The village pays for the tables & chairs, as well as long tables that encourage spontaneous conversation, so that anyone can stay as long as they want, and not feel the pressure to move on so a paying customer can take their place. Such a place will provide board games, newspapers, books and magazines, and corded electrical/internet outlets in the laptop zone.

Fun - Children play. Give them the simplest of things - a rope swing, boxes to make into caves or cast-off clothes to make into costumes and they will keep themselves happily occupied for hours. Give them a safe greenbelt where they can run wild without parental supervision and they will have the time of their life, all the while learning to become independent and autonomous. The VillageTown invests in many ways to compete with television and the latest electronic media. Some are as simple as a low wall around part of the plaza, so balls, skateboards, and bikes are separated from the adults. On each plaza, the village can provide a DVD movie theater with sofas that not only shows blockbusters but movies made by and about people in the community. There is something different about electronic media when it is shared in a public space. The most important element of children's fun is knowledge that the VillageTown is safe. Older people talking about their own childhood grew up at a time when no parent worried where their children were. Car-based societies destroyed this sense of security. Human-scaled VillageTowns where people know and look after each other restore this way of life. Investment advisor Catherine Fitts calls it the *popsicle index*, defined on her web site as *"the percent of people who believe a child can leave their home, go to the nearest place to buy a popsicle or snack, and come home alone safely."* The VillageTown aspires to have a popsicle index of 100%, but hopes the store offers better treats than a stick of frozen water, sugar, corn syrup, gum, and stabilizers.

Plaza Benches: a place to sit in the sun - Some elements of the village are simple. With no cars, the plaza is a social place. Comfortable benches can provide a place for people to sit – make sure they are not in drafty locations, and assure they have shading for days when the sun or air is too hot. Especially important for older people who no longer work full time, but seek the company of others, this simple piece of street architecture becomes a valuable thread in the social fabric of a community. Unlike the benches in shopping malls which are temporary places to take the weight off one's feet from too much shopping, or the benches in front of parking meters along a busy commercial street, plaza benches create communities. Regulars claim their space every day, filling a convivial need.

Theaters and performance halls - Conviviality is laughter and entertainment, although halls may also be a part of cultural enrichment. Society has become so used to the perfection of televised performance that it fails to excite. Yet when one attends a live

It's a marvel to see professional sports players, but they are not like us. Provide for homegrown sports, where the cost is little more than constructing a well-drained field.

Market day is more than shopping. It's an excuse to get out and meet friends, to make life vibrant.

When the circus comes to town, life is put on hold. Festivals, events, celebrations are something we all look forward to. For children they are magic; for adults they break routine. Enjoy them.

performance, where human talent is on stage, the entertainment becomes personal and the sharing of it during breaks and after the performance adds something special that television cannot match. The VillageTown invests in such facilities, some of which are built in connection with a Guild Hall, others as separate public spaces for the community.

Home grown sports - Conviviality is also about local sport; not tickets to sit in a large stadium watching professional super-humans, but the local fields and gymnasium where the players are one's friends, neighbors, or children. Villages will form teams to compete with other villages on the greenbelt's sports fields. Beyond team and ball sports, provided the climate & land is appropriate, equestrian fields serve as an important experience for a particular sector of childhood, notably school-aged girls. The VillageTown should also invest in sports places, both indoor and outdoor, and if it has access, to include natural places such as ponds or rivers where children can swim.

Markets - Europe does some of the best traditional outdoor markets. Some have been running since the middle ages, but they maintain all their vitality. The market in Vaison la Romaine in Provence, France (one of the best places to find famed Provencal fabrics) began in 1483, when Pope Sixtus IV granted a license. Subsequently in 1532 Pope Clement VII set the day: every Tuesday, which continues even now. Others, like the four-week Christmas market in Munich's Marienplatz, mark the season with special food and drink, as well as hand-made gifts that attract visitors from around the world. The VillageTown central town plaza is ideal for large markets, as are the village plazas for smaller markets.

Festivals - In the small island town of Deya, Mallorca in Spain, the local community maintains its identity in the face of tourism by putting on festivals to celebrate the seasons, historical events, religious dates – and in the absence of these, they make up new reasons. In one of the most unlikely places in America, the rural town of Ashland, Oregon in America's far west - a place where a rodeo might seem more fitting – they put on a Shakespeare festival that draws visitors from around the world. Ninety minutes from Brisbane, Australia, a city of 45,000 people instantly self-creates for one week each year, mostly living in tents. They call it the Woodford Folk Festival – although it is much more – on a festival field that now has grown to over 400 acres.

The best festivals usually begin out of passion. They usually have insufficient funds and rarely make money for their organizers, but they become loved events that everyone looks forward to. In order to make them happen, and stress out the organizers less, the VillageTown sets aside land as festival fields in the greenbelt close to the transport center to accommodate visitors. In providing for festivals it is important that the VillageTown not over-professionalize them. In one successful, comfortable planned town in America, they put on a parade and festival that never quite feels right; the marchers who come in do it for the money, then they go back to the old town where the real party happens. When it comes to conviviality, provide the basics and then let the magic happen.

When food becomes monetized, it loses its flavor. Traditionally, food was local. It had flavors many people don't even know are possible. When food is monetized, monocultures take over where chemicals are used to keep food growing long after the soil is depleted. The rich variety of foods that our ancestors grew and ate has now been reduced down to a select few that fit the transport and supermarket standard for food. For example, there are over 7,500 varieties of apples world-wide, but less than a dozen varieties typically found in the supermarket. When one re-establishes the relationship between town and country, by creating a single, local food market, food may be expected to regain its flavor.

More Detail – *On Conviviality and Health: The Food Systems*

Food: One of the prime elements of the good life is conviviality, which often revolves around food. Additionally, medical researchers constantly emphasize the importance of a healthy diet as the best way to maintain overall physical and emotional health. The food industry however works to a completely different set of priorities focusing on transport, yield and profits driving farmers to rely heavily on monoculture and chemical farming to stay in business. The farmers are not price setters but price takers. The unfortunate result is bland food that costs too much (over 80% of the consumer's food on the plate is paid to middlemen, not the farmer) and involves risk assessment as to the allowable level of illness and health using chemicals and processes known to be toxic to humans and to the planet.

Market Town: Traditionally, the 10,000 person market town was set in the middle of farm country and they were two parts of the same economy. Almost all food was local, seasonal and therefore was diverse. Transport and petroleum-based chemicals changed all that. Today, *Food Inc.* sees food varieties selected for durability as food is routinely shipped hundreds or thousands of miles from where it is grown. This completely changed the character and output of farming, and it broke the local town-country economy. Once broken, good farmland was bought for development and paved over with suburban sprawl.

In some places, activists pressed for rules to prevent further sprawl. What they failed to notice was the disconnect between farms and town. In essence, the protected farms became a pretty backdrop for city folk. Very little food grown on those farms feeds the people living in town, because the farms converted to monoculture. In Sonoma County California, an urban growth boundary was voted in as law, prohibiting sprawl taking more farmlands. However, the local farms that grew fruits, vegetables and local meats gave way to *grape sprawl*, as in this photograph, to the point where the rolling hills are now covered in seemingly endless rows of grapes. The peach trees that grew some of Sonoma's finest peaches are gone, cut down when the new boutique "farmer" planted more grapes.

Grape sprawl **now covers the formerly diverse farmlands of Napa and Sonoma Counties, Calif.**

The VillageTown restores the old town-and-country local economy, not out of sentimentality, but because it works better. The farmer knows who will eat the food they grow. VillageTowns can *anchor* the surrounding farmland, providing a local market for the full range of foods and cut out the middlemen enabling the farmers to earn more while lowering the retail price to the village customer. However, in places like Sonoma County, the very rules written to protect the farmland are turning it into monoculture sprawl. The VillageTown challenge is to enlighten those rule-makers so they will approve better rules.

Protecting the Food Supply: Securing a permanent, protected food supply to the higher standards of nutrition, health, and flavor requires the VillageTown lock in food-buying contracts and in many cases purchase development rights from participating farmers at the onset, even if present day law prohibits rezoning them. Once built, one can expect the very presence of the VillageTown to cause developers and politicians to press for rezoning of the surrounding rural farms. No matter how strong the law to protect the region appears, politics driven by pecuniary interest generally proves stronger. The only real protection is ownership of the development rights in a form that keeps it as farmland.

In today's economy, many farmers find they must go into debt to keep their businesses going. If the VillageTown offers to buy development rights, the farmer has the option to use the proceeds to pay off bank debt and start with a clean slate and a better business plan. Alternatively, some farmers may elect to take a discount to buy elder housing for the time when they plan to retire, or to buy a home for one of their children who has left home, and finds no other opportunities to return near the family and find work. All such options should be offered to the farmers who will choose what fits their needs best.

Farmer's Choices: In contracting for food, some farmers will prefer fixed contracts where they remain in control of their farms and can plan based on knowing the produce will sell for a fixed price. Their only risk then is the weather and other factors that can cause crop failure. Some farmers need to borrow to plant the year's crops. Some may prefer to borrow from the VillageTown bank. Others may prefer the VillageTown establish a consumer's fund where the farm's customers advance money as a conventional farm loan. A more recent innovation is Community Supported Agriculture (CSA). In this relationship, the consumers join in the farming risk in exchange for fresh foods at fixed prices. There are many web sites that explain the details of this system, so it is better to refer to them (such as www.localharvest.org) than repeat them in this book.

There are three separate facets to VillageTown food:

- **Home** - Food is becoming expensive, and economists tell us prices will rise as weather, transport costs, and increased consumption create more demand than supply. This is monetized food biting back. Home-delivered food lacks the social experience, but when the totality of the market is from farm direct to home, costs are contained.

- **Markets** - The shops and weekly farmers' markets become a place for social encounter, a way to catch up, to see and be seen. The rich colors of the market – the bright reds of tomatoes, the fresh greens of cilantro – add to the sensory delight, as farmers and fish mongers hawk their wares in loud voices. The food is fresh, the prices fair, and the experience a delight.

- **Public** - The plazas are designed for alfresco dining in good weather.. When the weather turns, public dining goes inside – entering a warm room, full of bustle, wafting odors of fresh bread, coffee, or cooked food is welcoming. The tradition of the long table encourages strangers to meet, and friends to join each other for a chat without an appointment. The VillageTown can become famous for its food, making it a wonderful place to live, and a great place to visit.

Consumer Food-Buying Systems: On a functional basis, the participating farmer becomes part of the local economy and the food-ordering system is part of the VillageTown intranet. A key element in making the system work better is to avoid weights and measures, and instead go to fixed container sizes. Instead of 20 pounds or kilograms of apples, a filled-to-the-top reusable box is used that one time may weigh 19.5 and the next time 20.5. In the end, it averages out, while the labor cost of filling, weighing and calculating is replaced by simple box filling for which a box-price is charged. Most food will be delivered in reusable packaging and bottles, just as people did for centuries before plastic was invented. They used to call this service *the milkman*.

With sophisticated software, farm orders can have the customer's delivery address on each box or bottle that arrives in bulk at the freight depot, where, along with the mail and courier delivery, it is loaded onto small electric delivery vehicles that run delivery routes within the villages. Since everything is within a 10-minute walk, these vehicles can travel at a walking pace and still deliver rapidly (being electric, they are more efficient than the stop-start-stop use of a gas-powered or diesel-powered vehicle). They deliver to a food box – locking doors in the wall-face of the building so packages and food can be delivered when people are not home. This delivery can be done by the same vehicles that deliver mail and courier packages.

Farmers' Market Day: The market towns of yore featured a large central plaza where once a week, an outdoor market would appear. The farmers would load their carts with food to sell at the market. This tradition is reviving around the world as it offers the freshest foods at lower prices, in a very colorful and social atmosphere. The VillageTown will have many places for such markets, including the fields in the greenbelt, the village plazas, or for larger events, the town-center plaza.

Food Shops: The food-box system provides for home delivery of food, which some will prefer because it incurs the lowest cost and the least effort. The food-box system competes with the discount chain supermarket, but not the more boutique specialized village stores such as the fruit & vegetable shop, the butcher, the baker, and the cheese maker. While the shops will probably buy from the same farms, the farmer may send the best of the crop to the shops. Because the plazas emphasize conviviality around food, it can be expected that small businesses will emerge and revive traditional methods for making cheese, breads, beer &wine, olives, and many of the other foods that used to define a particular region. The same may hold true for the cafés and restaurants that buy from the same food sources.

The Art of Food: At the core, food is fuel to keep us going. But when one thinks of travel to great places, one also thinks of food. Country cooking in France and Italy is famous. Often their best foods were developed not for the restaurant trade, but in rural homes from recipes served to families and friends. For most of human history, , one had to travel to different countries to experience different foods, but no longer. Now immigrants bring their local dishes to their new land. The focus on food adds to the convivial atmosphere, and it can become a distinctive attraction for visitors. As *Food Inc.* further monetizes food and makes eating more expensive, VillageTown food can become a distinctive feature.

Like other aspects of the VillageTown, the simple matter of food and drink touches the economy, conviviality, and citizenship, and it becomes the glue of artistic and intellectual growth. Even in spiritual matters, the feast of the religious holidays plays an important part.

Recycling: The back end of the food system comes in the waste. In the typical suburban community, what could be compost is put in the kitchen-sink garbage disposal where it then mixes with sewage to create a foul mess that must be treated before disposal. The rural alternative of putting food scraps in a compost bucket makes little sense when one is looking at sending a collector around every day to 4,000 houses. The best solution is to keep the garbage disposal unit, but have a separate set of pipes that take only kitchen waste and pipe it to a central location where it can be reprocessed for use by the farmers. It can be used to create mash to brew tractor-grade alcohol to free the farmer from petroleum dependency. It can be fed to Tilapia fish that eat waste products to make high grade fish fertilizer. Or, it can be processed into standard farm-grade compost. Whatever system is set up, it is recommended that it be a joint venture between the VillageTown and the farmers, so the VillageTown does not have to pay for disposal, and the farmers need not pay for fuel, fertilizer, or compost. You can read more about this approach on page 106.

Home-made entertainment is more engaging

MORE DETAIL – CONVIVIALITY AS ENTERTAINMENT

As people become consumers, they increasingly turn inward. The average-sized home in consumer societies grows as the consumer must have a video room, an exercise machine room, his and her computer rooms, and a three- or four-car garage to hold all the stuff that consumers buy. This *stuff* has the effect of isolating people.

The VillageTown seeks to offer alternatives to get people out of their homes by creating attractions that are fundamentally social. On the plaza, it is neither expensive nor difficult to have a video room that seats fifty people with a wall-sized projector, so when children do watch pre-made media, they do so socially. But rather than make it passive, make it village TV: show locally made video before the main evening's feature. Talent will emerge as villagers begin to record their own stories. Subtly the role of media changes – it begins to become our story rather than someone else's.

On some plazas, the villagers may decide to build a bandstand for dancing in the street. On others, the guild hall may request a theater for cultural enrichment – make it acoustically excellent, but design it to also function as a cabaret theater for entertainment. When furnishing the plaza, buy weatherproof tables that have board games built into the table top – chess, checkers, backgammon, and so on. Set them out so a small crowd can gather around and watch. In the youth zone, consider funding a climbing wall and perhaps a place for skateboards – but select a surface that makes the wheels quieter.

Pay attention to the weather. If it snows, set aside a hill for sledding. If winters are cold and long, build an arboretum, a greenhouse filled with tropical plants and birds intended for people, so you have a place to go, peel down to short sleeves, and feel warm. Install benches and tables, and build a glass-walled room where the children can play, make noise, and throw balls without disturbing adults sitting nearby. If the weather is miserable part of the year, consider building winter-walks where the buildings are closer set in the rear and covered with a glass walkway to the plaza. There was a time when people were tough and thought nothing of walking outdoors in foul weather. Today people are less hardy as they move from heated home to heated garage to heated car to covered parking garage at the mall or office. In the VillageTown there are no cars, thus, planning must consider design for outdoor weather protection that functions differently than when one uses cars.

Outdoor conviviality includes the sports fields, but plans should also consider such things as the fishing pond. If you are lucky, your location will have a river or the seaside. If not, build one, especially if precipitation is seasonal and water storage is useful. Plant shade trees of the sort that one can doze under with the fishing line tied to one's big toe. Also, build children's caves for the younger ones, and make sure there are trees ideal for tree houses for the slightly older children. If you can't remember what fun was, read *Tom Sawyer.*

CITIZENSHIP - IT'S MORE THAN POLITICS

Typically, when people think about politics, they think about elected officials, voting, laws, taxes, and too often about corruption, injustice, and ineffectiveness. Yet, in relation to *a good life*, the ancient meaning of *politics* is closer to our word *citizenship* than what we understand when we talk about politics.

Perhaps the true concept of citizenship was best expressed by Stewart Udall when he said *we valued education so we voted to tax ourselves to build a school and hire good teachers*. In this view, it is about mature adults agreeing on what they value and then agreeing to pay for it. The process they used was democratic – counting votes. At a deeper level, this kind of citizenship is about taking care – education of the young, care for the elderly and infirm, care for our physical and natural environment, care for society and civilization.

This view of taxation is rare in today's world where systems are so big that the ordinary person rarely feels they have a say in the matter. Most people pay taxes not because they want to pay for something they value, but because it is the law; failure to pay results in criminal prosecution. Many then complain about the ineffective or inefficient way taxes are applied, yet too often they feel those complaints are powerless to change the outcomes.

While there is little the VillageTown can do to change national or global politics, it can give its citizens more of a say over their local lives and can enable them to implement systems that actually work. Much of this is accomplished by de-monetizing citizenship. When one breaks a town up into smaller units of villages, taking care becomes personal. People look after each other. Conflict is usually resolved directly. Village decisions are made through direct democracy; sometimes by a vote, sometimes by consensus or the decisions of respected leaders.

On a town level, citizenship will be more formal and monetized. Not everyone enjoys participatory democracy; yet there are always leaders who thrive on the job of representing their constituency. Someone has to make the decisions what to do and how to pay for it (legislative). Another must get the work done (executive). A third autonomous authority needs to have power to step in and straighten out matters when things go wrong (judicial).

Common experience and formal studies to show that when a community grows over about 10,000 people, representative democracy becomes bureaucratic. One no longer can hold elected representatives accountable because one no longer runs into them in the street or standing in line at market checkout. It is for this reason that the VillageTown looks to limit its size to about 10,000 residents. It does this by fixing the number of buildings and the amount of land available for development at the beginning, with no room for further expansion. It may grow a bit in people per building, but probably not enough to matter.

Too often when we think of citizenship, we think of politics. Certainly electing leaders to make decisions is important, and the VillageTown will have its own internal governance system based on corporate, rather than municipal, law.

However, sometimes citizenship is about mundane subjects such as trash. At one time trash disposal was simple because there was so little of it. Food was delivered in reusable containers. Goods were delivered in barrels or boxes that were reused. Plastic, made from petroleum, did not exist and paper was too expensive to waste. Now, packaging is another form of externalizing the costs. The businesses that make the goods do not pay for disposal; they only calculate the cost of buying the packaging, leaving the disposal costs to the taxpayer and to future generations.

Good citizenship looks at trash differently. It asks *what is the purpose of the packaging?* and *is there a smarter way to approach it?* In the photograph below, the rear pallet in the middle is filled with compressed white-plastic milk containers. Used once, the container is then tossed out. In many places, the plastic ends up as trash in the landfill. In smarter towns, it is sorted to be melted and reused. But in a VillageTown, it may make more sense to go back to reusable glass bottles. If possible, the VillageTown will contract with nearby dairy farms and wash its milk bottles.

The same principle can be applied to many day-to-day purchases. If the VillageTown can specify the packaging, it should do so. If it cannot, it should work out the best way to reuse the surplus resource – not shipping it off to a third-world country for "recycling", but dealing with it at home. This approach is probably different from how trash is handled by the host jurisdiction, and it is another reason why the VillageTown will need its own internal governance. Of course, the host jurisdiction may be so impressed that it asks to join the VillageTown's surplus resource plan.

CITIZENSHIP - TAKING CARE OF ALL THINGS GREAT AND SMALL

Citizenship is about taking care. Citizenship is the social process of getting along with other people; it's about making and implementing good community decisions. What happened when we stopped calling people citizens and instead redefined them as consumers? Materially consumers *have* more, but as communities they *care* less. When one asks people to act like citizens rather than behave like consumers, change happens. Citizens take responsibility; it's their life, their community, their future. Also, size matters. In pattern № 12 of *A Pattern Language* Christopher Alexander observed: *Individuals have no effective voice in any community of more than 5,000-10,000 persons.* Limiting VillageTown size to 10,000-population made up of twenty 500-person villages and a town center creates a structure that gives individuals an effective voice. To foster citizenship, the VillageTown provides meeting halls, and a formal organizational structure that is representative. Beyond this, it provides the plazas, cafés and taverns where the discussion that enables and informs representative democracy has always occurred in an unstructured, spontaneous way.

More control over one's life and future - At one time, communities formed local governments to enable them to take care of local matters. As Village Forum's Chairman Emeritus Steward Udall said about his own small town of St. Johns, Arizona, *we voted to tax ourselves.* In most places today, that sense of taxing ourselves no longer exists. Citizens tend to see local government as a separate institution, no longer their collective will. Stewart also said *small communities are very intolerant of crime, and the neighbors looked after the kids as they carried on around town; they had little crime.* Note the sense of personal ownership in both these statements. Local governance was both personal and owned by all citizens, not solely by the elected representatives or the appointed bureaucrats.

There are reasons why communities like Udall's worked and why so few do today. The powers are still there, but developers do not take the time or invest money to claim those powers; it's neither their job nor their interest. The home buyers move into pre-cast format created by the developer that is not concerned with citizenship. In contrast, the VillageTown addresses governance matters – it invests in good citizenship and good governance.

No matter what local or regional government holds authority over the VillageTown, any community of 10,000 people will need governance powers that the host jurisdiction is unlikely to provide. This is especially the case given the different character and needs of a VillageTown. To accomplish this, the VillageTown embeds two levels of governance in its founding documents:

- *Village governance* is direct and personal, borrowing from the direct democracy model used in New England town meetings and New Zealand restorative justice.
- *Town governance* is formal and representational; using checks-and-balances. These details can be found on page 108 and page 250. This governance structure is supported by its strong asset base and resources. Without those, it is hard to get things done.

When cars are removed from the streets, and when the communities are small, where everyone knows everyone, children learn independence and autonomy and they become adults easier.

Teens need places to hang out with their own, to be more independent, but have plenty to do. When they come of age, they need a community that has a place and a role for them.

Education of the young - Education is how civilization sustains itself. The invention of the isolated school campus based on the factory and the commuter model of society is relatively new. In it students' only role models are overworked, stressed teachers. With the advent of widespread electronic media and what is generally believed to be a decline in public education, society is at risk of creating a nation of button pushers and test-takers. This can result in losing that sense of ingenuity and capacity that is essential to maintaining the inherent strength and durability of community and nation.

The VillageTown takes a different approach, not to the curriculum but to the location. Classrooms are in the villages, on the plazas next to offices and shops, part of the active life of each village. Some classrooms are in the guild halls or on the greenbelt. The VillageTown integrates education with the life of the community. The community operates full time; it does not empty out during the day. The same holds true for the children's school day.

The classrooms are in the community, not segregated from it. Students study in the context of a community. Looking out the classroom windows, they see adults using knowledge first acquired at school. They interact with adults at lunchtime, eating at the cafés or walking home to eat with the family. They learn acceptable behavior not through lectures by the school principal, but by the natural responses of adults at the café on the plaza. When it comes time to get a part time job after school, they are already known in the village.

With proximity comes involvement, and the teachers are expected to take advantage of the rich resources within the community. For parents of school-aged children, this attraction is key, indeed it can be paramount. Some parents will move home to get their children into good schools. In the VillageTown they not only *believe* it will offer a good education; by virtue of their proximity, they are able to *evaluate* that quality everyday.

Security for one's children - It is deemed normal today to live behind locked doors, to set the alarm when leaving home, and never let our children out of sight unless someone trusted or paid is looking after them. Children no longer learn to be autonomous or independent; they cannot play in the streets or be gone all day fishing or climbing trees. When they become teens, parents fear for their safety because normal life is more dangerous than it once was.

Some of this is due to a relatively new rite of passage – earning a driver license. In suburban culture parents find that they drive their children everywhere, so many welcome the day when the teen can do the driving. But car crashes are the number-one killer of older teens, who are inexperienced, lack the brain development that good drivers need, push the power too hard, and too often they combine driving with alcohol or drug abuse. In today's suburban culture, learning to drive is a necessity. In contrast, the VillageTown eliminates day-to-day car use and replaces it with a more enriched cultural and social life to meet the needs of its young. For parents, it reduces the fear of that phone call from the police saying there was terrible car crash. . In the VillageTown they know where their children are, and they know that it is a safer, more stimulating place than the suburbs or the city.

When you become infirm, it's hard to finish crossing the street before the traffic light turns.

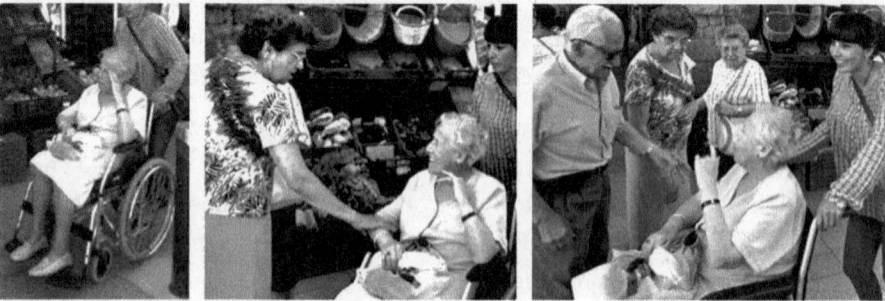

In this sequence of photographs an elderly woman's face brightens as she is greeted by friends while out in her village plaza. In suburban life, such people generally must move to a retirement or nursing home. Good citizenship means elders can remain living in their community.

For the baby boom, counting on state pensions or even the stock market and equity in a suburban home may be a gamble where the odds are not in their favor.

Boomers Reinventing Retirement - World War II delayed starting families, but afterwards they made up for lost time creating the Baby Boom – a generation self-focused in every stage of their lives. Many seemed to suffer the Peter Pan syndrome – they did not want to grow up. Now facing the elder years, they realize their parents' entitlements probably will not be there. Conventional care and secure pensions look most unlikely. They will need to reinvent retirement. They need to redefine citizenship because the expectation that the next generation will pay for their elder years runs into a demographic, non-negotiable wall.

The VillageTown offers Boomers a better opportunity. They will remain productive and be vital participants as long as they are able to do so. They will slow down, and eventually want to live more simply, but they will continue to be participating members of the community. Curiously, this requirement will be aligned with their aspirations. Few generations want to hang around old people, even when they are old themselves, but the Boomers seem to feel more strongly about this than previous generations. Under the circumstances, this is good.

Investing in Tangibles - In one sense, the 2008 crash was a blessing. Baby boomers saw 40% of their equity wiped out as previously soaring stock and real-estate prices crashed. The blessing comes in the warning it gives. The 2008 crash was caused by greed, lax regulation and banks giving out loans like candy in a parade. The next crash is more ominous. It's about demographics. When there are more sellers than buyers, the price goes down. In the USA, for example, when 79 million Baby Boomers go to sell their real estate and investments to pay for their retirement and there are 69 million next-generation buyers, for many the money they counted on will not be there. The government will be in the same shape, unable to provide the level of support enjoyed by the boomers' parents. What should boomers do?

For those boomers who invest in the VillageTown, their investment is in people, in wealth creation, and in a plan to enable those boomers, as they become elders, to live well in their last stages of life. In fact, it may prove so attractive that boomer housing may need to be rationed to prevent the VillageTown becoming a de facto retirement village.

Elder Security - The elders of society often live with fear, as they are seen by criminals and delinquents as vulnerable. The VillageTown inherently provides a level of safety and security than enables all its citizens, including its elders, to live normally: no cars, a thousand eyes looking at all times, a low tolerance for crime and elder-housing to meet their needs.

Care for Elders - Again quoting Stewart Udall, this time speaking about elders remaining in the community: *The old people were honored for their age and for the fact they had lived good lives and they had taken care of their community needs.* In almost every time and every place except in contemporary western society, the elders remain in the community and they have an important role to play, passing on the culture to the younger generation. The VillageTown provides three stages of housing for elders and it self-insures their third stage, nursing care. By doing this they never need to leave their community to move to an isolated, age-segregated retirement home.

Like the canary in the mine who becomes ill and dies when poisonous gasses become toxic, the honey bee that pollinates our fruit is another quiet way that Nature is telling us that we are in trouble. We don't know the cause of bee hive collapse, but the Theory of Unanticipated Negative Side effects (see page 215) would suggest it is a combination of corrosive effects.

Still life with stone and car by Cherokee artist Jimmy Durham presented at the 2004 Biennale of Sydney. Durham dropped a rock onto a 99 Ford Festiva purchased from a car dealer.

More Detail – Citizenship as Caring for the Environment

When we talk of environment, we speak about two different concepts. The physical environment is local. The physical environment is proximate: noise pollution, dust, traffic, noxious smells, and the health of soil and water we see. The natural environment is more *intellectual*, because it focuses on theories and scientific measurements. It is about Nature and Earth and how we treat both. Often it is about data. We must believe what our data tells us, or we must believe the scientists who read and interpret the data.

In matters of the physical environment, the VillageTown pays careful attention to making it good, beautiful and healthy. The building systems and schedule provide for this, as does the intent to build all at once, so that residents need not suffer the "temporary" nuisance of additions, demolition, and replacement construction. For both residents and neighbors, the greenbelt as a cross-boundary buffer zone creates a better physical environment, and it also filters the air to make urban life more pleasant.

For a long time, environmentalism was a lonely practice of the few, who for the most part were tolerated or marginalized by an establishment that externalized its costs. As industrialization expanded however, externalized practices grew and it became apparent that Nature was beginning to bite back. When Rachel Carson published *Silent Spring* in 1962, documenting toxic effects of pesticides on the US environment, and when Time Magazine featured the 13th time the Cuyahoga River in Ohio caught fire in 1969, the public became aware that environmental abuse was out of control.

In matters of the natural environment the VillageTown looks for synergy to provide tangible support for our belief in environmental scientists. In the matter of Climate Change, it intellectually accepts the majority view, but on page 70, we list 20 reasons why cars should not be used inside the VillageTown walls, all of which are based on tangible, not intellectual, benefits. The fact that the VillageTown takes over 6,000 cars off the road, and reduces driving demand by over a quarter-million miles a day should satisfy the Climate Change test for sustainability. But even if the world shifted to cars built entirely of renewables that ran entirely on sustainable energy, the VillageTown would still keep them out of the village, and keep everything within a 10-minute walk. The same environmental tests are applied to building materials and design, public utilities, and other places where humanity's footprint on Nature and Earth is too heavy.

When addressing the environmental effects of food production, the VillageTown combines economy with ecology. It's cheaper, faster and healthier to feed villagers from nearby farms and and the food should taste better. Unit food costs may be higher since yield no longer is the primary aim – squeezing the maximum from the soil through heavy dosing of chemicals. However, by cutting out the middleman, the actual costs may be lower, and certainly the total cost including externalized costs certainly will be lower.

Back around 2006, *green* became the new politically correct fashion statement, resulting in an inordinate amount of confusion as to the impact of humanity on the planet and Nature, especially the 20% richest of the world's population. The confusion has long been caused by the difficulty of measuring or evaluating the adverse impact of the supply line that stands behind almost everything we buy. In 2006, this began to get more complicated because one variety of environmentalism – concern about the impact of greenhouse gasses on the climate claimed center stage and shoved all other issues off the agenda. The carbon footprint became the number-one concern, almost to a point of obsession.

For example, one gallon of gasoline releases 19.4 pounds (8.8 kg) of CO_2 into the atmosphere. The average car in 2011 has a manufacturing carbon footprint of about 17 tonnes CO_2e^*. Using US DOT/EPA statistics, if the car lasts its average 13 years and gets the average mileage, the fuel burn adds an additional 78 tonnes of greenhouse gas during its lifetime. The US FHA tells us the average person drives 36 miles a day, which means that for a 10,000-population community, over a quarter-million miles a day are racked up. It's probably higher in the suburbs. That works out to about 136 tonnes of CO_2e per day, or 50,000 tonnes each year just in the fuel burn. But that's just the beginning.

The total environmental impact of a gallon of gasoline is an entirely different calculation, and to date we have been unable to find any reliable number. It would have to include the footprint for exploration, the drilling, the roads to get to the drilling, the offshore platforms, the blowouts in the Gulf, the shipwrecks in Alaska or the 7,000 oil spills in Nigeria, the trucks, ships and rigs to extract, the refineries, the wholesale-distribution network, the retail stores, and so on. It also includes for the USA, some indirect costs of the US military (the world's largest consumer of oil) insofar as the US fights wars in states that happen to have a lot of oil – its military protects America's strategic energy interests. This impact is more than just its CO_2e number. It involves fouled land, water, air and food, as well as sickness, suffering and death. And that is just for the fuel pumped into the tank. There's more:

Calculate the indirect operating footprint of the car. In order to drive the car, one must also calculate the footprint of the construction and maintenance of concrete or asphalt highways, roads, bridges and tunnels, the wear on the tires, brakes, batteries and mufflers, the oil changes, and the mechanical parts that wear out. One must include all the support industries including the people who commute to buildings that provide car insurance, the highway patrol and police/fire/ambulance attending crashes, car crash hospitalization, the court systems, the tow-truck business, the repair shops, body shops, car washes, the parking-ticket industry and so on. Again, these effects are more than just CO_2e.

Most of these problems will not be solved by cars that get better fuel mileage or that run on electricity, or by building transit-oriented-design (TOD) communities that use

---

*   **e = equivalent**

trains. The VillageTown offers a smarter approach. The transport environmental footprint of VillageTown citizens is literally a footprint. They walk. Their daily *home-range* (to borrow a word zoologists use to describe a wolf's daily territory) is covered on foot, not in extended-range machines. By moving destinations once instead of moving people every day, a huge environmental footprint shrinks to a much smaller one. Yet this lower footprint is not why the VillageTown is designed the way it is. It is instead a positive externality, a happy side-effect of creating a wonderful place to live.

Keeping with the carbon footprint for a moment, while there are many variables that complicate the calculation, it is estimated that the carbon footprint of the VillageTown's bulk material per average 3,000 ft² (300 m²) building is about 20 tonnes CO_2e. Considering this average house will take two or more cars off the road, the car-removal offset alone comes in a matter of months. When one adds the energy efficiency of the homes, the impact of supporting local food, the sequestration impact of planting native trees in the greenbelt (which is done for other reasons) and so on, the VillageTown earns one of the lightest environmental-footprint report cards possible. Even so, the Stewards endeavor to lower that footprint even more by looking at alternative materials and more innovative systems.

Having said all this, however, even if the VillageTown generates carbon credits that it could sell, we recommend not to do so. Selling a credit gives another polluter the right to pollute. While this may make sense on the global scale, at the VillageTown level it would be contrary to the ethos of treading lightly to provide for the needs of seven generations.

Perhaps the most important aspect of the VillageTown approach to a sustainable environment is in its initial purchasing power. There are many new bright-green technologies out there that are starving for customers. Some are still in need of development funds, but others are proven. The brief for the organizing company calls for conducting a world-wide search to find the best proven, affordable systems to implement. In evaluating such systems, they look beyond the greenwash to assess the real, long-term impact of proposed solutions. In other words, these organizing-company professionals come with an open mind, and, for the right solution, an open checkbook.

Further, while their fiduciary obligation to the citizens requires they select proven systems, they may also allocate a certain safe percentage of their systems budget to new, promising technology that still requires field development and testing. In some cases, the organizing company may invite such businesses to move to the VillageTown, receive capital funding and secure the opportunity to make the VillageTown a showcase customer.

The bottom line finds the VillageTown committed to implementing long-term, truly effective sustainable practices, but not highlighting sustainability as a trendy bragging point. In a sane world, all development would be sustainable, and it would simply be another subset of good citizenship. The VillageTown endeavors to be a sane development.

More Detail – *On Handling Water*

We are told that in the 21st century water will become as valuable as oil. Because it is a new development of 4,000 homes, 1,000 workplaces and 10,000 people, the opportunity to introduce new, sustainable systems presents itself. The VillageTown will have a development budget of a billion dollars, enough to implement a better approach to water.

Waste Water

Conventional developments use a single sewage pipe that mixes together all residential and commercial waste water that then must be expensively cleaned before disposal. It is further complicated by the medications people now take, especially antibiotics that pass through the body and slow the biological breakdown process at the sewage treatment plant. This is costly, wasteful and not sustainable. The VillageTown proposes to handle sewage completely differently, by analyzing what goes into the sewage pipe and then installing additional pipes to capture each separately. In the long view of 175 years planning, the cost of plastic pipes is negligible. *Out-pipes* are called *grey, yellow* and *black*. An additional pipe may come from each building's roof collecting rain water (*rain* pipe)

Food scraps (compost) and dirt from dishes, clothes and bathing (grey): Food scraps are captured in the kitchen sink using a conventional sink grinder and cleaned-grey water piped in automatically when the grinder is turned on. This pipe flows the compost to the processing center where the nutrient value is used to produce farm products, including fertilizer, compost and fuel. This same pipe can receive dirty water from baths, showers, dishwashers and clothes washers, provided that the VillageTown supplies its residents with a range of free or subsidized soaps and cleaning agents to prevent adverse-chemical-based products from entering and contaminating the system.

Urine (yellow): The average person expels about 500 liters of urine a year. That is about 5 million liters (1.3 million gallons) for the VillageTown, not including visitors. Urine is acidic, nitrogen-rich and contains most medications that pass through the body. It is anticipated that all toilets in the VillageTown will have urine-diverters that capture and separate urine. Urine will have its own pipes to the processing center, where it will be converted into crystalline form, dried, and converted into a white powder called struvite to fertilize plants. This process removes the pharmaceuticals as well.

Faeces (black): Captured separately, human faeces are nutrient rich; a surplus resource of significant value if processed to produce biofuel and fertilizer. The processing plant to handle this has a number of steps very different than the typical sewage treatment plant. There is a type of fish that eats faeces, thus the slurry begins in fish tank. The process also uses heavy-metal bacteria to extract the metals that pass through our bodies and would be harmful if allowed to return to the food system via fertilizer. Part of the process uses the mix to brew engine-grade alcohol that can be used by the farmers to power tractors.

Diapers: It is expected that a 10,000-population VillageTown will have about 190 births and 80 deaths per year, based on global 2011 statistics with average life span of 67 years. This means that the VillageTown will go through about 1.5 million diapers a year or 4,000 a day. Rather than accumulate disposable diapers, it makes more sense for the VillageTown to operate its own diaper service, and for this to be paid for out of general community fees, since a sustainable community needs its young. This diaper collection service is best run out of the processing center since the faeces should then go directly into the black-water processing system, and the washing of the diapers has special requirements that are different from washing clothes.

Fresh Water

Conventional developments provide a single pipe in, with all water processed to drinking standard, even if it is used for the toilet or washing. Having said that, the standard is not particularly good. Water can smell of chlorine, for example. When one looks at the average household, less than 5% of the water actually enters the body, thus it makes sense to have several qualities of water being piped in. *In-pipes* are called *pure, clean* and *dark*.

Drinking water (pure): In the best system, drinking water would come in glass-lined pipes to the kitchen and bathroom sinks. It would be highly filtered and not have residual chemicals in it. It should taste good. This would be water that is of a higher standard than municipal drinking water. It is expected that about 20 million liters (6 million gallons) of drinking water would be consumed per year.

Washing water (clean): Showers, baths and dishwashers can use water that meets sanitary standards but not be as good as drinking water. This would come from storm water, grey water and ground water that would be cleaned and pumped in to meet municipal standards. In drought regions, such as Australia, recycling would be especially important.

Blackwater option (dark): Depending on state regulation, the VillageTown will look into establishing a closed-loop system for black-water. Think about the oil in a car, that is filtered as it recycles in a closed-loop system. In-pipe water would be the carrier for the faeces, and when it arrives in the processing plant, this black water would be separated, cleaned and recycled as dark-water. This is an area that may benefit from research, as it may turn out that a different liquid than water may be a better carrier. If such a system is used, the toilets may have automatically closing lids to keep pets and babies from getting into them.

Conclusion

For the host local government, the VillageTown water handling system will be a learning curve. It may ask if the broader community may tap into the system. Provided the local populace is willing to learn new habits, this may work well and be a win-win.

More Detail – *Citizenship and Keeping the Peace*

Traditionally, law in community focused on keeping the peace and protecting private property. Keeping the peace is an ancient, ambiguous, yet convenient concept, especially in small communities of 10,000 or less. In such communities, keeping the peace also is the best way to protect private property, since it sets up expectations of respect for people and possessions. Keeping the peace shapes how people live and work together.

It only takes one or two individuals or families tearing at the fabric of a community for the quality of life in the community to decline. Traditionally, communities had the means to protect themselves from such people, but over time, this personal accountability has given way to detached, over-worked, monetized systems that are less effective. At one time anti-social behavior was summarily dealt with – get along or move along. In too many communities, this is no longer the norm. Instead communities are asked to tolerate the erosion of the social order. Contrast this with a private company where anti-social conduct is grounds for termination of employment. Society has given up enforcing expectations that enable people to live together in a community, but has not given up those expectations when people work together in a company. Something seems wrong about this.

In regard to respect for private property, the public is asked to tolerate crime and rely on locks and insurance rather than live in a safe and free place where one can leave valuables in public view, knowing they will not be taken. Contrast this with a private company where valuable property, tooling and supplies are part of the office or workshop, yet few employees would think of stealing such things. If they did they would be summarily dismissed and banned from returning. Why is it that within the company but not the community, the old standard remains?

In the VillageTown, therefore, the means to restore peace and protect property is written into the fundamental contract upon which the legal structure of the community is established. This can only happen at the beginning, before the first villager buys a home. It must permanently embed in the purchase agreement and the ongoing title to buildings the rights of the community to protect itself – to keep the peace and protect private property.

Rather than invent new approaches to such protection, the VillageTown looks to the proven system of checks and balances to implement its system of judicial governance. In essence, the VillageTown will have the right to make and enforce rules that keep the peace and protect property.

Keeping the peace is social in nature. It is about preventing and resolving conflict. On the village level, this tends to be informal, in part borrowing from Maori principles of restorative justice where respected elders facilitate dialogue and accountability. At the town level, it is formal, with what is in effect a court system, although it is based on the law enabling a corporate disciplinary committee rather than the state court system.

The key to this system is in its enforcement powers, which can be summarized as *get along* (with each other) *or move along.* Individuals or families who tear at the fabric of society to the point where the peace of the community is disrupted, are first dealt with informally. If this fails, it is then escalated to a formal process where the ultimate power of VillageTown includes the ability to force the sale of their home and require they leave the VillageTown permanently.

In regard to this matter, a correspondent to the villageforum.com web site asked the following question: *"I want to know your views in regard to cultural upheavals in Europe due to low birth rates and incursion of Islamic values that do not seem to integrate with the local populace. How does a VillageTown go about dealing with the members in the community who bring a political cum religious agenda of subversion? Can a VillageTown reject any such groups and not be politically incorrect? This risks being accused of racism and religious bigotry. It's such a delicate balance. I wonder if you have thought about the implications?*

This complex question makes a number of doubtful presumptions, most notably that religion or national origin of a migrant group is the cause of subversion. The problem of migration clashing with bigotry tends to come when a settled group of powerless locals finds a migrant group moving in without the rituals of welcome and hospitality. The locals feel imposed upon and the migrants feel isolated and unwelcome. In Europe this is further aggravated by migrant poverty and a tendency for the migrant elders to lose control of the conduct of the young, who may run wild in the streets, with higher incidences of crime.

None of these circumstances would apply in a VillageTown where everyone is a migrant, and where some villages may intentionally form around cultural or religious identity. The design of a VillageTown does not have the outsider-versus-local-populace structure that requires integration; the whole point of different villages is to enable citizens to experience contrasts, different ways of life, the cultural experience of travel within a 10-minute walk. However, the line in the sand is drawn at the word *subversion.* If this means breaching the peace, then it does not matter what the reason. The drivers may be political, religious, maniacal ego, greed, bullying, power-plays, but all are irrelevant. The decision to insist that one get along or move along is based on breaching the peace. It's about conduct, not beliefs.

While we use the word VillageTown and speak of *citizenship*, the older word comes from ancient Greek. The word *Polis* refers to what sociologists would call the *common locality*, a community of people that is defined by geography as opposed to a community of interest, such as a social network. From polis we get the words *polite, politician, policy* and *police.* It begins with good manners, a social expectation of treating others politely. While the word *politician* has developed a negative connotation, traditionally this referred to people elected to make *policy*, to make the rules that enable people to get along. *Policing* is the enforcement mechanism. While a society requires a very high percentage law abiding citizens, it must have the mean to do something when a few breach the peace. The VillageTown is the *polis* in every meaning of the word.

More Detail – *School Classrooms in the Villages*

Education of the next generation is essential for continuity and improvement of civilization. This should be an obvious and accepted statement that guides how we educate.

However, over the past century, we evolved a bizarre form of age segregation in which our children are taken out of society and housed in isolated, uninspiring structures where they have little contact with adults except for harried teachers trying to control 30 students. Instead of fostering a passion for learning, considerable energy is devoted to a power struggle as students constantly test the patience of the teacher. Outside role models come from pandering media and games, especially video, creating false expectations for children as to what life is about. This bizarre educational system evolved to serve pecuniary interest and private agendas. Unfortunately, the result was a poor education for the next generations while distressing parents and concerned members of society.

Children learn by observing and interacting. Children learn to speak at home; they are not taught, it's part of how human brains develop. They learn better if their parents talk not only to them, but, in their presence, to each other and to visitors. Children taken out into the community learn how to behave, not because someone teaches them, but because anti-social conduct elicits an adverse response. This is natural, it is how human beings are wired, and in every traditional society, children, adults, and elders all share the same space. This is how culture, knowledge, and expertise are passed from one generation to the next.

In our civilization, we developed advanced knowledge, such as mathematics, the sciences, and the arts, that are not so easily learned in day-to-day living. This is why childhood learning evolved into formal schooling. We need more focused learning environments, with teachers who mastered their particular subject matter. While in theory, this is why we need schools, somewhere along the way, the system got hijacked. It now is directed to serve the interests and agendas of special-interest groups and to serve as babysitters for parents who must commute to somewhere else – away and unavailable all day long.

The VillageTown intends to use public education – unless the state system proves so intractable that the organizing company is forced to look at alternatives. However,

Bussing students to school takes time, costs money, burns fuel, and is anti-educational

It makes so much more sense to educate our children where they live; they learn how to live.

it will not accept building (or bussing students to) separate campuses outside of the villages. Classrooms will be on the plazas, in the guild halls, and in the greenbelt. In this way, students observe the life of the community as a natural backdrop to their day-to-day learning. Instead of eating in an institutional cafeteria, they will dine on the plaza, in the affordable café, with their parents and other adults, or perhaps they will walk home for a family meal. Sports will be in community gymnasiums and on the greenbelt using the same facilities that adults use, although the schools have priority during the day. Parents will naturally be more involved with their children's education, and the classes will make use of community resources in teaching. People running businesses will observe the students and in time some will be offered work after school and on weekends.

Through proximity, parents and the wider community become more aware of the children's education. The teachers should welcome this and take advantage of it. Within a community of 10,000 there will be people with remarkable stories. When the curriculum calls for a particular lesson plan, the teacher may use word of mouth or the VillageTown intranet to put out a call for someone to augment the lesson. The learning becomes real, personal and meaningful when instead of just a teacher and textbook, a member of the community comes in and talks about the subject. This applies at all levels of learning.

The change is simple – change only location. It saves capital-development costs. It requires less overhead. The school system should contract with the VillageTown corporation to provide for management of the paperwork, thus freeing teachers to focus on student learning rather than administrivia. It is simple and logical, not ideological or pedagogical.

At the same time, these changes are subtly profound as they remove so many obstacles to learning. Once again they are obvious, normal ideas in a world that has become abnormally dysfunctional. It really does take the village to raise the child.

This walk-to gathering place attracted teens, children, adults and elders. On a car-free plaza, teens socialized in public, having fun but not getting into trouble; they enjoyed being together.

More Detail – *Teenagers: A Safe, Stimulating Place to Grow Up*

At one time, children at puberty joined the adults in the work of the community; they became participating members of society. In the 20th century this began to change as the skills for work required more education. With blue-collar work now shifting to third-world and emerging nations, even a high-school education is no longer enough for many workers in first-world nations. Instead of moving into adulthood at puberty, teenagers enter a peculiar and sometimes dysfunctional period of part-time study and mandatory leisure.

This also is a period when their bodies are radically changing, and scientists tell us the teenage brain literally breaks down and rewires. During this time, teens may feel they are losing their minds; scientists say this is not a bad description of what is happening. Children's brains are wired to read adult body language since the child's life depends on those adults. At puberty, the body becomes adult-like, and the brain breaks down the old wiring and rewires for independence and autonomy. While this is underway, it can be an exceptionally difficult time both for teens and their parents.

The focus of the teen turns inward as they deal with sexuality, body, looks, and their sense of place in the world. Belonging becomes important – not to family, but to their peer group. They need to feel they are a part of that peer group. If that group is structured, with guidance from caring adults (often in their 20's and 30's) it can be a healthy form of belonging. If that group is unstructured, it very often devolves into something unhealthy and potentially damaging or lethal. The unstructured environment is especially notable in the modern world where the adults drive away to some other place to work and do not return home until late. It is easy for teens to say they are going out, and be in an unattended place where adults are not present, and where the traditional social checks and balances no longer exist. This is especially the case in a car-based society where teens drive.

Caring parents find they spend an inordinate amount of time driving their children to activities, to places where teens can occupy their time in a safe and healthy manner. The parents will seek out a place to live where there are a wide range of structured activities to keep their teens occupied and hopefully developing some skill or passion along the way. They seek to direct their children to worthwhile friends, clubs, sports, youth groups or other peer groups they trust. Meanwhile they compete against commercial media driven by pecuniary interest that panders to teens' fantasies, creating dissonance between the parents' reality and the media's fantasy. Usually the fantasy wins.

Caring parents fear their children taking up with "bad" friends, meaning teens who lack structure and whose parents are not present or who let them run wild. This can involve drug or alcohol abuse, crime or dangerous gang or cult type activities. In many places it now involves hollow sexuality where the often under-aged partner is seen more as an object and less as a feeling, loving human being.

When their children begin to drive, the opportunity for parents to structure their child's activities lessens. Not only do parents worry about what their children are doing, they read that the number-one killer of older teenagers is car crashes (the second is suicide/homicide).

In England, theaa.com writes "1 in 5 drivers are involved in a crash during their first year on the road. Male drivers aged under 21 are 10 times more likely to have a car accident than male drivers aged 35 or over. Young drivers have a higher proportion of crashes at night than older drivers, 1 in 8 British drivers are under 25, but a quarter of drivers who die in traffic collisions are in this age group. In 2007, 40% of passengers killed or seriously injured – meaning lost limbs, paralysis, brain injury and other life-changing injuries – were in a car driven by a young driver.

Mall rat is a disparaging term for teens who frequent shopping malls. Their lives have been monetized; they wear brands on their clothing; they must drive or be driven to get there. They don't know what they are missing. It is a sad, hollow, vacant way for children to become adults.

With the advent of electronic media, some teens grow physically passive as they spend their leisure time in front of the tube. The Kaiser Family Foundation tells us teenagers today spend 7.5 hours a day indoors using electronic media and doctors write specific prescriptions for outdoor activity. While this places less burden on parents having to drive the kids to various activities, parents remain worried: It is unhealthy for a body to be seated for so long, and the content of most electronic media is passive and vicarious. Watching teen videos is different from living what the actors are doing on the screen; listening to bands through headphones is not the same as making their own music. While technology offers great powers to people, the *black-box* phenomena (where people yield knowledge and understanding to an engineer who packages the function in a black-box with a start button) takes away the opportunity to learn.

Parents share these concerns. They ask how a VillageTown could address the needs of their children. If the answers make sense, they will see that moving to the VillageTown will give their children a better environment in which to grow while relieving family pressures.

There are concrete answers to these questions, some of which are inherent in the design, and others that may emerge based on how people in the villages choose to live.

1,000 teens in a VillageTown - In a 10,000-population VillageTown that matches normal demographics, there will be about a thousand teenagers. Most teens tend to have a small group of close friends and a larger community of perhaps twenty-five or fifty peers with whom they identify. Thus with a thousand teens in total, there should be a wide range of social choices.

20 Villages and the Town Center - A child will grow up in and identify with their home village. This is natural. However, with the onset of puberty, they begin to explore further afield. In the VillageTown they have 19 other villages and the Town Center, each of which will have its own special character. This gives the teen more choices, more places to develop friendships, and a new sense of belonging consistent with their developing independence and autonomy. However, each of these villages will also have adults present 24/7. It's not that the adults are spying, but that they are there going about their day-to-day life. When the teen travels to these other destinations, some of which may have different activities, worthwhile friends, clubs, sports, youth groups or other peer groups, one should remember, they all are still within a 10-minute walk, as are the sports fields in the Greenbelt. The parent need not drive, nor worry about the older teen driving, as cars will not be a necessary part of daily life.

Secondary schooling - the location of the High-schools - the secondary schools are placed in the Town Center, not in the villages. It is recommended that there be several high-schools, even if they are side by side; they should be more like several colleges in a university. One should be academic, preparing students for higher education. A second should be vocational, preparing students who will leave and find employment working with their hands, perhaps in the industrial park. A third should focus on the creative arts, an alternative school for those who do not wish to fit within the normal constraints of the educational system. In support of this, we recommend one of the top ten TED talks by Sir Ken Robinson *"who makes an entertaining and profoundly moving case for creating an education system that nurtures (rather than undermines)."* With the high-schools in the Town Center, VillageTown living expands the teenager's home-range in a way that supports the innate desire for more independence and autonomy. It mixes students together, so they meet new people and more easily find a good group with whom they feel they belong.

The Youth Zone and the SUVIE village - Teens often like to hang out with *older kids*, actually young adults in their early 20's, and they find support from even older adults who are not like their parents. The VillageTown is encouraged (for other reasons) to provide parallel market housing for young adults so they can afford to buy their first home. When surveyed, these young adults said they would rather have their own zone than be scattered among the other villages. For a start, they said, they will be noisier. They want dancing in the streets, climbing walls, skateboard places. They do not want, and will not have, disapproving older people judging them because they live next door. They want to be in a place more like college, where they can meet, party, date and perhaps marry and move on to a more family-oriented village. For this reason, it is recommended that a youth zone be established and that it be in the loudest end of the noise overlay. This zone will be a natural attractor for teens, and provide another place where they can develop independence and autonomy in a safe and healthy environment.

---

*   http://www.ted.com/talks/ken_robinson_says_schools_kill_creativity.html

These two young men formed a saw-violin & tub-base band – talent adding to street color

The youth zone may be its own village, or it may be part of what is called the SUVIE village, an acronym that originally meant Single Unattached Villager, but was renamed by its target audience as Single Unencumbered Villager. This is a village that will have non-traditional housing, since the presumed family average of 200 homes for 500 people will not apply. Instead, some housing will be small apartments; others what was once called the luxury bachelor pad and a third type that resembles the Oxford college hall with privately owned rooms or serviced apartments that share formal dining, a great-room, and other elegant or bohemian commons space. These single adults can be of any age, some who live single by choice – preferring the company of others rather than the commitment of a relationship – and others who suffered divorce, separation or death of a partner, or who are simply impossible for anyone to live with. Experience shows that these single adults can be an excellent source of volunteers to guide youth groups, clubs or other teen activities.

Transition to Adulthood - When high school is finished, today's teenagers find the transition tough. Fifty years ago, in many countries a teen could walk out of school, find a secure job the next day and within a year have the resources to marry, buy a home, start a family and live a secure life. Today, it is not uncommon for that same demographic group to be living with their parents well into their twenties or thirties, even for those with a college education. They can't afford to buy a home; good jobs are hard to find, security is elusive and in many countries it is socially acceptable to conceive a child without a partner or spouse; having the grandparents raise the child is becoming more commonplace.

Part of the VillageTown's purpose is to create opportunity for all, including youth transitioning to adulthood. Some will leave the VillageTown to go to college or university;

some will never return. Others may go out to seek their fortune in the wider world, but when they are ready to start a family may return to their VillageTown – especially if their parents offer them the family home in exchange for a life-pension in elder-housing (including elder-housing on the ground floor or back half of the family home). A third group of youth will find work in the VillageTown. Some may have held part time work while in school. In the village, one is known. Proprietors of small-to-medium-sized businesses will have watched the youth grow up, and some will smoothly transition into work. Another group will have studied in the vocational high school, and if the VillageTown Legacy Fund managers are doing their job, there will be entry-level employment with a business in the industrial park or one of the workshops in one of the villages.

The Legacy Fund managers should also be working with the high school, and should be encouraging entrepreneurship. Some young adults may move into the youth zone, buy a house and become successful before their 21st birthday. Remember Alexander the Great studied under Aristotle when he was 13; at age 16 he put down a rebellion, stormed the rebel's stronghold and renamed the city after himself. By age 17, Mozart was engaged as a court musician in Salzburg. By age 19 in 2004, Adam Hildreth was named one of the U.K.'s 20 richest teens (net worth of approx. $3.7 million) by starting Dubit Ltd five years earlier, the most visited teen web site in the Great Britain.

When the first VillageTown is built, one can expect that more VillageTowns will follow, and when this happens, it is likely they will become trading and exchange partners. If they are located in other countries, this will open the possibility for safe travel; a distant destination where one is welcome and has an automatic introduction.

Reality Check - The VillageTown is not intended to be its own universe. It is embedded in larger holons – its surrounding region, nation, and continent. It is not intended to be a utopia, and just like other places, there will be teens who do not do well, and in some cases, teens who may not survive to adulthood for reasons having little to do with their community. However, it should be a safer place because people are present all the time, and because small communities tend to have lower tolerances for crime and the sort of conduct that makes it easier for teens to damage themselves. Because cars are not necessary, teen driving will be discretionary, not something parents must provide. Because of its density, it will offer alternatives to vicarious living through electronic media. It can be expected to be a place of enriched culture and social activity, thus offering day-to-day life where boredom is less of a problem than in the car-based, media-reliant suburbs. With adults present, teens can be expected to have more role models, more mentors, and more champions. With its economic foundation, the VillageTown should provide youth both with a transition to adulthood and an independent, autonomous future. For parents, living in the VillageTown means less time spent driving children, and it should reduce the cost of raising children. The VillageTown will not fit everyone, but for many it offers a new and better choice.

Single people and childless couples tend to have more discretionary income for entertainment, dining out, fashion, and some of the luxuries of life. They add to the wealth of the community and they add different energy to it. However, often they prefer to be surrounded by others who share their lifestyle. For this reason the Village Town encourages villages for such people.

Suburbs were designed for families. They were designed to raise children. When the kids finish school, they are supposed to move away. Some parents will hang on to the empty nest, but they no longer fit in as they did when raising children. Likewise, adults who do not marry and raise a family, or who have different sexual orientation, do not generally fit well in suburban life. This results in social segregation. This explains why much of society lacks complete communities.

The VillageTown is intended to be a complete community, and it is the distinctive character of each village that makes this possible. One village may be for families with many children, with grandparents living next door, but the next village may be completely different. When adults live alone or live as childless couples, their focus is different. They tend to have more discretionary income, as well as the time and interest to focus on their own pursuits. Fashion, furnishings, parties, evenings out with friends or at the theatre are all pursuits for which they may have more time. Because they have the time and the resources, they enrich the VillageTown through their support.

Alternative lifestyle refers to different forms of housing for people. A village made of 500 single persons may require 500 residences. Alternatively, twenty of those single persons may chose to build a large facility with privately owned very small apartments and a larger commons area for formal dining, a great hall and even a private library or concert room. Alternative lifestyle also can mean a tribal way of life in which an extended family lives and works in a much larger, somewhat rambling building with home workshops and less clear boundaries between family and work life. This could be one such family in an otherwise mainstream village, or it could be a whole village made up of such extended families. In the New Zealand VillageTown project, for example, the Maori leaders who have expressed strong interest in forming a village said they would do so by bringing in their tribal values, family structure and architectural traditions.

The driving force behind villages comes from the village coordinator who steps forward and declares what sort of village they want. If the coordinator can recruit enough buyers who like the idea, such as designing for alternative lifestyles, it can happen. The organizing company will encourage diversity, including alternative lifestyles, because this is what makes the VillageTown a complete community. However, its job is not prescribe a particular outcome, but rather to enable the coordinator and future villagers to make it happen. It does this by making them aware of their architectural and design options.

As seen after dark in this ancient village, when elders can no longer live at home, it is kinder to place their nursing care within the village, not isolated from the rest of society. The full length doors have curtains if they need privacy, but often they are open, and if the weather is good, the doors are open so the elders can greet and be greeted, even if they cannot speak.

In such places, their loved ones live nearby; instead of being left in a wheelchair in the nursing home day room, elders are taken out into the community. It is not so difficult when all one does is wheel the chair out the street-level door to arrive in the plaza.

It's not easy being weak and infirm at any age, but it is especially difficult for the elderly, as for the most part, recovery of their strength and mobility is unlikely. However, it is cruel to make it worse by segregating them, cutting them off from the community and concentrating them among others who also are suffering. The end of life should be a peaceful time.

More Detail – *Care for the Elderly, the Weak and the Infirm*

In almost all cultures but our own, when people come to a certain age we call them elders. They are respected for their experience, the wisdom that often comes with age, and for the lifetime of service they gave to family, community, society and the economy. In today's monetized culture however, we tend to call them *old people, retired, pensioners, golden oldies* or if we are politically correct, *senior citizens*. Our suburban communities have no place for them, mostly because they can no longer drive, so we segregate them into ghettos we call retirement homes – or if upscale, *retirement villages*. These places cut them off from society and deprive the community of their assistance and the transmission of culture that traditionally went from grandparent to grandchild. This model also promises to be unsustainable in the future when there will be too many old people and not enough young to pay for segregated retirement and expensive health care.

The VillageTown begins by calling them elders, although in doing so, it acknowledges that the dividing line is no longer so absolute. At one time, 60 was old. Now it may be 75 or 80 before one looks and feels the same as an earlier generation did at 60. The VillageTown focuses not on age, but on elders' mobility and their capacity to care for themselves.

As discussed elsewhere in this book, it will become essential to de-monetize elder care. When demographic projections suggest that we will be going from five working adults for every elder down to two, it is likely our present-day elder-care systems will fail. De-monetizing is much easier in a complete community. There are many relationships that develop between old and young when they are in close proximity, not solely those of parent and grown child. Often elders become surrogate grandparents to a child with whom they happen to click, or the elder becomes a mentor – able to take time that the parents cannot. Later, when the elder becomes weaker, and that child is a teen or adult, the relationship reverses, becoming one of young caring for old – this is natural and involves no payment.

Care Contracts: Young people often find it difficult to afford to buy a home; elders have the money, but worry if their savings will provide for their remaining life needs. In a care-contract, the elder takes their life savings to pay for a three-story home. The ground floor becomes their settled home; it's all they want and need. They contract with a young family, perhaps their grown children or someone else they trust, for a lifelong pension as well as payment of the property taxes, utilities, and other home expenses. At their death, the home becomes the property of the contract family. The payment is probably less than mortgage payments or rent but enough to live on comfortably, making it a good solution for both. The elder need not worry about paying bills, home maintenance or security, and the young family gets a good neighbor as well as a future home. The VillageTown would monitor such care contracts to assure there was no abuse of the contract that would make life difficult for either party. This sort of innovative contract is another way that the VillageTown provides for good citizenship without looking to the taxpayer for help.

More Detail – Medical and Health Facilities

The VillageTown focus is on maintaining good health, not on illness. This means that if people exercise naturally by walking outdoors, and they have the opportunity to eat fresh, local, healthy and affordable food, they can expect to remain healthier. If they live in a lower-stress environment, where people naturally support each other, they can be expected to remain healthier. Additionally, the health facilities owned and operated by the VillageTown will have a focus on keeping people healthy rather than becoming involved only when illness strikes. It's cheaper and better to keep people healthy.

Access to Hospital: In most cases a 10,000-population community is too small to support a large hospital for severe illness and injury. This is another reason why it makes sense to locate less than a two hour drive from a major urban center.

Primary and Village Health Facilities: The organizing company builds and pays for two levels of health facilities. The neighborhood facilities serve three to five villages with doctors, nurses, and health practitioners. These provide the normal GP services as well as a focus on diet, exercise, and other practices that maintain good health. It is recommended that the staff is paid by the VillageTown and receives bonuses for exceeding average health statistics (pay for wellness). The primary health facility would offer a higher level of services, including urgent care for injuries and illness. It is recommended that the primary facility be located near the motorpool and the helipad for rapid transport to a regional hospital.

Medivac: It is recommended that the VillageTown run a helicopter service for the region or contract for the same. Local ambulance service would use custom electric vehicles.

Funding and Medical Insurance: While each country's laws and programs are different, it is reasonable to expect that publicly funded, or even privately insured, medical services will become more expensive or decline in quality. Thus, it is recommended that the VillageTown self-insure on the majority of medical services, employing its medical staff, and purchase group catastrophic medical insurance for all VillageTown residents as a part of the annual fee. It is recommended that it buy drugs at a wholesale rate. Finally, if it is legal to do so, it is recommended that the threat of litigation be controlled.

Litigation control: Access to medical services would be voluntary, but would be owned by the community to lower prices and increase quality. Thus, if a client sues for malpractice, they are suing themselves and their neighbors. Out-of-control litigation results in excessive testing and a substantial portion of the doctor's fee going to malpractice insurance. This is not in the interest of the community. It is recommended that as a condition of belonging to and using the medical services, the member waive the right to sue for malpractice. Instead the VillageTown should establish a very active checks-and-balances system that includes peer review and citizen feedback to uphold standards so that bona fide malpractice is exceptionally difficult to happen undetected.

Anti *slow-suicide* provision: If the VillageTown provides its own medical services and self-insurance, it should consider a provision to offer only hospice care, not expensive treatment of illness caused by smoking, consumption of excessive alcohol or illicit drugs or other voluntary choices which damage health and cost the public money. If it may legally do so, it is recommended to exclude such coverage. If someone chooses self-destructive habits, they would be encouraged to purchase private medical insurance outside the VillageTown plan.

Healthy Environment: The first thing the doctor says to the patient is *"eat healthy foods, get plenty of exercise, go outdoors more often, don't smoke, and if you drink, do so only in moderation."* The problem we face is that our physical environment and modern systems conspire to make this more difficult. Healthy foods are harder to find because so many foods are laced with chemicals and lost in packaging. The number of steps between farm and plate are longer. Thus, the VillageTown makes a priority of restoring the single, town-country local economy and cutting out the middleman so the farm can make a profit growing affordable, healthy food. By designing a walking home-range, outdoor exercise is a given. It is natural, necessary, and socially more enjoyable. It does not take long for the body to remember the purpose of its feet, legs, and torso. Further, the surrounding greenbelt should have long walks as well as exercise and sport areas. Finally, while alcohol will be enjoyed by some in the convivial atmosphere of the village squares, drunkenness is generally deemed anti-social conduct and one may expect that such excess would not tolerated by most villagers.

Healthy infrastructure: In addition to these active prescriptions by the doctor, we are increasingly seeing people become ill due to the mix of industrial chemicals and other toxins that are a part of modern society. The VillageTown will build homes using safe materials that have been around for thousands of years. Similarly, we recommend that until the cumulative effect of thousands of people using wireless devices in high density areas is known, the VillageTown use wires and cables to reduce the need for wireless devices. In cafés, for example, provide ethernet cables, and, for wireless only devices, install low-power-signal transmitters with very limited range of perhaps half a room or less.

Safer environment: Obviously, the first aspect of safety is the walking home range. Remove cars from day-to-day life, and injury/death from car crashes is significantly lowered. This is especially the case with young people who are overly represented in car-crash statistics. Additionally, a chemical free environment, and one that does not fill the air with pollutants, will have long term benefits on health. Finally, the organizing company is instructed to consider injury risk in design. With more people walking, design for real safety not solely to meet the safety requirements of building codes.

Alternative Health: In western society, the pecuniary interest of the medical establishment is so powerful that it shoves aside what is called *alternative health*. This is not in the interest of the people who live in the VillageTown. It should use its autonomy to enable those who are open to alternative approaches to be both providers and users of such services.

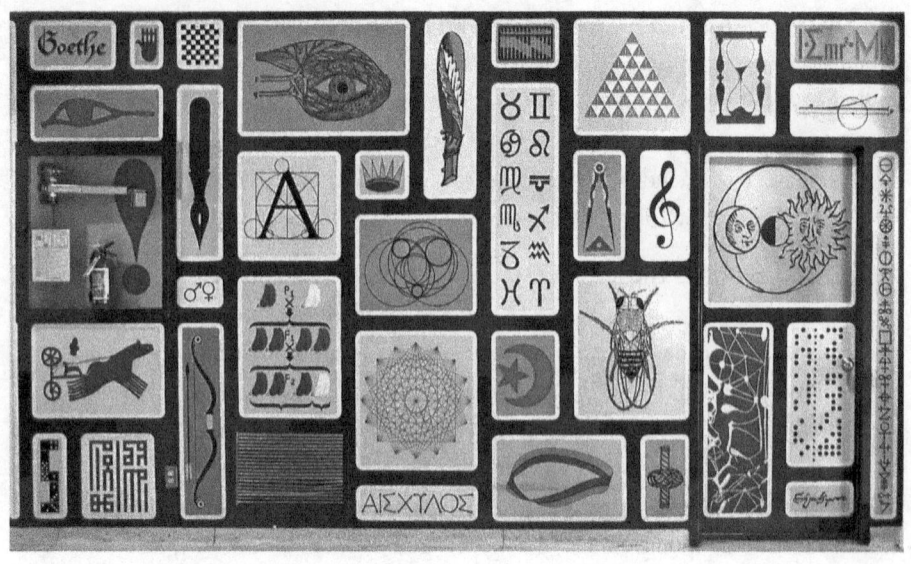

The intellectual pursuits give us languages so we may think – these languages can come in unfamiliar forms.

The artistic pursuits give us a mirror so we can see through another's eyes what our eyes would not see.

ARTISTIC AND INTELLECTUAL GROWTH

Small towns can be deadly boring places where gossip becomes a contact sport. Such towns can drive their creative people away to the cities as soon as the law allows them to flee. But some small towns are different. They are vibrant and colorful, with many things happening all the time. It is not size that makes them different, it is the character of the place.

This difference rarely happens by accident. In some cases it is the outcome of trade and wealth, where wealthy patrons came to value artistic and intellectual pursuits. That is the story of the Renaissance and more recently the story of New York City after the Second World War. In some others it may be because a college or university was located there. In the Italian town of Pietrasanta, before it was gentrified, it is due to its proximity to a marble quarry that attracted sculptors.

The VillageTown creates such an intention from the onset. It identifies people who pursue creative growth and then examines what they need in order to be successful at their pursuits. The most obvious need is to close the gap between income and cost of living so the creative person does not need to work at a maintenance job to keep going. It makes sense to lower the cost of living first, as it is always cheaper to save a dollar than earn one.

Beyond this, for creative people to thrive, they need a concentration of other creative people, not necessarily in their own field, for creativity often begets creativity. There must be a critical mass.

In addition to affordability and a peer group, creative people need resources. Sometimes they find these resources when the economy changes. When a warehouse district loses its tenants, the creative class will move in because the spaces are large and the rent cheap. The problem comes when their presence turns it from sordid to trendy and they are gentrified out. The color dies as the money moves in.

The VillageTown proposes a smarter way to approach this. It lowers the cost of living, working and provides free-base housing to ensure that at least 5% of the VillageTown population is of the Creative Class. And it pays for purpose-built facilities where the members of those artistic or intellectual clusters define what they need within a fixed budget that allows both for creativity and chaos (unorganized potential).

The VillageTown also seeks out institutions of higher education, inviting them to run a year-abroad program or an advanced research center in one of the villages or in the town center. By doing so, it further enriches the population, encouraging more diverse views of life and bringing in different people who add to the vibrance and color of day-to-day life.

Street Performance is as old as the town:

POWER OF MUSIC/William Wordsworth (1806)

AN Orpheus! an Orpheus! yes, Faith may grow bold,
And take to herself all the wonders of old;–
Near the stately Pantheon you'll meet with the same
In the street that from Oxford hath borrowed its name.

His station is there; and he works on the crowd,
He sways them with harmony merry and loud;
He fills with his power all their hearts to the brim–
Was aught ever heard like his fiddle and him?

He stands, backed by the wall;–he abates not his din
His hat gives him vigour, with boons dropping in,
From the old & the young, from the poorest; & there!
The one-pennied Boy has his penny to spare.

Buskers, street performers – once called minstrels or troubadours – sing, play music, juggle, clown, eat fire, dance, stand still as a statue or break-dance with trash-cans drums. They tell stories, tell fortunes and read poetry. They draw three-dimensional works in chalk on the pavement. They set up, they perform, the crowd gathers. They do it for love & coin.

When creative humans perform on the streets and plazas something marvelous happens, something no video screen on the billboard or amplified music from a shopfront can match. It's real, it's authentic and it's been going on for thousands of years.

CULTURAL ENRICHMENT

Artistic & Intellectual Growth – not everyone is interested in the artistic and intellectual pursuits, but a town that lacks them becomes homogenous as it loses some of its best and brightest to the better cities of the world. People need to be both participants in and appreciators of creativity. To be a complete community, the creative pursuits are essential. The VillageTown borrows the term *Creative Class* coined by Richard Florida, to encompass both the traditional creative professions – music, theatre, art, film, and the creative minds: designers, architects, engineers, scientists, inventors, and entrepreneurs.

Classical Athens was car-free, waste-free and carbon neutral, however, it was known not for those environmental qualities, but for its democracy, philosophy, theater, music, geometry, poetry, and other creative arts. The primary artists who make music, theater, poetry, paintings, sculpture, and performance add to the cultural enrichment of a place. A place with a stimulating intellectual atmosphere becomes a magnet. As Richard Florida demonstrates, the Creative Class builds a stronger economy. To attract the *creatives*, specific investments should be made. To sustain them, specific legal protections should be adopted; gentrification is the enemy of the creative class. Providing an artistically and intellectually enriched environment attracts a wide range of people who enjoy living amidst that enrichment. To attract and retain such creative people, the VillageTown invests in artist guild halls, artist residences, public performance buildings, and outdoor facilities.

"Growth": Notable is the fact that in describing the artistic and intellectual contributions to a good life, the word *growth* is the object. The artist who cranks out the same works over and over goes stale. The university that teaches the same knowledge without doing research often finds it slips behind. This is not to say all must be interested such pursuits; there are people whose sole passion is sport, or fashion, or gardening. However, the community that has neither artistic nor intellectual growth becomes a segregated and more barren place, as those who pursue and those who enjoy creativity flee it for more interesting places. The VillageTown aspires to be a complete community. To achieve this, it invests significant capital in facilities and a sustainable economy to foster both individual and community artistic and intellectual growth.

Culturally enriched - More than any other investment, providing affordable space for the Creative Class promises to make the VillageTown a primary attraction. Artists, musicians, actors, writers, scholars, scientists, engineers & inventors all add to the buzz that makes a place stimulating and interesting. The challenge such people find comes in reconciling their passion with their ability to earn a living. The starving artist is more than a cliché. In traditional societies such people were honored by their community, and more importantly supported by them. In the case of the VillageTown the primary support comes in capital investment during development, and it is done in such a way that the initial investment pays for itself forever.

The Artist Guild Hall on each plaza should be a commanding building in scale. The Village Town may seek out patrons to make it more beautiful than the Village Town budget could provide. Likewise, for the academic buildings; they too should be prominent as they will be permanent.

Artist Guild Hall: On each plaza, the VillageTown builds a public building known as an Artist Guild Hall. It has about 25 members who share a common art, and who determine what amenities they will need to do their work. Musicians need practice rooms, recording studios and performance halls. Painters need studios and galleries. Inventors need a widget store and fast food delivery 24/7. This hall is paid for by the development, and it includes rental accommodations for visitors. The rentals generate income to cover maintenance.

Freebase Artist Housing: In addition to the hall, the VillageTown solves a technical design problem by offering *freebase housing* for the guild members. The VillageTown design rejects the grid plan for streets in favor of visually interesting curves that create more dynamic views. This means that when the streets curve, either an extra wall must be built, or a house must have trapezoidal rooms. The VillageTown makes the curve with a building of one-room loft flats that are trapezoidal. It then offers them rent-free to guild members. The net cost of constructing these is minimal. The guild member may live in it rent-free or lease it out, keeping the proceeds. It's not free of course; in exchange the artist must do their art. By lowering the cost of living, the artist can spend more time doing it.

Benefit: The benefit of this to the community should be obvious. The very presence of the cultural creatives, in their artistic and intellectual endeavors, adds to the richness of the community. The musicians will provide music both in the performance halls and on the street. The actors will put on live theater and possibly create a thriving recording industry of both video and audio. The artists will add color and texture with paintings and sculpture. The writers and scholars stimulate minds with poetry and intellectual debate and discovery.

Academia: In addition to funding the Artist Guild Halls on every plaza, the VillageTown will seek to anchor a college or advanced university program on its main town square, thus incorporating that distinctive social atmosphere that comes with higher education. This has an economic component in bringing in students and faculty, and a social component as youth of college age add a wonderful spirit to a community, keeping it forever refreshed and vital. Not every VillageTown will have its own college or university, but every one can host a one year abroad program or an advanced research center.

Festivals & celebrations - With 500 free-base homes provided rent-free for the creative class, with the plazas and part of the greenbelt designed for festivals, celebrations and market days, the VillageTown may expect an annual cycle of events that break the routine of daily living. For the VillageTown it's about conviviality, but for the creative class, this is good business; a way to generate interest in their arts so they may make a living at it.

Festivals and celebrations add authentic, locally-made experiences that can be focused on anything: seasonal, religious, rites, craft, food & drink, sport, whimsy, or high art. In today's world, people travel to wonderful places on their two week vacation, and then return to the drudge. In the VillageTown, villagers experience year-round wonder and celebration at home. They need not travel far for great experiences; instead others come to visit them.

In a ground breaking set of books, including *The Rise of the Creative Class*[*], Richard Florida shows that the most successful cities and towns are those that provide for what he calls the *Creative Class*. In addition to the artists, musicians, actors, writers, film-makers and other front line artists, in his definition of this class he includes inventors, scientists, engineers and the associated professions that support creative work. This class seeks places to live that are affordable, culturally supportive, and authentic – that elusive quality rarely attained by franchises, chains or planned communities.

He showed that attracting this class to a community does more for the economy than any of the conventional political ideas such as stadiums, shopping malls, convention centers, or master-planned developments. To this end, the VillageTown plan includes investment by the organizing company in one artist guild hall per plaza.

To attract and protect the creative class – which the VillageTown deems essential for many reasons – the development invests in a creative infrastructure in the same way a gated-golfing community builds greens and a club house through a premium applied to each home sale. In the VillageTown this involves developer-funded Artist Guild Halls – large buildings designed by and for a cluster of artists (one for musicians, another for film-makers, for example). The hall contains the rooms and facilities the artists deem important (for example rehearsal rooms and recording studio for musicians), as well as income-producing rooms, such as visitor accommodations so the hall can cover its own on-going expenses.

Some guild halls will be for primary artists – musicians, actors, painters, and crafters. Others will provide for the broader definition of the creative class – inventors, scientists, designers, film-makers, the rapidly expanding digital industries; with this latter class being tied into themes for particular villages such as entrepreneur and hothouse-industry villages.

Engaging artists begins in the first stage of development. It is essential that this part be set out with clear boundary conditions of what is negotiable and what is not – because artists are often not business people, yet the building of a guild hall involves money – the development's money. A fixed budget is provided to build the Hall, another to provide what is needed to outfit the Hall with furnishings, technology and tools of the trade, and a third budget provides for *free-base artists housing*. This third budget requires explanation:

Many forms of art pay badly. Many in the creative class are not skilled in the art of money-making. Artists tend to be the pioneers that transform localities into stimulating, happening places, but then the place becomes trendy, forcing them out. More affluent people move in, gentrifying the neighborhood. Any plan for a VillageTown *must* presume gentrification will happen unless protective measures are put in place. At the same time, and completely unrelated, the VillageTown has a design problem in that it seeks to avoid a

*   ISBN 0-465-02477-7 ©2002

The Village Town will invest in different sorts of theaters for arts and for entertainment such as music, live-acting, dance, cabaret and film. It may link these with one of the guild halls where the guild looks after the hall to assure it is always in use.

The free-base artist housing is intended to provide rent-free accommodations for members of the artist guilds. Necessarily, it will be basic, perhaps a single open room with high enough ceilings that the artists can create their own platforms for sleeping, as shown in this artist loft. As in this one, the walls are expected to be trapezoidal in shape to follow the curve of the street. Some artists will buy a home, in which case they can rent out the free-base and keep the money.

grid design of attached buildings in straight lines. It needs to turn the streets so they curve, but to do so, some buildings either must have wedge shaped gaps with an extra wall, or some buildings must be trapezoidal rather than rectangular.

The solution for both problems is to build *free-base housing* for the members of the guild. These are single-floor, single-room flats, trapezoidal in shape, that provide a small-but-comfortable living space intended for a single person. These are provided rent-free to guild artists. The artist pays no rent; but does pay for utilities. If the artist does not wish to live in the free-base unit – perhaps they have a family or they want to buy an open-market home to enjoy capital gains – they may rent the free-base unit out and keep the income to help them focus on their art.

It is said that people don't respect that which is given to them free. The guild members are not getting something for free. Rather they are getting the kind of support common in tribal culture before life became monetized. The guilds are expected to do their art, to make a contribution to the enrichment of the VillageTown.

Forming the guild requires a three-way dialogue among the villagers and their coordinator, the organizing company, and the group of artists that clusters. It is likely that in the same way a coordinator emerges to call a village into being, there will be an artist who puts out the word to his or her fellow artists. The organizing company will maintain some controls during this phase to assure that the guild does not become a clique and that it has artists in the three stages of new, emerging and the master. It may also encourage and set aside space for visiting artists to keep the guilds refreshed and dynamic. Of course, once several VillageTowns are built, one may expect artist exchanges to occur among them.

Once the guild is formed and approved, the organizing-company staff works with the guild members to prioritize and implement the construction budget. One may presume that no matter how large the budget, it will never be enough, thus the guild will need to establish a strong and self-supporting business plan to ensure it can do what it does best without needing bailouts. For example, the organizing company will build visitor accommodations in the guild hall that will generate ongoing income for the guild and provide a unique place for visitors to stay. It may recommend an actors guild run the next-door theater to generate income as well as work. It may construct classrooms for the primary and secondary schools that generate part-time employment for its members. Note that the financial affairs of the guild are to be managed by the VillageTown administration to assure the books are in order and funds prudently managed.

The guild may also elect to seek out sponsorship and patronage. The budget allocated by the organizing company should provide for a proper hall, but may not be able to cover the additional expenses of greatness. The arts have traditionally attracted wealthy patrons, and this should be encouraged by the organizing company for particular guilds.

Spiritual Development and Fulfillment

There was a time when writing this page would be simple. Every reader would be in the same denomination of the same religion, and it would merely be a matter of discussing the budget for the buildings. This is no longer the case for the first VillageTowns.

Thus, we first must make a distinction between the practice of religion and the buildings designed for spiritual activities. The VillageTown sets a boundary. It builds and maintains the holy places (which we will call chapel, church, and cathedral to denote size, not religion) but does not meddle in or concern itself with matters of religion or belief.

If a particular village comes together around a shared religion, the VillageTown will pay to build a church for their use. It comes out of the amenity budget, in the same way that the guild halls and plazas are funded. If that village wishes for a more expensive building or they need more land than is allocated as standard, they may elect to either pay for it out of pocket, or assess a higher base price for their village to pay for it in their mortgages.

If another village forms for secular reasons, the VillageTown will still pay to build a church, meaning sacred architecture for use in rites of passage as well as a calm place for private contemplation, for song (acoustics are important), and for other non-profane uses. In some cases, the secular village may request a smaller building, chapel-sized. In the Town Center, the VillageTown will build a cathedral that can seat many more people.

Sacred architecture is a known and important specialty within the architectural profession. It ranges from the simple vernacular to the highest art form of the great cathedrals of Europe and mosques of the Islamic world. Some tend to emulate the great forests with columns rising like tree trunks drawing one's eyes to the heavens. Others more resemble the womb-like feeling of holy caves. Some of the ancient buildings tend to follow lines that run across the earth, upon which man has erected stones and built altars, churches, and cathedrals for thousands of years.

The decision on the chapel or church for each village is made by the people who will live there. For those founders who say they are not interested, we say *trust us on this one.* Do it for future generations or to honor your ancestry when such buildings were deemed important. Make it visually and acoustically beautiful. Make it comfortable to sit in peace. Make it a safe place to go to be alone, or for a quiet talk that would not feel comfortable in the café or out on the plaza. Invite artists who work in the sacred to adorn it. Design it for an adult or youth choir. Build a bell tower and find a homeless church bell at *www.keltek.org*, an English charitable trust that saves such bells.

Holy space is important for human beings. The VillageTown will have both buildings for holy space and outdoor places, including a cemetery in the greenbelt.

MATTERS OF SPIRIT

Spiritual matters – In traditional societies, when the community shared beliefs, *religion* was a useful word. This common sharing is no longer the case, and proposing any religious affiliation in a development immediately enters controversial grounds if it aspires to represent the broad cross section of society. Because we no longer live in a homogeneous religious culture, the religious experience as both an individual and shared activity must stand outside the scope of a real-estate plan. However, sacred architecture both in buildings and in outdoor landscape is important to all people – architecture that combines beauty and awe.

When we speak of spirit in a community, it is something we immediately sense, and it may have nothing to do with the religion of the place. When we walk into a building that was built with spiritual qualities, or even a natural place – a cave, a waterfall, a field of flowers, or a grove of trees, it can have a spirit that inspires. One need not be religious to be affected by the experience of entering one of the great cathedrals of Europe when a choir is singing. In Japan, the gardens of sacred architecture engender a heightened sense of peace and tranquillity. In Cornwall, dowser Hamish Miller mapped out what he called *earth energy lines* crossing the length of England. He reported that at the spot where masculine and feminine lines intersect, he found altars in ancient churches where vows of marriage were spoken. Finally, over time, a cemetery becomes important to people, marking the passing of generations as they finally live in a place they can truly call home. Providing holy space becomes important for some people when deciding where to live. In these examples, sacred architecture plays a role not well understood by most contemporary designers.

Rites of Passage: People need places that are sacred and holy, even if they hold no beliefs or religion. Some people get married in a church, others on a beach or in a field, but very few would choose a profane place, even if they described themselves as atheist. Communities need holy spaces. They need them for rites of passage including birth, coming of age, marriage, and death. Such places must be big enough for all to fit in, to hear and see, and they need a certain holy feeling about them, appropriate to the occasion.

Holy Places: For these reasons, the VillageTown funds a smaller church-sized holy building on each village plaza and a larger building – cathedral-sized – on the Town Square. Sacred architecture is a subset of the architectural profession, and the VillageTown would seek out qualified architects to assist in such designs. The decision on classical, traditional, modern, or post-modern is made by the villagers when they set out the design code for their village.

Religion: The buildings are non-sectarian and open to all who come in peace, and respect the code of conduct set by the villagers. If a village is formed by people whose defining theme is their shared religion, they may request that their holy building be a church, temple, mosque, sanctuary, or shrine of their denomination. Further, while the central cathedral is also non-sectarian, if a particular religion requires part to be consecrated for them to use it, they may pay for construction of a smaller attached wing that is theirs.

Roots: The traditional Maori culture of Aotearoa, New Zealand defines itself in part by its connection to land. A tribe for an area is called *Tangata Whenua,* where tangata is the word for people and whenua is the word for both land and for placenta. In this view, the land owns the people, not the other way around. At the heart of their lands is a square of communally owned land called the *marae,* and its building, the *whare nui,* is their central meeting place. This valuable tradition of connecting with the land gives them an identity and stability that modern culture too often lacks. The VillageTown learns from this model, providing the opportunity for generations to establish themselves with such a connection, yet to do so within the context of modern life.

Optimism: Around the world, people are gathering to voice concern about the trend away from what they deem important in life. They see that to reclaim what is important, they can no longer look to someone else, to some authority or official body. Instead, they begin to see that all power lies within, dormant until it is awakened into action. This is not the same as the 20th-century struggle for power of one class against another. It is something completely different. The power to create requires no permission, the freedom is already there. Just do it.

Often, organized religious groups find their spiritual attention is preoccupied with earthly matters such as fund-raising to fix the roof. In the VillageTown, building repairs and maintenance are part of the operating company's budget. This makes it easier for religious groups to focus on spiritual matters. It also assures the building will not be neglected if the membership declines, as is happening in many parts of the world today.

Such buildings may serve more utilitarian uses as well. The Maori *whare nui* holy building is not only used for rites of passage, but for community meetings *(called hui)* and as a place where hundreds of visitors may sleep on floor mattresses. It is not unusual for a whare nui to be pressed into use with two-hours' notice. By tradition, such use is free. This model may prove very useful for villages when a large group on a limited budget comes to visit.

Roots - We live in a transient society where people move many times, to the point that they don't come from anywhere anymore. This produces a deep-seated feeling of hollowness and can have terrible consequences when one grows old. There is an ancient concept that one does not own the land, the land owns the people. *As you drink the waters of the land, as you eat food grown from the land, as each night you sleep on the land, as your children are born unto the land and as you bury your loved ones in the land, the land becomes a part of you, and you a part of the land.* Some yearn for this connection. Others accept rootlessness as normal, but when they encounter this deeper relationship, something stirs in them. This is especially the case when one asks *"where do you want to be buried?"*. It is important the VillageTown has a greenbelt, and in that greenbelt a cemetery. It changes one's understanding of time. It builds for many generations. Cemeteries are an important marker of connection to land.

And another Spiritual View: An Optimistic View of the Future

As of late, prognosticators, pundits, and politicians have been painting a gloomy picture of the future, as if the golden era is over and future generations may expect a world where Nature bites back, energy runs out, and affluence collapses. This is a new mood. For people who grew up in or after the Great Depression, every year seemed better than the previous, and the future looked bright. But we now have the first generation of young adults who have been told since kindergarten that the Earth is in decline, and that it is mankind's fault.

The VillageTown takes a different view. It shows how people can take back control of their community, their wealth, and the future for them and their children by investing in the ultimate tangible, the things that influence their own day-to-day lives. It does not propose to solve all the world's problems, because history shows that most change for the better comes from local change rather than some grand sweep of nation-states. The VillageTown proposes what in essence is very simple; what is doable in today's world.

We have more power, more tools at our disposal, more access to knowledge and resources than any generation in the past. If we can free ourselves from the muddle that we call reality, wake up and look around, we see that we can make change for the better.

It is important to understand what wealth is, and how wealth is created and how it is preserved. For ordinary people, the way to develop and protect economic security is to create a local economy that creates wealth and then protects it from outside interests that try to leach it out.

Not only were cattle an early form of wealth, words like *pecuniary, fee, capital, in-kind* and *chattel* derive from old Latin and Germanic words associated with cattle.

The Importance of the Local Economy

"When several villages come together to be self-supporting or nearly so"

As Aristotle observed, the initial purpose of villages coming together is to enable them to become **economically self-supporting**. Back then this meant that everything they needed – food, clothing, tools, household goods, and some luxuries could be made within their common locality. Obviously, self supporting means something different in a global economy where our advanced technologies would be impossible to replicate on a local level.

In the 21st century, it means *to generate and sustain wealth that benefits the common locality and community wellbeing.* This includes analyzing every transaction and every system to maximize its contribution to the local economy. This is especially important in hard times. It was said that during the Great Depression, rural France hardly noticed, while Australia which lived on its exports, suffered great hardship. The VillageTown will participate in global trade, but avoid dependency on global systems that could hurt it.

Thus, the VillageTown focuses on ways to strengthen local wealth creation and create resilient systems that protect against outside forces and interests seeking to erode or leak away its wealth or the wealth of its citizens. It pays attention to the impact of economic hard times, providing locally for many of the basic needs, such as good food, warm homes and a way to keep people employed and active. The old word for this is *commonwealth*.

(COMMONWEALTH: The English noun commonwealth in the sense meaning "public welfare; general good or advantage" dates from the 15th century. The original phrase "the common-wealth" or "the common weal" (echoed in the modern synonym "public weal") comes from the old meaning of "wealth," which is "well-being." The term literally meant "common well-being" (reference Wikipedia)

The Legacy Fund – Hundreds of millions of dollars to start out the local economy: In the introduction on page 37 we discuss the Legacy Fund. In this section, we provide more detail about it because it potentially is one of the most important parts of a VillageTown.

When built at the same time, the cost savings of twenty villages of 200 homes each (4,000 units total) is huge, perhaps a hundred million dollars or more. Those savings are due to 4,000 buyers pre-identifying; thus it is community, rather than individually, generated. It is the collective pre-identification that makes economy of scale. It could not be achieved by building one home because its cost will be close to the market value. But if 4,000 individuals and families commit to build at the same time and share a common building system, the economies of scale create a large *cash differential* between cost and market price.

Question: Who gets to keep this big pool of cash?

You (all) keep it: If a developer does the project, they keep the differential and take it out of the community. But when an organizing company does the project, the organizing company that becomes the operating company keeps the differential and the operating company ownership passes to the community in the form of stock and voting rights. The large pool of money not only stays in the community, but it is invested in the economic and social wellbeing of the community. To put it another way, you not only get a home, you get a cash-rich capital corporation established to serve you and your fellow citizens.

Tax Note: How this is actually handled will be decided by lawyers and tax accountants based on applicable tax law. Looked at one way, the differential can be understood as the profits, which makes it taxable as corporate income. However, in another way, it could be seen at as an investment made by the buyers, where they are buying the home and making a mandatory capital investment in corporate stock. In this way, the differential may turn out to be nontaxable, which means the VillageTown starts out with a larger pool of cash. Some of the legal work in the first stage of the project will be directed to answering this question.

Create a Legacy Fund and a proactive fund management team: While the local economy is likely to do well just by virtue of people bringing their businesses and jobs to the VillageTown, this differential in the form of a *legacy investment fund* can enable the VillageTown to invest in local businesses, not just with capital, but with expertise and the combined sales and buying power of five-thousand to ten-thousand people.

Plan for seven generations: The differential amount varies by project. For simplicity, let's say the fund starts out with $100 million (which may be low). This begins as cash, money in the bank that came from the sale of the homes and workplaces. It is 100% owned by the VillageTown, to be used in accordance with its charter or founding document. That document will say that it must be prudently invested to serve the foreseeable needs of seven generations (175 years), which means the current generation can and should benefit from the fund, but not loot or squander it. Further, the fund managers will be prohibited from cashing it out and paying a dividend to the current stockholders, or drain it down by paying ongoing expenses that should be paid by the current citizens. This would be prohibited in the founding documents because it is commonwealth, not personal. The core principle provides that commonwealth funds may be used to invest in private enterprise (both in the form of loans and capital investment) that contributes to *wealth creation*, but not be used to support activities that are fundamentally *wealth converting*.

Question: How can the Legacy Fund be used?

The scope of wellbeing is wide, and the potential of a large fund is phenomenal. Typically, large investment funds such as insurance or pension funds work on a 40-40-20 rule where 40% is in very conservative, very secure holdings, 40% is in normal-risk investments such as blue chip stock; and 20% may be used as venture capital for higher risk, but more lucrative returns. In the case of the VillageTown a similar formula should be developed by the organizing company, based on best practices, except it should focus on investing in ways that directly benefit the people, villages and businesses of the VillageTown. It also should assess risk differently because its investing includes support professionals to enable the SMEs to attain success. It should invest in creating resilient systems and businesses to assure VillageTown wealth and well-being for seven generations.

Investing in small to medium enterprises (SME): The VillageTown needs SME's. The organizing company seeks to attract and foster SME industries for the same reason that Nature creates diversity rather than foster monoculture. Monocultures have a much more difficult challenge figuring out how to survive. The strengths and defenses of monoculture are more narrowly formed, with less resistance to unanticipated challenges and threats. Diversity fosters survival and resilience. If the company of a company-town goes bankrupt or is sold to overseas interests who decide to close the town's factory because it is not sufficiently profitable, the local economy can collapse overnight – with catastrophic economic, social, and cultural impact on the people and their town. However, if the VillageTown has a thousand SME businesses, even if some fail, the economy will continue in a resilient fashion. Further, because the VillageTown has an economic enterprise fund with both money and expertise, it may be able to keep those potentially failing SME businesses from closing their doors. This could be accomplished in a variety of ways, such as by providing bridge capital, expert advice of various sorts, new channels for sales and marketing, and/or improved information systems for efficiency.

The challenge SME's face include attracting capital and expertise, opening markets and securing competitive prices to buy goods and services. Administered by skilled fund managers, the Legacy Fund can invest directly in these SME's – as loans, joint ventures or paid-in start-up capital. This is a prudent use of funds as long as the fund managers can assure that most SME's will not fail and can help guarantee zero unemployment.

This is a 19th-century example of wealth creation. The investment is in the locally-made adobe building, the chute and the waterwheel. The energy source is free: gravity combined with rain water, strong enough to turn a water wheel that first ground grain for bread and then was used to generate electricity for the ranch. It was built in the 1870s and was used until 1949. It was probably discontinued when rural electricity came to northern New Mexico, USA.

VillageTown Inc.: The VillageTown is a private enterprise. Its stockholder citizens own it. Thus, it holds the right to protect its local economy in ways a public local government cannot. When a big-box store forces its way in to a small community and wipe out the downtown businesses that cannot compete, there is little the local government can do about it. If they try, they will face crippling litigation. If a big-box store, a franchise, or a chain-owned coffee shop tried to force their way into a VillageTown they would not get permission to conduct business because the VillageTown's purpose protects its commonwealth, including preventing money leakage. If they threatened litigation the VillageTown would have the money to prevail in court, but probably the case would be thrown out – the VillageTown is private property and has the right to protect what it owns. Its purpose includes protecting its stockholders – including protecting citizen-owned local businesses from outside predatory businesses that endanger VillageTown industry. Even if a franchise were sought by a VillageTown citizen, it may be blocked because of the money leakage inherent in franchises.

Investing more than just money: To gain some assurance of success, the fund managers would not solely invest passive money. They would also provide a full range of professional expertise, advice, and services in all of the relevant areas in which the SME would need help, including legal, accounting, human relations, etc. A complete *back office* could be provided by the VillageTown fund-managers for an SME, so it could focus on its area of expertise.

The *Mondragon Model*: In the Basque region of Spain one finds the seventh-largest corporation in the country. What makes it unusual is that its stockholders are its employees, so instead of sole focus on generating profits for its stockholders, it puts the wellbeing of those stockholders as paramount. It brings a strong focus on education to enable its employees to be more effective. Curiously, it takes a distinctly capitalist, businesslike approach while using left-wing rhetoric. This model may be applicable to VillageTown blue-collar manufacturing businesses that otherwise would be vulnerable to buyout and relocation to a cheap-labor, third-world country, harming the VillageTown local economy. To implement such a model, the organizing company would need to take a stronger role in the initial start-up.

Overseas Field Offices: Over time the Legacy Fund managers can develop a world-wide presence where the VillageTown opens field offices in different countries that do not just represent one VillageTown business, but take on a broader portfolio of many goods and services offered by private businesses in the VillageTown. These services can become joint ventures between the private SME businesses and *VillageTown Inc.* The Fund can use its capital to benefit the local economy with strong SME businesses and to grow the legacy fund for the benefit of future generations. The fund managers are aware of the SME businesses in the VillageTown. They have a bird's eye view, and they can see synergies that may not have occurred to the SME entrepreneurs who sometimes are too close to their work to see the bigger picture. The fund managers suggest the SME expand its market, and their proposal includes an international business plan that uses the international sales force already in place. Done right, this can greatly expand the VillageTown's markets.

Purchasing Power: In addition to the sales end of business, the fund managers can harness combined purchasing power to put an SME's purchasing on par with a large corporation. The most obvious area is in insurance and legal aid, but price breaks can also be found in the tools of the trade, in supplies, and in materials. This can be especially beneficial if *clusters* form in a VillageTown. A cluster mean a place known for a particular trade because many independent businesses locate in the same region and find that even though they are competitors, all do better because of proximity. For examples: Silicon Valley is a high-tech cluster, Mumbai & Wellington are newer film clusters in the prototype mode of Hollywood, and New York and London are global money clusters.

VillageTown Trading Partners: Eventually one may expect that when the first VillageTown is operational, and others see the huge benefits offered in all aspects of life, the idea will catch on. The fund managers may decide to work with the VillageTown Stewards to co-invest in starting new VillageTowns in other parts of the region, country or globe, and in doing so seek to create trading partners. This is especially the case where the new VillageTown is located in a region that has a different climate or access to different raw materials that the first VillageTown needs. These sister-city relationships can also extend to social connections: student exchange, sabbaticals, house-swaps, artist residencies and other social, cultural or recreational exchanges.

It's more than a home: Given this potential, when one buys into a VillageTown it becomes more than a home and more than a lifestyle. Because it is backed by a potentially large pool of liquid capital, buying into a VillageTown becomes a comprehensive business proposition. Business is not the purpose of life, but the foundation of a good life is built on it and the VillageTown comes with both a focus and a fund for building a strong foundation.

Social Investments: It is important to remember that the above discussion is only about the profitable investment aspect of the legacy fund. Some of it will be used as an endowment for social benefits that enrich life but do not turn a profit or break even.

There was a time when a male high-school graduate in many first-world countries could collect his diploma, walk out of school and get a good job that enabled him to marry, buy a home and raise a family in a solid blue-collar job. This is no longer the case.

Staying with American examples since their statistics are easy to access, the common view holds that in the 1970's the US job market began to erode as America and much of the west move its large-scale manufacturing to third-world or transitional countries such as China. Many of the big icon corporations died unless they were bailed out by taxpayers. The Radio Corporation of America (RCA) died in 1986. The jobs in the Bethlehem Steel Mills are gone; the company went bankrupt in 2001 and its assets became foreign owned in 2005. General Motors would be no more had the government not bailed it out in 2009.

Today, this suggests that the high-school graduate will find work in a big-box store selling goods made overseas, but will not earn enough to have the stability his or her father enjoyed. Now, we read, even a college education does not guarantee one can find a job, making it exceptionally difficult for young people to start out in life. At the same time, the next generation of third-world workers are not as willing as their parents to work long hours for low wages. The western nations can expect that the cost of goods will rise, and that they become permanent debtor nations unless they begin to make things once again.

There is another story. According to the U.S. Department of Commerce, in 2007, there were over a quarter-million American companies exporting merchandise and 97 percent of these companies were small and medium-size enterprises (SME's). Among these companies, 29 percent, over 75,000, were manufacturing firms.

One of the reasons countries like the US, EU, New Zealand, Australia and similar countries have an edge over the Asian and third-world countries is a tradition of innovation: in the US it's called *Yankee ingenuity*, in New Zealand it's *number 8 wire*. Innovation tends to do best in small-to-medium enterprises. Statistics show these businesses can compete even if they pay higher wages and pay more to run non-polluting businesses.

In the VillageTown, land is set aside for a walk-to industrial park that targets these SME's. The option to sell or lease the property is a decision of the organizing company, but either way, it is extremely important that the organizing company attract a wide range of businesses that require industrial buildings. In places where the industrial real-estate market is high, and businesses are reluctant to move in due to high cost of doing business, the organizing company may elect to subsidize the industrial offerings through the profits earned on residential sales. The prime attraction of the VillageTown to the company owner is personal. Most SME's have hands-on ownership, where the principals work long hours at the office or plant. Having the VillageTown quality of life within walking distance gives them the best of both worlds. At the same time, having a permanent housing stock for their workers means the workers' cost of living can be lower. If the VillageTown uses its collective purchasing power to provide better health care, old age care, lower cost for consumer goods and food, and no need to drive, then workers may discover they can make products that are more globally competitive. This enables them to keep their jobs and their quality of life. This is especially important if the businesses need to compete on price with third-world countries.

In America and most of the affluent Commonwealth Countries, the typical SME is entrepreneurial, owned by the person or family that started the business. In Spain, however there is a different model known as Mondragon. Started in a small town of the same name over half a century ago, it applies left wing rhetoric to what normally is considered right wing capitalism. It also has become phenomenally successful. In essence, the people employed by Mondragon are also its stockholders. All corporations tend to pay attention to the needs and interests of their stockholders, and this is no different when the stockholders work for the corporation. In the case of working stockholders, they are interested in more than quarterly returns; they want the corporation to pay attention to and provide for their wellbeing.

Without subscribing to the ideology that accompanies the Mondragon model (it's important the VillageTown avoid ideological alignment), the functional model is worth exploring as a potential customer or model for the Industrial Park. The idea of the workers being the stockholders is similar to the idea of VillageTown citizens as stockholders.

Permanent, affordable industrial-park-worker housing

The industrial park requires housing for its blue-collar workers. It is important that all who work in the VillageTown live there and not commute by car or bus, including its blue-collar workers. However, like other target groups who cannot compete for VillageTown housing on the open market due to their pay range, blue-collar housing that is built but not protected runs the risk of gentrification. For this reason, the VillageTown should offer a parallel-housing market for blue-collar workers in the Industrial Park, and if the target group prefers, it may cluster those in a blue-collar village that would have its own special character. As an example of such character, this photo below is of the *Hun Festival* in an old, blue-collar neighborhood in Baltimore, USA, where the colloquialism *hun* (as used by waitresses when serving customers in diners) has become a cause for local identity and annual celebration.

Special Tutorial: How Money Works

Because the VillageTown plans for seven generations (175 years), understanding how money works and knowing how to protect capital for *commonwealth* is paramount.

If we spend what we earn, understanding how money works may not be important. If income equals spending, and if we keep our job and income flow, why worry? Of course, the reason to worry is the "if". If things go wrong, we need some resources set aside to assure we get through the tough times. If we want to take a break that stops our cash flow for a while, we need to know our cash savings are protected.

This is a concern for a VillageTown that plans for 10,000 people today and for seven generations. It is especially a concern because we live in financially perilous times when old rules no longer apply. There was a time when people were encouraged to save, which meant depositing cash in the bank and earning interest. This worked as long as the cash remained stable, meaning that the face value would buy the same quantity of goods from one year to the next. The low interest earned was a measure of risk when the bank loaned the money out. It was low because the bank was prudent, and risk was spread.

However, when the Great Depression struck, the meaning of money and currency began to diverge. Today they are so far apart that the ordinary person may find that what they are told about money and what really goes on are very different. In short, the system no longer looks after the ordinary person. Banks are no longer what they once were. The result is that personal purchasing power is constantly under assault by the very financial systems that at one time existed to protect that same purchasing power.

The concern is best stated by the US Treasury* which wrote: *Federal Reserve notes are not redeemable in gold, silver or any other commodity, and receive no backing by anything. This has been the case since 1933. The notes have no value for themselves, but for what they will buy.*

What are commonly called US dollars have no value for themselves, and the decline in what they buy is called inflation. As we will see, over a 75 year period since 1933, the dollar lost a lot of value. This loss applies to almost every currency in the world today.

In order to understand this, it is helpful first to clarify essential terms. *Currency* in US dollars means Federal Reserve notes and coins, and has a similar meaning in Pounds, Euros, etc. Currency is cash. *Money* means something different. Interestingly, like the question on why we build communities, one of the more useful starting points for understanding the meaning of money comes again from Aristotle, written over 2,300 years ago.

Aristotle wrote: "*When the inhabitants of one country became more dependent on those of another, and they imported what they needed, and exported what they had too much of, money*

---

*   See http://www.treasury.gov/resource-center/faqs/Currency/Pages/legal-tender.aspx

necessarily came into use. For the various necessities of life are not easily carried about, and hence men agreed to employ in their dealings with each other something that was intrinsically useful and easily applicable to the purposes of life, for example, iron, silver and the like. Of this the value was at first measured simply by size and weight, but in process of time they put a stamp upon it, to save the trouble of weighing and to mark the value."[*]

Aristotle cites metals as useful forms of money because metal:

- Is easily transportable (unlike land)
- Is divisible & fusible (unlike diamonds)
- Holds an intrinsic value (unlike paper)
- Remains relatively stable (unlike food)
- Is homogenous (unlike the goods that make up the Consumer Price Index)

Thus he focuses his attention on money as metal coin (gold, silver, copper, iron, bronze, etc.). However, it is important to understand that money is not only coin. Money is anything of tangible value. Money is any tangible good that holds a stable value in relation to all other goods. Note that this concept of stability is a complicated by the fact some things can increase or decrease in relative value (food values increase when crops fail and drop when too much food is harvested) which is independent of the stability of the unit of measure that is money.

As the US Treasury makes clear, US currency (dollars) is not money because it makes no commitment to fix the value to a measure that is stable. Cash used to be minted or printed; today the big money is created by computer keystrokes. It is created out of nothing and is only worth what it will buy. When currency is printed faster than the economy grows, the result is real (as opposed to reported) inflation. If at this point your eyes are beginning to glaze over and words fade into fog, let's try an example:

Let's take a nomadic tribe whose sole measure of wealth was in cattle. Each person's wealth was counted by the number of cattle they owned. However, it became complicated to re-brand each cow each time it was sold – hot branding hurts the cow and living cow-skin was not seen as the smartest way to record owners. So instead, each cow was branded with a number and the tribal elders issued notes: one numbered note would be issued for each cow. As long as the herd remained stable, a fixed number of notes would be in circulation, and ownership of the cattle would be represented by matching the capital notes with a herd count. When a new calf was born, the elders would give the cow's owner a new capital note, sort of like a birth and ownership

---

[*]   Politics, Book 1, Chapter 9: 31. Note: quoting Aristotle does not imply Village Town endorsement of Aristotelian philosophy (or ideology). His observations on community & money are useful because they are historically some of the first written, and remain remarkably relevant over 2,300 years later. Some of his other views are not so useful.

certificate. When a cow died, or was slaughtered for a feast, the elders would take back the capital note and destroy it. In essence, that is how currency is supposed to work. One capital note is always supposed to buy one cow.

However, when the nomadic tribe becomes a nation of millions of people, and the things of value explode into the dizzying array we have today, the connection between the capital note and the value of the thing bought becomes a disconnect. The people in charge of the capital note printing business know this, and they know how to turn that disconnect into something that benefits part of society at the expense of other parts of society. Going back to our tribal analogy, the elders stopped recording matching numbers, since the cows were all in the same herd anyway, and it did not matter who owned which cow. The capital notes began to become a currency. To enable buying and selling of smaller units, they began to issue fractional notes where a hundred fractional notes (pence) would buy one cow. Thus one could buy a quart of cow's milk for one penny.

This system maintained integrity as long as the holders of all the capital notes and pence matched the audit. This worked for generations, and gradually they stopped doing the audits. One day, a young citizen complained how it cost ten pence to buy a quart of milk, and an elder standing nearby mentioned how at one time a capital note would buy a cow and one penny would buy a quart of milk. The young one researched the old rules and called a tribal assembly to conduct the ancient audit. They discovered that in total the tribal members held ten-thousand one-cow notes, but had only a thousand cows. The purchasing power of their capital notes worth one tenth of what they were worth when they entered into the agreement to use capital notes. It was not that the cows died faster than calves were born, it is that the elders' descendents began to print more notes than they had cows. Who got those newly-printed notes remains a mystery that the tribal mainstream media avoided discussing. What is for certain is that the ordinary members were the losers; somehow the ten cows they thought they owned was now only one.

The equivalent of that tribal audit was done recently on the internet where on hubpages.com a blogger going by the name of Zsuzsy Bee in Ontario Canada transcribed prices she found in a stack of 1933 newspapers and then compared them to the same newspaper that still prints similar ads in 2008. Coincidentally, 1933 was the year cited above by the US Treasury and the last year the US minted a $20 gold coin that had the same purchasing power as a $20 bill. By 2008 the melt value of that one-ounce coin was $850. To put this in perspective, divide 20 by 850, and you see the purchasing power of a 2008 dollar is 2.3¢ in 1933 value. This is closer to real inflation, however the official US Bureau of Labor Consumer Price Index (CPI) Inflation Calculator say that twenty dollars in 1933 has the same buying power as $330 (6¢ or 6%) in 2008. Let's transcribe those prices into a chart to show the erosion of purchasing power.

This chart was made up from prices posted on hubpages.com where a member wrote: "*I found a couple of dozen old newspapers in the far corner of the attic back to the years of 1933 to 1934. I made up a list from the ads that were in these papers, comparing the prices to today's.*"

For source data see *http://hubpages.com/hub/life-75-years-ago-compared-to-now*

	1933-34	2007-8	Purchasing Power
New Car pricing starting at	$ 445.00	$ 13,500.00	3.30%
Men's shoes	3.00	49.99	6.00%
Men's Slacks	1.95	39.95	4.88%
Women's blouse	0.39	29.95	1.30%
Women's wool coat	6.75	199.95	3.38%
Prime roast beef	0.27	6.99	3.86%
Chuck roast beef	0.05	3.99	1.25%
Minced veal	0.06	4.49	1.34%
Chicken whole	0.19	2.29	8.30%
Duck whole	0.22	4.39	5.01%
Lamb chops	0.21	8.99	2.34%
Bacon	0.21	4.29	4.90%
Atlantic sole	0.09	3.99	2.26%
Salmon	0.25	5.79	4.32%
20 oz white bread loaf	0.06	1.59	3.77%
Corn Flakes	0.07	3.99	1.75%
Dozen eggs	0.14	1.99	7.04%
5 pounds Sugar	0.24	3.29	7.29%
50 lbs flour	1.03	18.99	5.42%
Coffee per pound	0.23	5.99	3.84%
1 quart milk	0.16	1.19	13.45%
Cheddar Cheese	0.23	12.99	1.77%
Quart of Ice Cream	0.39	2.29	17.03%
California Oranges	0.21	3.99	5.26%
Iceberg Lettuce	0.10	1.29	7.75%
11 oz bottle Stuffed Olives	0.25	4.49	5.57%
2 lb jar Peanut butter	0.25	3.99	6.27%
12 oz can Tomato soup	0.07	0.89	7.87%
Light bulb	0.18	1.19	15.13%
Six 21 x 42" towels	1.00	41.94	2.38%
Soap bar	0.05	1.39	3.60%
Unfinished Adirondack chair	1.98	129.00	1.53%
Bamboo rake 18"	0.15	18.99	0.79%
Gas Range	68.25	689.00	9.91%
Refrigerator	96.00	989.00	9.71%
Average 6 room home	4,750.00	100,000.00	4.75%
Apartment for rent per month	22.50	875.00	2.57%
Banana Split	0.16	4.29	3.73%
Dance at a Club (per couple)	2.50	50.00	5.00%
Lunch at a diner	0.50	7.99	6.26%
Evening movie ticket	0.20	9.50	2.11%
Minimum Wage	0.33	8.00	4.13%
Melt value 20 US gold coin	20.00	850.00	2.35%

For comparison in June 2011 the Melt Value of a $20 one ounce coin is $1,500 (1.33%)

In regard to the 1933-2008 buying power chart, an economist may object that this chart from Ontario newspapers must allow for the USD - CAD exchange rate; that at times of instability the price of gold may rise too high, and over a 75-year time frame, not all products are equivalent – all of which are valid points that serve to further confuse the ordinary person. However, for the purpose of understanding purchasing power, the numbers are adequate. The one place where the chart probably is not representative is in the price of a home. It states the average Ontario home costs 100,000, whereas the US Census put the average price of a new home at 263,000. This is probably due to the rust-belt effect, where the value of community has seriously eroded since 1945; true market value of Ontario homes is lower than elsewhere.

Another measure of the declining value of currency's purchasing power can be calculated by taking our same ounce of gold and plotting how many barrels of crude oil it would buy. This chart runs from 1946 to 2011. Unfortunately it is difficult to find the spot price of oil prior to 1946, and given the war it would not be relevant.

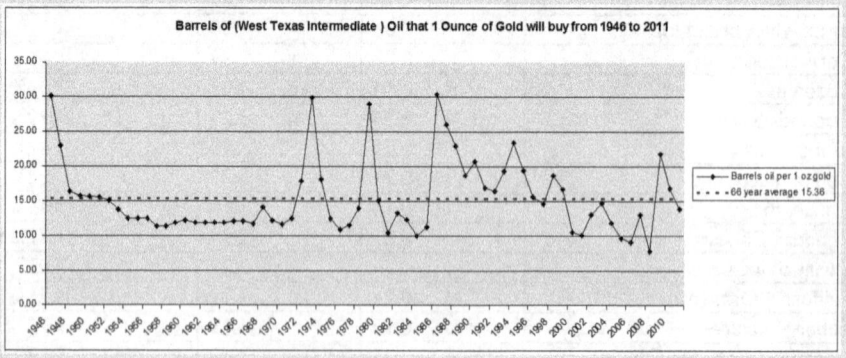

The average number of barrels of oil our one-ounce gold coin buys since 1946 is 15.36 barrels. As of this writing, one ounce of gold buys just about 15 barrels yet in US dollars, the price of a gallon of gas at the pump is $4 and two years prior was $2. In other words, it's not that oil is rising, but the purchasing power of the dollar is dropping.

Prices at the pump fluctuate not because the fundamentals change, but because the dollar is no longer a stable currency. While petroleum really will go up in price when the easy oil is pumped dry and it becomes more expensive to extract it from tar sands or deep below the oceans, the chart shows that for now, it really has not changed much.

To complicate matters more, during the sub-prime era from about 2001 to 2007, the Federal Reserve printed out trillions of dollars to fund new mortgages on new homes. While there were many losers as these mortgages defaulted, the dollars printed did not self-destruct, but flooded into the national and global economy. Most ended up in the hands of speculative investors who moved them out of cash and into tangibles, including oil futures. These investors have so much money washing through the system that they are creating a new boom and bust cycle that wreaks havoc on the family budget of ordinary citizens whose weekly paycheck is not structured for $2 gas one year and $4 a couple of years later. Essentially, the only way to deal with this is to decouple your salary from oil by eliminating driving from your home range.

Back to the larger question, the implications of currency versus money are important for a community that starts out with a legacy fund and intends to plan for seven generations (175 years) not the 75 years from 1933 to 2008. For the community to protect its commonwealth, it must understand the disconnect between money and currency and incorporate its understanding in its planning. While individual members of society may earn and spend fast enough not to notice, from the broad view of the economic wellbeing of the community, the currency question must be addressed.

Further, technology can help. If we look at the five characteristics of money that Aristotle cited as important, we see that technology has made some of them redundant. As long as the currency represents things of value that hold intrinsic value which remains relatively stable, a computer system can manage the rest. The intrinsic value that backs the currency no longer need be easily transportable, divisible & fusible, or homogenous. Mutual funds in the stock market (when not being manipulated) are a good example of a new-technology currency, as are on-line gold companies that let members instantly transfer ownership of gold-grams. For that matter, we can go back to owning a herd of cattle and include a radio collar on each one to assure the chattel notes match the audit.

This is the new reality of currency and money. For the VillageTown that intends to start with a large Legacy Fund and a citizen-owned bank that can be expected to handle many millions of dollars in personal and business savings accounts, it becomes extremely important to use advanced computer technology to implement a system that protects people's savings while maintaining the sort of audit trails that not only are expected of a fiduciary, but also provide comfort for the tax collector who conducts audits in the currency of the state.

The role of the bank in society has changed over the centuries, and since the advent of computers has changed drastically. In the 19th century, banks were imposing buildings designed to give an impression of stability, permanence, and security. The vault doors were visibly prominent behind the counters to say to customers *your money is safe with us*.

Today, the real bank is not the counters in front of vaults, but the computer screens connected to a central database. The bank's database is connected to the national and the global monetary systems, and the ordinary person has no idea how the system works. At one time, the image of the banker was a local, upstanding citizen; conservative, prudent, and trusted by the community. Today, the image is of high-fliers somewhere else, in New York or London, drawing bonuses that would set most people up for life. Unfortunately, this stereotype has a ring of truth to it. Banking and financial investment have become predatory and so complex that the regulators do not seem to understand, much less know how to safely regulate, the industry of money and currency.

It is important for the Village Town's economy that it not only knows its bankers, but that it owns its bank. It will begin with both an asset base and its mortgage base, and in today's predatory environment, it is prudent that it maintain local control over both.

WEALTH CREATION AND PRESERVATION: THE BANK & INNOVATION

The term *bank* has two meanings – the traditional definition and the legal meaning as governed by the laws of the state. Thus while the term bank is used, it may turn out that in a particular state the bank legally must be called by some other name such as Community Bank, Credit Union, or Savings & Loan. In this book, we use the traditional meaning.

Capital Preservation: From a functional standpoint, the reason to start a bank is to retain the profits that come from the retail mortgage business. If 4,000 homes take on an average $250,000 mortgage, that adds up to a billion dollars in mortgage assets. A community bank can take decades to reach assets of a billion dollars, but for a VillageTown that can be the starting number. Servicing those mortgages provides jobs and pays the expenses to operate the bank on an ongoing basis.

Next, consider the VillageTown Legacy Fund that comes from the differential between the construction cost and the market price of the buildings. The VillageTown may open for business with hundreds of millions of dollars in cash. Why give away the profits on managing those funds when its own bank can manage those profits to benefit the VillageTown?

With these two financial foundations derived from home sales, the bank can cover the normal day-to-day operations costs of offering a full range of banking services to the citizens and businesses of the VillageTown. It can offer a few innovative services as well.

The Stewards will establish a bank to process and package the construction loans and mortgages. During construction, it will have its own board of directors, operating at arms length from the construction arm of the organizing company. It will serve as the fiduciary disbursement authority, making progress payments based on goal attainment, but does not issue final payment until the job is done. In this way, it assures both the home buyers and the institutional buyers of prime mortgage-backed securities are protected. Its stock will pass to the operating company when the construction is complete, so it too is citizen-owned.

VillageTown Insurance - Like the mortgage business, it makes little sense to give away the substantial premiums villagers will pay for insurance. Some insurance is required during construction, other types are ongoing. At a minimum, the VillageTown initiates wholesale buying of insurance or reinsurance, and in some cases it may elect to offer self-insurance where it deems the market not competitive. Like the bank, this business would operate at arms-length from the organizing company to assure checks and balances remain in place.

Money-turn - Because the whole community will be wired with an intranet, every business can have a point-of-sale terminal for electronic banking. Where it becomes interesting is what can happen within that closed loop system. The first principle of creating wealth within the local economy is to encourage voluntary money turn – buy local. To enable citizens to make local decisions, it is helpful if the local content of every transaction is displayed. What sometimes appears to be local may involve more money leakage than one might expect. Local content can easily be estimated and displayed on preprinted labels, but with a closed-loop computer system and the right software, it can be calculated and displayed dynamically, provided the cost basis can be tracked. If all transactions are done through the same system, this is possible and it gives precise local content.

Save money not currency - The special tutorial on how money works (starting page 148) makes a distinction between money and currency, noting that national governments make it clear that currency is backed by nothing and is only worth what it will buy. (The US Treasury, for example, states *Federal Reserve notes...have no value for themselves, but for what they will buy).* The problem comes when, consistently over time, the same unit of currency buys less every year. The most extreme example of course is Zimbabwe which got to the point where it was issuing one-hundred-trillion dollar bank notes whose only value was for collectors buying them on ebay for their novelty value. While reserve currencies such as the US dollar are seen as more stable, in the average person's lifetime of 75 years, the dollar given to them when they were born will be worth mere pennies when they die - if even that. The old system encouraged people to save money; the new system encourages them to earn and spend – and to borrow when earnings don't cover spending.

When currencies were backed by something that had value in itself, it was deemed good to save money in the bank. Now, to use the vernacular, that's a chump's game. The interest paid by banks does not keep up with the erosion of purchasing power. Deposits may keep up with the official rate of inflation, but there is a divergence between what the Consumer Price Index says cash is worth, and what that cash will buy in the market. Instead of saving money for a rainy day, the system now encourages spending that exceeds earnings and thus debt. This is good for the banks, but unless borrowed money is invested to realize a higher return, it tends to make people and their commonwealth poorer.

For the ordinary person who earns, spends, and does not save, this is not a big problem.

But for a VillageTown of 10,000 people seeking to preserve its wealth, where collectively there is substantial cash on deposit in the bank, this becomes a greater concern.

Therefore, in today's global economy, currency should be understood as useful only in the short term, and as inflationary pressures increase, the meaning of *short* gets shorter. If the VillageTown wishes to preserve the wealth of its people, villages, and local businesses (including the surrounding farms), then it needs a way to enable individuals and businesses to transact in currency but save in money (tangibles).

At present, it's interesting to see that the technology exists to do this, but not many people are taking advantage of it. On the Internet there is a company based in the Channel Islands called goldmoney.com that enables its members to buy gold by the gram, stored in Swiss vaults. Nothing new in that, people have been owning gold in Swiss vaults for centuries. However, because goldmoney.com is Internet-based, one member can pay another member instantly in one of several currencies, and the bank instantly moves ownership of the equivalent amount of gold from the buying member's account to the seller's.

This new technology has profound implications. Gold has value for itself, but it is not useful to buy and sell with coins in an era when most transactions are electronic (even a paper check is ultimately an electronic bank transfer from one account to another). A gram of gold is about the size of a large match-head, but it will buy a copy of this book with almost half the gold match-head left over in change. In old technology it would be unrealistic to conduct business using too-small gold grams, which is why lesser-value silver and copper coins were minted. But today, few people physically move metal; the change of ownership is nothing more than an automated, digital entry between buyer and seller. It opens up a whole new way to think about money in contrast to currency.

In our special tutorial on money, we quote Aristotle's definition of money that focused on coins made of gold, silver, copper, or bronze. He gave reasons why coined metals were useful, but some of those values apply only when one buys and sells using real coins in a purse. With computers, money no longer needs to be easily transportable, it only needs to be mathematically divisible & fusible, and it need not be homogenous. However, it is important that it hold an intrinsic value and that its value remains relatively stable.

For sake of simplicity in suggesting how the VillageTown can encourage savings while protecting its citizens against inflation, let us stick with Aristotle's fondness for metals. Let us examine a simple system in which money is based on fixed units of silver and gold. It just as easily could be based on a wide range of commodities located anywhere in the world, but that additional complexity may serve to confuse the point. So let us imagine the VillageTown bank building has two clean-room vaults – one for gold and a second larger vault for silver, each with its floor being a precision scale that measures the actual contents within a milligram at any time.

The bank would purchase a vault full of what today is called precious metal tokens, not coins*, and offer them to citizens as a tangible investment – silver and gold tokens in 1/4 to 1 oz weight. The tokens would remain in the vault unless someone wanted to withdraw their property. Integrity of ownership would be assured by matching the vault scale and electronic or ultrasonic audit with the computer record of ownership. Again, like the Swiss vault, there is nothing new about this. In fact, except for people wanting to withdraw their money to keep it at home or carry it around, it would not matter if the metals were in the VillageTown bank or a Swiss or Perth vault. We use the local example to keep it simple.

Where it gets interesting is when the all members of the local community become members of the bank, and instead of needing to go on-line and enter a password for internet banking, they have a normal-looking cash card that is accepted in every business in the community. For visitors, the electronic system works just like a normal debit card/credit card payment system. But for locals, it has an extra twist:

This part may sound a bit complicated, so stay with us. The point of it is to not evade taxes, for any banking system that makes it easier to cheat the tax collector is an invitation for trouble. If numbers are not your cup of tea, skip this example.

Mary, a Spice Café customer pays for a meal costing $35. Both Mary and Spice are bank members. Let's presume that the current bank spot rate for an ounce of silver is $35.

- Mary owns no cash; she currently owns 1,000 silver one-ounce tokens in the bank
- Mary has previously arranged with the bank to sell her silver to buy currency
- Spice has previously arranged with the bank to buy silver with its deposited currency
- Mary pays Spice for her meal with her bank card, paying $35 in currency (cash)
- The bank electronically buys 1 oz of her silver and deposits $35 into her cash account
- The $35 cash is instantly deposited into Spice's cash account paying for the meal
- The bank electronically sells Spice a 1 oz token of silver for the $35 just deposited as cash
- The computer record of Spice's cash account showed they earned a taxable $35 sale
- The record show now Mary owns 999 ounces of silver, and the café owns 1 oz more.
- The tokens in the bank did not move, but the ownership of one of the tokens changed

---

*   As Aristotle noted, to save the trouble of weighing, the minter marked a value (such as $20) on the coin. In modern times, the right to make such a mark is reserved to the state and a private bank can do so only by license. However, there is no such limit on marking with weight (1 oz). Confirming the purity and weight is no longer the technical challenge it was 2,300 years ago. Such metals are technically not called coins (with a denomination) but *tokens*. They look like coins, work like coins, but unlike coins anyone can mint them without having to pay a franchise tax to a sovereign government. Of course, this idea of using weight not an assigned value is also not unfamiliar to historians. At one time, a British Pound meant a pound of sterling silver.

In essence, this is a double entry transaction. The buy-sell of the food is handled in currency, thus keeping the tax collector happy. Separate from that transaction, the buy-sell of the ounce of silver is a normal investment transaction that happens all the time. What makes it different is the instant nature of the two independent transactions, which in effect allows normal transactions to occur using money, not currency. Thanks to computers, instead of a single buy-sell transaction, two buy-sell transactions occur sequentially but simultaneously without any extra cost or delay. And, of course it is not necessary that the tangible be in silver or gold (since governments from time to time outlaw private ownership of gold and silver) but anything (or a mix of things) that have stable value. It can be a mutual fund or even a herd of cattle.

Tax Neutral: What makes this transaction important is the fact that it is not proposing to use an alternate currency or to evade the tax due. The taxable transaction occurs in the national currency, and it is fully recorded for reporting purposes. This keeps the tax-collector happy. However, the second *invisible tax* – inflation – is avoided. Since the VillageTown plans for seven generations, this unseen, un-legislated and therefore insidious tax must be both understood and mitigated. Of course, some may object that the bank spot rate keeps changing – that the price of gold or silver keeps going up or down. What those objectors miss is that what is changing is not the value of the tangible asset, but the purchasing power of cash. The asset is not *worth* more or less. Confidence in cash keeps changing; its purchasing power is unstable because it is worth only what it will buy.

Earn Interest on Tangibles: There's more – the new technology potential becomes even more interesting. When one deposits currency in the bank, the bank then loans it out. The saver is paid 3% interest, the bank loans it out at 5%, making its profits on the difference, less expenses and losses from default loans. Typically, the person who has gold in a Swiss vault makes no interest, but has to pay storage charges for the use of the vault and its security services. However, with a local bank, there is no reason that gold and silver (or whatever) cannot earn interest as well. Once the whole community is working off of a tangible-based money system, your deposits can be loaned out to others for interest.

A Private Bank: While further analysis may change the view on this next matter, at present the recommendation is that to be a customer of the VillageTown bank, one must be a citizen or business in the VillageTown, or a nearby farmer participating in the VillageTown's local economy. No doubt visitors or people living in other places would like to deposit their savings in the VillageTown bank, but this introduces a new level of oversight and paperwork due to global post-9/11 regulations seeking to control terrorism, drug trafficking and money laundering. The maxim *know your banker* cuts both ways. It is better if the bankers not only know their customers, but know that their customers are (indirectly through owning the VillageTown corporation) the owners of the bank. Therefore, visitors pay in currency and are not permitted to open local tangible accounts.

PART 3: YOUR NEXT STEP

In this next section of the book, we cover some of the details of what will happen as you proceed from your initial enrolment to the point where you move into your new home and your new life. In the previous section, we described some of the investments that will be made using some of the cost savings that comes when everyone pre-identifies and the net profits are used by the VillageTown for the VillageTown and its people. Now it is time to cover the process and some of the boundary conditions, or as we prefer to call it, the *framework* that sets the parameters within which the VillageTown will form.

This is important to what one may call the *buy in*, so that you will have a fairly good idea what to expect before you make the decision to commit. While there is a great deal of latitude that each village will have in self-defining, there are aspects that need to be set out and held to in order both to achieve the desired outcome and to stay within budget and on schedule.

For example, except for the town-center district which may have fully custom-built homes (at a considerably higher price), most homes will be slab-constructed using a poured-mold-and-form system that makes a very thick, fully insulated wall in a single pour. The modular nature of the forms allows for some variation in height, depth and width, and the carve-able nature of the inserted forms offers the opportunity for a wide variety of surface treatments from the simple to the most complex. The shell walls are expected to be fully load bearing, meaning that all interior walls can be moved in the future as housing needs change. The shell walls, floors, and roof will be built in a serial fashion, one house after another, working down the street. This means homes will go up rapidly and inexpensively, yet still provide for considerable variety and beauty. It is within this framework that your decisions about your home will be made, in accordance with the architectural code you and your fellow founders set out for your village.

It is the intent of the organizing company to reduce the elapsed time between when your construction loan begins and the time when you can move in, to minimize the carrying cost of money while you live in and pay for your current home. Further, it is the intent of the organizing company to build the villages in parallel, so the VillageTown achieves critical mass for the local businesses which require a certain population in order to stay in business. This requires planning that verges on choreography and is one reason why most construction workers will be on full-time contracts, prepared to work day or night as the project will run 24/7 until completion.

To ensure the best outcome, considerable thought went into developing the framework. The Stewards' intent is to find the best professionals money can buy to run the project from start to finish. So with this preface, let us begin the journey toward your new village.

More than the sum of its parts: Building a VillageTown is best understood as a framework. It needs to be seen as a whole. While intended to be flexible and adaptable, its core foundation is based on the timeless unchanging purpose of communities. Many of the aimless practices of our time will be found not to fit.

In 2008, when *How to Build a Village* came out, many people around the world were attracted to the concept. Founding steward Claude Lewenz was invited to speak at conferences and tour various locations to speak to planners, politicians, communities and developers. He found that some of the professionals professed to love the idea, but then sought to "tweak it". One said loved the idea, but insisted that people would not give up sleeping above their cars parked in an attached garage, and then insisted that at least some of the roads should permit car use. A number of people made similar comments, and curiously they always were speaking in the third person, saying that other people would not give up their cars, as in *"There is no way you will convince an American [Australian/Kiwi, etc] to give up their cars."* When asked, they said they personally would love to live in a place without cars, and probably would only keep their car in the motorpool until they felt comfortable with the rental car arrangement.

This emotional attachment to their car is understandable, but we make it clear that the no-car policy is non-negotiable. If this becomes too distressing, the organizing company will assure the driver that it not asking people to give up their cars, it only asks that they not sleep next to them. All that changes is the garage location and where the car is driven.

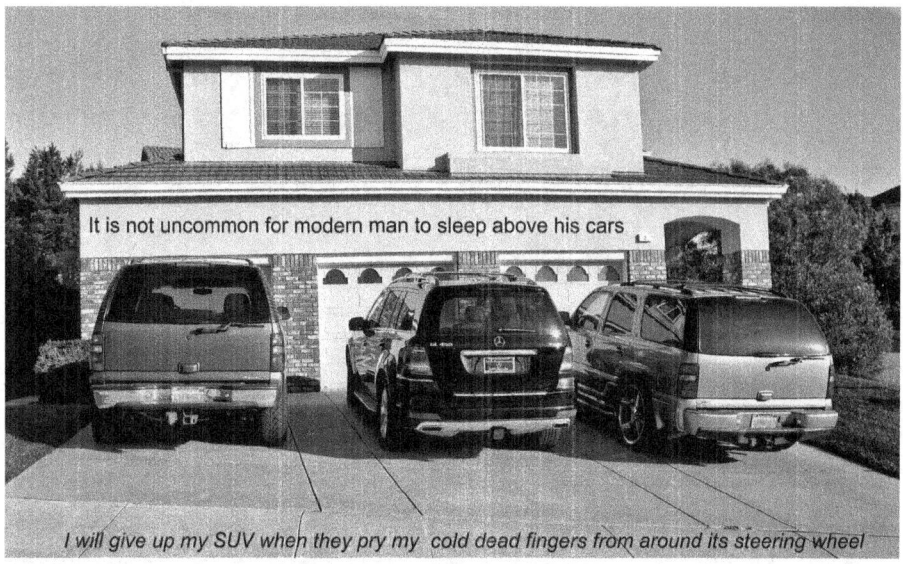

It is not uncommon for modern man to sleep above his cars

I will give up my SUV when they pry my cold dead fingers from around its steering wheel

Another person listened to a talk and then came to the front afterwards to pitch building a VillageTown in the remote Australian outback for his mining company.

When Cars Take Over the Village: Lacock in England is a 15th century town preserved by the National Trust. In its preservation, they required that the exteriors be restored to an earlier time – to the point that the telegraph pole visible in the earlier photograph from the 1920's was removed. Only the trees have changed.

The later photograph, taken in 2006 from the same location shows how the historic preservation succeeded, and how it failed. The character of Lacock is completely changed with the presence of parked cars and vans on both sides of the street. The pedestrians look out of place – they are there to walk back to their car, crossing the street, rather than properly belonging in the middle of it. In earlier times, the road joined the buildings on both sides into a single entity. Now because of cars, the very same road severs the village, destroying its sense of wholeness.

Apparently he was busy twittering during the part on the diverse local economy. A number of listeners proposed that they owned the perfect land (one pitched 14 acres, covered in a mature native forest, more vertical than flat). Then there were the eco-villagers who saw the VillageTown as the answer to their lack of traction– albeit a larger and more sophisticated idea than they had considered. But they brought their own limiting ideas of sustainability, for example: composting toilets in each home. For some reason, composting toilets seems to be a major test for ecovillages. Problem: The typical composting toilet must be emptied once every six months. If the average home has two toilets and there are 4,000 homes, this means 64 toilets must be emptied every day, all year long, forever. This requires access to the homes, full-time staff, trucks to transport the compost, and management problems for improperly maintained systems. Not a great idea.

Of course, if 200 families (500 people) want to come together to form an ecovillage within a VillageTown, they should feel free to organize their buyers. They may choose to be near the greenbelt to have their shared gardens, they can install a composting toilet on the roof garden (in addition to normal plumbing), and they can run their village meetings with value-based consensus protocol. Odds are, they will prove to be good citizens and lovely neighbors, and provide expertise in permaculture and other green innovations for the VillageTown.

Synergy - Therefore, in understanding the VillageTown as a framework, each distinctive feature must be understood as part of a whole, connected with other features. Changing one may change the character of the whole, and some changes may have such an effect that in the end, it is no longer a VillageTown.

Non-negotiables - For this reason, there will be certain aspects of a VillageTown that are nonnegotiable. Cars in the villages mean it is not a VillageTown. School classrooms located on a separate campus or busing students to schools in the host district because they have schools with low enrollment guts the core of a VillageTown. A VillageTown with commuters walking to the train station every day is a bedroom community, not a VillageTown. Beyond these non-negotiables however, there are certain desirable aspects that may simply not

The school classrooms belong on the main plaza in the village

fit in a particular location. If that happens, the organizing company looks for alternatives that adhere to the principles; to find another way. This is called having an open mind.

WHAT YOU SEE IS WHAT YOU GET (WYSIWYG)

When the host government writes the rules that govern what can be built in an urban plan, their planners must look to the future and not only write rules for what the developer wants to build, but for what limitations will be placed on further development when private owners wish to change their buildings – sometimes adding on, sometimes tearing down and rebuilding. This crystal-ball exercise slows down the approval process. It also adds to its complexity. The planners must set out controls to anticipate the future, and to prevent the developer from exploiting loopholes that are not in the public interest.

The VillageTown takes a different approach. It first notes how frequently wealthier communities always seem to have someone tearing down, adding on to or remodeling their home. While it is classified as a temporary annoyance, over time it becomes a constant background to daily life - especially in good weather when people wish to be outdoors. Someone in the area always seems to be doing construction. The parked trucks of the workers and double-parked delivery trucks, cranes, jack-hammers and general noise and dust become an annoying part of everyday life. Given the density of the VillageTown, this is deemed unwise and a problem that demands smarter thinking from the beginning.

Building demolition is noisy, dirty, and disruptive. Design smartly to avoid tearing down later.

Instead of providing for future expansion of the building shells (changing the exterior walls and roof), the VillageTown builds an extra story. Instead of two-story homes, it builds three, with the top floor left empty as a single big room, unless the initial buyer needs it to be finished initially. If built when the walls go up, the cost of one more story is minimal.

The exterior walls are load bearing, but the floors are designed to need no further support inside the perimeter walls. Most interior walls may use a system that uses the same mix as the exterior walls but which may be built with a lightweight locking brick that keys together in a way similar to Lego© blocks. This system means that as times and needs change, the buildings can change without having any impact on the exterior. It also means planning officials will not write rules for future growth or for exterior change.

Instead of rule-making, the VillageTown uses a *WYSIWYG* process called Dynamic Engagement: the development is set out on a scale model that, once locked, becomes the fixed plan. The plan lays out twenty villages and the town center. It establishes the Greenbelt, Industrial Park and Transport Center. The streets and plazas are precisely placed and each home or workplace is cut to shape for the 100:1 scale model. Two villagers who set their homes next to each other on the model just met their next door neighbor.

All issues of height, scale, sunlight, public-activity level, noise zone, road width, and other planning issues are proposed, negotiated, and agreed upon using the scale model. The planners are in attendance, not as designers but as approvers signing off on what is acceptable, and dynamically identifying what will not be accepted in the final plan.

Neighbors and other interested parties from the host community are invited to attend and to discuss any concerns they may have. However, the Greenbelt is designed to prevent cross-boundary conflicts. This, and the fact that there will be no commuter traffic, no cost to local taxpayers and no costs loaded on local services should mitigate most concerns.

Dynamic Engagement works on the same principle as the jury system, namely that ordinary people, when placed in a formal, structured environment with professional support, generally make the best decisions. The ordinary people are the future villagers, so they have a stake in getting it right. The formal, structured environment means that the tendency for mob rule, when the loudest or most egotistical gets their way, is prevented from gaining a platform. The professionals include group process experts who keep Dynamic Engagement moving forward. It also involves professional architects, planners, designers, engineers and other necessary experts who guide, but do not direct, the process.

One of the most important empowerment tools is Christopher Alexander's *A Pattern Language*, which gives ordinary people a language to articulate what they need and love in design terms. After considerable testing to identify the best way to make this language accessible, it was found that computer-printed photo *fridge magnets* worked as a way to summarize each pattern so participants could identify the patterns of importance to them and then advocate for those patterns. Coupled with the 100:1 scale model, a medium that ordinary people can understand (as opposed to an architectural plan, which requires skill to visualize), Dynamic Engagement accelerates the planning process, making it easier and faster to get the final plan. This process is discussed in detail starting on page 221.

In part, the ease of planning comes from reducing the number of variables. Except for the town-center zone where taller buildings may be detached (and much more expensive), all the village buildings are attached on the sides. They may vary in depth, but all will share side walls. This makes better use of land, is more energy efficient, and saves on construction costs since two buyers share the cost of one wall. Thus the design considerations focus on the visible front and rear walls, and the roof, which may include outdoor living space.

Common Design Elements

Each village founding group determines its own Architectural and Design Code that lays out the look and feel of their village. This can vary widely, but it works within a general framework. Some of the important design elements include:

Single Bulk Material: All buildings must be constructed at the same time; they need to be completed rapidly in months, not years. This means that a fixed set of parameters becomes essential, including dimensional restrictions and choice of materials. Dimensional restrictions means something to the effect that building width is in increments of say 4 feet (1.2m) so the forms can be of a standard module size. Bulk material means that all the buildings use the same raw material rather than one made of timber frame, the next steel studs and the one after that brick. Building material must be non-combustible with a high earthquake & fire rating (low heat-transfer rate). It must be durable, moldable, flexible, non-toxic, easy to work, fast to build, relatively low in cost, easily obtainable, and easily stored in bulk. It also must be familiar to building inspectors, so that approval is uncomplicated. In Pattern № 207 of *A Pattern Language*, architect Christopher Alexander writes *we believe that ultra-lightweight concrete is one of the most fundamental bulk materials of the future*. The Stewards agree but prefer to call it *Variable Density Aggregate*.

Narrow and deep is not the way to go   Instead build wide and shallow - let more light in

Attached 2-3 story buildings: In order to maintain a livable scale and to assure sunlight streams into the intimate village streets, the attached homes should be wide and shallow, not like the old urban row houses that were narrow and deep. The narrow design saves the developer money on building streets, but means a dark home that is not good for people. Limit village homes to three floors, but recommend a flat roof that becomes an outdoor living space for gardens, private greenspace or tiled patio, and perhaps partially shaded with by a solar or rain collecting open-air roof. Design most village buildings as attached, meaning they share a common side wall, but sufficiently thick so neighbors do not hear each other. The front and rear faces of buildings may be stepped in or out to break the flatness of the streetscape, and some villages may prefer to also have balconies and porches.

Courtyard Design: Depending on the total land available and the climate of the region (especially in tropical or very hot regions), a village may decide to permit courtyard homes. These are homes built around a central courtyard, and there are a wide range of

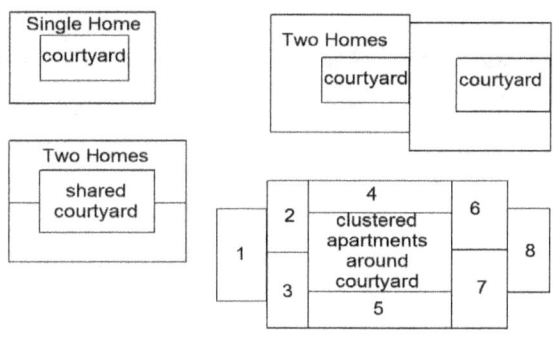

designs to consider. Do note that such designs may add to the cost of construction and slow down construction time.

4 story Town Center: The Town Center is the showcase for larger buildings: the town hall with a five-story, walk-up clock tower; the high school; perhaps a college; the cathedral; perhaps a concert hall. The Town Center is the place for taller, bigger buildings, including apartment living and larger commercial and office buildings. The town-center area is also the appropriate place for detached buildings, including grand homes and mansions for the rich who wish to show their wealth – for the rich are part of a complete community, and, if civic minded, make disproportionate cultural contributions. The organizing company would price mansions and grand homes accordingly. Further, it would ensure they would not be invasive monuments to vanity, but would add to the overall beauty of the town.

No front or back yards: For the most part, it is expected the homes will not have front or back yards for a number of reasons:

Land use: Finding enough land will be a challenge, especially if 60% needs to be a greenbelt and 10% for the industrial park. Expanding the urban core to provide for front or back yards means the urban core has to be bigger. In tropical areas this may be negotiable.

Backyard issues: Suburban or row-house backyards tend to have good & poor uses

- Good: Play areas for children
- Good: Place outside during summer for outdoor dining
- Good: Flower or food gardening
- Poor: Storage of big things, like cars or boats
- Poor: Toilet and enclosure for barking dogs
- Poor: A dumping place for trash to be disposed of "later"

VillageTown Alternative: In a VillageTown, the plazas offer better alternatives for play and alfresco dining; the greenbelt provides better space for larger gardens. Rooftop flat living space is a recommended design option for pets, private gardens and outdoor living. Cars, boats, and other motorized or trailered possessions are kept in the motorpool or in storage near the industrial zone. The VillageTown will seek to minimize trash or the need to store it.

Eliminate Conflict Zones: VillageTown research found the prime place where conflict occurred between next-door neighbors was the fence between back yards. The second conflict zone was the same line in the front yard. Defensible space can become a war zone and seemingly decent people can turn into neighbors from hell. By moving the personal outdoor space to the roof, with higher side walls, the issues that create conflict diminish. It is harder to cart trash up to the roof, thus the tidy next-door neighbor is less likely to become annoyed. For villages that want front space, add raised porches & upper decks.

Social Access: When open front doors, sitting balconies, and porches are slightly above the street, people make better connections with folks walking by, especially if the street is car-free. Likewise, if the back door is on a green-street, social interaction flows.

Green Street: The term *green street* refers to a back-door social concept that begins with a footpath for walking, and then on the sides may have plantings of grass, flowers, food or trees. It is an attractive alternative to the back alley, which too often becomes a depressing place that fosters trouble. It is publicly owned by the VillageTown; it is not the home-owner's private property. The adjacent owner is permitted to plant flowers or dwarf trees, or set out potted plants, and tend the part near their home, but they will do so differently than if it was their own exclusive domain.

If in grass, the green-street may include end-of-street fencing so the VillageTown may use a shepherd and sheep to cut the grass, instead of noisy lawn mowers. In regions with many months of snow or below-freezing temperatures, the green street may be roofed over with glass and heated with some form of renewable energy so that its citizens may enjoy a pleasant walk outdoors when the front street is inclement.

Narrower Streets: Human-scaled streets tend to be less wide than streets made for parked and passing cars and considerably narrower than the streets the fire department wants to drive its trucks to the fire and then turn around to return to the station. Human-scaled streets should be wider than old European medieval streets designed to defend against marauding invaders (that also blocked the sun). Design of VillageTown streets will seek to be narrow, but still let sunlight in. Some street width will be determined by the initial construction requirements – the heaviest use those streets will have during their lifetime.

Curved Streets: Grid streets, beloved of traffic engineers to move cars and by military strategists to suppress insurrection, have few redeeming values in terms of human-scaling. In human-scaling, it becomes desirable to curve the village streets. This introduces a design challenge because most people seem to prefer rectangular rooms and right-angle homes. When one makes a curve either someone gets a trapezoidal room or an extra wall must be built and a wedge of wasted space introduced. The answer for the VillageTown is to go with the trapezoidal building that is then allocated as free-base apartment living for members of the artist guild halls. See an example of a free-base apartment on page 132.

Microzoning: When one zones for a walking community, zones become tighter, but the same principles of separation remain. Some people enjoy walking to high energy places, but prefer to live in quiet places. Being able to walk to a destination in under ten minutes is important, but other times, luxury is a two-hour stroll through the town, never crossing the same place twice. Sometimes people want to walk where they connect with people, where they stop for an unscheduled conversation. Other times they prefer to take paths that enable them to be alone, or walk with another in private conversation.

- **Noise overlay:** Some villages are quieter than others. Within each village some parts are more active than other parts. This is called a noise overlay and is crucial in planning.
- **Plazas:** Each village has one main plaza. It is the village's busiest place, with people entering and exiting constantly. Its buildings are microzoned with busy ground floor businesses and the option of lesser-visited businesses on the upper floors (perhaps offices or shops), or private residences of people who enjoy the buzz of the plaza.
- **Primary Streets:** The less-visited, ground-floor commercial establishments are found on the primary streets. Here, people may enter buildings every few minutes, perhaps walking into a shop, an office or a café.
- **Secondary Streets:** On these streets, one would find private homes with no more than a home office with few visitors during the day and no sign except a small name plate.
- **GreenStreets and Quiet back-streets:** The quiet streets would be purely residential; farther away from the core. Some alleys may be green-streets (see page 168).
- **Footpaths:** In addition to the streets, a VillageTown needs footpaths exclusively for walking – no bicycles, nothing with wheels; a labyrinth for strolling, not point to point.

Participate in the Design of your own Home

Visit the most beautiful villages and towns in the world, the ones people love. Look carefully at the architecture of the buildings. Note the appeal of even the simplest buildings, ones obviously not designed by professionals; they feel authentic. Learn the history of the building and you will find that it was built by a family to suit their needs, but also to add to the character of the neighborhood, since they and their neighbors would live with it for all of their lives; having built it to serve their needs and the needs of future generations – their descendents. They took care because their roots were in their home.

Contrast this with what we find today. The builder, designer, and planners are all motivated by pecuniary interest – they are in it for the money. Very few of them will live with the results. Even if the designer attempts to make it a masterpiece, it feels *off*, because too often it comes from the wrong place: *I am the artist and this building is my canvas.* Also, too often prime consideration is given to the real-estate agent's advice as to what sells easiest. Ornament is no longer the work of a skilled artisan, but whatever pre-manufactured details are available from the building supply store or catalogue. This is especially the case with doors and windows that at one time gave a building its personality.

In all of this one gets a sense of detachment, as if the people living there are just passing through, which sadly in our modern society is too often the case. If they are tenants, this sense of disconnect is even greater – it's harder to make a rental into a real home.

To achieve authenticity and character within a framework that still allows the VillageTown to be built, the people who buy a home are encouraged to shape its design. This is not to say they are to become amateur architects or neophyte interior decorators, but that they will be given a pattern language and a design process that engages them in the design. It works a bit like the jury system, where ordinary citizens are asked to make the key decisions. If they worked without a framework, they would be like a lynch mob. But by working within a formal structure supported by professionals and protocol, they get it right more often than the professionals, which is why the system is used.

The framework sets out the parameters within which they must work:

- Homes are attached, as in the traditional town or city. This is necessary to keep the walking distances compact and allows for better energy efficiency, better use of land.
- The walls are thick enough to not hear the neighbors.
- House depth is set from street-side to alley, with some variation to break up flat surfaces, to allow balconies and outdoor living space in upper floors, and so on.
- Building height is limited to 2-3 stories in the villages and four stories in the town center.
- Building materials must use non-combustible, non-toxic materials that are easily formable. Wood is used only as ornamental, e.g. doors; when used as flooring, will be over non-combustible aggregate to prevent the wood becoming a conflagration.

Within this framework, the intent is to build a load-bearing shell where all interior walls are non load-bearing so that people can place rooms where they desire, and when needs change, move them without disturbing the neighborhood. We recommend buildings include a corner chute going from top floor to bottom that could house a personal elevator or to drop down the laundry, but be easily converted to quietly drop and dispose the old building materials removed when remodelling the interior.

Shaped by location, the view, and how the sun will shine in, each home will be different. Individual needs and personal preferences come into play. One family looks back on their life and finds they spend all their time in the kitchen, and the dining room ends up being where old papers are stored. So they decide to build a country kitchen with a large stone slab counter – one side for food preparation; the other side for family and friends to sit, talk while food is prepared, and for all to eat together. Another couple loves to entertain in a formal, elegant way; their kitchen is small. A family raising children can expect the chaos of toddlers and young ones running everywhere; so they design their rooms to be easy to clean, and not be easily damaged or cause injury.

Beyond the functional questions that shape a home – the equivalent of asking how many pockets one needs in clothing, or if the design should provide for an ever-changing waistline – we come to style. What should it look and feel like? What should it say? One person likes a neat, orderly and precise place; the next family prefers something warm, embracing and welcoming. A third prefers something comfortable, like a pair of old shoes they love regardless of how unfashionable.

The exterior style comes with some constraints. During the Dynamic Engagement process, the future villagers will decide on their architectural code that describes the overall look and feel of their village. As a condition of designing a home in that village, the code sets the boundary of what is designed. It may set color limits, or prescribe traditional doors and windows rather than wide sweeps of green-tint plate glass. Within this code, the individual or family decides on color, ornament, detail, decoration; on where they want the windows. In a pedestrian society, the front door becomes the primary social feature. Will it be a special investment, beautifully hand carved, or will it be simple? Will it be a *Dutch door* where the top half is left open to the street? The same style questions then turn to the interior, where there are fewer constraints. In all of these questions, the intent is to make a house into a home – to make it personal and to make it fit, and in doing so to quietly improve life.

Because of the need to avoid future exterior construction, the design process proposes including low-cost expansion space inside the shell. Instead of a two-story home, add a third-story empty shell with no interior walls or finish. When funds become available, and need grows, expand internally rather than deal with the dust, noise, and traffic, and the necessity to write more complicated zoning rules that come with future exterior expansion.

Stewart Udall, Chairman Emeritus of the Village Forum epitomized the role of the Steward. Committed to a higher purpose, he devoted his life to making the world a better place, and when he heard about the VillageTown vision, he fully supported it, lending his name but also providing the younger stewards with a deeper sense of importance to what they were doing.

It begins with the VillageTown vision – here being discussed by two Stewards in a public presentation. From that came a meeting at another person's home, exploring how to move the vision forward. At that point, most work is done by volunteers – by people who want to live in a VillageTown.

Eventually, it gains enough momentum to secure funding and shift into a more formal, professionally run corporation called an organizing company.

Engaging the Future Villagers

Different Approach to Development

From a practical standpoint, the project begins with the need to find capital. In the period from about 2001 to 2007, much of the world was awash in investment capital for real-estate development, allowing construction of multi-billion dollar projects based on speculation and as it turns out in some cases, dishonesty.

Flying over America in 2010, I saw abandoned homes built — unwanted, never occupied, bank-owned and next to them still empty lots on culs-de-sac roads that may never be finished.

Even good projects now find it difficult to source conventional funding. Ironically, this works in favor of VillageTowns; the VillageTown has a different set of needs that require a different approach to financing.

For a VillageTown to work, it needs to know who will live there before it begins, because those future citizens lead in the design process. Once those buyers are identified, the project ceases to be speculative; this has very different implications for financing.

There are two ways to begin.

    i.   Secure stage one financing, or
    ii. Identify the buyers for at least one village in the VillageTown.

It's a bit of a *which comes first* dilemma. To identify buyers without financing means the Stewards will use volunteer time, internet *spiral marketing*, and good will.

However, at one point cash needs to be found, and this is done in three stages. The first stage is the initiation stage where the two primary jobs are to identify the buyers and set up the business end of the project. Make no mistake about the professionalism required in this latter job. It involves hiring the most experienced and talented professionals one can find, making sure they are the right people for the job.

The Buyers Self-identify

Nothing attracts Stage One funding faster than having full enrollment of committed buyers for one of the twenty villages in a designated VillageTown. Commitment at this point is moral, not legal, meaning that a village coordinator has identified a theme, made it public, and enrolled 500 people (usually 2.5 persons per home for 200 homes) who say they are in. They must be able to demonstrate they have the ability to buy, to move and to earn a living. At this point in the process, there is no contractual obligation – that would be premature; there is not enough on the table. Many of the enrollees already may be involved in a dialogue through the Village Forum; talking about the character of their village. Such a group becomes a powerful force; more convincing than any business plan. If the median home in a village sells for $250,000, that represents $50 million in purchasing power. That attracts attention. It also provides inspiration for the next village coordinator who will focus on enrolling a group around a different theme.

At this stage, no contracts have been signed. No one has locked themselves into a buying agreement, and anyone can back out for any reason. As a practical matter, it would be prudent for the village coordinator to set up a waiting list for oversubscription, not cut off applications when the limit is hit. While no legally binding documents exist, the presence of the buyers is convincing. It should be a major priority of any project.

Note that in some cases, this can happen in very short order. The right person, the right media story, the right village theme could fill its enrolment list in a matter of days or weeks if the right message connected with the right audience. While this would not be something to count on, it can happen, especially in today's global climate when people are feeling anxious about large and threatening social, environmental, economic, and cultural forces over which they have no control.

Choosing the Right Region - An International View

In finding buyers, a region can be new territory, or it can be near a populated area likely to draw from the region. For the first VillageTowns the latter is the more prudent approach. For example, in Australia both Sydney and Cairns proposed hosting VillageTowns. Sydney has a regional population of over four-million people. In contrast, the Cairns region has less than a quarter-million people. Thus, a VillageTown in the Sydney region could find it easily draws its full population from the surrounding region, whereas in Cairns one would need to expect that almost all buyers came from other parts of the country or the world. For the first VillageTown therefore, it is smarter to choose Sydney than Cairns. The people are there already, and for the first VillageTown in a country, it is important to make it as easy as possible to get the job done right. Keep it simple.

However, once several VillageTowns have been built in Australia, the Atherton Tablelands (near the city of Cairns, but at higher altitude with better weather) may be an excellent VillageTown site. The climate is warmer than Sydney and provides a more pleasant outdoor experience much of the year. The soil is fertile and the food production is prodigious and varied. Local-to-global businesses focused on Asia will find that it is probably the closest location to the major Asian destinations where the native tongue is English and Common Law reigns. It has ample water, which for a decade was a major issue in Australia. When it was examined as a possible site, it was found that if a VillageTown was placed every ten miles (covering about 1/500th of the available land and securing the surrounding farmland to prevent sprawl), about 5% of drought-stricken Australia could relocate to the Tablelands without having adverse effects, due to the vastness of good available land and the compactness of VillageTown land requirements.

The first regions should be ones that have everything going for them. Later, when the concept has become popular, other more creative sites may be considered.

Where to Find the Buyers

- **New Zealand:** With a population of 4 million, and an open immigration policy that seeks migrants in skilled categories appropriate for a VillageTown, New Zealand can be expected to look overseas for a significant portion of its buyers. Some will be expatriate Kiwis wanting to return home, especially those with young families. Without VillageTowns, the challenge for expats is that after London, New York, or other overseas destinations, New Zealand life can be viewed as lacking in cultural and social enrichment – a bit dull. The VillageTown provides for that. New Zealand VillageTowns can be expected to have more village themes based on nationality, as immigrants come from almost every nation on earth. A small country, New Zealand is an attractive alternative, especially as other parts of the world experience economic, social and cultural deterioration. It is an English-speaking nation ruled under Commonwealth Common Law. New Zealand consistently ranks as one of the least-corrupt countries in the world. The air is clean, the waters pure, the views exquisite, and the outdoor life offers a broad array of activities in a mild climate that ranges from sub-tropical to alpine in less than a day's drive. It offers a desirable quality of life at all times: food is fresh and abundant, population density low, and the country's location means it is safer in times of global chaos.

- **USA:** The United States population is large enough that most buyers will come from the 50 states, or from US citizens living abroad. The buyers will be looking for a higher quality of life, more control over their personal lives and the lives of their families, and more protection from the economic shocks that make investment in local tangibles attractive.

GLOBAL SEARCH – IMPORTING A WHOLE COMPANY

Imagine what it would be like to search the world to find companies doing the most exciting and innovative work and invite them to live in your village. Imagine what it would be like to be the owner of such a business and to be approached by a future 10,000 population community who says *We need you, come join us*, and in saying that back it with money and plans intended to help that business attain its maximum potential.

In the first VillageTown, this will be part of the job of the organizing company. If the site is in a country that supports open immigration, such as New Zealand, it will include a first-world business-talent search. This means the company will seek a special relationship with the immigration department to secure VillageTown visas for whole companies. Find a brilliant business, a small-to-medium enterprise, employing for example, twenty professionals. Offer to the owners and management the invitation to move to a great place, with a lower cost of living, a higher quality of life, and a lower cost of doing business. Invite them to move everything – the business, the tooling, all the staff (other than clerical or unskilled) and their families.

Focus on particular migrant countries, so that enough migrants move from that country to form a complete village. This removes one of the big concerns to migration where one instantly becomes a foreigner in a new land. This is especially important to the families, where the familiarity of home is retained in the 500-person village, but the cultural experience of the new land is just beyond. For example, we have one Steward focusing on Germany where they have a 50% tax rate, 20% VAT and a number of people who would love to live in subtropical New Zealand where the tax rate is 28-33%, the GST 15%, and the population density is much lower. If that plan proceeds, it would involve recruiting 200 families, enough to form a 500-population German village within the VillageTown. This would probably involve perhaps ten or twenty German businesses renowned for their quality, innovation and important models such as their apprentice systems.

By uplifting whole businesses, the host nation realizes an economic boost both to GDP and its tax base. In most cases, such a business will be international in focus, and thus serve to improve the balance of trade. In the specific case of New Zealand, many of these businesses may be ones already conducting business in Asia, where the prospect of living in Western culture based in the Far East gives one the best of both worlds.

Rather than do this in a random fashion, the organizing company should look at creating clusters. London and New York are financial clusters, Hollywood and Mumbai are film clusters and Silicon Valley is a high-tech cluster. By inviting businesses that share an industry, the overall outcome is excellence and greater levels of success by individual businesses.

The same approach should be applied to the Artist Guild Halls. The organizing company should seek out the best artists and invite them to form a guild. Usually this involves several senior artists who then enrol some seasoned artists as well as younger emerging artists and those promising young ones just starting out. This proactive approach to recruitment will make a great difference in the character of the VillageTown.

In a US VillageTown themes may include a few nationality villages, but most can be expected to be about different interests, some clustered around the arts or lifestyle.

- **Australia:** Buyers for an Australian VillageTown would for the most part be domestic, although many may be drawn from immigrant populations already holding Australian visas or passports. The country is reported to have a housing shortage, yet in its population centers the continued suburban sprawl is placing great strains on the systems. If the VillageTown is built in the Sydney or Melbourne region, most buyers will be local.

- **European Union:** It was interesting recently to read in a Swiss magazine that suburban sprawl is becoming a national concern. Car-based sprawl is showing up in the most unlikely places. Even though much of the VillageTown inspiration comes from the proven patterns of old Europe, new Europe is going in the direction of sprawl. With 27 member states and almost a half-billion citizens, the EU can be expected to attract almost all its buyers internally. The core question for a VillageTown in the EU will turn on language. Will the VillageTown be national in focus, where one in Germany will attract mostly German-speaking buyers, or could a site be selected that truly attracts the breadth of the EU, with villages speaking different languages. Mallorca in Spain has been proposed as a potential site. As a resort island, it has air connections to most of Europe and with the shift to tourism some of the older villages have been completely abandoned. One of these villages may serve as the core of a new VillageTown that would be built following the traditional stone design indigenous to the island's architecture.

- **England:** Within the EU, England presents a special case, as it struggles to deal with the Thatcher years when the middle class boomed and England's roads suddenly had to deal with an explosion of cars. An island with limited land, England was trashed with ill-conceived sprawl. In response, planners in England embrace green architecture, transit-oriented communities, and other innovations that seek to domesticate the car and save the world from climate change. VillageTown development in England would seem to be an ideal solution, except that it will require a mind-shift by planners. Its proposal for a walking home-range and restoring a single town-country local economy is not part of the planning vocabulary. If approval could be secured, perhaps the most likely site for the first VillageTown in England would be Cornwall, where local communities are being destroyed by hollow-house syndrome.

- **Asia:** A large continent with many different nations, the most likely first candidate is China, where one can expect that all buyers would be Chinese, and many from the wealthier classes able to afford such a life. The VillageTown concept has received strong interest from China, but would need to be adapted to their different culture.

Be Careful about Finding the Land Too Early

Identify the region, but be cautious about starting with a particular piece of land unless that land already has the medium density, mixed use zoning required for the VillageTown.

In many cases, the owner of a piece of land will step forward and press for it as the site of a VillageTown. While it may be perfect, it could bog the process down if the project commits to it too early. The problems include:

- **Wrong motivation:** The land owner wants to sell. Their motivation may be altruistic, but in many cases, pecuniary interest will be the driver, and that drive will get in the way, especially if the vendor has a strong personality.

- **Wrong location:** Too far away, to difficult to get to, not the right climate (which in some places can vary with micro-climates), lacking amenity values, not near food sources, insufficient or too difficult to secure water or energy, hostile neighbors (personal) or noxious neighbors (such as open mines, noxious smelling or sounding factories, farms, toxic activities), too close to commuter links (likely to attract commuters), etc.

- **Wrong site:** Not enough land, too hilly, wrong shape, geotechnical problems, soil is too good to be covered with housing, has important flora or fauna that should not be destroyed, the land is too expensive, contaminated, etc.

- **Wrong local jurisdiction:** This can be a large concern. Some jurisdictions are approachable from a policy level (the elected officials want the VillageTown) but can become a nightmare if approached with land, where the regulators (bureaucrats) have their own ways of doing things and can waste massive amounts of time and developers' funds through the way they do business. Other jurisdictions are a closed shop, meaning there are local relationships between vested interests and the elected politicians, and an outside project like a VillageTown will encounter a hostile welcome. Having the buyers, but not the land, means the jurisdiction must compete to win the VillageTown.

Caveat

Reality has a funny way of disrupting plans. Sometimes a local government gets it, wants it and will do whatever is necessary to help make it happen. In such cases, make sure the idea can be made to fit, in whole or in part and get moving. As long as the core features remain active, it's worth moving forward.

Location – Selecting the Right Region, Jurisdiction and Land

Unlike a new suburban development that depends on regional job growth to generate home sales, the VillageTown brings its own local economy. Therefore it can be located anywhere it can secure high-speed broadband and be within a two-hour drive or one-hour shuttle flight of a major airport (if the latter, the VillageTown may chose to own and operate its own shuttle airline to assure competitive pricing). Close access to existing rail is a bonus. This frees the VillageTown from the usual geographical constraints of proximity to urban centers and suburban rings. The best location is one with a cooperative local government that will provide rapid approvals and will not tax for services the VillageTown intends to provide internally. Beyond that, a rural setting with nearby farms prepared to enable the VillageTown to secure its food supply is important. Access to permanent and affordable water is important, noting that rain water will be harvested and waste water will be recycled as much as possible. It is important the building land be relatively flat to enable the mobile factories to move from house to house with ease. Later VillageTowns may build on hills, but the first one should avoid making it more difficult. Climate becomes important, as alfresco life adds an important quality to the village life. Finally, access to outstanding natural amenities is a luxury a VillageTown may pursue. This may include bucolic countryside, or nearby waters, or mountains or forests.

The importance of the rural farmland Market Town

In the old countries, set among farmland one will find numerous small villages with perhaps a general store, a church and two pubs. Among them, one finds a larger market town, often 10,000-population, that anchored the countryside and provided the market for the surrounding farms. The town-and-country relationship formed a single local economy.

This system breaks down when the farmer's market shifts to the supermarket chain buyers. The farms become monoculture, and once the middlemen put together a monopolistic cartel, they press the farmers to grow more food for less money. This results in dosing fields and animals with chemicals, and producing food not for flavor and nourishment, but to survive transport to distant places and look good in the stores. Over time, the market towns lose their economic basis, and unless they turn to tourism (if they are pretty), they tend to decline. If the district is within driving distance of a city, the suburban ring then begins to expand and both the farmland and the old market town undergo conversion to wide boulevards lined with big-box stores, malls, fast food and drive-in franchised restaurants, car dealers, and motels. Branching off from the boulevards new tracts of suburban homes go in, ranging from the luxury *McMansion* on a postage-stamp lot to transient-living,soulless apartment blocks surrounded by off-street parking.

For many farmers this is the new end game. They do not make much money on farming, and they look to cash in when their farm is rezoned for development.

In some places, when the general public begins to realize this sprawl will eventually wipe out the bucolic countryside they pass laws that protect the farmland by prohibiting development. In places where prescriptive zoning is allowed, they set the barrier high, perhaps requiring a referendum to change the rules. Unfortunately, these protective policies never considered the possibility of a VillageTown. In effect, a VillageTown set in the middle of farm country restores the traditional role of the market town. It provides choice of markets for the farmer. Given that the middleman takes over 80% of the consumer's plate (only 19% of what the consumer pays for food goes to the farmer), shifting farming practices to sell to the VillageTown enables the farmer to once again focus on growing food, and to make a good living doing so.

Restoring a single town-country local economy brings back diversity to the farms, so fields no longer resemble an endless carpeting of monoculture. The air, water, and soil is cleaned as the farmers stop blanketing food with sprays and chemicals. Delivery becomes more local, and the option of farmers-market days adds a social component to shopping.

To achieve this, however, the rules must either permit it, or be carefully rewritten to allow country market-town VillageTowns without opening the door for suburban sprawl. It may be that the best way for this to happen is on a case-by-case basis, meaning the whole package must be proposed and approved rather than rezoning laws rewritten.

Development Finance

Building the VillageTown – Financing and Investment

In order to develop a self-supporting local economy, the VillageTown cannot begin to build until a critical mass of buyers has committed to the project. Thus the typical process of securing large-scale investment capital and doing a staged development over decades is not applicable. The bare minimum size for a VillageTown is 3,500 persons, and the lower target should be 5,000. While it is possible to have a strong economy with 5,000, it is recommended to target the larger population of 10,000 unless the land or other factors preclude this. The 10,000-population VillageTown cannot begin until half of the citizens have committed. It is desirable that all units are presold. Otherwise part of the VillageTown will remain a construction site longer. This critical mass is also essential to make the Dynamic Engagement process work. Therefore the development has three stages of financing.

- **Stage One: Initiation** – Critical path: Buyers self-identify but do not legally commit until the end of this stage. Key employees hired, business plan and legal documents drafted, marketing of the project initiated, village coordinators recruited, village themes defined, bank set up, jurisdiction and land confirmed, infrastructure planning initiated. Venture financing: $5 million and twelve months' duration.

- **Stage Two: Organization** – Critical path: Buyers complete financing applications. Land acquired, Dynamic Engagement planning completed, infrastructure built, stage three tooling designed and ordered, bank organizes buyers for mortgage-backed securities (MBS). Capital requirement around $20 to $50 million, with variable depending on land price and acquisition terms. The principal (but not ROI) on stage 1 funding repaid with Stage 2 funds. Estimate twelve months for stage two.
- **Stage Three: Construction** – Critical path: MBS funding in the bank, construction begins. For a village to be started, all buildings must be spoken for, either sold, or if a few remain unsold, then the organizing company or village buyers cover the cost as a speculative venture. Each village is a single project of about 200 homes. A minimum of ten villages (5,000 population) must be presold. Each village will be built as a single project, so that partial occupancy can occur as soon as each village is completed, thus reducing the time the new construction interest is accruing while the family, individual, or business is paying rent or mortgage.

Limited Investment Risk

Risk is inherent in the first VillageTown project but it is staged, and, relative to the full project, minimal. In a conventional development, land must be acquired and rezoned, all utilities and roads installed, building platforms set out, and often a block of homes built before the developer's risk is covered. In 2008, developers around the world saw the credit crunch destroy the market for their projects; the risk turned on them and they lost.

In the VillageTown, risk decreases much earlier as the critical path calls for the buyers to self-identify and commit before the land is paid for, rezoned, or developed. By stage two the risk is substantially lower because all residences are pre-sold, and by the time construction begins, the risk capital is paid out as the project funds itself.

Development Approvals

Implications of the Organizing Company not being a Developer

Similar to a developer, the organizing company's brief includes providing fixed returns to its Stage One and Two investors, as well as paying a 10% reinvestment premium to the VillageTown Stewards and Co. This reinvestment premium is to be used for future developments, thereby avoiding the need for future Stage One financing. Beyond this, the organizing company keeps all net profits, just as a developer does. However, when the project is complete, the VillageTown Stewards and Company, who technically own the stock in the organizing company and in the VillageTown bank, turn that stock in and issue new stock, one share per dwelling, with voting rights granted to the citizens living in that dwelling. In this way, the Stewards fulfill their stewardship role, which is very different than that of a typical real-estate investor/developer.

VILLAGETOWN ORGANIZATIONAL STRUCTURE

By this point, you the reader are presumed to have a fairly good understanding of what a VillageTown is, based on the several books, the web site, videos, FAQ, forum, public talks, and direct conversation with Stewards. The next step is to understand how to get there, and to understand some of the choices along the way.

The first thing to understand is the value of different organizations to help make it happen. Some are advocacy-focused volunteer groups and. Others are businesses with particular functions. These should operate under the same principles of checks and balances that will be instituted in the VillageTown itself.

ORGANIZATIONAL DEFINITIONS

- **The VillageTown Vision** is the pure idea for VillageTowns. Ideas exist in the higher form of reality, and the role of all involved with the idea is literally to cast the idea in concrete, so people may call a VillageTown their home. The vision is a framework, not a franchise planned down to minute detail. The framework sets the boundary conditions within which people work, but it does not prescribe the outcome. Each VillageTown will be different, because the people founding it are different.

- **The VillageTown Stewards** (sometimes called the *village stewards*) are the volunteer guardians or stewards of the VillageTown Vision. The Stewards are located and focused globally - they want VillageTowns to happen anywhere & everywhere, although some will have a regional bias, by virtue of living wherever they live.

- **The Company.** *Company* literally means *group shares bread*. The Company was set up by founder Claude Lewenz to hold the intellectual property on VillageTowns and establish the various organizations necessary to make a VillageTown happen.

- **The VillageTown Stewards & Co** - The Company sets up The VillageTown Stewards & Co to initiate projects and to hold reinvestment funds to start future VillageTown projects world-wide. It owns the tooling developed when a project is complete, so that tooling can easily be transferred to the next job site. The Stewards hold in trust the stock in the organizing company until the project is complete. The Stewards appoint the organizing company's board of directors, who understand their decisions are made to serve the best interests of the VillageTown's future citizens. The Stewards write the business plan for each local organizing company and license that company to build one VillageTown. There may be several such stewardship companies in different continents depending on legal requirements and tax implications.

- **The VillageTown Organizing Company** - Each organizing company begins as a name, not a corporation. The organizing company is incorporated in the state where the VillageTown will be built when funded. The organizing company is the only organization legally constituted to make *offerings* (a term with legal implications). Until the organizing company exists and is legally mandated to make offerings, there are no financial or property offerings, and no promises or commitments made to the public or to potential buyers. The organizing company buys the land, secures development permission, builds everything, and sells to the public. It borrows money to start the project and it pays the money back. In lieu of paying profits to stockholders, the organizing company pays a 10% reinvestment fee to the VillageTown Stewards & Co to make VillageTowns self-replicating. The organizing company's successor, the VillageTown *operating company*, keeps all net profits and all VillageTown assets to benefit the people and villages of that VillageTown. To be clear, unless state law blocks it, in lieu of a developer, there is an *organizing company* and the stock is held in trust. On completion of construction, the organizing company is recast as an *operating company*, and the stock is issued to the buyers of the homes with voting rights by citizenship (see below for details). The organizing company earns the net profits; its successor, the operating company, keeps and invests them through its Legacy Fund managers.

- **The VillageTown Operating Company, also known as the *VillageTown Council*** - The VillageTown is built all at once, not over the years or decades. It is built by the *Organizing Company* that is recast as the *Operating Company* on project completion.

  Private Corporation: Subject to legal advice, the VillageTown Council is a private corporation established to serve the interests of the people and villages of the VillageTown. It may run both for-profit subsidiaries and non-profit organizations.

  Name: Subject to state-law restrictions on the use of the word *Council*, the desirable name for the operating company is the local name followed by VillageTown Council (if the local name was *Vilton* the name would be *Vilton VillageTown Council Inc*).

  Shares: On completion, the buyers secure title to their homes and workplaces. Each title is accompanied by one share in the operating company. The share is intended to have no independent market value (although it will make the property more valuable), and cannot be sold separately from the property.

  Voting: While the owner of each residence is the legal owner of the share, the voting rights to that share are by the adult residents (citizens) living in it. This is not a new idea: local government tax the building, but grant the right to vote to the citizens living in the property. Landlords only vote if they live in the VillageTown.

  Municipal Government: In some locations, there may be benefit in the VillageTown becoming its own municipal government. If appropriate, the VillageTown may elect to do so. However, it shall still take advantage of the greater powers accorded to private corporations and operate itself primarily under corporate law. This is recommended because corporations have more power and suffer less interference from the state and from international treaties.

Legal Details: The structure and details of the operating company is a complex subject beyond the scope of this book. Substantial funds are set aside by the organizing company to receive the best legal and tax advice money can buy.

- **The Village Forum** serves several functions. It is intended as a non-profit organization, but is unlikely to register for tax-exempt status, as this brings in government compliance regulations that make its work more complicated with no commensurate benefit. The Forum also is the name (www.villageforum.com) of the informational web site. Additionally, when a project is funded, the Forum represents the buyers with funds provided by the Stewards. The purpose of this representation is to establish checks and balances to the organizing company. These separate funds enable the Forum to speak on behalf of the future buyers who are registered with the Forum. The Stewards appoint and fund a small group of willing volunteers, future buyers who become the collective voice for the potential buyers in a named project. Those funds are then used to retain independent expert professionals to assure the interests of the buyers are always kept in the forefront.

- **The VillageTown Coordinator** starts out as a volunteer appointed to call attention to a particular region; to attract a VillageTown project. If successful, this work may (or may not) evolve into a job with the organizing company. The coordinator contacts the Stewards and proposes a particular region. The coordinator agrees to take on the role of primary contact and local advocate. The first job of the coordinator is to call into being a Village Circle, as discussed next:

- **The Village Circle** - Typically a project begins for a VillageTown when someone in a region contacts the Stewards or the Forum and puts together a convincing case why that region should be considered for a project. If the Stewards agree, the project becomes *named*, and a web page is set up. A coordinator or project manager is identified who will work on a volunteer basic, and that coordinator sets up what is called a *Village Circle*. The circle consists of volunteers who focus on spreading the word, with the goal of having a VillageTown in their region. The members of the circle are always volunteer, driven by passion, with no expectation of profit or inside track to employment. Their primary job is to introduce the word *VillageTown* into the regional language so that decision makers and key influencers know what it means when the subject comes up. Their purpose is to establish local legitimacy so the project is understood not as some outside group coming in with all the answers, but as a local desire to secure more choice on community design. It should be noted that the power of such a group may be more than its members think. It changes the sense of the project. When it becomes clear to the public that the idea of a VillageTown is being put forward by a local group wanting a VillageTown in their territory, it is usually received more kindly.

- **The Village Coordinators** - When a project gains momentum, people emerge who respond with passion; in one form or another, the vision has been on their mind for years, and they may have a strong sense of the kind of village they would like to live in. Their passion has a power that no developer can match. Thus, a special and perhaps pivotal role is created. In essence, they articulate a vision for their village and then they attract others to the vision – potential buyers who not only want to live in a VillageTown but in that particular village. In some cases, the coordinator already has a network of friends who share that vision, and with two degrees of separation, they fill their quota of approximately 500 people (typically 200 homes). In other cases, the idea is set forth on the web pages, and connection comes through the internet. These village coordinators are volunteers who work under the supervision of the VillageTown Coordinator. Each village coordinator sets out a vision for their village – its look and feel – and they spread this vision to attract other people who would like to live in such a place. If they are successful, resulting in millions of dollars in sales, there may be some form of in-kind exchange in thanks, but this is not set in place at the onset both for legal and motivational reasons.

BEGINNING WITH A VILLAGETOWN COORDINATOR & VILLAGE CIRCLE

Typically, a project begins with a contact made via email after a person or group learns about the concept of the VillageTown, buys and reads the books, and resolves to bring a VillageTown to their region. These contacts go to the Stewards, who take a closer look.

Some proposals lack the qualities for consideration in the first round of projects. For example, land was proposed on the Atherton Tablelands above Cairns, Australia. The land is attractive, fertile, with a lovely climate (much more comfortable than tropical, humid Cairns at sea-level). However, it was not named as a potential project because the first project should be within two hours of a major city, one with at least a million population, rather than a place that is too remote. Thus, certain locations go into the file as worthy of another look once the first series of VillageTown projects are completed.

Presuming the region passes this first set of tests, the Stewards begin to look for a local person prepared to take on the role of coordinator. This person becomes the local contact, and their first job is to pull together a circle of supporters called the *Village Circle*. The role of this circle is relatively simple – to introduce both a word and an understanding of that word – VillageTown – into the regional language. Once an idea has a name, it is easier to put into action.

The circle does not exist to find land or represent themselves as the organizing company. They are not there to recruit buyers or make promises. They exist to advocate for a VillageTown in their region and to spread the word; literally: spread the word *VillageTown*.

Typically, the coordinator invites people to a meeting where the VillageTown idea is put forth. Before the meeting, the people are encouraged to go to the web site, read the information, watch the videos, and, if they find it of interest, to buy and read the books. After the first meeting, those who decide to stay in are strongly encouraged to read the books, because web sites, videos, and talks can never cover the detail of an idea as different as the VillageTown. For circle members unable to afford the expense, budget copies of books are available to the coordinator, typically for less than five US dollars plus postage.

The circle then looks at its talent base and develops a strategy for getting the word out. Often the circle attracts people in the industry – planners, ecologists, activists, brokers, and consultants. This can be a double-edged sword, as the circle brings good contacts in the realm of the decision-makers and the key-influencers. This is helpful. However, these people also bring *baggage* from their industries. Their expectations can cloud their vision and lead them to turn the VillageTown idea into something it is not. Their expectations can lead them to implement ideas that keep them within their comfort zone, but would undermine the framework and intent of the VillageTown.

The circle works as an open system, meaning people will come and go, gradually sorting out the less committed, too busy or financially-interested parties. Ongoing meetings can be helpful, but can also become tedious if nothing happens in between the meetings. The best way to be effective is for the coordinator to establish a way of measuring how far the word VillageTown has travelled. The idea is to create what some call a *buzz*, or awareness of what the VillageTown is and can do. This buzz can be shared through multiple channels of communication: face-to-face, presentations, print and audio-visual media, etc.

While the circle proceeds to spread the word, opportunities will come up. Land will be found; a local-government official will get it, love it, and offer to do what they can to help make it happen. A sponsor will emerge, perhaps someone or some organization prepared to provide funding. But the most powerful thing that could emerge is a group of people who want to form their village within the VillageTown.

During the market testing phase for the VillageTown idea from 2008 through 2010, many people and groups emerged who already were formed in what could become the core of a new village group. Some already had the sort of leader who could become a village coordinator to set out the special character for their village and call together individuals and families who would like to live in it. With no more than two degrees of separation, the core group contacts its friends who contact their friends, and with no formal structure in place, 200 buyers materialize around a good idea.

This should be encouraged, and when it happens, the coordinator links these leaders and their group with some of the other Stewards. Two hundred homes at an median of $250,000 each is $50 million. While the potential future villagers have signed nothing, and committed nothing, this level of coherent, well-defined interest speaks volumes to both funding sources and decision-makers. From a publicity standpoint, this becomes a news story. It is interesting that a group has a good idea, but it becomes news when 200 families say they want to live there.

At this point, so there is no misunderstanding, "a *median* of $250,000 each" does not mean the *minimum* home price is $250,000. The intent is to have what we call a *complete community* which means that it reflects the full socioeconomic scale in the region. This means affordable homes, rentals, average homes, eccentric homes, and luxury mansions. Home prices are set to correspond to the regional market, and every effort will be made to offer the full spectrum of housing including affordable rental accommodations (which for the most part will be managed by the VillageTown operating company on behalf of private investors to assure a high standard of landlord and of tenant). Thus, as long as those first 200 families are living somewhere already – either paying a mortgage or paying rent, it is likely they will be able to afford to live in the first VillageTown.

GAINING MOMENTUM – ENROLLING VILLAGE COORDINATORS

At one point, a passionate person will step forward. They have a strong sense of what their village will look and feel like. They may have been dreaming about it for years, yearning for it. Their personality will be attractive, meaning they can attract others and enrol them in the vision. In some cases they will self-identify; in other cases the VillageTown Coordinator goes in search of them.

We call this person a village coordinator because their focus is on their village. Their passion is their vision for it; their job is to people it. Their primary driving force is not to make money, but to live there.

In reading this job description, a conventional business person may have some difficulty working out what a village coordinator is because they may seem more volunteer than employee, more amateur (in the sense of the French word *amateur*, meaning *one who loves*) than professional. This is OK, live with it. In a world that is becoming increasingly monetized, the VillageTown seeks to go in a different direction, in which people do some things because they are good, rather than solely because they are profitable.

In the next section, the text is written as an orientation for the village coordinator. However, it is worth reading by all.

The Village Coordinator

About you - Clarity, Passion, Leadership, Discipline.

You want to live in a village. You are passionate about it. You get along well with people, and you communicate your passion effectively. You listen well. You are not a pushy sales type, but you attract people to an attractive idea. You are well enough organized to keep communication lines open and projects on task. You lead by weaving people into harmony. You can enrol 500 people.

500 people

Your job is to enrol about 500 people for your village, typically about 200 families. This means 200 families who will actually follow through, buy or lease a home, bring or find a job within the VillageTown and live in your village. This means you also need to establish a waiting list to accommodate legitimate drop-outs. The statistical average suggests 2.5 people per home; thus 500 people means 200 homes. However, if a village has a high number of single persons, for example, you my find the need for more homes or alternative forms of living space such as the elegant, university-hall, shared design where individuals own a small apartment and share commons space.

The 500 number is approximate. Studies and experience that suggest a face-to-face community works best with 250-750 people.

Theme

Each village has a theme. As coordinator, you set the theme – with the caveats that the organizing company must approve the theme, and the theme must be sufficiently attractive to enable enrolment of 500 people.

The theme is perhaps the most important aspect of VillageTown planning. The variety in the VillageTown comes from having 21 themes (of which the 21st - the town center's theme is architectural: grand buildings in a larger scale setting).

Some themes will be based on nationality, especially in countries that rely on immigration (such as New Zealand or Australia). In the USA, nationality may be based on ancestry for some villagers (e.g. people of Italian ancestry who are Americans by birth and accent, but would love to live in a village that reflects their ancestry – or non-Italians who happen to enjoy the quality and character of life that Italian villages offer).

Other themes may focus on activity – a filmmaker's village or an entrepreneur's village that joins inventors with people who turn ideas into businesses. With appropriate sponsorship, a village theme could be research-oriented, a kind of extended think tank.

A village theme could be one of the elements of the good life, for example a slow food village that celebrates conviviality, a village built around a college, with a focus on intellectual and artistic growth, or a village formed by a group that shares a common religion (provided, of course, that such a group is able to get along with other villages that do not share their beliefs).

Alternatively, people who share a love of music may decide to create a village where amateur music is the theme, and it would not be surprising if they elected to call for a music guild hall in their village. Sport can be a theme – either a shared passion for participatory sport, or watching. In some locations there may be a critical mass for an equestrian village which would be located on the outer ring next to the greenbelt, so the horses would be close by. Such a village may include equine studies in their local school electives.

A theme could be about a way of life – families may want a children-and-old-people-everywhere village that supports extended families. Alternatively, another village may be for single people who wish to live their lives without the constant pressure to couple. This group seems to have been nicknamed as Suvies (single unencumbered villagers). To support entry-level housing, a youth zone may be its own village or it may be blended in with the Suvie village.

There may be situations where there is sufficient demand that two villages have very similar themes. The organizing company would facilitate a dialogue to decide how to manage this, including questions of proximity – side-by-side, or on opposite sides of town?

The theme becomes a major focus in the design phase, as the professional support designers challenge the villagers to translate their theme into architecture. In the New Zealand project, the German village coordinator is having a great deal of fun trying to work out what the archetype of *German* is for contemporary German migrants who would form their own village. It's not the Disney version. The questions focus on what the buildings look like. What are the sounds and smells? What shops are essential? What colors? What window shapes and designs? What fonts are used on street signs? It was amusing that when Germans were asked what the archetypal German village would look like, the most common answer was *Italian*. Apparently those replying much preferred the convivial Italian model to their own Teutonic style.

Attraction

The village coordinator creates an *attractive* vision - a vision that attracts. In some cases, a coordinator may actually know 150 people who would move into their village, if all the questions were answered and it was affordable. Most likely those 150 would know one or two more people, making the enrolment of 500 easy. In other cases, the coordinator will create a story that attracts people using viral (or spiral) marketing – one person hears about it, and that person tells another, and so on. For this kind of marketing the web site becomes an essential tool. The coordinator may choose to have a video made – perhaps of them talking, or if they have access to the talent, perhaps a You-Tube-type entertainment video that tells the story. There are many attractive elements of the VillageTown, and these need to be woven into a story that generates interest, provides answers, and secures enrolment.

Building Confidence

It's a major life decision, not only moving to a VillageTown, but designing it. The decision-making process must be gradual. The role of the village coordinator is to slowly build confidence, not put on the hard sell. It is a process that unfolds, a journey to a new place in a future time. The village coordinator is not expected to have all the answers, but is there to help keep the unfolding occurring in its time and according to its pace. It's about building relationships, from which confidence naturally emerges.

Initially, people are asked only to make an expression of interest in which they confirm they have an interest in living there, can afford to buy in and to earn a living. They then go through an education phase in which they not only learn about the village and the VillageTown but about the business of making it happen. They learn that an organizing company is different from a developer, and that as citizens they have a very different level of participation in the invention of their future. This process builds confidence as they begin to commit emotionally to their village.

During this period, the organizing company leverages their commitment to secure the location and concessions from the local government. Everything is still provisional rather than contractual. It is the coming-together phase. Finally, when the numbers come clear, the costs are locked down, and the agreements with the local government put in place, the future villagers are asked to make a contractual commitment. By this time their confidence should be high, as they see themselves as central to the process.

Even at this point the contract has out-clauses; the investments made by the organizing company are still limited. As the project proceeds, commitment levels rise.

Instant Oversubscription

Despite the expectation that the process is gradual, it is possible that the idea will catch fire, go viral through the Internet, social networking such as Facebook or Twitter, and conventional media, and find that a village, or all the villages, reach oversubscription in a matter of days. The village coordinator needs to be prepared for this possibility.

The level of dissatisfaction in the world is high. Parents seek better places to raise children, and will move to get into a good school zone. Baby boomers are waking up to the next stage of their lives, and beginning to worry. The creative class rarely finds places where they are honored and offered an enriched environment to pursue their art. All over the world, people yearn for something more. They find it hard to articulate, but many report they find in the idea of the VillageTown the answers they seek. They find it hard to believe such a way of living is possible, but the gradual commitment process allows them to become involved without undue risk.

This has the potential to compress the enrolment up to warp speed, requiring the village coordinator to have plans in place for rapid response. Among other things, the coordinator needs to have already decided how to give priority in the event of rapid oversubscription. Is it first come, first served? Or does the coordinator rank applications by skills, range of ages, mix of character, or some other criterion? Will it be personal – people the coordinator likes, or a lottery left to chance? What happens to those not accepted? Are they put on a waiting list, or spilled over to another village, or possibly even another VillageTown? There are many choices, and the Stewards and the organizing company will be there to help. Should this spiral event happen, it becomes a delightful problem, but one that requires contingency planning not to reflect badly on the project or create excess pressure on the village coordinator.

Economic Mix

While the coordinator is not expected to be an economist, and the VillageTown relies in part on self-selection for the economy to evolve, getting a good mix of jobs and employment is important. The organizing company should have a policy of open information meaning that applicants state how they intend to earn a living, and this is made available to all applicants. In this way, if there are too many applicants for a particular occupation or profession, the applicants should be informed, introduced and encouraged to work it out.

However, some village coordinators plan to actively recruit the best in the world – seeking people who are known for their excellence and who can add much to the VillageTown and their particular village. The potential here is unlimited and exciting. Many people with extraordinary talent, highly respected in their field, nevertheless feel they live in mundane environments. The idea of being invited to move to a place intended to become a hothouse of excellence is both appealing and an honor.

Some village coordinators may choose to create a job roster, and some organizing companies may choose to develop a town-wide job roster to identify what critical jobs need to be filled and to note when some may be oversubscribed.

About Baby Boomers

The demographic bump of people born between 1946 and 1964 can pose a problem, as the VillageTown is not intended to become a retirement village. Boomers are at the peak of their earnings power and net worth. They are worried about their future as they are told there are too many of them to support current retirement-pension levels and medical care. The VillageTown offers solutions for them, but this runs the risk that too many of them will enrol. Subject to legal advice that it does not transgress anti-discrimination laws about aging, the village coordinator may establish a quota system that generally reflects the national census in terms of age in order to assure the VillageTown maintains a well-balanced age range.

About Commuters

A CBS reporter read *How to Build a Village* and then asked "What happens if someone moves in and then decides to take a job thirty miles away where they commute every day by car?" The answer is that unless there is a requirement from the host local government to control outbound commuters, the VillageTown uses design to encourage behavior rather than rules to enforce it. If someone chooses to be a commuter, they are free to do so, but unless the site selection is poorly done, most are unlikely to so choose. The design of a walkable home-range, a strong local economy, and a site selection (hopefully) outside the commuter belt should be enough to discourage many commuters. There may be a few who commute out to the surrounding farms in country-town VillageTowns. Beyond that design, however, if citizens choose to live in the VillageTown and commute by car, generally it is best if no rules are set in place to prevent this.

It is important to explain to future villagers that the VillageTown is not an intentional community where the group makes rules that place a value system upon the residents. Rather, it is a free community where rule making is limited to enabling people to get along with each other, not telling people how to live.

It is expected that a portion of the villagers will need to travel longer distances from time to time, and for this reason good access to a major airport is essential. In some cases, this can be by road, but for other sites, it may be more efficient for the VillageTown to establish its own commuter airline that runs a regular schedule from the nearest regional airport to the hub.

After reading *How to Build a Village*, the mayor of a large city in New Zealand proposed a site within his jurisdiction. He marked it on a map; some of the Stewards had a look, and found its center was an under-used commuter rail station. The site was politely declined. Access to rail is helpful, but not rail so close to an urban center that the VillageTown runs the risk of becoming another bedroom community that empties out during the day.

One site under consideration in California is located on an island connected to the mainland by a tunnel and bridge that could easily be overwhelmed by new commuter traffic. The host city may not be convinced by the mere statement that the VillageTown will have no outbound commuters. In such a case, it may require the VillageTown to adopt and enforce rules. It's not hard to determine who is a daily outbound commuter; all the cars will be parked in the motorpool and the guard at the gate will get to know everyone passing through. If the conditions of securing permission from the host jurisdiction included a prohibition on-road commuters, violating commuters would be easy to identify, would be charged, and, if found guilty, evicted. Knowing that the power exists, such people will either permanently move away, find a way to move the job to the VillageTown (such as using Telepresence) or temporarily find accommodations outside the VillageTown nearer work, until they can sort out their career. This sort of enforcement is not desirable, but may be necessary in certain situations.

Pricing

Buyers want to know the cost. The price of open market homes will be determined by comparable market values. Parallel market homes will be determined by median income of the target market. In each village, open market homes and workplaces will be priced based on location, footprint (the amount of land required), floor area, number of floors, height of walls, complexity of roof, door, and window style, interior walls, level of finish, and amenities. In this way, buyers will be able to tailor homes to fit their budget. Because the village will be treated like a historic district when completed – meaning no further structural additions or conversions – buyers who typically would add on as they can afford it, instead are encouraged to purchase the largest basic shell they anticipate needing, and finish it later. For example, they may order a three story shell, where the top floor is left unfinished with only stairs and street-facing windows. Relative to the total cost, the cost of taller exterior walls and another flight of stairs is not that significant, but it allows expansion later as the buyer's budget allows.

Early on in a project, variables such as land prices, or infrastructure development and construction, will be estimated. We hope pricing will use an on-line price calculator that allows the buyer to put in their specifications to calculate what they can afford. Similarly, when the mortgage financing is in place, it is expected the on-line system will provide a finance calculator to specify the maximum mortgage for which the buyer qualifies.

Construction

The coordinator then explains to the buyers that almost all homes and workplaces will be built by the organizing company and its construction subsidiary. This is necessary because building 4,000 homes in short order (target is 12 months) requires precision coordination that resembles a NASA space shot or building for the Olympics. Workers cannot be tripping over one another, supplies cannot be arriving at the wrong time, streets cannot be blocked because different crews have their own priorities. It also means that the price of construction will benefit by quantity purchase of materials and builders who work full time so they turn up to do the work when it is scheduled to be done. The only exceptions to this will be some of the grand homes and commercial buildings where the organizing company may build under custom contracts.

Fun

The village coordinator should not be so focused on their own needs that they override the interests of the hundreds of people who will live in their village. Some people who start out as coordinators may find they are asked to step aside if they create too much drama. One of the core values of the Stewards is enjoying one another's company. The village coordinators need to enjoy what they are doing, and those who work with them need to find them enjoyable. People who offend easily or are easily offended will not work out well as coordinators. Manipulative behavior results in short tenure. The role of a village coordinator is intended to be a dream job, don't make it a nightmare for yourself or for others.

In contrast, for people who enjoy others, it can be one of the most fulfilling projects one will do in a lifetime. Think about it: you call people together, you help turn a wonderful vision into an even better reality, and then you get to enjoy the fruits of your labor. If approached with the right mindset, this part of village-building can be a lot of fun.

Compensation

Even though it is called a job, the job of village coordinator is not intended to be such in the sense of employment covered by employment law. The village coordinator comes to the job out of passion, not pecuniary interest. Yes, it is the Stewards' view that the successful coordinators should be awarded for their <u>successful</u> efforts, perhaps with some form of *credits* to exchange for a building site or even perhaps a home. Decisions on credits are made by the organizing company and depend on variables such as the number of parallel-market homes (the youth zone, for example, will consist almost exclusively of subsidized housing which means it will be built close to a cost basis; thus fewer credits are available). The accountants and lawyers will work out the tax and contractual arrangements. Success means completion, not getting half way. If a coordinator recruits half a village before the villagers and the organizing company finally feel they have had enough of that coordinator's dysfunctional antics, the errant coordinator will not earn any credits. From the Stewards' perspective, effectiveness is the measure, and relationships must be simple and set out to avoid entanglements or litigation.

Being a Part of History

History is a funny thing. When it is happening, few people notice. It is only later when the bards write the songs, or in today's world when masters- or doctoral-level students do their thesis on what happened, that the mark is measured. Calling a village into being is a happening. But when it is built, if done well, it may last for centuries. In corporate culture, planning for five years is considered long-term, as the demands of the quarterly report place immediate expectations. In contrast, older cultures, such as the Maori of New Zealand plan for a minimum of seven generations; about 175 years. The VillageTown sits better in this scale. It is humbling, but inspiring, to consider one's work in this context.

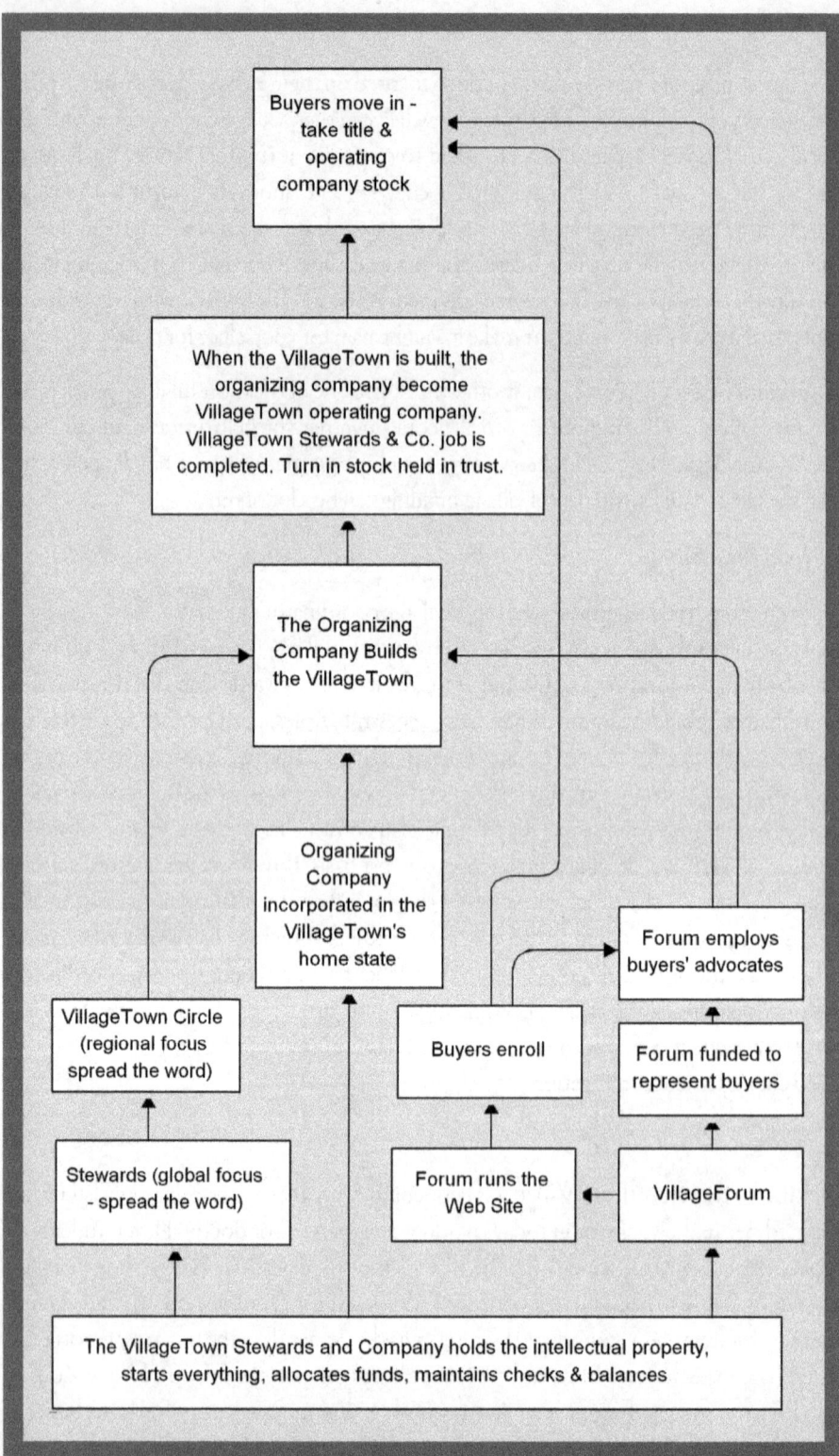

Buyers move in - take title & operating company stock

When the VillageTown is built, the organizing company become VillageTown operating company. VillageTown Stewards & Co. job is completed. Turn in stock held in trust.

The Organizing Company Builds the VillageTown

Organizing Company incorporated in the VillageTown's home state

VillageTown Circle (regional focus spread the word)

Forum employs buyers' advocates

Buyers enroll

Forum funded to represent buyers

Stewards (global focus - spread the word)

Forum runs the Web Site

VillageForum

The VillageTown Stewards and Company holds the intellectual property, starts everything, allocates funds, maintains checks & balances

THE PROCESS

There are several ways to begin, and it ultimately depends on who or what steps forward first. The variables include the funding, the circle, the region, the land, the politics, and, most importantly, the passion of the people and where they happen to live. How a project will emerge can be driven by one or several of these forces.

FUNDING OF A THREE-STAGE PROCESS

Funding is secured by the VillageTown Stewards and Company. The first five million is the hardest. Before that, the first VillageTown must start with nothing other than passion and commitment. Everything must be done by volunteers who, out of their own pocket, pay what needs to be paid. Some funds come through book sales, but for book sales to be a significant source of revenue, the books must become bestsellers. After the first project, the reinvestment premium is expected to provide the start-up capital, thus making the future projects internally funded by an organization dedicated to the purpose.

Funds are required in three stages, with two stages involving lesser amounts of risk capital and the final stage being self-funded in the billion-dollar range.

- **Stage One** - $3 – 5 million. Buyers self-identify. A project begins when it receives funds to establish a named project. *Named* means a region has been selected (such as North of Auckland, New Zealand; Northern California, USA; or Greater Sydney Australia) and a project leader or coordinator has stepped forward and agreed to be the local face of the project before the organizing company is incorporated.

The budget for the first stage includes hiring top professionals to manage the project rather than rely on early volunteers. The VillageTown is a complex billion-dollar project. This team will engage experts in a marketing-and-PR campaign making heavy use of internet and viral (spiral) marketing to get the word out and attract prospective individuals, families, and whole villages to the project. During this stage, these people self-identify, but are not asked for any legal or financial commitment.

Dialogue is opened with local governments and interested local parties. Extensive preparatory work is initiated, including starting the bank and the insurance programs, and marketing the Stage 3 funding packages to the wholesale buyers.

The legal framework is written. The founding documents of the VillageTown are essential to secure a long-term future in which the people and communities of the VillageTown maintain control of their lives, their assets and their community. It is essential that these documents be clear, simple, and unbreakable, and that they attain what the VillageTown concept and approach are intended to achieve.

The planning process is agreed upon with the host local government and the tools and procedures to be used are identified. This involves finding or building a large hall to house the Dynamic Engagement process. By the end of the first stage, the target land will have been identified, the purchase agreements executed and the local government agreement on approval process will be in place. The site plan will include density, various building heights, and other negotiated general limitations and approval for infrastructure agreed in general, noting that specifics will come in Stage 2.

At the same time, the engineering and tooling work begins. Building a VillageTown is more akin to mounting a project like the Beijing Olympics than a conventional suburban sprawl development. It is most likely that few if any subcontractors will be used – with full-time on-site contract workers, there is more assurance schedules and budgets will be met. The tooling is designed in Stage 1, ordered in Stage 2 and put into production in Stage 3.

Planning in the first stage also includes specifications for the *intranet* computer system and software, identification of the public utilities (which may include renewable energy and closed-loop management of sewage and solid waste).

Stage 1 includes negotiation with state and local authorities for the school system, and similar negotiations with farmers to secure the permanent supply of local food.

By the end of Stage 1, the buyers pay a deposit into an escrow fund, refunded if the project does not happen. This deposit is important to separate the talkers from those who are serious; essential to establishing the credibility of the enrolment list.

- **Stage Two** - $20 – 50 million. Buyers qualify. The critical path of the second stage is to move buyers to their commitment point and to approve them for appropriate financing. The bank or equivalent finance institution will have been established by the organizing company and will take and process construction-loan and mortgage applications. It will have secured provisional placement of this financing in packaged, prime mortgage-backed securities (not to be confused with toxic <u>subprime</u> mortgage-backed securities) so that by the end of Stage 2, full funding is secured to build.

At the start of Stage 2, at least ten villages will have been named (their special character defined) and will have full subscription (all homes spoken for). It is hoped that all villages will be subscribed; however, the local economy requires at least 5,000 people in order to support local businesses. Estimating 2.5 persons per household, and 200 homes per village, this requires ten villages. Partial subscription in one village is unacceptable, because it means the villagers end up living in a construction site. However, if the subscription for a village is close to 100%, the citizens of that village, an investor or the organizing company may elect to fund construction of the unsold units as lock-up shells, so finishing work is done inside where noise, dust and the large-scale machines used for shell construction would not be an issue. When sold, those who provided the funds will receive the profits as a return on investment.

Described in more detail on page 221, the Dynamic Engagement process serves multiple purposes. Its prime purpose is to secure character and authenticity that comes when the people who live with the results are engaged with the planning – where they take the lead, and the professional advisors are there to provide them support. Its second purpose is to generate a plan to secure permits. The method is similar to what the professionals call *charette*, where a scale model of the site sets out the location of everything. The participants are introduced to a *language* developed by Christopher Alexander's team called *A Pattern Language*. The problem with Alexander's book is its lack of accessibility – it's thick, both literally and in access. This is solved by reducing the patterns to business-card-sized *fridge magnets* that allow the group to become fluent in the language of planning their own village. By the end of the process, each village will have been set out on a 100:1 scale model that can be reduced to conventional paper plans required by local authorities for approval. In this way, therefore, the application for permits will be precise – what you see is what you get, with the further understanding that once locked, there will be no significant changes. This latter condition makes it much easier to secure approval, since local-government planners need not write complex, future-proofing conditions.

Also in Stage 2, the land will be prepared. This will vary greatly depending on circumstances, and this variable will have a large impact on the budget. Some manufacturing facilities are required to build the VillageTown; these must be built. Some public utilities may need to be installed for construction. The road base must be in, even if they will not be paved (sealed) until the heavy equipment has left.

- **Stage Three** - $1 – 2 billion. Construction. Unlike the first two stages that require start-up investment capital, the bulk of the project is self-funded. In essence, each buyer's financing on their home is pooled by the bank so all will realize substantial efficiencies of scale that stay with the VillageTown. If the median mortgage is for $250,000 and there are 4,000 homes built, this works out to $1 billion. These funds come through the VillageTown bank that issues progress payments in the same way any construction loan is structured.

The primary activity of the third stage is construction. Presuming all villages achieved full subscription, the projects would have a hub (the industrial park) for some processes, such as mold-making and batch-processing of bulk materials. It also will run parallel job sites with their own equipment for construction. In Stage 1, the engineers would have determined how many buildings each project can construct in 12 months based on the investment in tooling. If one mobile factory can build 200 buildings in a year, then there would be 20 such factories. If it can turn out a full village in 6 months, then ten mobile factories and teams would be required.

There are many benefits to rapid-build, but the compelling requirement has to do with the local economy. To make a profit and stay in business, many of the local businesses require a certain critical mass of customers. Thus, in a matter of weeks after opening, not years or decades, the villages need to be fully populated. This of course is not unprecedented. At noon on 22 April 1889, the cities of Guthrie and Oklahoma City in the United States were bare land. By sunset each had a population of 10,000. According to Harper's Weekly*, "*In that time streets had been laid out, town lots staked off, and steps taken toward the formation of a municipal government.*" While the Oklahoma land rush happened in a day, and the VillageTown process is expected to take three years, it is a useful reminder that with good planning and clear intent, people can make things happen rapidly. This of course is not to compare the rather bland results of the land rush with the more comprehensive intentions of the VillageTown – they are very different concepts for development.

In addition to construction, the roads are finished (and paved when the construction equipment leaves), utilities installed, and public facilities in the greenbelt and the industrial park built. The balance of the industrial park is built in accordance with the needs of its tenants, with un-leased space built to shell-specifications only.

The implementation plan may be staggered to enable some villages to be occupied prior to the 12-month deadline. These decisions are made by the engineers who write the complex plan required to keep on schedule. Construction is expected to run 24 hours a day, seven days a week, with workers living in dormitory housing much like those who work on oil rigs or in the mines of Australia's Outback.

IF THE LAND COMES FIRST

There are jurisdictions where building is simple, but in the most beautiful places, the local governments sometimes become bastions of complexity with thick volumes of regulations, complex procedures and time-killing processes that earn the word bureaucracy a bad name.

The disadvantage of buying land before securing an agreement with the host local government is the shift from policy to bureaucracy. A VillageTown is an attractive boon for most local governments. It has minimal adverse impact on the neighbors, the roads, the infrastructure, or the taxpayers. It brings construction jobs and an ongoing economic engine that is not dependent on the regional economy. Thus, it can be expected that once local elected officials understand the idea, they will offer concessions to win the VillageTown for their jurisdiction. Rather than seek tax breaks or other concessions that burden the host's taxpayers, the VillageTown will ask that as policy makers, the elected

*   Harper's Weekly 33 (May 18, 1889): 391-94

officials commit to a different way of doing business that protects the local community, but frees the process from the downtime and circular time that hurt the outcome.

If the land has already been acquired and the VillageTown commits to building there, political leverage may be lost. The process then shifts to the bureaucracy where appointed staff have procedures in place designed for the adversarial developer-versus-the-public proposed developments. The official's job is to protect the public from the excesses of the developer whose job is to make a profit. The problem comes when the profit is not made through *wealth creation*, but is made instead through *wealth conversion*. Conversion is what accountants call *externalized costing*, where someone else, usually the taxpayer or general public, pays for the impact costs of development or suffers loss of amenities. Unfortunately, such adversarial processes, established by policy and implemented by officials to manage or control traditional development, are not helpful for the VillageTown concept and approach. This is because the VillageTown uses a planning model that is fundamentally based on creating alignment between the project and the public interest.

There are times when the land will be there, and the conditions will be right for its use. In some cases, it will be owned by a person of good will who loves the idea of the VillageTown and is prepared to structure its sale to work within the three-stage funding. In other cases, it will be a failed conventional real-estate development that collapsed when the market and funding sources dried up. Or, it may work when surplus government land is placed on the market. This is especially the case when advances in military technology change the location of land (especially coastal) needed for defense, although such land may require careful examination to assure prior use does not bring its own problems.

Finally, there may be land from brownfield industrial sites or urban redevelopment where a local government has taken charge and is seeking a better solution. In all these cases, it is is better that the VillageTown not commit to the land until it has come to an accord with the host local government.

This is the main Town Hall building for Auckland Council. Every floor contains the desks of civil servants who control local government. The face of local government can be daunting, yet nothing will happen without securing its permission. Thus, the first question to ask is: *If it looks daunting, is it easier to go somewhere else?* Of course, this is not supposed to be the purpose of local government, but sometimes it is. Eventually, local governments will compete to win a VillageTown, but not for the first project. Pick the jurisdiction most likely to help make it happen.

The Key - Local Government Approval

No matter how great an idea a VillageTown may be, or how many people are ready to sign up, nothing will happen without the permission of local and sometimes state authorities. In almost all circumstances, the land use will need to be changed. It would be most unlikely that the zoning will permit a development of this magnitude, especially with its mixed-use planning principles - people living and working in close proximity. Matters such as car-free design will prove challenging, as most land-use planning presumes a driving home-range. The proposal for the VillageTown to implement advanced water, multi-pipe waste-water systems, innovative solid-waste handling, energy systems, and other technologies will be new for the host jurisdiction. And then, the desire to get it all done in months, not years, may be a bit challenging for the typical local-government official.

It is important that these permissions, consents, approvals, licenses, subdivisions, and other pieces of government paper are processed with a level of efficiency generally unknown within the typical bureaucracy. Thus, it is most likely that the VillageTown proposal will have to begin at the policy level – with the elected officials who vote resolutions to set the direction that the administration then follows. The issues the elected officials will need to evaluate include:

- **Opportunity:** The prime reason for a local government to host a VillageTown is its benefits. It brings a showcase billion dollar development that generates new income in the range of $250-350 million per annum. Yet it does this without the adverse impact of traffic, road use and congestion, or the cross-boundary conflicts of noise and lights, and it not only pays its own way, but adds to the local government coffers.

- **Requirements:** The time frame, scope and home-range of VillageTown is unlikely to fit the business-as-usual procedures of the host government. Because it does not use a developer, it lacks the profit incentive to slog through years of bureaucracy to win the prize. Thus, if the local government cannot agree to a highly efficient and effective process of approval (without compromising the principles of protection inherent in the government's role), the organizing company will look elsewhere.

- **Speed:** Because the development is funded by the buyers' construction loans, time is of the essence. If possible, all approvals should be granted in 3 months or less. Then once construction begins it must run 24/7 under large moveable structures that provide lights and weather protection. This means inspections at any time and without delay – all of which is paid for by the organizing company, of course.

These matters are easier for the elected officials to resolve because the VillageTown principles and plan are intentionally aligned with the purpose and function of local government.

BACKGROUND: ORIGIN OF VILLAGETOWN PLANNING PRINCIPLES

In New Zealand, the Resource Management Act (RMA), its national zoning law, states its purpose is to enable people and communities to provide for their social, economic and cultural wellbeing while protecting the environment for present and future generations.

The actual text of the purpose of the Resource Management Act 1991 reads:

The purpose of this Act is to promote the sustainable management of natural and physical resources.

In this Act, sustainable management means managing the use, development, and protection of natural and physical resources in a way, or at a rate, which enables people and communities to provide for their social, economic, and cultural well-being and for their health and safety while—

(a) sustaining the potential of natural and physical resources (excluding minerals) to meet the reasonably foreseeable needs of future generations; and

(b) safeguarding the life-supporting capacity of air, water, soil, and ecosystems; and

(c) avoiding, remedying, or mitigating any adverse effects of activities on the environment.

The New Zealand-based Stewards pondered the challenge of the RMA. While the law spoke about enabling people and communities, in practice it seemed to enable the developer's planners to argue with the local government's planners that the adverse effects of the proposal would be minor, and if the parties disagreed, for that same argument to be put forward in a special Environment Court. The people were generally left out of the equation unless they were prepared to spend hundreds of thousands of dollars on lawyers and their own expert witnesses. We asked, *What does it mean to enable people and communities?*

To implement the law's purpose, it seems obvious that first the people and communities need to be identified and enabled. Then a framework would need to be created in which they would focus on their social, economic, and cultural well-being while paying attention to the natural and physical environment and the needs not only of themselves, but that of future generations. From this the understandings emerged:

- **The people** are the people who will live there; the villagers and the host neighbors.
- **The communities** are the several villages and the VillageTown as a whole, built within the context of a larger community that will host the project (such as the county).
- **Economic wellbeing** is the strong local economy and the legacy fund, as well as the surrounding region that benefits from the VillageTown's presence.
- **Social and cultural wellbeing** is understood as the social pursuits of conviviality, citizenship and artistic, intellectual, and spiritual growth.
- **Health and safety** is self-explanatory, but includes healthy food and drink.
- **Foreseeable needs** borrow from Maori, who speak of planning for seven generations.
- **Safeguarding, sustaining and protecting the environment** is self-explanatory in principle, but requires sincere commitment and funding to implement.

For the project to move forward, the host jurisdiction must vote certain resolutions:

1. **Invitation:** To agree in principle that a VillageTown would be desirable within the jurisdiction, and to instruct their senior management to pursue it as a top priority. In consultation with their senior management and the VillageTown Stewards this resolution should set deadlines. If consultation with the electorate is required or advised, the host would agree to initiate it in a timely fashion, with minimal partisan politics. This resolution may begin in the form of what is sometimes called a *Heads of Agreement* that outlines the general terms of agreement from which negotiations on details can proceed.

2. **Cooperation:** To agree in principle that the relationship should seek at all times to be amicable and cooperative, understanding that the intent of all parties is to align the jurisdiction's public interest with the VillageTown's future citizens public interest – in other words, no inherently adversarial relationship.

3. **Acceleration:** To agree to the importance of providing all approvals in minimum time and with minimal costs going for regulatory (as opposed to valued) studies, reports, etc. Such an agreement would vary state by state, as some governments establish onerous regulations as a way of slowing down conventional adversarial development. Unintentionally, such regulations can bar good ideas because of their prescriptive nature. Where appropriate, the host jurisdiction handles the regulatory applications.

4. **Allocation:** To negotiate and agree on detailed terms that will form an ongoing contract between the VillageTown and the jurisdiction. This may include agreements on matters of authority over, and payment for, services that may normally be provided to localities by the jurisdiction but not wanted by and therefore not provided to the VillageTown. These may include public utilities, use of existing schools, public-safety services, etc. This also should include an agreement on decision making and taxation so there is no overlap of decision making or taxation/fees/rates in areas where the VillageTown intends to manage its own affairs, and is justified in doing so because of the services the VillageTown provides internally using its own resources.

5. **Collaboration:** To agree on areas where the VillageTown may install larger systems as a joint venture with the jurisdiction and to agree on cost sharing. For example, the VillageTown may propose a recycling-and-solid-waste-disposal system that is better than what the host jurisdiction has, and they may prefer to have the VillageTown take over the service for the whole jurisdiction.

6. **Concession:** Often small developments are required to make payments to the local government to secure permission, while the opposite happens when local governments compete to win a large project – they make concessions. The VillageTown fits in the latter category, but seeks cooperation and efficiency rather than cash. It will pay its own way. Other concessions, such as land set aside for parks and open space, affordable housing, elder housing, health care services, and similar concessions will not be paid for

TUTORIAL ON POLICY: REDEFINING THE WORKING RELATIONSHIP

Nothing gets done without permission from the host local government and other officials who must give their stamp of approval. Ironically, those regions most committed to sustainable development will be the most difficult to work with as permission for the most sustainable of developments is sought. For this reason, the fundamental basis of permission must be understood and, if necessary, challenged at a policy level.

On page 221, the Dynamic Engagement process is described in some detail. At a policy level, it seeks to find a better way to engage all of the interested parties to achieve the outcome of a VillageTown in their jurisdiction. It does not begin until the policy makers for that jurisdiction have committed to both the idea and the process to get the VillageTown approved and built. To do that, it examines the fundamental purpose of local government and seeks to clarify distinctions that sometimes become blurred.

Policy vs Procedure: It's disturbing to visit some local governments and observe how the employees act as if they are the government. They develop such a stake in what happens that sometimes they regard elected officials and a vocal citizenry as obstacles to overcome rather than the reason they have a job. Thus, it becomes important to restate the separation of powers granted to the elected as opposed to the appointed.

Elected officials make policy. Appointed officials carry it out. While elected officials may rely on the appointed officials for advice, they are not obligated to do so. The staff tends to work within a framework of policies and procedures, rules and regulations, that for them becomes what is real. Too often rules become more important than outcomes.

When an outside-the-box idea like VillageTowns comes along, bureaucracies tend to fail to respond appropriately. Individual officials may like the idea, but they see it in terms of prohibitions, of what cannot be done because of the policy, procedure, rules, regulations. At such times, it becomes important that policy makers reassert control. They are elected to look at the big picture, not to be bound by rules written to address other issues.

The VillageTown strategy examined the principles behind planning rules, and evolved to meet or exceed the expectations of those principles. Most rules presume a car-based development, but the VillageTown is not car-based – rules on traffic and congestion do not apply. There are rules on street widths written for fire departments; but a VillageTown is designed to be non-combustible. Rules focus on future growth and expansion, but a VillageTown is designed to expand internally, but to add no buildings, additions, or redevelopment in the foreseeable future (at least 50 years). Again, the rules don't apply.

We recommend a policy designating the VillageTown an exception to be judged on its own comprehensive plan according to the principles behind the rules and regulations. Only if there is demand for more VillageTowns should new rules be drafted.

because the VillageTown intends to provide these as part of its development. The more typical set-aside or cash payment to the jurisdiction would not be applicable.

7. **Facilitation:** To negotiate and agree on the terms of Dynamic Engagement as the way to secure a comprehensive plan that may require rezoning. Specific issues such as *design by fire truck* must be resolved at the onset. This may mean suspending normal planning processes or regulation, and in some states may require state-level approval including possible changes to the law*. It also may mean employing and training special planning and inspection staff to focus fully on the project.

8. **Implementation:** To assist in locating the right land and assuring that the price negotiated is fair to both buyer and seller. This can be a delicate problem if the vendor of a potential site gets wind of the resolution and tries to hold the sale to ransom.

In addition to these resolutions, to move the project along, the jurisdiction may decide to assist in the first stages of funding. If this is done, it is important that it be a simple, direct investment with an expectation of a return, rather than a state grant that comes with onerous requirements that make it more difficult to accomplish the VillageTown's purpose.

Details: Planning Schedule and Personnel Matters

Time Frame: When one examines the bureaucratic-approval process, one finds the use of time to be counterproductive. The actual work takes perhaps weeks, but the process can take years because of *down time* (the paperwork sits on a desk because the worker is too busy) and *circular time* (the paperwork is returned to the developer to answer an issue, the approval process stops, and it is placed at the bottom of the pile when returned). In some places, approvals can take a decade. Given the social, economic, and environmental challenges civilization is facing at present, delaying plans that address them is unacceptable.

Three months: There is no reason the planning process cannot be accomplished in three months or less, provided the land selected does not present difficult engineering challenges. Early on in the negotiations with the local government, this needs to be put on the table and an agreement locked into place. If the law provides for community input, it too should be adjusted so the objections and concerns have their day to be aired, but

---

* If changes to law or state regulation are required, it is recommended that they be proposed as a test case in which the state agrees to appoint a Board or Commission to apply the principles behind the regulations while considering different ways to accomplish them. For example, instead of *design by fire truck* where public fire safety means making the roads big enough to take big fire engines, the VillageTown would propose a town of completely non-combustible buildings (International Building Code Class II-a [masonry noncombustible]) with all rooms sprinkled and fire-fighting equipment (hoses, etc) permanently stationed on each block. Instead of a fire department, the VillageTown would employ a public-safety department trained both in fire fighting and emergency medical response, and it would provide them with custom-designed electric vehicles appropriate for rapid response in the urban core and the Industrial Park. The Board or Commission would consider such a proposal, and if in its opinion it would provide equal or better public safety than the fire truck regulation, they would permit it on a single-case basis.

FOR LOCAL GOVERNMENT PLANNING, A NEW CONCEPT: HOME-RANGE

In the second half of the 20th century, local politics tended to be highly centralized and local plans tended to serve vested interests – often those of real-estate subdivision and construction. Urban planning favored suburban-housing subdivision, road building, boulevard enhancements, and centralized infrastructure. Planners tended to come with engineering degrees and a limited and generally conservative outlook on social and environmental issues.

In recent decades, this began to change as the planning profession became an academic discipline of its own. It took on a more liberal ideology that began to focus on ethnic, racial, and class disparity, and then more recently on environmental concerns. This ecological systems-approach looks at a wide range of environmental factors, ranging from protecting natural systems to the carbon-dioxide-equivalent footprint of various ways to house and transport people and goods. Unfortunately, as is often the case when ideology takes hold, once the planners have fixed on what they believe to be good or bad, it becomes a challenge to introduce something outside the scope of their experience or thinking. This is the challenge facing VillageTowns.

Almost every planning document used by the industry makes the presumption that mechanized transport is necessary. Because few, if any, in the industry consider transport in the context of what zoologists call the *home-range*, one of the most important critical distinctions that could help improve planning is not part of their language or jargon.

As discussed in this book on page 23, the Home-Range concept was first coined in 1943 by zoologist W.H. Burt, who mapped out the territory that an animal covers to provide for its day-to-day needs. While the concept is applied to all sorts of animals, the curriculum to train urban planners fails to apply it to humans. This is a serious omission. The human home-range describes a particular subset of human travel – the territory covered by a community of humans every day. It is their every-day territory. A suburban freeway will have a mix of home-range drivers (commuters, shoppers, parents driving children or school buses, etc.) in addition to its extended range drivers conducting business as well as a smaller number of folk driving beyond their home range.

From all research we can find, no planner has ever made a distinction about or a map of the home-range of a car-based community. We suggest that such a map would show that in the typical 10,000-population car-based community, thousands of people were driving in circles, passing each other constantly (and occasionally crashing into each other), as they wasted time and valuable resources in an exercise few enjoy.

By isolating the driving home-range from the balance of transport issues, we remove ourselves from the car-versus-transit debate – from the dictates of those planners who want to force people to ride together versus the pro-car advocates who see car ownership as a matter of freedom. In planning a walking home-range for a community by moving all daily destinations closer together, we avoid the issue entirely. Cars and roads are still used for business, deliveries, and discretionary driving beyond the home-range, but walking home-range removes a whole class of drivers. Zero home-range transport is more sustainable than moving people in trains or buses, but people are free to travel point to point when they want to – at no cost, not subject to flu-sneezing folk in the next seat over, striking transit workers, or unfortunate mechanical delays that inevitably happen at the worst possible time.

The implications of a walking home-range are different than those of closing off Main Street and discovering the merchants howl because their profits are down. A walking home-range implies all the other details incorporated into a VillageTown. It requires an economic critical mass through a complex mix of local wealth-creating and wealth-circulating businesses. It implies a different sense of security, especially for the weaker and more vulnerable members of society. It needs a different location – closer to its food sources, but with no need for access to typical suburban amenities like shopping malls or commercial boulevard streets. It involves a very different concept of local zoning: microzoned, narrower streets, non-combustible buildings, and a different approach to managing public utilities such as energy, water, and waste.

This may be a challenge for some professionals, especially for those who allow their ideological values to dictate outcomes through the use of rules. For example, California counties that set out Urban Growth Boundaries are counterproductive when seeking to restore the single town-country economy important to the VillageTown's health, economy, and quality of living. It's better for the rural community to place the VillageTown in its midst rather than trying to shoehorn it into a suburban-sprawl zone.

Before getting into the details of how a VillageTown fits or does not fit their rules, it becomes important that the professional planners conduct a survey – or at least consider the likely outcome of a survey – that maps out the home-range of their residents. Then they must evaluate the impact of future developments that add more car-based home-ranges in contrast with the walking home-range of a VillageTown.

are not permitted to be used as delaying tactics in hopes of breaking the project. In the case of a VillageTown if there is a vocal minority that is able to hijack the political process for their own private agendas, it may make more sense to look elsewhere unless the host community can get its own house in order.

Policy Agreement with the Planning Commission (or equivalent): In advance of the planning process, it becomes essential that a protocol is negotiated and set out to instruct the staff on their role and how they are to work with the process. A core part of this is working in the Dynamic Engagement process (see page 221).

The most challenging part of Dynamic Engagement may be the desire of the staff to assess effects not on the spot, but back in the office where their level of accountability is significantly lower. Their job is to assess where any part of the evolving plan may have an adverse impact that must be avoided, mitigated, or remedied.

The staff is not part of the planning process; while they may find making a suggestion helps move things along, they maintain an arm's-length separation. They are like referees in a sports match – enforcing the rules but not playing in the game. The point of Dynamic Engagement, however, is for them to articulate clearly the adverse impact, so that the people participating in the planning process can understand the problem and immediately solve it. This is not an unfamiliar process for such officials, except that it usually comes at the end, when a planning matter is brought before the court, and the judge pressures both sides to work out their differences. At that point, and with great speed, they have the same dialogue that the Dynamic Engagement process seeks to move to the beginning.

Prior Pre-Plan - Certain aspects of planning do not need to involve the people who will live there, and those parts should be addressed first, but equally expeditiously. Most notably this involves an assessment of the site to assure that it is suitable, and any concerns, such as endangered species or archeological finds on the site are appropriately avoided, mitigated or remedied*. Some conventional issues, such as cross-boundary conflicts, or the effects of commuting are automatically resolved by the nature of the VillageTown. It is designed to eliminate significant outbound daily traffic and the greenbelt creates a boundary that separates human activity that may otherwise bother the neighbors.

Beyond negotiating these planning matters, the same dialogue with the host government should include specifics on the ongoing working and tax relationship as well as a clear agreement on concessions.

---

* In some places, such as California, heavy-handed regulations were adopted to slow down or block the kind of suburban sprawl that has transformed many of the most beautiful parts of the state into seemingly endless tracks of homes and commercial boulevards. The procedures do slow down development, but they also make it more difficult to do good development of the sort the VillageTown proposes. In such places, it may be necessary to go to the top, to the lawmakers, to propose that an experiment be tried where the VillageTown is held to the same (or higher) standard, but not to the prescriptive process to attain it.

Taxation matters

In rezoning rural land for urban development, the host jurisdiction enables the developer to realize large profits. Often they ask for concessions such as cash payments to cover future jurisdictional expenses, or in-kind concessions such as park land or reserves. On the other hand, to win an attractive development, such as a new corporation, the local jurisdiction and the state offer concessions such as land, cash or a lower tax rate.

Tax and fee neutral: Unless automatic concessions are offered that would be foolish to turn down, it would be inappropriate for the VillageTown to ask for tax breaks or other concessions that burden the host taxpayers. The odds are that the VillageTown will be in better financial shape than the host, and it would be wrong to exploit the locals in a bidding war to win the VillageTown.

On the other hand, the host government should not look at the VillageTown as a cash cow to be milked. There will be sufficient economic, social, environmental, and cultural benefits merely by having the development proceed that will make it a net-positive outcome for the host and its constituents. If a host begins to show greed, look elsewhere.

In some locations, fees are charged for new development following the theory that the development is not covering all its costs, and the taxpayer will otherwise carry the burden. This can include assessments to provide for open-space land, parks, affordable housing, road upgrades to handle more traffic, and, where it is a local matter, building new schools and increasing law enforcement.

In these areas, the VillageTown intends to fund directly. 60% of the land is designated as permanent greenbelt. 25% of the housing stock is to be designated as affordable housing for essential target groups, as well as elder care, first-time-buyer housing, and support for artists and for the disadvantaged members of society. As noted, the VillageTown will not generate outbound traffic that would cause daily congestion, and it intends to build its own schools that it hopes may be run as public schools. In many cases, the investment the VillageTown will make in these features would exceed the concession expectation.

No double taxation: In a scholarly article called *The Puzzle of Double Taxation: Why do Private Community Associations Exist?*[*] Professor of Public Policy Robert H. Nelson finds that *from 1980 to 2000, about half the new housing built in the United States was subject to the private governance of a community association.* He observes that in many cases the homeowners pay the association for services that are also included in their local jurisdiction property tax bill; thus giving the local jurisdiction tax income without needing to pay for the service. In some regards, the governance system of a VillageTown is similar to the private community association, except that it is more sophisticated and has a broader scope. It is a priority to

* http://www.independent.org/pdf/tir/tir_13_03_2_nelson.pdf – The Independent Review, v. 13, n. 3, Winter 2009, ISSN 1086–1653, Copyright © 2009, pp. 345–365.

select a final site where double taxation never happens. The VillageTown is not looking for a free ride, but if it intends to take care of its own services, it would not want to pay for duplicate services it will not use. Of course, in some cases, it may go the other way, that the host government finds that the systems the VillageTown will implement would be better for the larger community, and thus enter into a contract or joint venture.

Often, gated communities form a private association that duplicates services offered by the local taxing authority; thus their citizens pay twice. The VillageTown would negotiate such matters. The VillageTown will pay its own way, but it is inappropriate for its citizens to be double-taxed.

Consolidated tax bill: To maintain an amicable working relationship, it is recommended that the VillageTown collect all local taxes/fees/rates and pay a single bill to the host local government for all properties. When the VillageTown CEO hands the host jurisdiction a check for the tax bill on a billion-dollar development, one may expect the amicable relationship to continue. From the host government's perspective, this lowers costs as it sends out only one bill and is not concerned about individual property owners who fail to pay.

Other matters

Competition to win a VillageTown for a jurisdiction: The concept of a VillageTown and its walking home-range generally is outside the long-range plan of most local jurisdictions, and for this reason it may be better to begin with target region, rather than purchased land. In this way, at the legislative (elected) level, multiple local governments are invited to compete to win the VillageTown project. The benefits to the jurisdiction are obvious: a billion-dollar development that adds hundreds of millions annually to the regional economy without adverse environmental or social impact.

The problem with resolutions: In part this can be accomplished with resolutions adopted by the host jurisdiction. However, experience shows that when politicians change, problems can crop up. Unfortunately, when the parties become opponents, a resolution can be revoked. Insist on contracts. A contract is enforceable in court. The VillageTown will have the resources to fight, which should remove the temptation for future politicians to tamper with what should be an amicable and permanent agreement.

Securing rapid permission and approval

There was a time when folks would migrate to new land, mark out boundaries and build their community. The builders knew how to build, so it was a matter of the owner deciding on the size and function so the builder could find the materials and get on with the job. This is not how it works today.

At one point the number of white-collar-paperwork people involved (who build nothing) begins to become counter-productive. Too much money and energy goes to paper rather than product; too much is laden with added cost but not added value. Originally such paper costs were to assure checks and balances, but over time they begin to grow a life of their own, and become counter productive as they leach the energy of good projects. Money that could have otherwise gone to make a more beautiful and functional building went to pay for reports and approvals that contributed little of lasting value.

For this reason, we analyzed the many aspects of paperwork in permission and inspections in order to reduce the time and variables so that more money can go into making more beautiful buildings and villages, thus creating more commonwealth.

- **Planning**: Five-hundred acres are needed: 60% in greenbelt; the balance for development (urban core and industrial park). In planning this, care was taken to avoid adverse effects that stand in the way of an easy approval: traffic, noise, tax burden on locals, cross-boundary conflicts, etc. The VillageTown removes the planning barriers.
- **Fixed Zoning**: By implementing *what you see is what you get,* the need for complicated rules about future development are replaced with one page that says that once built, the job is complete and will not change. Limit exterior change, and design building interiors for future change – build an extra floor and no load-bearing interior walls. The VillageTown does not require rules on changes to the built environment – there will be none.
- **Subdivision**: Using the 100:1 scale, 3-D model (and possibly walking and staking the land in some cases), form will follow function rather than have surveyors arbitrarily staking the land based on a paper exercise. Unless there is some good reason, it is unlikely the VillageTown will subdivide land ownership into separate titles; there are many good reasons to keep it all in one. It may turn out that in some places, it works better to have only one title for all buildings, with the VillageTown granting contractual rights that are equivalent to unit titles, but without the red tape.
- **Structural Engineering**: All buildings (except the few custom-designed ones) will use a single bulk material (variable density aggregate is recommended). The exterior walls will be load-bearing and the floors made of full-span, pre-tensioned concrete. Thus, the structural engineering requirements for the VillageTown become less complex. This reduces both engineering and inspection complexities.

- **Design**: The Dynamic Engagement process is intended to enable the people and villages to work within a professional framework to design their homes and communities in a way that results in authenticity and a special character. The local-government planning officials participate in this process, not changing their responsibility, but changing the manner in which they discharge their duty. In effect, the sort of negotiations that often occur after a zoning application gets to court and the judge orders the parties to sort out their differences, is moved to the beginning of the process, where the parties engage in a dynamic process to find solutions that will receive approval and satisfy the local people and their representatives.
- **Building Permits**: Securing permits for 4,000 buildings promises to be a paperwork nightmare, especially if the host local government is a small rural jurisdiction. The VillageTown will seek to create a set of minimum-maximum specifications on items of interest in the permitting process, to allow a set of master permits to be used for many buildings. Alternatively, the application may be for multiple buildings to be approved under a single permit – as much as a whole village on one building permit/consent.
- **Inspection & certification**: While it is important to have active checks and balances to assure proper construction, it will be crucial to the VillageTown that the inspectors are on duty 24/7 and that they stay with the project from beginning to end. In some jurisdictions, this service can be performed by third party inspectors.
- **Materials, specification, and certification**: By using a single bulk material, mixed and poured on site, the variables are greatly reduced, especially as the variable density aggregate provides structural support, insulation, and weather proofing all in a single material. This also enables an on-site factory with on-going materials testing and certification to ensure quality control.

In some cases, the local jurisdiction has the power to make all of this happen. In other cases it can be more complicated. What is essential is that all parties understand what a VillageTown is, agree it would be of value in the target location, and then agree to work out as efficiently as possible the details that otherwise could slow or stop the project.

There is urgency. As discussed in many parts of this book, the issues of aging, economics, environment, and resources are pressing on civilization at this time.

Further, because the VillageTown Stewards do not keep the net profits of a development, but instead leave them with the VillageTown itself, they lack the willingness that a developer has to keep slogging through a regulatory morass to earn the hundreds of millions in profits at the end.

The fact that there is no developer has wide ranging positive implications that may not be fully appreciated by the approving local government. In essence, the project is one where a community builds itself. Thus the idea of protecting the community from the pecuniary interest of the developer goes out the window, and with it a whole set of issues.

TUTORIAL: THE THEORY OF UNANTICIPATED NEGATIVE SIDE EFFECTS

Think of a gun and a grenade. A gun points in a specific direction with a very narrow field of vision focusing on the target. In contrast, a grenade blasts searing shrapnel indiscriminately in every direction.

The theory of unanticipated negative side effects suggests that we tend to be unidirectional (like the gun) when we plan (focused on a narrowly defined specific outcome), but the effects of what we do are more like the grenade. The obvious toxic negative effects, such as a hand grenade with a 100 yard/meter kill range, are picked up in the design stage; the plan is modified or the idea is abandoned. The positive side effects are usually promoted by the marketing department.

However, the grey area of negative side effects is conveniently ignored, especially the closer it gets to the neutral line. This may be because some negative side effects take longer than normal human observation to have an obvious impact. Or it may involve complex interaction with other forces, so that the cause is not obvious. Or it is noticeable, but may have adverse effects on the career or earnings of the evaluator or expert if they speak up. This theory applies to many inventions such as money, medicine, transport, industrial-farming methods, product development and manufacturing, energy, housing, elder care, welfare, shopping, dining, recreation, and education to name but a few.

Unanticipated negative side effects are cumulative – slowly corroding quality of life. Over time the corrosive effects may be noticed, but by that time the plan, product, or practice has powerful advocates, is entrenched in society, and passes for normal. Bodies, communities or nations that seem worn out, damaged, tired, or suffering malaise are often victims of unanticipated negative side effects.

Today, in modern society, we have problems and challenges that were hardly known a century or two ago. We spend billions trying to solve social, medical, and environmental issues that were unknown in the past. However, usually we treat the symptoms, rather than going to the root cause. In a rational society, this would be deemed insane. In a monetized society, however, this is profitable to some sector, industry, or vested interest, and therefore deemed good business. The negative side effects are classified by accountants as externalized costs, and therefore do not show up as a liability on the balance sheet – instead the liability is transferred to the general public. This normal conduct in modern society fails to address the question of whether it is sane or not.

Before introducing any technology or processes into the VillageTown or its local economy, pay careful attention to any and all negative side effects that will have an adverse impact on the wellbeing of the VillageTown and its people. The negative side effects will not be printed on the package.

TUTORIAL: ON PLANNING, POLARIZING & FINDING A BETTER WAY

In addition to examining *how* the planning and the permit process works, it's important to understand *why* it works as it does, to understand what changes may be needed.

How bad outcomes come into being

Few people believe they are bad; they feel they do what they do for good reason. Polarized politics occurs when two groups of people develop opposing views on a particular subject because they view the subject from different perspectives, with different outcomes in mind. Their potential for communication then breaks down when they begin to demonize the other side – they allow themselves to become enemies.

The theory of unanticipated negative side effects on the previous page examines the problem of linear thinking and linear vision. Doing so opens the potential for a dialogue between polarized groups by asking all parties to consider a different way of thinking.

In the theory of unanticipated negative side effects, the obvious negative outcomes, such as the example of a hand grenade with a 100-meter/yard kill zone, are not seen as the major challenge. As long as checks and balances are even slightly functioning, some party will point out the obvious failure and something will be done about it.

The problems arise in the less obvious cases. Our example is the US Interstate Highway Program. Adopted by the US Congress in 1956. It set America (and then the world) on the drive toward seemingly endless suburban sprawl. It had a good linear intent. America had suffered the Great Depression and was pulled out of it by the largest war the world had ever seen. The economy was on everyone's mind. The target was clear: do not relapse into a second Great Depression.

As discussed above in the History section (page 45), VillageTown Chairman Emeritus Stewart Udall told some of us at his kitchen table when he was 89 years old, *"Most people today don't realize the Depression lasted eleven years. We got out of the Depression when the Pearl Harbor attack occurred – when we realized we were in a global war and we had to convert our economy....We supplied the equipment that won the war. That gave us faith in technology and it also gave us faith in education... There was a kind of aura about America's future."*

Consider what Stewart described: First came the trauma, the Great Depression. Next, came the crisis that ends the trauma; it ended in triumph – they won. By winning, they developed faith that which enabled them to win, in this case technology and education. Neither event was planned or desired, and the responses were reactive, not proactive. When peace comes, one has the luxury of looking back and deciding what to do next – to plan. However, that planning gets mixed up for three reasons. The old trauma remains and gives linear focus to planning – it becomes a rifle shot, in this case

216

aiming at the prospect of a relapse into the Great Depression. Second, private agendas distort planning – the scope is intentionally narrowed to benefit those with power. In this case it benefited the petroleum, car, and chemical companies that won the war. Finally, planning suffers the *aura effect*, meaning faith is not questioned, but acted upon.

Stewart was describing the theory of unanticipated negative side effects; no debate, no checks and balances, no examining the partial negative side effects. Stewart became one of the earliest to talk about those side effects and spent the rest of his life raising the alarm, but by that time the vested interests were well and truly entrenched.

Therefore:

Observe all and take care: Since side effects tend to be omnidirectional, the way to avoid unanticipated negative ones is to introduce omnidirectional observation, analysis and thinking into the process. Create a matrix of all aspects of human life and test each proposed component against the full matrix. Include the test of *a good life* in addition to the more familiar tests on the health of people and the environment.

However, even this omnidirectional test fails to address all negative side effects, when insufficient information is available. Not all adverse effects can be foreseen, and some may be sufficiently obscure to never stand out. The explosion of previously rare cancers suggests something is going wrong, but with so many new toxins it's almost impossible to isolate what toxic mix is responsible.

Adopt the Precautionary Principle (Risk Management): *Prudence* is the second tool in the planning kit. If you have the choice, select materials and processes that are time-tested; avoid unproven components that may have unanticipated negative side effects. If you wish to explore new materials or processes, do so in a prudent, scientific manner. Test fully before adopting. Do not allow profit motive to undermine scientific integrity.

De-polarize the working relationships: While omnidirectional analysis and prudence can go a long way toward better planning, before they can work effectively, people need to cease demonizing those seen as the *other tribe*. As part of a test of the Dynamic Engagement process, the facilitator introduced a model called *HBDI brain dominance* which identifies and color-codes four ways people use their brains. Participants were first amused to see how it confirmed their social biases (the participants knew each other), but then saw how the group would be stronger when those with opposing brain-types worked together by blending their strengths. It demonstrated the *wisdom of crowds*.

Align interests: Bring together the various groups who must live with the results. Put the here-for-the-duration-of-the-contract professionals in their place: they are here to serve, not to dictate outcomes. Align profit motive with the people who will live with the results. Align all interests. Take the time to do it right the first time.

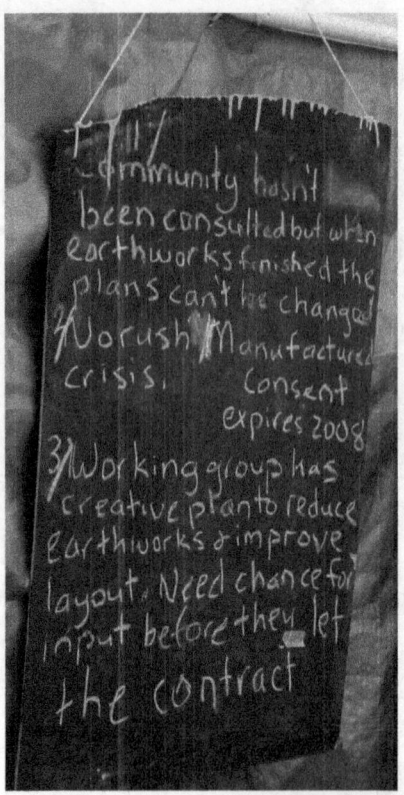

Property Development can rile the locals when they see that it comes in from the outside to make a buck at the locals' expense.

In contrast, during the market-testing phase for VillageTowns, two activist community groups, one in New Zealand and a second in Australia, invited some of the VillageTown Stewards to make presentations for their community.

As the elected officials looked around the room to see the locals in attendance, in both cases they said they were astounded. They said the most vociferous and sometimes effective opponents to development were not only in support of bringing a VillageTown to their region, but had paid the expenses and bought the books to present the VillageTown vision to the public and the officials. Several times officials commented that with the activists in support, it promised to be a completely different experience than any real-estate development they had ever seen.*

It's another example of VillageTowns turning real-estate development upside down.

---

* Both proposed projects are still on the books but are deemed too far away from a major urban center to be a good candidate for the first VillageTown project.

The sign taped on this guitar may seem like a bold claim, but in the case of this picture, the guitarist and united opponents actually succeeded in killing the largest development their community would ever have seen. The developers were completely misaligned with the community; thus they succeeded in uniting factions of the community that previously felt they had nothing in common with each other – until the threat of outside development brought them together as one.

Consultation - Listening to the neighbors

The fastest way to bog down a project is to ignore the neighbors and bulldoze your way through the planning process. The fastest way to get approval is to have the neighbors asking the government officials and planners to please approve the project.

Not only will the 10,000 VillageTown citizens have to live with the result, but so will the host citizens who will have a new VillageTown nearby. To align them with the proposal, their concerns must be heard and, as much as possible, addressed. Of course, many of these concerns are addressed in the core principles:

- **Noise and lights**: By surrounding the urban core with a greenbelt, neighbors should not see or hear the urban or industrial activities. They should see trees, fields and hedgerows. The greenbelt is an effective ways to eliminate cross-boundary conflicts. In addition, direct urban lighting downward; do not pollute the night sky.
- **Traffic**: By focusing all day-to-day activities inward, villagers should not need to drive. Thus, the usual 6,000 cars that can be expected from a typical development will not be part of the VillageTown. There will be some additional traffic for deliveries and the occasional villager driving outbound, but no congestion. The highest traffic count may end up being the neighbors driving to the VillageTown, attracted to its amenities.
- **Higher taxes or fees**: It is of the utmost importance that the VillageTown be tax neutral (or even tax positive) to the host jurisdiction. It can and will pay its own way, and it may be able to offer the host jurisdiction joint ventures to save on costs.
- **Catalyst for suburban sprawl**: The VillageTown would be as concerned as the neighbors that its presence would attract hit-and-run developers, and it intends to use its Legacy Fund to buy critical development rights to prevent this from happening.
- **Environmental protection**: The point of separating the urban core from the greenbelt is to establish and contain human activity so it can be made fully sustainable while creating a natural environment where Nature can thrive. The VillageTown seeks to be a showcase, especially in how it manages its public utilities (water, sewage, energy, etc.).

This is an abbreviated list of the issues that concerned neighbors raise. One of the first things a project needs to do, even in the VillageTown circle period (page 186) before a project is named is not only to identify the decision-makers and key-influencers, but to open a dialogue with potential neighbors. If that dialogue is successful, some of them may even join the circle as they see the value in attracting a VillageTown as a new neighbor. Then, during Dynamic Engagement (page 221), make a point of including the neighbors in the invitation and engaging them in the process. If they raise concerns, seek to address them immediately.

Be a good neighbor from the beginning.

DYNAMIC ENGAGEMENT PLANNING PROCESS TO SECURE ALL PERMITS IN 3 MONTHS

On the book flap of Christopher Alexander's *A Pattern Language,* the authors write "*At the core... is the idea that people should design for themselves their own houses, streets and communities. This idea... comes simply from the observation that most of the wonderful places of the world were not made by architects but by the people*". This observation is supported in a more recent book by James Surowiecki entitled *The Wisdom of Crowds: Why the Many Are Smarter Than the Few and How Collective Wisdom Shapes Business, Economies, Societies, and Nations.* Perhaps the best example of crowds or groups of people making better decisions than professionals is found in the jury system, where for over a thousand years, it has been shown that ordinary people, when brought together in a formal and structured system, supported by a framework of conduct and by professionals who know their place, consistently get it right more frequently than do judges. What is important to emphasize here is the qualifier "in a formal and structured system, supported by a framework of conduct and by professionals". Without that structured, supported system, it's a lynch mob.

Dynamic Engagement is the process whereby the people and communities are enabled to plan the look, feel, and design of their village and their own homes. They are supported by a team of skilled professionals including architects, master planners, engineers, designers, etc. The process is so named because it includes dynamic engagement with the approving local government officials, who are in the room to identify adverse effects, and to suggest how the planners may resolve them through avoidance, mitigation, or remedy. Because the officials are present, they comment on these evolving proposed plans in *real time.* Obstacles are identified and negotiated when they are set out, saving considerable time.

100:1 Scale model: Typically, plans are made on paper – easily read by professionals, but more difficult for ordinary people and communities to visualize and comprehend. In contrast, the scale-model plan is fully accessible. It resembles the hobbyist's model train set with its buildings, streets, trees and ornament, but without the trains. Such a model would be correctly oriented and have helpful details like moving spotlights to represent sun angle.

Scale Model Numbers: In testing different scales, 100:1 works best. 200:1 is harder to visualize. HO model train scale of 87:1 may be an alternate if you use pre-made train set buildings. Alternatively, projects in the USA may use a scale of 1 foot = 1/8th inch (96:1).

The scale model of 150 acres (60 h) will be large. To be manageable it should be cut apart like a big jigsaw puzzle where each village is a puzzle piece. At 100:1 each village is roughly the size of a full sheet of plywood. Each piece should be built on a rolling table and the tables should fit together to form the full urban core and industrial area when complete. If a full model of the 500-acres (200 h) is built, this could require a large room. 500-acres at the recommended scale works out to about 46 feet by 46 feet (14 x 14 m).

Pattern Cards:

In *A Pattern Language*'s introduction, the authors further explain about its sister book: "*The Timeless Way of Building* describes the fundamental nature of the task of making towns and buildings. It is shown there, that towns and buildings will not be able to become alive, unless they are made by all the people in society, and unless these people share a common pattern language, within which to make these buildings, and unless this common pattern language is alive itself.

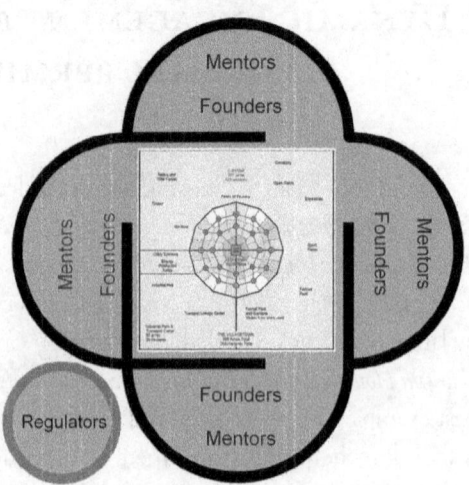

The Stewards agreed with Alexander's analysis and found his book to contain the seed of the tools required. Unfortunately, while the book was supposed to enable "*all the people in society*," its very thickness tended to make it difficult to access – it's a bit overwhelming. After testing several different methods, the Stewards developed what they call *Pattern Cards*. These cards are made using ink-jet magnetic paper known as *fridge magnets*. They are the size of a business card, can be printed using an ordinary color printer, and magnetically stick to a steel-backed whiteboard.

On each card, a pattern is summarized into words that will fit on the card. If the pattern refers to one of Alexander's patterns, it also uses that title and number. For example the detail for this card below can be found on page 436 of *A Pattern Language*, where four pages provide detail about the Street Café.

This particular card will appeal to a member of the group, who volunteers to become its guardian, the one who makes sure the pattern is remembered and done right. They will write their contact details on the bottom, so the group knows where to find them.

88 Street Cafe
The street café provides a unique setting, special to cities: a place where people can sit lazily, legitimately, be on view, and watch the world go by. Encourage local cafes to spring up in each neighbourhood. Make them intimate places, with several rooms, open to a busy path, where people can sit with coffee or a drink and watch the world go by. Build the front of the cafe so that a set of tables stretch out of the cafe, right into the street or plaza. Note that cafes on the sunny side tend to be busier.
Guardian   @   372-_____

Note that at the bottom of this card, there is a place for a name and contact details. Each pattern may attract a person who's passionate about the idea it puts forward. They become its advocate by signing up on the bottom of the card. They are then asked to make sure the pattern is not overlooked.

In the Dynamic Engagement process, one of the first tasks for the participants is to examine all the cards and then to organize them into some sort of order. They do this by picking them up from the table

and placing them on the magnetic whiteboard.

In doing this, they engage the others in discussion, as they try to determine what

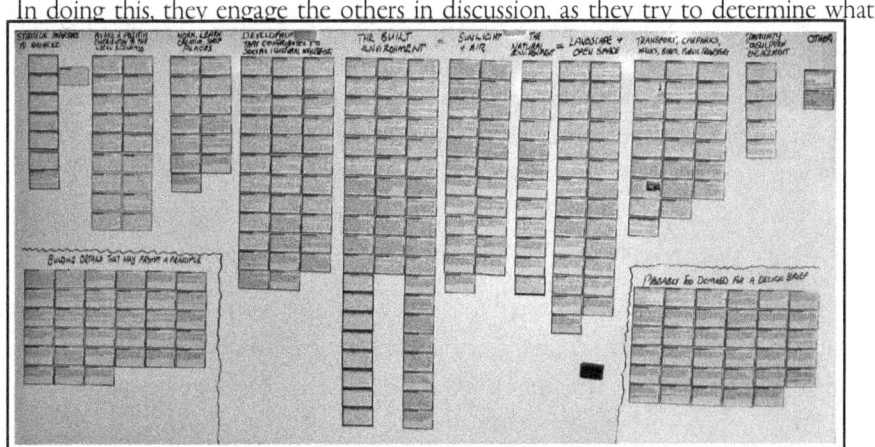

headings should be defined, and what patterns fit under them. In this process, it is important that the professional advisors do not take over – indeed that they refuse to lead when people ask them – but instead they seek to teach the villagers how to become fluent in this new and perhaps initially unfamiliar but easy-to-master language.

When the patterns on the table are all placed, the facilitators then engage them in a process of identifying their own vernacular patterns – showing them what makes a pattern, how to word it, and then how to have the support staff prepare and print a new magnetic pattern card to add to the board.

The facilitators then run a session based on the HBDI system or equivalent that demonstrates how people who think and work differently can either act like warring tribes or acknowledge they need each other's differences to work together.

After that, the real work begins as they set out to complete two critical work products:

1. **The Code**: Each village will develop its own Design and Environment Code that sets out the general look, feel and design expectations for their village. This will be developed in workshop mode, and then reduced to a written document by a qualified planner who sets the boundary conditions for both public design – the plaza, the streetscape, the public buildings – and the visible faces of the private homes and workplaces. A sample code is appended to this book on page 270.

2. **The Plan**: Each village will create its own 100:1 scale model of the village that later is reduced to conventional planning documents by an appropriately licensed or registered draftsperson. The plan will be precise and show all significant details, including the location and size of the plaza and all streets, buildings and other improvements. The planning process will be supported by model makers who cut individual buildings to scale for placement on the model.

It should be noted that technology is moving rapidly, and the Dynamic Engagement process may find that it uses the internet as a secondary or even a primary tool. Commercial virtual-reality systems such as Second Life may enable the same process to occur using software on line. As a secondary tool, so that future villagers who cannot travel to the workshop may participate, such virtual reality may be extremely helpful, especially if it can be coupled with telepresence for live video and audio feeds. However, its role as a primary tool to replace the 3-D physical model, still remains as an open question.

Not all 200 families are expected to participate in the workshops. Typically a much smaller group fully engages, a middling group is happy to observe with some participation (such as using on-line Internet tools), and the remaining people are happy to let others handle the process and live with the outcome.

The Code: Architecture that is Loved

When Christopher Alexander wrote, *This idea... comes simply from the observation that most of the wonderful places of the world were not made by architects but by the people* it is important to remember that some of the awful places of the world were also made by the people. As noted above, it is important that the people who will make the decisions work within a formal structure supported by the right professionals. Some of this support will come around the question of architecture.

The VillageTown seeks character and authenticity of the sort found in the most wonderful places in the world. However, it acknowledges that these places are often old and took decades or centuries to evolve. The VillageTown does not seek to be a historic replica, but to capture that essence of the wonderful places of the world. When one looks closer at those places, several factors seem to be important:

- **Elapsed time** – usually decades or centuries
- **Personal wealth** – discretionary resources to pay for beauty
- **Imagination and education** both of the individual and society
- **Skill and talent** of local artisans using the local vernacular
- **Stakeholding** in the community, where the individual or family commissioning the construction of each building expects to live there for generations.

Of these, stakeholding is the most important; a completely different attitude emerges. In suburban life one buys a home based on resale value – putting down roots into the land would be unlikely. In contrast, when you live in a place you love, you establish a deep relationship to place. You no longer owns the land so much as the land owns you. In setting out the process for a VillageTown, securing this deep connection becomes important.

Elapsed time is not a critical factor: Surprisingly, the factor people usually focus on – the elapsed time that seems to endow a certain patina – turns out not to be essential. The front cover of *How to Build a VillageTown* shows a lovely timeless pedestrian street in what appears to be an ancient Greek village. In fact, that village Oia in Santorini was flattened by a severe earthquake in 1956 and much of what looks timeless was built at the same time as the American suburbs. The same story is told in Germany, where American warplanes levelled many classic buildings in the towns and villages. Many of the timeless buildings standing now were built after the Second World War - as new as America's suburbs.

Conclusion: While elapsed time does add a patina, with the right intent it is not essential to securing character and authenticity.

Culture not Cult

In a VillageTown, authenticity and character come from the ten thousand people who will live there, not a strong-willed individual. This implies a very different process during the founding stage, where the principals who lead the project may not know how it will turn out, only that it will turn out successfully. The best analogy is that of an old ship intentionally sunk to form an undersea reef. The ship provides the framework upon which whole communities of sea-life will emerge, but the ship itself is inert; it has no ego.

These two photographs exemplify the challenge the design process will face, and there will be many contrasting images like these that will be part of the educational process of mastering the pattern language. The upper buildings are a 1990's California showcase of new urbanism architecture. Without a doubt, it is a vast improvement on the dying town that pre-dated it. However, when compared to similar buildings in the Spanish fishing/holiday village of Cadaquez, the cartoon-like architecture of Windsor becomes apparent. The windows all appear to have come out of the same catalogue. The details that an owner would add are missing. Cadaquez has functional balconies, in part because the pedestrian street is worth watching, whereas Windsor's home-range view is of parked and moving cars. *(These photos are a duplicate of those on page 34)*

Without such a framework, life could not grow, but the framework does not make any decisions. This is different from the history of many planned communities.

Over the centuries, many planned communities follow a common pattern whereby a charismatic or persuasive individual articulates a vision and then becomes the CEO to make it happen. Such places strive for *culture*, but often result in something closer to a *cult* – most benign and well-meaning, but nevertheless clearly showing the stamp of the founder. In these planned communities, control is focused on a single person, and several generations later it still can feel like one man's dream rather than a community that has that special feeling of character and authenticity.

The VillageTown seeks to implant the personality of each citizen on each private home and the community's shared identity on the character and culture of each village. This seems to be the only way to secure that most difficult of qualities, authenticity. Therefore, the perceived founders need to be the people who will live there, not the visionary who starts it.

The Challenge of Architecture and the Drive for Newness

Perhaps the most challenging part of getting it right will be designing the streetscape – what the buildings look like from the street. The people who will live there make the decisions, but they will need guidance. The challenge will be to get the balance right. Let us consider what might be called the dark side of architecture.

Architects have been criticized for placing too high a value on accolades from their peers, where awards are given not on buildings lived in, but on a portfolio of photographs submitted. Too often the professional incentive becomes newness, to do something bold, edgy, or quirky, rather than something that fits and serves the human character. On the next two pages, we provide another tutorial in which we quote from some of the more critical views about architecture, not to alienate the profession, but to reset the expectation. The VillageTown has no place for architectural vanity; such architects need not apply.

This 1960's showcase village in Reston, Virginia designed by architect James Rossant, a student of Walter Gropius, is highly intellectual in rendition. It shows little individual character of the people who live there, and it suffers by having a split home-range: walkable intent, but car-scaled.

The architect George E. Hartman observed:

The architectural profession gave the public 50 years of modern architecture and the public's response has been 10 years of the greatest wave of historical preservation in the history of man.

Or hear architect Christopher Alexander, who more recently wrote:

In the 20th century we have passed through a unique period, one in which architecture as a discipline has been in a state that is almost unimaginably bad. Sometimes I think of it as a mass psychosis of unprecedented dimension, in which the people of earth – in large numbers and in almost all contemporary societies – have created a form of architecture which is against life, insane, image-ridden, hollow. The ugliness which has been created in the cities of the world, and the banality and pretentiousness of many 20th century buildings, streets, and parking lots have overwhelmed the earth. Much of this construction is caused by developers, housing authorities, owners of hotels, motels, airport authorities. In this sense architects might be considered blameless, since in some degree the ugliness of what has been created is caused by new relations between time, money, labor, and materials, and by a set of conditions in which the real thing – authentic architecture that has deep feeling and true worth – is almost impossible.

But architects are not blameless. For the most part, architects have stood by, content to play their role as part of the 20th century machine. In many cases they make it worse. They guild the lily of commercial development with pretentiousness. Many architects have raised the designer-consciousness fashion of building to new levels, have invented absurd ways of thinking about architecture, have altogether poisoned the earth with an abundance of terrible and senseless designs which have few redeeming features. *

In a controversial speech by a critic of contemporary architecture, HRH Prince Charles spoke (www.princeofwales.gov.uk/speechesandarticles) in 1987 at Mansion House:

In the space of a mere 15 years, in the Sixties and Seventies, and in spite of all sorts of elaborate rules supposedly designed to protect that great view, your predecessors, as the planners, architects and developers of the City, wrecked the London skyline and desecrated the dome of St. Paul's...

You have, ladies and gentlemen, to give this much to the Luftwaffe: when it knocked down our buildings, it didn't replace them with anything more offensive than rubble. We did that...

I believe I have been accused of setting myself up as a new, undemocratic hurdle in the planning process – a process we are supposed to leave to the professionals. But the professionals have been doing it their way, thanks to the planning legislation, for the last 40 years. We, poor mortals, are forced to live in the shadow of their achievements. Everywhere I go, it is one of the things people complain about most and, if there is one message I would like to deliver this evening, in no uncertain terms, it is that large numbers of us in this country are fed up with being talked down to and dictated to by an existing planning, architectural and development establishment.

...architects and developers have the wrong kind of freedom – the freedom to impose their caprice, which is a kind of tyranny. Competitions even encourage them to come up with the voguish innovations and fashionable novelties that appeal to nobody but other architects. One prominent architect recently confessed, airily and with no apparent sign of

*The Nature of Order- Book 1 p6 by Christopher Alexander: ISBN 0-9726529-1-4 © 2002

shame, that some of his earlier buildings have ceased to interest even him, now that the thrill of creativity has worn off.

Well, what kind of creativity is that? To put up a building which other people have to live with, and leave them to live with it while you wander off saying you're tired of it, and then to put up another one which you will presumably get tired of too, leaving yet more people to live with the all-too-durable consequences of your passing fancy. There is a terrible fecklessness to all this, when grown men can get whole towns in the family way, pay nothing towards maintenance, and call it romance.

And finally, the full quote from Christopher Alexander again:

At the core of these books [*A Pattern Language, etc.*] is the idea that people should design for themselves their own houses, streets and communities. This idea may be radical (it implies a radical transformation of the architectural profession) but it comes simply from the observation that most of the wonderful places of the world were not made by architects but by the people.

Architecture often becomes a source of public discussion, debate and sometimes controversy. Timeless architecture has proven itself, but even then, when one goes to the extreme of Poundbury, whose design code is almost entirely retrospective, the professional domination of the streetscape fails to deliver the wonderful places that Christopher Alexander and his coauthors praise.

The key comes in his observation that the development of the wonderful places comes from the involvement of what he calls *the people*, meaning the people who must live with the results, and therefore call for design that fits their needs and aspirations. When a profession awards prizes and accolades based on photographs of works as printed in peer magazines, the profession runs the risk of not being aligned with the people who live in or walk by those buildings.

To align the profession and the future citizens, the citizens must be involved at the beginning, and as Alexander suggests, the role of the architect must be transformed from the artist who views the building as his canvas to the mentor who provides the professional guidance to inspire and guide the citizens to a wonderful outcome.

For the most part, suburban development does not use architects. Rather, developers pick from a catalogue of house designs that tend toward cartoon imitation of historic designs.

Rapid Construction: 4,000 homes in 1 year

Flat ground is helpful. Each village is a separate project; 200 attached homes need to be built in a matter of months, finished and ready to inhabit in 12 buildable months (buildable means no adverse climate that stops construction, such as months of freezing weather). It can be done, it has been done, but it means that everything follows a well-planned system. It requires each job site be lit and covered with a massive mobile tent, where work progresses three shifts a day, working around the clock seven days a week. It presumes a single bulk material for almost all buildings and it presumes cutting out unnecessary complexity.

While the final decisions will be made by the organizing company and its engineers, at present, the proposed approach will use steel forms laid flat on the ground, perhaps including hydraulic lifts rather than solely relying on cranes to lift the walls into place. The form will have a carved plastic (recyclable) mold inserted that shapes the outer wall face. Doors, windows and utility chases (for pipes, cables and wires) are installed, and then the whole wall is poured. It may use a sandwich pour with a strong first layer, a higher-foamed middle layer for super-insulation, and a top strong layer for the inside wall. This inner wall may have gypsum plaster poured on it as well to make the inside micro-climate drier.

As soon as the walls are sufficiently cured, they are lifted into place, locked together, forming a four-wall exterior shell complete with all its doors and windows in their final position. Then a second team sets up a hydraulic platform to pour the upper floors and optionally a flat roof that becomes a roof garden. The top floor is poured first. When this, including the roof, is completed, the house is a lock-up shell, ready for stairs, interior non-load bearing walls and inside finishing. The wall and floor makers move to the next building, working outward in spiral fashion to always have ground space for the forms. Each street- or alley-facing wall can be a different size and because of the carved molds, each will look different, reflecting the character of the person or family who will live in it.

Such a system works only because of the volume. With 4,000 units to build in short order, sophisticated tooling becomes essential. Approximately 36 walls must be poured and lifted in every day, twelve walls per eight hour shift to meet a 12-month schedule. If there is urgency, such as Christchurch, New Zealand where 10,000 homes were destroyed in an earthquake, the Steward in charge of that part estimates he could deliver 4,000 shells in 150 days with the right tooling and staffing. The Industrial Park becomes a critical part of construction both to stage the raw materials required, and to make the accessories such as the plastic mold carving system.

For people in the trade this may seem an impossible task. This is because the project is not like house-building, but more like building a major airport, freeway bridged intersection or perhaps the Beijing Olympics. It is a 21st-century approach to construction.

Matters of State and National Interest

In a curious way, certain aspects of the VillageTown have been developed in response to the failure of state/national governments to achieve their stated goals. VillageTowns seek to avoid entanglement in government programs and are unlikely to enter into programs that come with too many government strings attached. However, from the government's perspective, the VillageTown can offer hope and a way of solving challenges that otherwise fall to the government.

- **Higher tax revenue** - The VillageTown focuses on economic development in seeking to foster wealth creation through full employment and high levels of productivity. While it does this for its own commonwealth, it has the happy side effect of generating taxable income. It is estimated that the minimum income a 10,000-population VillageTown will generate is no less than a quarter-billion dollars per annum; possibly considerably more. The 50-acre (20h) walk-to Industrial Park will be home to tax-paying businesses as will the office-based and workshop-based businesses located on the village plazas and in the town centre. Where sales, goods-and-services, or value-added tax is collected, the VillageTown's local economy can be expected to be a significant revenue source as well.

- **General and Diverse Industry** - Ultimately, the health of a state and nation is dependent on the productivity of its people and industries. Small-to-medium enterprises (SME) are an important part of the national and regional economy, and have the benefit of resilience. If one goes down, not all follow. Just as Nature abhors monoculture, healthy economies abhor dependency on single industries. In the VillageTown SME are recruited for the industrial park and the village workplaces located on the plazas and pedestrian streets. Some will move from other places in the country or state, which may make them tax neutral. But the VillageTown Legacy Fund* supports new and expanding enterprises that contribute to the gross domestic product, create new jobs and improve the economic health of the nation. Unlike economic stimulation based on speculative bubbles, the VillageTown plan is long term, and it will become a permanent contributor to regional and national wealth.

- **Visitor industry** - Unlike tourists, who tend to concentrate in the best places during high season, paying to be entertained by locals, visitors come to destinations all year round with a pre-planned intent. They tend to spread out more evenly, not focus solely on the popular spots. They tend to give as much as they take. Because of its inherent attractiveness, the VillageTown projects that at any one time about 10% of the people in the villages will be visitors – coming either to learn about the VillageTown or to enjoy the social pursuits of the good life. When many VillageTowns are built in a smaller country or state, this can create a new purpose for visiting that state or country, and redefine the visitor industry.

---

* $100 million+ cash investment fund derived from profit realized by building 4,000 units at the same time

- **Lower state childcare and education costs** - The public life of each village occurs around its central plaza which is surrounded by adults in workplaces, cafés and shops, and by school classrooms and childcare for younger children. The intent is to adopt public education unless the school board or education department proves intractable, but to do so without burdening the state with the construction of a new high school and several primary/elementary schools. Instead, classrooms are on the public plaza, and sports fields are community use facilities on the greenbelt, with priority for students during school hours. Education on the plaza exposes children to the full breadth of adult role models. Instead of eating in school cafeterias, they will join adults dining on the plaza, or walk home to dine with their families. Classroom enrichment is possible where teachers can invite local adults to assist or to talk about their experiences in life. What for an elder is their past, for the classroom curriculum may be eyewitness history. As these students grow, they have the opportunity to secure part-time work in village businesses – the adults have watched them grow and will feel comfortable employing them. The same elements hold true for younger children in offering a more enriched form of day care. The plazas are safe for children; they can play outside under the watchful eye not only of their minder, but a thousand eyes of the other villagers. Parents will work nearby and can share child care if they prefer to de-monetize the costs. All of these qualities can be expected to reduce the cost of education and child care.

- **Opportunity for young adults** - Increasingly, high-school and university graduates find it difficult to become employed in meaningful, career-track jobs, to buy their first home, or even to afford to live where they grew up. For university students, educational loans are becoming increasingly burdensome – mountains of debt for an education that offers no guarantee of a job commensurate with their degree. The Legacy Fund managers work with its small-to-medium private enterprises (SME) to incorporate apprenticeship for those who seek a career path after graduating high school and internship for those pursuing a university degree. The SME companies are asked to develop a youth employment plan to assure entry-level jobs are available for their young adults. Beyond this, the VillageTown sets aside a youth zoning that offers special low-cost housing specifically designed for single young adults. Initially priced as affordable, small housing, they come with a restriction that when they are resold, the buyer must be under age 26 and prove they earned the down payment legally and that it was not a gift or loan from family or friends. Since most young people lack the purchasing power of their elders, this assures youth housing stock always remains affordable for the young.

- **Zero Unemployment** - Using its Legacy Fund, the VillageTown establishes a set of *standby-jobs*. When the Fund invests in local enterprises it includes a condition that they plan for situational unemployment to provide work for VillageTown citizens who lose their jobs. It also establishes its own stand-by work space, outfitted with appropriate tools and materials, that enable such workers to immediately take up productive work while they seek permanent employment. The intent is to assure that such workers can earn enough to pay their bills, their rent or their mortgage while still having time to look for work or retrain for another job. In this way, the damaging psychology of unemployment does not kick in; the worker has a place to go, work to do, and brings home pay for creating wealth. The benefit to the state is clear – far fewer unemployment claims.

- **Zero Poverty** - Similar to the zero-unemployment plan, zero poverty is a Legacy Fund program that intends to give a hand up to individuals and families suffering in *economic poverty*. The qualifier *economic* makes a distinction that views poverty caused by alcoholism, drug abuse or mental/emotional/physical disability as a symptom needing different protocols than for those who lack the resources, education or breathing space to move themselves off of government welfare. At the onset, the VillageTown organizing company is expected to take on a number of clients presently receiving welfare benefits where the individual or family makes a commitment to shift from a beneficiary to a productive member of society. The organizing company will arrange for transitional housing, training and support, and work with the Legacy Fund and private VillageTown businesses to develop a career track. Once operative, the VillageTown will provide its own safety net so that people who suffer some setback that otherwise may drop them into poverty – such as death of a loved one, divorce, disability or trauma – are caught before they fall and with community support helped back on their feet. This may involve housing as well as stand-by employment. This should mean the VillageTown places less of a burden on the state welfare funding.

- **Low Crime Rate** - *Small communities had a low tolerance for crime* said the VillageTown Stewards' Chairman Emeritus, Stewart Udall. In the VillageTown model, the core community is a tight, 500-person village that is active 24/7. People know their neighbors and they watch as the children grow into adults. In such an environment, delinquency – often the first stage that leads to crime – finds it hard to get a toehold. The VillageTown pays attention to its children as they develop a sense of autonomy and independence; they are unlikely to turn to crime. Further, the VillageTown is established with powers that enable it to keep the peace and protect private property. It protects its citizens from those who would seek to tear the fabric of society. While a 10,000-population community may find it hard to monitor criminal activity of adults, it's much harder to hide in each village of 500. Further, while criminal activity is shunned, aspiration is rewarded – crime usually takes hold when healthy opportunity is in short supply. The state and national benefit of such an approach is obvious and easily quantified. In the USA, for example, the cost of housing a prisoner is nearly equal to the median national income of an individual. In New Zealand it is over three times the median income. The VillageTown should result in lower police, court, prison, parole and home-detention costs.

- **Lower Traffic Costs** - No commuters and no cars in the villages means lower traffic-police costs (including highway patrol), lower court costs, and lower costs due to injury and crashes. It means less congestion, less pollution, and less wear and tear on highways. It means a very small carbon footprint and cuts the state's overall need for petroleum.

- **Teen health and deaths** - In a society that is not at war, is not starving and does not suffer plagues, older teens should not be dying. But in modern societies teen death by motor vehicle and suicide is shockingly high. For many teens a rite of passage is the driver license; a rite not relevant in the VillageTown. Teens alcohol-abuse and drug-abuse statistics are overwhelming. Much of this stems from the boredom, alienation and peer pressure that characterizes the *un-communities* they call home. In the VillageTown teens will live among adults, not be isolated as they are in suburbs. In the VillageTown, there is a concerted intent to make life for all ages engaging and interesting. Teens will have no need to drive and renting cars comes with more limits than taking the family car for a spin. When one examines the structure of a VillageTown it becomes apparent that one of the underlying benefits for all ages living in a VillageTown is the sense of belonging; it is this belonging that will enable more teens to survive to adulthood.
- **Aging and retirement** - *"Over the next five decades the 65+ dependency ratio is projected to more than double, from 18 seniors (people aged 65+ years) per 100 working-aged adults (people aged 15-64 years) in 2006 to 45 per 100 in 2061. This means that for every senior, there will be 2.2 adults in 2061, compared with 5.4 adults in 2006."** The demographic tsunami of an aging population is coming, and policy makers seem paralyzed. In many countries, elders look to a social contract where government provides for them. This contract is likely to be broken because of the sheer numbers now paying into the system who soon will begin to draw on it. The VillageTown provides for elders, with several stages of housing and encouragement to continue in settled work. It lowers their cost of living, eliminates their need to drive, and brings them back into the community where they become contributing members and where they are supported by social networks of friends and family rather than paid social workers. This works under a concept of de-monetizing society, where people take care of each other as a part of day-to-day life rather than as a job. It's worked for thousands of years.
- **Aging and Dementia** - Dementia covers a wide range of symptoms for which contemporary society is not well designed. As the population ages, dementia cases will increase at a time when government revenue is in decline. The VillageTown approaches aging differently and in a more humane way that lowers costs while increasing quality of care. When one builds a walking home-range, the cost of care for people with dementia can be lower. They are part of a community and the longer they remain in familiar surroundings with supportive friends and family, the less likely they will become depressed, the better it can be for them and the lower the cost to the taxpayer. If they wander, they are less likely to get lost or harm themselves. If they do require locked care, such facilities still remain in the village, near to those who love and remember them. This is another example of de-monetizing society.
- **A National Model** - the first VillageTowns will be more than a habitat solution for 10,000 people. They will also become national models and research centers to prove the solutions needed for today's changing world. They will have the money and the will.

* http://www.stats.govt.nz/tools_and_services/services/schools_corner/activities/secondary/teacher-our-ageing-population.aspx

How central/state government can help

While it should be possible to establish a VillageTown within existing state law, there are specific changes to law and regulation that can make a difference. These will vary state by state*, but the general issues will remain the same. The core reason to make such changes is to assist in the success of attracting and retaining residents. From a government perspective, the VillageTown can be an economic engine that solves problems rather than add to the burden of the state. Some areas include:

Immigration: This is especially important in smaller countries like New Zealand. A VillageTown visa would enable qualified migrants from other countries to qualify for a VillageTown residence visa subject to the ability to pay for a home and bring a business, employment, or sustainable pension to the VillageTown.

It would require the visa holder live in the VillageTown for no less than five years before they would qualify for permanent residence. This would prevent applicants who had no intention of living in the VillageTown from using the visa as a loophole to get into the country.

It should allow a business to be moved along with some or all of its permanent, professional employees. For example, if a company employed skilled engineers, finance and marketing people and wanted to bring them all as a team, the visa would extend to them. But the jobs that could easily be filled by citizens of the host state, such as clerical and warehouse, would not qualify on their own. Such applicants could still qualify if they could show permanent employment and be able to buy a home, or if they were married to a qualified applicant.

The visa would also apply to prospective members of the artists guild halls who will be provided with low-cost living and a work place funded by the development. Some of the world's great artists and intellectuals may not qualify for normal visas because they focus on their art, not their net worth. In some cases this may involve older applicants where the benefit to the state should be balanced against the potential liability, noting that the VillageTown will take care of many of the expenses that the state normally accrues.

Legalize *Parallel Housing*: In most states it is legal to restrict certain housing sales and rentals to people over 65. Creating parallel markets to benefit people under age 26, workers in the industrial park, essential workers such as teachers and lower-skilled, lower-paid staff of local businesses such as cafés, may breach anti-discrimination laws. Since the purpose of parallel housing is to permanently assist those disadvantaged, and to assure a complete community that reflects national or regional demographics, there may be a need for law change to accommodate this rather than try to find ways around present law.

---

*   When we refer to the "state" this means the relevant legislative body. In the USA it means a state government, not the federal. In New Zealand, it means central government not local government. In Australia it means both national and state. In Europe it means the national government, not the EU.

Legal Status: It is expected that the corporate structure should be adequate to perform all the roles the VillageTown intends, but there may be some benefits in special legislation.

Permissions: Ironically, in some states and regions, regulations intended to control suburban sprawl and reduce the adverse impact of a car-based society make it more difficult to implement a VillageTown project that will do a better job of reducing those adverse impacts. This is the case in the Bay Area of California where the regulations add substantial costs to the point where a good project such as a VillageTown faces unnecessary obstacles that are not in the interest of the people, state or the region. For the first VillageTown, it is recommended that rather than change the regulations, the VillageTown project be designated as an experiment where the regulations are suspended. Instead, establish a high-level authority to examine each element of the proposed project and test it against the principles from which the regulations stem. The standard should be equal or better than the intent of the suspended regulation – it is not the intent of a VillageTown to subvert the original purpose of environmental, social or economic protections. This is made easier by the What-You-See-Is-What-You-Get plan that once set, is not changed.

Tax Status: The economic engine of a VillageTown intends to head-hunt the best businesses and people in the world to encourage them to move to the VillageTown. However, in some cases, the state has adopted short-sighted tax regimes that make it less competitive. A project proposed for Slovenia is unlikely to get off the ground due to their tax regimes. This was best explained by an OECD report which said *When taxes on labor are introduced, a "tax wedge" appears between the labor costs paid by the employer (gross wage) and the net wage received by an employee. At a certain level of wage, a higher tax wedge increases unemployment and decreases employment, all other things being equal. Slovenia has an unreasonably high tax wedge; in the EU only Belgium and Germany have a higher tax burden. According to previous and our empirical findings we suggest that Slovenia could benefit from a reduction in the tax wedge.*[*]

The VillageTown may be an ideal test site for innovative approaches to taxation. It has precise boundaries, clearly defined citizenship, and a corporate structure as its foundation. We recommend designating it a free-trade zone and offering a low-rated or zero-rated tax on migrant businesses that conduct all their business and generate all their profits overseas. The employees would pay tax, but the businesses moving from some other global location would not. The same should apply to start-up businesses.

Education: The VillageTown would prefer to use public education, but wishes to change the venue, so the classrooms are in the villages, not on a separate campus. It may offer to pay for the buildings, but it may also require changes to the rules governing public education to make it compatible with village life. It would propose to be an experiment in public education, seeking to achieve better results at lower costs, where real and useful learning becomes paramount, not assessment or administrivia.

---

[*]   http://ideas.repec.org/a/ipf/finteo/v29y2005i3p229-243.html

Appendix 1: Project, Tasks, Milestones

Stage 1 – Getting Started

1. **Setup:** When initial funding is secured, accomplish the following:

   a. **Incorporate the Organizing Company** – Legal and accounting advice will determine the appropriate legal structure of the organizing company. Unless there are legal or accounting reasons to not do so, the organizing company will be recast into a community-owned hybrid operating corporation when the villages go live.

   b. **Office location** initially near the regional center, later in the selected jurisdiction.

   c. **Chief and Staff** – Leadership requires a chief executive officer of the highest caliber with a commensurate salary and incentive package. This should be a recruited position. The CEO runs the project from start-up to title transfer and windup, at which time the project and contract will end. Incentives encourage the CEO to meet the three-year schedule. The CEO cooperates with the VillageTown Stewards and Company to assure the project remains aligned to its principles and goals, and works at arms length with the Village Forum that speaks for the buyers.

   d. **Budget** – In effect, part of Stage 1 is to establish the confirmed business plan. Reasonable projections and estimates need to be quantified and substantiated to secure Stage 2 funding and to prevent surprises or delays down the track.

2. **Core Legal Documents** – Legal work is essential to establish the right founding instrument to assure the VillageTown is able to run its own affairs in accordance with its own standards. Corporate or land law provides this more effectively than relying on local government law. In the absence of empowering state or national law, one of the more effective structures has the VillageTown owning the land in a single title freehold, and then provides land to each privately owned building on a permanent and perpetual leasehold basis. In this way, it can establish rules from time to time, collect fees to operate public services and retain certain enforcement rights to preserve peace and maintain order. This legal documentation needs to start as soon as the project is funded as it will have implications on securing stage three funding that needs to understand governance in-so-far as it potentially impacts on mortgages.

3. **Target Market Planning**

   a. **Active recruiting** – Instead of passively waiting for random applicants, the first VillageTown is expected to actively seek out the best people and businesses they can find, and deliver the message that the VillageTown needs them. It is rare in today's world for people to be recognized in this way, and it may result in what might be called a reverse brain-drain. No matter how talented or successful a person may be, the drudge of commuting to work amid a gradually deteriorating general quality of life may be enough to cause such talent to make the move.

b. **Critical mass** – Because the brief includes creating the framework for a strong local economy, documentation of the right mix is important. Money importers are those businesses who sell local to global. They bring the cash into the community from the world. They will be businesses that work by wire and businesses that make something in the industrial park. The VillageTown project needs to know the right mix of how many such businesses need to be recruited, as some may involve specific personal invitations to persons and businesses that may be located in other states or other countries.

c. **Local businesses** – For the VillageTown to attract money importing businesses, it must be an appealing place, which includes having the right mix of goods and services locally. Proposed local businesses will need coordination support. How many of what types of businesses? The plan needs to know these things to assure it enrols enough local skills for a self-supporting economy, but also to inform applicants if too many of a particular skill apply. (If this happens, its best to introduce each of the applicants to the other and let them sort it out, rather than make arbitrary paternal decisions).

d. **Over-subscription policies** - If the VillageTown concept takes off, there is a risk of oversubscription from subgroups, especially Baby Boomers realizing their elder years cannot rely on government or global financial systems to provide. Plans need to include how to address sales balance to assure the VillageTown does not end up as a retirement village.

4. **Marketing** – VillageTown marketing should be elegant, punchy, nurturing, effective and fast. The VillageTown lifestyle will appeal to a critical mass of buyers. Marketing is getting the word out. It will go viral: good ideas sent on by third parties to their friends. Village coordinators will establish their theme and then feed their networks to get the word out. Build a wave of interest that takes on its own life. If done well, full subscription could take place in short order. The audience for VillageTowns is world-wide. With mobility today and ability to move to find a better life, potential buyers can come from anywhere.

a. It is essential that the idea capture the imagination of many, and that it has no poorly thought out parts that might attract criticism. This requires clarity about certain presumptions about the economy, social structure and critical mass that are subjected to professional review by incontestable respected experts.

b. Web – The website villageforum.com contains most of the important information and a rudimentary enrolment screen, but it was volunteer written primarily to establish presence. A professional web system makes the primary screen work like a vortex – capturing interested parties coming with all sorts of different interests and moving them toward the objective of qualifying them and then enrolling them in the project. The purpose of the Village Forum is to open a global dialogue on VillageTowns with the intent of honing the ideas to attract the widest audience.

c. Buyers are identified though media and Internet, including viral/spiral marketing where the principals give up control over the message. Experts in spiral marketing and social networking need to be retained and their plans established in a manner that is consistent with the strategic intent of the VillageTown concept, framework and approach.

d. Buyer markets will be segmented. For example Baby Boomers worried about their elder years are looking for a different message than parents seeking a safe and stimulating place to raise a family. These messages need to be articulated separately.

e. Women: Do not underestimate the concerns of women. In the testing phase, women expressed caution along the line of *this is our life savings... let's be careful.* Their questions were different than those asked by men. The organizing company would be well advised to employ women in key roles to assure the marketing messages address the concerns of women. This is even more important if the move involves migration to a foreign land where one's native language is not spoken. In these cases a village of one's own nationality becomes an important element of security.

f. Village Coordinators are recruited. Each one puts forward a different theme for their village and enrols the required number of buyers for it. How their vision for their village is presented must be reviewed by the organizing company to assure that the message is consistent with the VillageTown promises and offerings.

g. Marketing to politicians is different as it seeks both to secure a specific site, and also to generate state interest in the prototype. The project profile needs to be higher than that of the typical 10,000-population suburban subdivision development. The political marketing campaign may require local or regional knowledge.

h. A media campaign extends beyond the real-estate pages. It should get into the social pages, green pages, cultural pages, business pages and immigration and tourism pages. For this reason, the CEO and advisory group will need media-charismatic representatives and speakers to present the idea as worth doing. Determining the right mix of media stories is region-specific. Groups include:

i.   Housing media – real estate, architecture, design
ii. Environmental / Green / Sustainability / Academic

iii. Political – this concept appeals to both the left and right wing

iv. Aging Baby Boom (currently key influencers and decision makers)

v. Parents, education and youth – parenting media

vi. Creative Class – the cultural parts of media

5. **Buyer Commitment** – Committing to buy, build and move to a VillageTown requires understanding and building of trust. Few people could be expected to examine the plan and then sign purchase commitment documents, and the organizing company does not intend to use time-share type hard-sell. Instead, the VillageTown uses a gradual commitment process where the initial step is an expression of interest. Subsequently contracts and funds commitment come in appropriate stages, by which time the buyers have confidence in the program and understand their role in it.

However, it is important to separate the serious buyers from those who sign up but do not intend to follow through. At the end of Stage 1, we expect the buyers will be asked to post a good-faith bond to be held in trust by a fiduciary. This bond will be returned if the project fails to complete, or it will be applied to the down payment when financing is completed. However, if the buyer fails to follow-through the bond would be forfeit and would pay to the VillageTown operating company to the benefit of the people who did fulfill their obligation. Such a bond would have out clauses for good reason, such as death, divorce or bankruptcy, etc.

6. **Jurisdiction Selection and Agreement** – Once the critical mass of buyers has provisionally committed (no money deposited, and no locked-in agreements, only a verbal commitment and intention), that potential purchasing power is leveraged to secure a provisional approval and a contract with the winning jurisdiction that sets out the policies that will guide the process through to completion.

7. **Construction Planning**

   a. **Construction systems** – Christopher Alexander in *A Pattern Language* finds that a single bulk material that provides durability, flexibility, insulation and an almost infinite range of surface ornament in a fast-pour, easy to shape system is the best way to build the 4,000 homes. The Stewards' experts in this area confirmed variable density concrete is the right way to go. However, confirming research needs to work out the precise details and costings to establish firm pricing and processes that will be used in construction, including the local source of the bulk aggregates. Variable density concrete, slab or in-situ form construction and 3-D molds to form surface treatment and ornament on buildings are all proven systems. For the project to proceed without surprises, these methods need to be priced, then precisely set out and integrated with confirmation of which systems and processes will be used to assure the buildings are beautiful, the results meets standards, and work-flow fits meets the organizing company objectives.

b. **Molding systems** – The front face of a building makes a large difference in the visual amenity – it can be beautiful, boring or downright ugly. The secret is the surface treatment. When using poured concrete, a mold inserted in the form can be used to creative effect to provide almost any shape, including embedding stone tiles that are cemented into the poured wall when the mold is removed. The mold may come from a low-melt plastic cut by a 3-D CNC Router to produce custom carved profiles that can then be inserted in the form to provide almost any visual effect on the wall, including window sills and architraves. Their utility in high volume production needs to be confirmed in Stage 1 so the tooling can be ordered in Stage 2 for use in Stage 3.

Caution – One only needs to look at stamped concrete trying to look like a fake stone patio to realize the danger of bad mold systems. Great care needs to be taken to assure the result looks good and authentic.

8. **Financial and I.T. Systems Planning**

a. **Banking** – With a billion dollars in mortgages to process, it makes sense to start a bank (or equivalent institution depending on legal and accounting advice) rather than giving the profits away. Establish a retail mortgage bank to process the billion dollars of construction/mortgage applications. After the VillageTown is built, it is converted into a community-owned bank. Transforming this bank from VillageTown Stewards & Co ownership to VillageTown owned makes the package more attractive to the buyers – profits go to their corporation rather than an outside bank. The bank would become a full service bank offering both personal and business banking with overseas correspondence as the VillageTown local-to-global businesses can be expected to be active in overseas sales.

b. **Software and Hardware Systems** – When the bank is established, we recommend implementing software to track the local content of goods and services. This enables informed purchase decisions to encourage buy-local.

c. **Intranet** – An *intranet* is a private network of computers, not connected to the Internet. At one time, most business systems were closed systems, where displays connected to a central processor. Unless a system needs to connect to the Internet, it makes more sense to provide a closed system that performs a particular purpose. The *intranet* is a wired system that goes to every home and workplace that allows the community to manage its own affairs. This may include on-line biometric voting to support direct democracy with no election or referendum costs. In Stage 1, begin writing specifications. Actual coding occurs in Stage 2 and Stage 3. Some of it may use already available open-source or packaged software.

9. VillageTown Services and Amenities

a. **Public utilities** – VillageTowns will have the funds to purchase state-of-the-art, proven sustainable practices in the areas of energy, sewage, solid waste, drinking, fresh and grey water, and telecommunications among others. Some of the hard work in these areas has been done by permaculture experts and others in the green engineering industries. Best practices have many different models found around the world, and the VillageTown intent is to seek out the best and most proven to implement in the VillageTown. This is a complex area that will require a coordinating engineer.

b. **Food** – A core component of the VillageTown focuses on food. The food component involves experts in food production and in permaculture. Food will begin with farmer negotiations seeking contracts for long-term provision of food to the VillageTown meeting the VillageTown's standards. It should include negotiations to purchase the development rights on those farms, to assure they never get rezoned for suburban sprawl. It then ties into the Intranet software development to write food buying, billing and delivery software and then to establish the actual delivery systems of farm to depot and from depot to door. Finally, it ties into the waste recovery areas discussed above.

c. **Schools** – The VillageTown seeks to have public schools in the VillageTown, but not the public school campus. This is often well received because many school systems lack funds to build schools for 2,000 students moving to a new town. The VillageTown citizens and parents can be expected to want a higher involvement in the education of their children, and this may be part of the negotiations. The alternative is private education for the VillageTown.

d. **Guild Halls** – What would make the best guild halls and how does one recruit the artists? The guild halls are understood not to be a generator of money (indeed they will require a non-recoverable capital investment, similar to a gated golfing community where the developer pays for the club house and greens through a premium on home sales) but as a primary attractor to create a culturally enriched environment, that among other things, drives initial sales. Thus, they need to be identified early.

e. **Elder Housing** – The laws for elder housing are well established; one may build housing restricted to buyers over age 55 to 65. Determine if public funds are available for elder housing, evaluate any compromises accepting such funds entails.

f. **Youth Housing** – Unlike elder housing where discrimination is allowed by age, restricting home sales to young people may require more complicated legal work to not be challenged as breaching anti-discrimination laws – ironic, to be sure.

g. **Essential Worker and Affordable Housing** – Same problem as with Youth Housing because the intent is to create permanent parallel markets with little bureaucratic interference or costs.

10. **Conclusion of Stage One** - At the end of the first stage of the project the following will have been accomplished:

a. At least 50% of a 10,000-population project will have self-identified and posted the good-faith deposit – all within viable villages (each village filled to capacity). This means that at least ten of the 20 villages are subscribed. It is desirable that all 20 villages and the town center are sold, but the critical mass requires 5,000 people.

b. A jurisdiction will have been identified, and will have executed a contract committing to a site and to the Dynamic Engagement process to provide all approvals required to build and complete the project.

c. The site plan with density, height and other negotiated general limitations and standards will have been approved, complete with roads and public works to be executed in Stage 2.

d. The 100:1 scale model will be prepared and ready for Dynamic Engagement. This may be backed by an on-line virtual simulation of the scale model as well. An appropriate planning facility will be ready for the planning workshops that begin in Stage 2.

e. Stage 2 contracts will be in place.

f. The engineering plan will be complete and specifications for Stage 3 tooling orders ready for tender.

g. The mortgage bank will be established and ready to process mortgages in Stage 2. The funding of the mortgage-backed securities will be in place.

h. The business plan will be complete and will contain all details, documents, expert analysis and direction to execute the project to completion.

i. Stage 2 funding will have been secured and when cash comes in, the principal, but not the ROI on Stage 1 capital will be repaid. The balance of all investment funds, principal and ROI, will be paid at the beginning of Stage 3 when the mortgage-backed securities are sold and the cash is in the bank.

Stage 2 – Staging

Stage 2 begins the physical work as site preparation starts, detailed planning is initiated and the tooling to build 4,000 homes and associated workplaces is ordered. The target for completing this stage is set at 12 months, noting that this is an aggressive schedule. The major work includes:

1. **Buyer Commitment** – After a year of gradual involvement and confidence building in the reality of the project, buyers now must begin to execute contractual and financial commitments for the project to proceed. The financing process shall resemble that where a family buys a buildable section (lot) and contracts for a new home, except all of this is handled on a larger scale by combining purchasing power.

2. **Dynamic Engagement Process** – The Dynamic Engagement process, described on page 221 begins. Where and how depends on available facilities and technology. The process will be repeated 21 times, for each village and the town-center cluster, effectively laying out each village as a large set of jigsaw puzzle pieces that are fitted together to create the whole VillageTown. When it is complete, the results are reduced to conventional planning documents and the project is "locked". After that, except for correction of errors and omissions, it is hoped that the plan (and the built VillageTown) would not change for at least 50 years.

3. **Master Building Permits** – In attached housing, the number of variables in building design is more limited with the primary ones being non-structural. Rather than apply for 4,000 separate building permits, the organizing company intends to seek approval for approximately 25 master building permits from which almost all homes will be built. These use "min-max" specifications to allow for field variables without amendment. For example, instead of engineering a separate design for each lintel over a door or window, min-max would set a maximum span allowed by a specific engineered lintel, allowing it to be that span or less without a permit change. Most building designs will seek to minimize interior load bearing walls to allow maximum flexible use of interior space especially in placement of walls. These permits are issued in Stage 2.

4. **Roading and Infrastructure** – The actual site will determine layout of the urban core, greenbelt, industrial park and associated facilities. While the design shown on the back of this book calls for round urban inner core and attached industrial park surrounded by a wider greenbelt to provide a buffer zone for cross-boundary conflicts, the actual plan will be determined by the geography. Once approved by the local government, work begins on shaping the land. Depending on the funds available, some of the primary roads and plazas will be built, the underground utilities installed and work

begins on the outer urban core walls (which may be living walls made of hedgerows or soft adobe-type poured walls). The land shaping will also consider water storage as all runoff from roofs will be collected. All utilities will be underground and future proofed. The final surface of the roads may be left unpaved until construction is complete, as during construction the roads will have heavy equipment, whereas when done, they will have only pedestrian and ultra-light vehicle traffic.

5. **Motorpool** – Toward the front of the VillageTown a covered facility will provide parking, fuelling and repair for cars and trucks. Future villagers will state if they intend to own vehicles, and if so how many and what parking requirements they have. The motorpool will also provide parking for a rental car fleet to be run as a private enterprise of the VillageTown. Such a facility could be built in Stage 3, except that it may be needed for another purpose earlier, as described in this text box.

> NEGOTIATION ITEM – Projections suggest that in Stage 3, about 500 construction workers will be needed for one year, working shifts 24/7. The mobile construction platforms may have roofs and lighting to enable working at night and inclement weather. Consideration is being given to building what will become the motorpool to initially serve as dormitory or barracks housing for the one-year builders. Discussion with the local government may include making permanent the dining and bathing facilities provided for the workers to be converted into standby Civil Defense facilities in the case of a regional emergency. If these eventuate, then the motorpool would be constructed in Stage 2, not Stage 3.

6. **Industrial Park** – Stage 3 construction of 4,000 homes and associated workplaces will create an instant market for large volumes of components required for house building and furnishing. Where possible, the plan will seek to capture this market for new manufacturing businesses operating on site. For example, the VillageTown will create demand for 100,000 windows and doors, all to be supplied in one year, and to have a character and beauty higher than utility grade. For this to happen, the Industrial Park will need to be at least partially built and operational in Stage 2. In Stage 3, a market will emerge for soft and hard home furnishings, where the appropriate manufacturers may wish to take early orders and set up business in Stage 2.

7. **Industrial Workers' Village** – In Stage 1, logistical planners may find that one of the villages, the one providing housing for blue-collar employees working in the industrial park may need homes completed in Stage 2, not Stage 3, in-so-far as they will be needed to make the components required for house building. If so, this village, or a part thereof, may be completed as part of the industrial park project. This village needs to be designed in a way that discourages gentrification as otherwise, the higher buying power of future citizens may create an employment problem for the local industries.

8. **Freight Depot** – The ideal VillageTown site would include a rail spur off a nearby

railroad line that runs freight and could run passenger trains. The bulk material to build Stage 3 may involve ship-loads of raw material where delivery by rail offers a better alternative to handle the volumes. Whether by ship, rail or truck, a high volume of goods will arrive at the project, mostly in raw material form to be processed and made locally. It is anticipated that the industrial park, freight depot and motorpool will all be under roof, and possibly covered with a flat turf top to allow the surface to be used for recreational purposes. The depot will need to be completed, at least partially in Stage 2.

9. **Order Stage 3 Tooling** – Subject to engineering design in Stage 1, we are allowing a year for the manufacture and delivery of the tooling required to build 4,000 homes and workplaces in Stage 3. Subject to confirmation by engineers, one may expect to commission large scale platforms to enable forms and molds to be erected adjacent-slab or in-situ so the walls, upper floors and roof of buildings can be poured in volume, in place, in hours. Given the prospect of constructing thousands of buildings at one time, the economy of scale supports the idea of using a single bulk material (variable density concrete) poured using what is in effect a mobile factory. This tooling allows placing of heavy forms, pre-installation of reinforcement, doors, windows, pipes and ducts, and pumps to pour the concrete. The mobile units are expected to have wheels or tracks. The mobile units probably will be portable tents for weather protection and lighting so three shifts may work around the clock. They may use 2-hour steam curing instead of 24 hour cold cure.

In addition to the cranes, CDC cutting tables will be ordered to produce the molds that will fit inside the wall forms. These should allow highly detailed ornament to be cut in minutes (or be hand cut), to assure that the walls will be beautiful and distinctive.

10. **Food contracts** – Negotiation of the food supply and development rights contracts needs to be done as soon as Stage 2 begins, with payment coming at the end of Stage 3. Some citizens may want to develop CSA farms (Community Supported Agriculture) where the customers take an active investment role in the farm which is then run on a different economic basis, but with the same intended outcomes. Food systems also include waste management, and these systems need to be proven, and operational toward the end of Stage 3.

11. **Conclusion of Stage 2** – Everything will be ready for construction of the villages:
    a. Construction/Mortgage Funding – in place
    b. Infrastructure – built
    c. Permits – approved
    d. Staging and tooling – ready
    e. Temporary builder accommodations – ready and approved
    f. Industrial component manufacturing – operational

STAGE 3 – CONSTRUCTION

When all the ground work, both literally and figuratively is completed, it is time to begin construction. There are many reasons to seek rapid build. Paramount among them is to reduce the construction loan time span – the time when the home buyer is paying an existing mortgage or rent, while taking on the new loan to build their future home. Additionally, this reduces the risk of exposure to future shock while the project is in development. It also responds to the demographic race where by 2018, the baby boom shifting from contributors to system draw-down may create a global fiscal crisis, where alternative solutions (such as the VillageTown offers) need to be proven and operational.

Stage 3 work includes:

1. **Financing** – The organizing company begins drawing on construction financing that is supervised and allocated by the bank on progress payments.

2. **Construction** – Each Village will be built as single project, preferably in a way that the whole village is completed at the same time, to allow early occupancy without compromising resident safety.

3. **Interior Finishing** – As soon as the shell is completed, a second finishing team follows behind to build interior walls, install cabinets, utilities, flooring and so on. One of the unusual aspects of the VillageTown is the desire to have all exterior shell construction done at the beginning, after which the development is treated as equivalent to a historic district. This means very little if any structural construction is done after move-in. To accommodate the needs of owners who cannot afford everything at once (who normally would add on, over the years) the maximum house shell may be built but not finished inside. Thus a buyer may order a three story home in which the upper one or two stories left as a raw, lock-up shell where subsequent finishing would be indoor work that would not disturb others. This is feasible because the cost of upper floor structural exterior walls and street facing windows is not a significant part of the overall building cost if it is erected when the primary walls and roof are built.

4. **Special Buildings** – Certain buildings including the Guild Halls, Sacred Halls (churches, temples, etc.), public and commercial buildings and some of the mansions in the town center will be built by different teams using custom construction methods and permits, while adhering to the same schedule and non-combustible code.

5. **Curved roads** – The overall design shall seek to avoid grid design where streets are straight and intersect at right angles. This means that where streets curve, a building must be trapezoidal. As part of the amenity related to the artist guild halls, what is called free-base housing is provided to the guild hall member artists. This is a small

home owned by the VillageTown and provided rent-free to the member artist. These trapezoidal shaped homes will be built where the roads turn. Additional turns may be provided using staircases and light shafts. In addition to artist housing, these bend-in-the-road buildings may provide other low budget parallel market housing.

6. **Utility services** – The VillageTown water and wastewater systems will be built and installed with processing plants in the greenbelt. These include more complex systems than the typical development with multiple pipes going into and out of each building. Processing of black water will involve a closed loop permaculture design operating in the greenbelt. See page 106 for more detail. Electrical systems will be installed and may include advanced locally generated power.

7. **Utility connections** – Hook up of water, waste water, telephone, broadband including intranet (internal to the VillageTown), electricity, storm water collection, possibly shared climate control systems, and other utilities will be completed.

8. **Conclusion of Stage 3** – Job Completed

   a. VillageTown built, cleaned, ready for move in.
   b. Tooling removed and stored for next project. Tooling is owned by the VillageTown Stewards & Co as part of its licensing the organizing company. When the stock is passed from the Stewards to the buyers, the tooling is returned to the Stewards for use by the next VillageTown project. All contract workers discharged – some may seek jobs in the VillageTown or with next project. Note that while the corporate structure remains intact, there is no promise of continued employment as the function of the corporation changes completely.
   c. Books closed, taxes paid, final reinvestment fees paid, organizing company stock passed in by the VillageTown Stewards and Company.
   d. The organizing company is recast into an operating company called the VillageTown Council (VTC) with assets (other than construction equipment), legal documents and the bank remaining with the VillageTown.*
   e. Titles issued on properties, each accompanied by a share in the VTC
   f. Ribbon cut, the ceremonial key to the VillageTown handed to the caretaker CEO
   g. Three-day celebration, invite the neighbors, fill the plazas and festival fields.
   h. VTC elections held (this could happen earlier if systems are in place)

---

* Note: The VillageTown Stewards & Co maintain a permanent legal interest in the VillageTown for the purpose of protecting the brand. As part of Stage 1 legal work, a form of certification will be issued that establishes a certified VillageTown. The importance of this comes if the VillageTown later breaches the principles to the point where it no longer serves as a model VillageTown. It is difficult to imagine what could cause such a revocation of status, but the interest will remain. This interest may be held by the Stewards. In addition to this regulatory function, the Stewards will establish a network of VillageTowns for the purpose of trade and good will relationships.

Appendix 2 - The VillageTown Charter

This section discusses the founding document of the VillageTown; its *Social Contract*. It needs to be drafted by the best lawyers the organizing company can find. It is essential that it is written in a form that is unbreakable (to be so tight as to allow no successful challenge in court), flexible (to allow the VillageTown to evolve), empowering and just.

Instructions for the Lawyers

A 10,000-population community living in medium density housing with its own local economy requires a level of governance that cannot be expected to be provided by the host jurisdiction. Local government law is generally established by the state, and it is subject to future change driven by political agendas that can have adverse effects on the VillageTown. It no longer effectively works as a Social Contract. In contrast, contract, corporate law appears to be less political, more stable and provide more certainty and control.

The decision as to what law to use is a complex one. The VillageTown encourages active citizenship and democratic capitalism, meaning people take advantage of shifts in technology to run their own show rather than be part of the 20th-century economy characterized by power struggles between the boss and the worker, the landlord and the tenant, etc. When one is in a power struggle, typically the left writes laws and regulations that protect the little guy, and when the right gets into power, they draft laws that make it easier to do business. Neither dynamic is particularly useful when developing the legal foundation for a VillageTown because the VillageTown intends to be a complete community. It provides an environment intended to enable people to thrive, with sufficient personal connection that its citizens will take care of the weaker members of their community out of concern, care and self-interest rather than by bureaucracy.

The general sense of the VillageTown Stewards is that the strongest and most applicable law is contract and corporate law. Following this approach, the VillageTown citizens own the corporation, thus are its stockholders rather than its customers or employees. This sense is based on the perception that as soon as law goes near customer rights or tenant rights, it gets back into the power-struggle cycle where the state writes regulations that make it more difficult for the VillageTown to achieve simple active citizenship.

For simplicity, rather than change share holding every time a citizen moves in and out, it makes sense to provide one share per title, with voting rights granted to the adult citizens who live in the titled building. The share cannot be transferred independent of the property title, thus has no book value independent of the property. By granting voting rights to citizens, it precludes the risk of corporations or non-resident landlords disrupting the democratic process.

A potential difficulty in writing the charter arises from anti-discrimination laws that are written to protect the rights of minorities and disadvantaged peoples. The VillageTown seeks to offer parallel markets for housing. It targets groups of people who work in fixed-income employment, such as public servants, or people working in unskilled but necessary employment, as well as youth, artists, disabled persons and other comparable groups. It seeks to create permanent housing markets for these target groups insulated from the high-earning buyers who otherwise may gentrify a desirable community. Prohibiting permanent affordable housing was certainly not a target of anti-discrimination laws, but the charter will need to be carefully structured so it does not run afoul of such laws in creating parallel markets for affordable housing.

Another important aspect of the charter is to return appropriate community control to the community. As crime and delinquency statistics show, communities are now asked to tolerate anti-social behavior, live behind locks and depend on insurance rather than live in peace. In contrast, private corporations do not tolerate such conduct, and they are allowed to remove people from the premises and secure court orders prohibiting them from returning. The charter document must establish a formal system of checks and balances that protects the individual from abuse, but also enables the community to protect itself from an abusive individual. Instead of law enforced by life, liberty, property (execution, prison, fines), the power granted to the community should be that of forced sale backed by involuntary public auction and a court order preventing trespass in the VillageTown.

We believe this may work best if the land is held freehold by the VillageTown corporation and sold leasehold to the buyer with the lease conditions remaining in perpetuity passing both legislative and judicial powers to the corporation under a system of checks and balances. This belief is not based on legal training or research however, and the VillageTown will take legal advice on the question.

The authority to secure sufficient powers of local governance to keep the peace and run the VillageTown can be written into the charter if it becomes a permanent condition of title to property. But this can only be done at its onset. If at some time in the future a VillageTown citizen were to bring a case before the court that nullified such powers, it would be extremely difficult to recover them. Thus it is of the utmost importance that the legal charter be a well-written document that can stand both the test of time (ability to evolve) and aggressive challenges in the courts. While it may be possible to develop a prototype founding document for VillageTowns, at this time it is expected each VillageTown will require its own legal work to address the governing law of its host state.

This work must be done early in the first stage of development to make it clear to the buyer the terms under which the VillageTown is established. In this appendix the needs of VillageTown governance are set out, from which the legal experts would generate what in this section is called the VillageTown Charter.

INSTRUCTIONS TO THE LEGAL TEAM

Recast Corporation

It is desirable and in some cases mandatory that the organizing company be established in the state where the VillageTown is to be built. It will be a private, for-profit corporation established by the VillageTown Stewards & Co, which will hold the stock in trust. The organizing company will purchase the land. When the properties are sold and titles pass hands, it is desirable that the Stewards turn in its holding stock and new shares be issued, one per house title to the buyers of the VillageTown properties with voting rights by VillageTown citizenship (over 18, permanent residents). The organizing company is then renamed as the operating company, perhaps called the XYZ VillageTown Council (if that term is allowed) and it serves the interests of its citizen stakeholders.

Therefore:

Draft a legal document (known herein as the Charter) that sets out the social contract between the VillageTown corporation (known herein as the VillageTown Council or simply the VillageTown or the Council) and its citizens, that gives the VillageTown the power to raise money (similar to fees/taxes/rates), run both for-profit and non-profit operations, and to make rules that are enforceable.

Ownership and Voting

Each title to a building in the VillageTown comes with one share of stock in the VillageTown Council. The stock can only be sold with the building. Voting rights to the stock is by citizenship, meaning one vote per adult citizen of the VillageTown. A citizen is a permanent adult resident of the VillageTown, not a visitor. Students studying full time for over six months in the VillageTown are considered citizens if they are over the legal age of adulthood, as defined by the State (for its voting role). If this is technically problematic, adjust ownership so that each citizen has an equal vote. Corporations and other non-natural "persons" may own buildings, but may not vote.

Three Part Governance

The VillageTown shall govern its own affairs using a time-tested form of representative democracy that provides checks and balances through separation of powers. It shall have

- A rule making function (legislative)

- An implementation and operations function (administration)

- Enforcement powers (judicial). In addition to a judicial panel, this includes a prosecutorial office to advocate on behalf of the VillageTown against the individual (the public prosecutor) and a second office that advocates on behalf of the individual (or corporation) against the VillageTown (the ombudsman).

For Profit Businesses best run by the Village Town

In addition to the governance functions, the VillageTown shall run for-profit ventures and subsidiaries (collectively known herein as the VillageTown Company) that engage in for-profit business ventures that combine the purchasing power of the citizens for their mutual benefit. Some may be governed by subsidiary boards appointed by the Council.

Governance

The Rule Making Function (Legislative)

The citizens shall elect a rule making body of representatives, referred to herein as the VillageTown Board (or the Board). In a 21 village project (20 villages/1 town center) seven representatives (one for each three precincts) plus the Mayor (see below) with a tie-breaking vote only, is probably a good number, and these representatives will serve in an unpaid, volunteer, part-time capacity. The Board shall run under normal rules of order as conventionally used in that state or country, and shall speak by resolution.

The Board shall vote an annual budget, and has the right (by contractual terms on each property title) to vote annual fees that are the equivalent of taxes or rates. Elections shall be held every year with a term of office of three years, meaning two/three of the seven representatives stand for election each year. Any representative shall be subject of a recall vote at any time*. The elected head of the Administration (herein referred to as the Mayor) shall chair the meetings, but only has a vote to break a tie. The Charter shall provide that the Board may make any rules on any public matters of the VillageTown.

The Administrative Function (Executive)

The citizens shall elect a Chief Executive Officer (known as the Mayor) to run day-to-day business of the VillageTown. This shall be a full-time paid job with no tenure and subject to a recall vote at any time. If state law make this difficult, the contract for services may need to be subject to a rolling month by month review conducted by vote, or some other device to achieve the intent. The Mayor shall be authorized by the Board to hire a staff in accordance with the annual budget. The Administration shall provide all normal municipal services such as street and public building maintenance, public utilities, revenue collection and contract management, and shall conduct litigation on behalf of the VillageTown.

In addition to these non-profit services, the Mayor shall supervise subsidiary for-profit companies that combine the purchasing power of the citizens to benefit the citizens. These companies shall have their own board of directors upon which the mayor sits, and the after-tax profits from these business ventures shall be paid to the VillageTown to offset the need for higher annual fees. These companies will employ their own CEO, and their boards serve at the pleasure of the Board.

---

* The VillageTown will have an intranet computer system in every home and workplace, thus enabling referendum and recall to happen without administrative costs. The charter should contain a process for such voting to prevent abuse, but to provide checks and balances.

The Enforcement Function (Judicial)

In order to enforce rules and contracts, certain powers must be set out at the onset. Of these, the most effective are those used by corporations and landlords – the right to demand someone leave. Corporations have the right to terminate employment and require the employee vacate the premises. Landlords have the right of eviction, requiring the tenant move out and not come back. Provided strong protections and due process are embedded in the Charter to protect the individual from capricious enforcement, the power to ask any citizen, resident or visitor to leave the VillageTown and not come back, is essential. Built upon such enforcement power, lesser enforcement penalties, such as paying a fine or making a written promise to cease and desist, can then be implemented.

The corporate judicial function consists of a hearing body (known herein as the Court), and a legal spokesperson both for the community (known herein as the Public Prosecutor), and a defender of the individual (known herein as the Ombudsman). The Court should have three judges plus two alternates (perhaps semi-retired), and the Board shall establish rules that specify what cases are heard by one judge or all three. The Board may also specify jury trials for certain offences.

Terms should follow that of the Board, three year terms, staggered for annual election. The judges serving the Court shall have legal training as a pre-qualification for election. In some countries, such as New Zealand which uses Justices of the Peace to hear lesser court cases, such qualification may be sufficient. The prosecutor and ombudsman should be duly qualified and registered lawyers. The prosecutor should be appointed by the Mayor and the Ombudsman appointed by the Board, but once appointed they should serve a term of three years, and (to preserve their independence) can only be removed from office by a referendum vote of the citizens. All positions should be part time.

Commentary:

Rule Making and Enforcement

In 2009, at age 89, VillageTown's Chairman Emeritus Stuart Udall commented on video that when he was young in the 1930's, small and medium sized communities had a low tolerance for crime. He observed that this no longer is the case. When he opened the local paper the front page stories reported serious crimes. This is not progress.

Communities tolerate crime not out of choice, but because the systems that provided community protection gradually failed to deliver on their promise. In small communities the size of VillageTowns, the people know who tears the fabric of their community, they lack legal means to deal with them.

Even if the VillageTown were to become a legally designated municipality under appropriate state law, it would lack effective power to control criminal conduct.

Systematically the power of local communities to protect themselves, their property, and their quality of life is taken away by agencies that fail to deliver.

However while municipal law is weakened, we see corporate law being strengthened. A corporation may make rules that it can enforce. It can protect people and property. It can work for the interests of its people; its stockholders, clients and employees. It also can engage in both non-profit services and for-profit businesses that can reduce the cost of living for its citizens (a.k.a. stockholders).

After examining many different ways to address this, it became apparent that corporate law offered the strongest protection. Buildings may be privately owned with a freehold title*, but ownership of the underlying land is owned by a corporation 100% owned by the property owners, the sole stockholders of the corporation. The underlying land ownership accords freedom to use the land for habitation (placement of a privately owned building), but retains the right of the VillageTown to make and enforce rules for the community.

Once this right is set up with appropriate checks and balances – emulating the traditional three-part separation of powers rather than inventing some new and untested form of governance – the VillageTown Board would have the right to make rules that enable its citizens to get along with each other. When a person or group breached those rules, the VillageTown Executive Department would investigate, and if it found a potential breach, it would ask the VillageTown prosecutor to bring charges before the VillageTown Court. If convicted the Executive Department would execute the decision of the Court.

These rules should include the power to set automatic triggers for certain convictions in state or federal courts. For example, if a citizen is convicted of murder, rape, or other named serious felony, the prosecutor would invoke automatic eviction without having to prove the offence, deeming the criminal conviction as sufficient.

In addition to criminal protection, some rules will relate to parallel housing markets. The VillageTown proposes to include low-cost housing designated for certain target markets. The VillageTown will hold a subsidy to assure the homes can only be sold to buyers within those target markets. In the event a buyer and seller cheat, thus depriving the VillageTown and its stockholders (the citizens) of the benefit of the parallel market, the VillageTown Court would be empowered to act and to enforce.

In making rules, the citizenry depends on the Board to get it right. If a group of citizens believes the Board failed in their duty, they would have the right to appeal to the VillageTown Court to overturn a rule. The Court's decision would be binding over the

---

* The question of how to vest ownership of buildings opens up interesting possibilities. From a functional standpoint, the person who buys a home or workplace should "own it" with the same rights as if both land and building was in freehold title. However, it may have advantages in dealing with the authorities if all property was a single title in the name of the VillageTown where exclusive use, with all rights of ownership, were granted to the buyer in a contractual agreement between the buyer and the VillageTown. This is further discussed on Alternative Form of Building Ownership on the next page.

VillageTown. Finally, at the highest level, because of the technology that enables instant voting on any subject, the citizens could call for a binding referendum on any rule which could only be overturned by another referendum.

None of this is new or innovative. The principles of representative democracy proved their value over hundreds, if not thousands of years. They fail when the checks and balances fail. What is unusual is using corporate law to establish community democracy.

In setting out these powers, and anchoring them in the underlying land ownership, it becomes essential that the legal foundation is unbreakable. Buy the best legal advice available. If the underlying documents get broken in court, it would be exceptionally difficult for the community to regain authority to assert the common good.

Permanent Conditions on Title

What sort of enforcement powers does a corporation have? The most often used right when dealing with people is to ask them to leave. Unlike government, which has the rights of property, liberty, and life (enforcement through fines, imprisonment & execution), the ultimate power of a VillageTown court should be the right to ask, and then require, that a person leave. Under landlord-tenant law, this is called eviction. When the offending citizen owns property, it must include a permanent condition on the title to the property that gives the court the right to order a home be sold by the offender, and if the offender fails to do so within a prescribed period of time, for the VillageTown to order its sale at public auction. Accompanying such an order would be a court trespass order to leave both the premises and the VillageTown. This power would also extend to orders to landlords, in the event the offender is a tenant not a property owner. Landlords would be ordered to evict, and if they refused, they would be subject to court orders including auction.

The challenge for the lawyer who writes this title restriction is to assure the clause is written strongly enough that a court will not overturn it in the future. It needs to be simple and absolute, with no right of appeal to the external court system once a decision has been made.

Alternative Legal Form of Building Ownership

The presumption so far is that the land is best owned freehold by the VillageTown and leasehold by the property owner, but that the building or apartment is owned freehold by the buyer. There may be another alternative that has some attractive benefits. One aspect of the VillageTown is the fixed shell for each building, meaning that the exterior walls cannot be torn down or structurally modified. However on the interior, all sorts of changes can be made using non-load-bearing walls.

Over time, building owners may want to change interior use, subdividing or combining ownership by floor or even part floor. They may want to split off the ground floor into a separate apartment for their old age, and sell the upper two floors, for example. To do this under separate title involves the host local government that may have cumbersome or even prohibitive regulations. The alternative may be to have all land and all buildings under a single title owned by the VillageTown that then grants rights that give the same effect as title ownership, but allow subdividing or combining ownership by a simple paper filing with the VillageTown corporation with no interference from the host local government. Part of the feasibility analysis of this would depend on how mortgage financing worked.

Process - The Charter as a Social Contract

The best approach may be to draft the Social Contract in a legal document known as the *VillageTown Charter;* referenced in and binding on every property title in the VillageTown.

While legal experts may suggest a better way, at present the Charter would be based on a single title to all VillageTown land owned by the VillageTown corporation; with separate freehold titles for each privately-owned building built on the leasehold land.

The leasehold right to use the land should be almost as strong as freehold ownership, and it would only be in the area of balancing the community interest when it found itself in opposition to individual interest or conduct that it would be able to use those rights to enforce the community interest. .

The leasehold would serve as the basis for voting and collecting fees to provide the services necessary for the operation of the VillageTown. The leasehold would also serve as the basis for the writing of rules, enforcement of rules, and execution of action in response to transgressions of those rules.

The Charter would lay out the checks and balances structure of the VillageTown, and provide the framework for ongoing and evolving community democracy. The evolutionary principle is important. The Charter must provide the ability for a super-majority (say two thirds or three quarters) of the voters by referendum to change the Charter in a manner similar to amending the Constitution of the State.

Process - Prosecution of Offences

The VillageTown prosecutor shall have the responsibility to bring charges against citizens who breach the rules (including breaching *parallel real-estate market* terms – see page 259), noting in the powers that citizens are responsible for the behavior of their children, tenants and visitors*. Such charges shall follow due process of law as generally practiced, except that delaying tactics shall not be tolerated.

---

* This is important. If a person is a tenant who commits crimes or a family cannot control the behavior of their children, or a home is owned by a trust, corporation or a landlord, and the base of enforcement power is the power of public auction, it has to connect the building and the offending resident, regardless of ownership. If the owner does not evict the offender, the owner loses the property to auction, thus forcing the offender out.

Process - Judgment

The VillageTown Court (the Court) shall hear the charges, shall deliberate, and make judgment, the most severe of which is a protection or no-trespass court order, that requires the offender leave (and bans return to) the VillageTown. This order includes the right to sell at public auction any buildings or real estate owned by the offender, including ownership held in trusts or corporations controlled by or for the benefit of the offender.

Process - Auction

As noted in the footnote, the right of auction extends to the building as connected to the offender. The Court shall have discretion to set a period of time where the owner may privately sell the building before the auction is triggered. This time should be dependent on risk. If an offence is high risk, such as the offender being a real and present danger to the community, no time may be allowed. If it is a breach of the parallel housing terms (cheating), perhaps six months would be allowed. At the end of the allowed time, the VillageTown shall conduct the auction, and is entitled to recover from the offender or any related party all costs and losses associated with it, including losses related to a selling price below mortgage owed.

Process - Appeal

A decision of the Court may be appealed to the VillageTown Board's elected representative body, but not to an outside court system, and the Charter needs to be written accordingly.

Process - Property

The Court shall have the right to dispose of any personal (not real) property not removed by the offender and to recover costs through such disposal.

Process - Protection of Rights

In writing these rules and enforcement mechanisms, great care must be taken to balance the rights of the citizen to prevent abuse. Non-conformity is not a crime. Breaching the peace, cheating on parallel home subsidies or committing crimes that adversely affect the community are matters that require the VillageTown to protect itself. The Ombudsman should be assigned to the case on behalf of the defendant in all cases involving auction. It may be useful to write a Bill of Rights into the Charter.

Process - Ombudsman

The role of the ombudsman is to assert the interest of the individual against the community. This may include advocating for an individual who wishes to challenge a Board rule. It may be to challenge an action or decision of the VillageTown's Executive branch. In such cases the community pays the ombudsman to present a proper case before the Court. In society today, this form of checks and balances is often overlooked, resulting in those who can afford good legal council securing justice not available to those of more limited means.

The ombudsman may also use the discretion of its office to choose to defend at no cost an individual charged by the prosecutor with an offence. Not all cases will be so defended, and offenders may have to hire their own legal council.

Anti-Gentrification: Parallel Real-estate Market

As discussed elsewhere in this book, the VillageTown is expected to be a desirable place to live, and unless measures are taken to preserve affordability in housing, gentrification promises to destroy the intended character and purpose of the VillageTown. After examining various models, the model selected is one that creates a parallel market, so that two identical homes, side by side, may have different market values, because they sell in different, parallel markets.

Parallel Real-estate Market

In order to counteract the corrosive effect of gentrification, where important sectors of the society find they cannot afford to live in the community because they lack competitive purchasing power, the VillageTown seeks to create Parallel Markets in which it keeps an interest in the property to restrict who can buy.

There is legal precedent for this in the case of retirement villages, where one must be over a certain age to be permitted to buy and move in. However, anti-discrimination laws, written ironically to protect some of the very people the VillageTown tries to serve, may make it more difficult to cater to selective disadvantaged markets for other target populations within society.

These include service workers, such as teachers or municipal workers, whose pay is generally fixed in pay bands. The ideal is to designate a particular home as restricted to named professions (such as a teacher), where the organizing company sells the home at a discount, keeping an interest as opportunity cost. When the buyer goes to sell, they can sell at any price, but only to buyers in the target market, where the fixed salary band necessarily creates a maximum price range that may be significantly lower than the next-door, identical but unrestricted home. In this way, the market operates with a minimum of bureaucracy, while still accomplishing the objective of assuring essential workers can live in the community.

Other target qualifiers may include age such as under 26 for youth housing, location of employment such as worker in the Industrial Park blue-collar homes, or disability housing.

The legal issues include:

- Finding a way to create parallel markets without breaching anti-discrimination laws or other conflicting laws.
- Clearly defining the legal basis. For example, it could be leasehold land where the

organizing company establishes a permanent interest in the property that is then passed to the VillageTown where the VillageTown maintains a passive role that only asserts the home is limited in its resale to the parallel market.

- Allow the VillageTown to transfer the parallel market designation to another equivalent property. Example: A qualified parallel home owner owns a parallel market home worth $200,000. They develop an emotional attachment to it (the place where they raised their children), and wish to pass it on to their children (something not allowed unless the child is in the same target group). They arrange to buy a second, equivalent home on the open market for say $400,000 subject to the VillageTown moving the parallel market designation from their first home to the second home. They then sell the second home to a qualified buyer at the parallel price of $200,000. The parallel designation moves from their first home to the one they just sold, and the operating company releases its parallel market interest in the first home. Their first home, without the parallel designation, is now worth $400,000. It costs them $200,000 to stay in their home, but it is no different from selling their first home at the parallel price and then buying a second home at the open market price.

- Clarify under what circumstances a person loses the right to live in a parallel home. This is a delicate matter, as under most circumstances the person should not be required to move out of a home they have purchased. However, if someone makes a clear career change that deprives the VillageTown of its target population, and enough of this happens to defeat the purpose, the VillageTown should have some power to correct the situation.

- Prohibit the VillageTown from unilaterally disposing of its parallel market rights. To explain: The principle of privatization sometimes sees governing bodies targeting public assets paid for by one generation, and disposing of them for short term capital gains, or even as political favors, thus depriving future generations of their value. Checks and balances need to be written into the charter and titles so an elected Board cannot simply vote to dispose of its interest. This may be by referendum, or by an interest being jointly held by another organization, perhaps the VillageTown Stewards.

- Clarifying primary buyer qualifications to protect the public interest. To explain: In the case of a couple where one spouse qualifies for the parallel market, but the other does not, is the couple qualified to buy? As long as the VillageTown gets the benefit they seek (for example that one spouse is a full-time teacher in the VillageTown who can walk to the classroom), the intent is met. However the legal language needs to be clear so the VillageTown can draw that fairness line to assure the public interest is met. Such language must be simple.

- Defining cheating, where a buyer claims to qualify, but in fact, does not. This can be direct, where employment is defined as, for example, a teacher employed in the VillageTown public schools or a municipal worker employed in the VillageTown. However, over time, people will come up with innovative ways to cheat, and the charter should be designed to enable the VillageTown to block such unanticipated intent while remaining clear and unambiguous to protect the public interest.

- Defining the Court's power to set a time-frame in which the offender must sell the home, and set the date when the Court orders a public auction where buyers must prove qualification to buy in advance as a condition of bidding.

- Recovering from the offender the costs and losses related to the cheating. This needs to be clear and executable with the minimum of need for the state judicial system.

- To prevent use of the state court system to preclude delaying tactics by an offender using a sharp lawyer.

Target Parallel Markets

The organizing company will identify markets it sees as important; some include:

- Artist Housing: While the preferred plan is to provide freebase housing owned by the VillageTown, and managed by the Guild Halls, the Charter should provide parallel market housing for designated persons. A creative example may include the village gadfly. In Christchurch New Zealand, they had an official wizard, who greatly adds to the local color. In a VillageTown it would be good to have the right to provide parallel market housing for such characters.

- Essential worker homes: These include public employees in service to the VillageTown, and may include public employees living in the VillageTown but employed by another outside agency. For example, if policing is provided by the surrounding town, county or state, the VillageTown may want a local presence and offer subsidized housing to have a police officer living in the town.

- Private Service Workers: This is more complicated. Some jobs pay poorly, are low-skilled, but important to the function of society. The VillageTown will have citizens

who lack the skill to hold better jobs, and others who prefer to work in simple jobs without much responsibility. Provision needs to be made for such worker housing, both on a transient basis and a permanent basis. While the industrial park's village will be built for blue-collar workers, additional protections may be necessary to prevent its gentrification. Home ownership must be tied to earnings or employment group.

- Elder Housing: Must be over a certain age such as age 65 to occupy.

- Youth Housing: Must be under a certain age (say age 26) to buy and must be able to prove purchase funds were legally earned, not a gift from parents or inheritance, since the earning power of youth is limited, and the intent is to always provide first-time buyer affordable housing. Once in, the owner may live there no matter what age, but when it is time to sell, the new buyer must be under the threshold age.

- Disadvantaged Housing: The general class addressed by welfare systems, but structured in such a way that those who can step up live in it as a hand-up until they are able to regain a position of advantage in the community and take care of themselves.

Concessions and Pragmatism

Certain aspects of the VillageTown are not negotiable. For example, it cannot have cars within; it is not to be a one-company town or a retirement village. Other desirable aspects however may prove to be a "show stopper" in some jurisdictions. If after the best legal minds have determined a desirable VillageTown characteristic will prohibit the project from going ahead, pragmatism asserts itself. Find the closest way to achieve as much of the desirable as possible and move forward. Likewise, if during the initial stage a particular aspect proves too difficult for people to understand, put it off. Wait until there is sufficient funding and skill to raise the matter again.

AN ESSAY ON FREEDOM AND LIBERTY

Freedom is a word that applies to the individual, alone or in society. A solitary pioneer crosses the frontier into the wilderness and is free. In contrast, Liberty is a social word. It is the totality of all freedoms that an individual may enjoy in the context of society. When speaking about freedom in community, society, or civilization, one speaks of liberty.

In the 17th and 18th centuries, as nations evolved, liberty became an important concept. John Locke wrote *"The commonwealth seems to me to be a society of men constituted only for the procuring, preserving, and advancing their own civil interests. Civil interests I call life, liberty, health, and indolency* [freedom from pain] *of body; and the possession of outward things, such as money, lands, houses, furniture, and the like."*

When the American colonists sought independence from King George III and his Parliament, Virginian George Mason wrote in the Virginia Declaration of Rights on June 12, 1776, *"That all men are by nature equally free and independent, and have certain inherent rights, of which, when they enter into a state of society, they cannot, by any compact, deprive or divest their posterity; namely, the enjoyment of life and liberty, with the means of acquiring and possessing property, and pursuing and obtaining happiness and safety."*

Less than a month later, in one of the most famous documents in western history, the Declaration of Independence, drafted primarily by Thomas Jefferson, declared *"We hold these truths to be self-evident, that all men are created equal, that they are endowed by their Creator with certain unalienable Rights, that among these are Life, Liberty and the pursuit of Happiness."*

Note especially Mason's linking liberty with entering *into a state of society.* In other words, liberty is freedom in the context of a community or a society of what he called men, what today we would call citizens: adult men and women (except, of course, convicted criminals deprived by the state of certain rights that come from the social contract).

By the 20th century, in the name of taming the chaos of life, to give people a life that appeared well-ordered and familiar, we saw the emergence of a new set of values: society reinventing itself by creating new, larger, and more complex institutions, corporations, and bureaucracies. These new forms of society were intent on controlling Nature, individuals, families, traditional communities and traditional ways of life, and in controlling many of life's uncertainties and unknowns. We saw the emergence of rules and regulations, of layers of government and big business that organized life into hierarchies in which human beings became less important. Unfortunately, while this promised to provide a well-ordered utopian life, it failed to deliver on that promise, but did result in considerable encroachment on liberty. In socialist nations, too often this meant corruption, the rule of the petty bureaucrat or the authoritarian dictatorship. In capitalist nations, this often resulted in corruption, and the rule of private oligarchies where a few used the system to benefit themselves at the expense of a majority – a majority who found opportunity had been privatized; only affordable by the few who held or had access to the power.

In the latter part of the 20th century, the character of society changed again. Societies redefined their majorities not as producers, but as consumers. The security that had been built up by the hierarchies of government and corporations broke. A good example is IBM, which in the 1990s reversed its lifelong-employment policy and laid off many thousands of loyal employees. Not coincidentally, it was the invention of the pre-eminent consumer device - the personal computer (originally invented, in part, by Berkeley, California radicals who objected to IBM's paternalism and what it represented), run by an operating system licensed to IBM by Microsoft's Bill Gates - that contributed to this breakdown of the paternal corporation. At its core, the process of breaking trust began. The security that was supposed to be the trade-off for loss of liberty slowly began to evaporate. Many noticed the loss of security; few noticed what was happening to liberty.

In this new era of the consumer, social structure began to break down and individual life became fragmented. The abundance of things to buy, and for a while, the easy credit with which to buy them, masked the destruction of that sense of solidity built up over the centuries. Consumers gave up security in order to enjoy a debased form of freedom: freedom to purchase, to consume, and to enjoy material things. People would change jobs, homes, communities, spouses, and their core identity: their values, beliefs, their given and family names, and even the appearance of their face, body, or gender, according to the ever-changing demands of fashion and circumstance. Conspiracy theories gained new believers as individuals tried to understand their increasing loss of control. Insecurity and uncertainty became the new norm. Temporary became the new reality. At the top, the sense of obligation and stewardship of an older generation gave way to a new breed where the game is a fight for power, with little concern for effect on people or planet. In a deep sense, no one is in control anymore; leadership devolved to securing advantage. Life becomes the ultimate nightmare of the collective ego. At its core, trust in institutions, leadership, community, and society, even trust in marriage and family came under assault. Not coincidentally, the ancient principle of liberty was and is now increasingly in retreat.

Trust is an integral part of the glue that holds communities, societies, and civilizations together. They can be forcefully contained by fear, but then as has been seen in the Arab Spring, new technology, such as smart phones and social media like Facebook and Twitter, can empower ordinary people to overthrow regimes that rule through fear.

Trust is voluntary. It is an agreement that is established through words, and earned through deeds. Often, trust is maintained through checks and balances, meaning power is distributed so that when one person or party starts to move too far to an extreme, another person, party, or group brings them back into balance. In English Law, the Magna Carta of 1215 established checks and balances to secure the liberty of freemen. It was secured by force of arms - King John of England had a choice: sign or die. Over the subsequent eight centuries, rule of force gradually was replaced by rule of law; today the great battles over the direction and fate of communities, societies, and civilizations are fought by lawyers, bankers, and captains of industry rather than abbots, bishops, and barons.

Today, the great institutions of state still guarantee peace and protection from national invasion or rebellion in most first-world nations. The VillageTown depends on that security for its existence. Unlike the ancient city-states, no VillageTown would maintain its own citizen-army to protect against invasion. But within the context of the safety provided by the state, the VillageTown examines the concept of liberty, and concludes that it cannot rely on the large institutions of state, business, and industry to protect its liberty. As was seen in the near-crash of the global financial system in 2008, banks are no longer institutions of absolute trust. Or, another example: instead of freedom from home invasion, individuals are told to buy locks, security systems, and insurance to protect life, limb, and property.

As individuals, restoration of personal liberty in day-to-day life is difficult, if not impossible. It is achievable, however, if they enter into *a state of society*, to use Mason's words.

The VillageTown is a state of society. However, the VillageTown is not prescriptive, like an intentional community or a cult that provides a pre-determined set of answers. It is a culture, not a cult. Instead, it provides structure to enable the village citizens of the VillageTown to enter into a state of society. They set out their expectations for their village, and then negotiate with the other villages to determine the expectations of the town as a whole to create a *social contract*. By virtue of these many villages, checks and balances are introduced. The checks and balances provide a self-governance system intended to create a sustainable physical environment - meaning one that will provide for no less than seven generations - intended to foster life, liberty, and the pursuit of happiness. How it will turn out, or evolve, entirely depends on the people who live there, as individuals, as families, as communities, and as members of a society and a civilization.

Some freedoms are inherently more accessible in a VillageTown. For example, at one time, children were free to roam, to learn independence and autonomy because their parents were not afraid they would get run down by a car, or abducted by an anonymous predator driving by. This freedom is stronger in a VillageTown because the cars are kept outside, and predators will find the villages provide no cover for them. Similar is the freedom from economic control. Let this be explained by a story:

A number of years ago, there was a debate in the Costa Rican legislature over the downside of depending on an eco-tourist economy. Many of legislators were independent farmers who noted that they could say what they want as legislators, because their livelihood was their own. If they were censured for what they said, they may get tossed out of the legislature, but they would be able to return to their farm and take care of their family's needs - they were economically independent. Yet they noted that if their children took jobs in the tourist industry, they were reluctant to become involved in matters of citizenship, for fear of losing their job if they took a controversial position. They saw that their future liberty could be compromised by a shift in economic dependency.

In the VillageTown, the reasons to create a self-supporting economy are due to the failure of the national and global economies to deliver on their promises of security. Events over the past several decades have proved they cannot be depended upon. However, as a happy side effect, by creating a self-supporting local economy based on many small-to-medium enterprises that are privately owned by VillageTown citizens, the fear of losing one's income if one exercises the right to freedom of speech is lessened.

If this self-supporting local economy agrees to take care of its own; that the Legacy Fund managers are charged with the responsibility to provide "hand-up" opportunities for people who suffer a setback, losing their job, for example, then there is increased freedom. Economically, people will take more risks. It was Thomas Edison who is quoted as saying "I have not failed. I've just found 10,000 ways that won't work." That sort of inventiveness was possible only because Edison had structured his life so he and his family would not starve while he took the risks to find the way that does work.

The VillageTown concept looked carefully at liberty, to find that balance between freedom and enabling people to get along with each other. It took the long view, looking back thousands of years in history and looking at many cultures. While the language comes out of the European and American colonial experiences (which owe a strong debt to the philosophers of ancient Athens as well perhaps as the Iroquois Confederation and other nations), the cultures that were examined and whose best elements woven in is much broader. Essentially, the concept evolved through a pragmatic asking of what works, what does not work, and why. More importantly, the process is not complete. Each VillageTown will be established in a way that its citizens shape their own future. Each will be different, because the people will be different.

Throughout the history of humanity various forms of society have been tried and tested. In the 18th century, American and future President James Madison wrote a strong case for checks and balances, and indeed history has shown that as long as those checks and balances are upheld, extremes are avoided, and the state of society does fairly well.

History has also shown that the most effective forms of society are ones in which checks and balances are face to face. The elected or appointed leaders who regularly encounter their constituents on the street or in the check-out line face a direct form of accountability that can't be beat. This is one reason why the VillageTown seeks to cap its population size at about 10,000. Much larger than that and facelessness begins to creep in.

This is one reason why it is proposed to build a town made of villages. A village of five hundred people (including about 20% children) is generally able to run directly; not dissimilar to the 19th century New England Town Meeting or the New Zealand Maori *hui*, where the whole community meets to decide matters. In such communities, people will sort out matters according to their own ways, and each village may be run differently than the next. It is their business and their responsibility.

As can be seen, none of these ideas are new; all are time-tested. What is a bit different is the fact that the internal governance structures of these communities will in effect be private; based on contract and corporate law, not constitutional or municipal law. They will exist as a layer separate from the nation, state or host jurisdiction. They will pay taxes rather than collect taxes. If the VillageTown citizens decide they value services not paid for by the state or host jurisdiction, they will decide to assess themselves the cost to pay for them not as taxes but as fees based on ground rent.

There is a sound reason for doing this. Over time the checks and balances inherent under constitutional law have been eroded by pecuniary interest. At the same time, contract and corporate law has been strengthened. If a corporation signs a contract with government, that contract is binding regardless of whether the opposing party is elected to office. However, if that same government passes a law promising the citizens certain things and the opposing party is elected to office, the government can repeal that law. A VillageTown established under municipal law can find the state can disestablish it more easily than if the state tried to disestablish a private corporation.

Finally, it needs to be emphasized that this essay is not universally applicable. This essay speaks mostly to western civilization, not the much more ancient oriental civilization which has a very different set of values in which harmony holds a much higher position. There is considerable interest in VillageTowns in the Orient, especially in China, and the physical structure of the VillageTown is most appealing to them. However, the system of self-governance that would emerge in an oriental VillageTown may be expected to be very different. Since the VillageTown concept is an inert framework given life by the people who will live there, this should not create a problem.

To summarize, liberty is a concept that emerged in Western nations over many centuries. Around the beginning of the 20th century, large institutions and hierarchies began to emerge in which society gave up many liberties in exchange for order and personal security. Toward the end of the 20th century, the order and security began to break down, as anxiety was privatized, but the ability to do something about it remained centralized. In the 21st century, people are recognizing that if they want to do something about it, the law gives them the power to do so, but they can't do it as solitary individuals. Looking back to models that worked before the great centralization, the VillageTown offers a way in which people can create a free and just social contract.

AN ESSAY ON SUSTAINABILITY

The Maori of New Zealand plan differently than their many of their compatriots of European extraction. Maori plan for seven generations. What this means is they ask what the impact will be on not only themselves and their families, but what impact will their decisions of the day have for the next 175 years. Today, in asking this question, they speak not only of future Maori children, but all children.

Before it became a political buzzword, sustainability was a simple way of talking about planning for future generations. Will we, the present generation, leave to future generations a better world, or will we leave them heavy debts to pay for our living beyond our means? Will we leave them mounds and seas of toxic trash, fouled air, polluted waters and eroded soils, vanished species, and family stories of pain and trauma caused by our wars fought over who gets Earth's limited resources? Or will we leave them a world in which we took raw materials, made marvelous tools that not only feed, clothe and shelter us without the need for human slaves, but enable all of us to enjoy a standard of living that once was that of only the very few? Curiously, at present, the answer seems to be both.

If it takes a million years for the Australian aquifer to charge, and we pump it dry in a hundred, what are we leaving for our descendants? If, when we were born, oil was easy to pump out of the ground, but we burned so much that future generations have to extract it from tar sands to maintain the standard of life we set, have we been selfish and greedy? Do we have any obligation to our children and their children?

Does the maxim *do unto others as you would have them do unto you* apply in today's world, or is it now *survival of the fittest in a dog-eat-dog world*? Are we civilized or selfish brutes? If the golden rule is still relevant, would the corollary *Will unto your descendants what your ancestors Willed unto you* apply? For the VillageTown Stewards, the answer is yes, and this is our meaning of the overused and abused word, sustainability: to leave to our future generations a world in better shape, or at least in as good a shape as was left to us.

Fossil Fuel (oil, coal and natural gas) is the discovery our grandparents of the 19th and 20th centuries harnessed to provide us the energy to improve life on earth. At the time, it seemed an unlimited resource because our lifetimes are so short. A 60-year-old American will have enjoyed cheap oil almost all of his or her life up until the last few years. In that lifetime, every year brought new luxuries into the hands of the middle class. In 1849, it took four months to travel from New York to California by land or sea. In 1869, with the new rail, that time was cut to less than a week. In 1969, today's 60-year old, at the time an American student, could buy a student-standby ticket from New York to California for $100. Today, anyone can buy an advanced fare NYC-LAX ticket for $129 in 2011 dollars - adjusted for inflation since 1969, that's $20.

But fossil fuels are a limited resource. Every year we have to dig deeper and use more energy to extract them. In the lifetime of that 60-year old, today's fossil fuels require more energy and cause more damage to extract. Fossil-fuel energy is a gift from our ancestors, those who figured out how to harness its power. In asking the question of sustainability, we must ask how we can use that gift wisely. Since it won't last forever, do we burn it all up to provide us with immediate gratification, or do we use it as a bridge to new technology that provides future generations with all the sustainable energy they will need? Obviously, we, the VillageTown stewards, chose the latter. We regard it as part of the golden rule.

Having said this, we find the word sustainability has now unfortunately been taken up as a battle-cry between political factions. We wish to have nothing to do with either side. There is a battle between two factions who wish to gain control over the levers of the state - who gets to write what rules to tell people how to live and who pays for their enforcement. Sustainability has become the latest weapon in that battle that has been going on ever since the beginning of the Industrial Revolution. This is unfortunate because in a very quiet way, the Industrial Revolution is fading into history. The Industrial Revolution was about centralization. Cities grew because factories grew because the size of machinery to make things grew, needing cheap labor, abundant energy and raw materials and the right to dump the waste into the river or up a smokestack.

We are now in the early stages of the Telepresence Revolution where increasingly life is become decentralized and work automated. The next generation of this will be to shift to entirely automated manufacturing that no longer needs the cheap labor of third-world countries. Interestingly, much of this will probably come from China, as its younger generations begin to enjoy the luxuries of a middle-class life and have no interest in working in factories the way their parents did. Given that there are 1.3 billion Chinese, the American model of middle-class life (based on 5% of the world's population consuming 25% of its energy) won't work, and the Chinese know it. To attain it, they will need to replace human capital with automation. They are doing so at a rapid pace.

From the perspective of the VillageTown Stewards, these great questions are, as the bureaucrat says, *above my pay grade*. Like the hobbit, the Stewards do not concern themselves with things over which they have no control, but prefer to enjoy the simpler pleasures of life. Instead of trying to save the world, the Stewards listen to the injunction of Socrates that justice is when everyone minds their own business, and refrains from meddling in others. Thus the Stewards direct their energy and attention toward matters that they can do something about. The walking home-range is a good example, as are thick walls that keep homes warmer and quieter for free: *we need less energy and get a higher quality life.*

Most people love their children and want the best for them. Many people love a beautiful world, natural landscapes full of a wide range of plants and animals, and many love stimulating urban places where people may enjoy a good life. In the end, for us, sustainability is nothing more than expressing that love through deeds.

Appendix 3 – Model Design Code

The VillageTown design process begins with a design code that both governs the VillageTown as a whole and provides the starting framework for the Dynamic Engagement process where each village designs itself. This code is a model that can be used as a starting point for a VillageTown project. Typically, it is completed by the professional support team in collaboration with the organizing company and the village founders.

What we are trying to achieve

We seek to enable people and communities (villages and the surrounding neighbors) to provide for their social, economic, cultural and spiritual wellbeing, health and safety while protecting and preserving the natural and physical environment and its life-giving qualities both for the present and the foreseeable needs of future generations.

These noble aspirations are taken from the purpose of New Zealand's Local Government Act, where we observed its de facto implementation seems to have devolved into granting developers permission to proceed with their plans with a higher sensitivity to landscape, flora and fauna, water, visual amenity, heritage, noise, dust and traffic. While this is a step forward, it hardly seems to be about enabling people and communities or about wellbeing.

Thus, we seek to look at the bigger picture of human beings living on earth within an environment of holons embedded in holons: from home to village to town to region to nation to globe. In economic wellbeing we analyze how to foster a diverse, robust local economy that de-monetizes certain aspects of life and avoids vulnerable dependencies on predatory global economic systems. We expand social wellbeing to be defined as *a good life*, understood as the social pursuits of *conviviality, citizenship and artistic, intellectual & spiritual growth*, with specific infrastructure investments made in each area following the principle that physical form (what you build) shapes social interaction – if you build a café, people will talk; if you fund an artist guild hall and provide affordable housing artists will come.

For safety and health, we propose non-combustible buildings that create healthy interior micro-climates and are earthquake and tsunami resistant. We propose to revive a town-country local economy where most food is grown on nearby farms, where by cutting out the middleman, the farmer can make a profit growing chemical-free food that is healthier.

In protecting and preserving the natural environment, the VillageTown acts both locally and globally. In local, part of the Greenbelt, occupying 60% of the 500-acre (200h) site protects or creates a natural environment where Nature is allowed to thrive. Wetlands, native preserves and other aspects are enhanced. Globally, the VillageTown seeks to reduce its footprint by removing the need to drive, reducing energy needs, and avoiding use of toxic materials and transport-dependent goods including their supply chain.

ENVIRONMENTAL CODE

In 1986, the World Health Organization's Ottawa Charter for Health Promotion declared, *"Our societies are complex and interrelated. Health cannot be separated from other goals. The inextricable links between people and their environment constitutes the basis for a socioecological approach to health. <u>The overall guiding principle for the world, nations, regions and communities alike, is the need to encourage reciprocal maintenance – to take care of each other, our communities and our natural environment.</u> The conservation of natural resources throughout the world should be emphasized as a global responsibility."*

Land selection and protection

Principle

The closer land is to its natural state, the more protection it may need. The natural state includes wetlands that clean water and reduce flooding. It includes streams that teem with wildlife. It includes native forests and bushland that are home to a wide variety of native flora and fauna. When land is converted to human use, especially farmland, it loses many of its natural qualities as the trees and bushes are cut and the land converted to growing mono-crops. The quality of the land often determines what is grown: better soil for vegetables and poorer soils used to grow grass for cattle and sheep.

When a site is identified for a VillageTown a tiered environmental land survey is necessary. Tiered means it depends on existing land use. If the land is in cow pasture, for example, one can expect there will be little to preserve, thus a lesser survey is required. If pockets of bush or timber remain, or it has wetlands, consideration should be given to preserving and enhancing these pockets, which may create a different shape to the urban design than the theoretical ideal as found in the diagram on page 30.

Rules

A site survey will map the following aspects of the land:

- Wetlands and water courses, including evaluation of water quality
- Topography with attention to storm water runoff and storage for VillageTown use
- Vegetation including an evaluation from quality native to weed/exotic infested
- Native fauna habitat, including an evaluation from protected fauna to pest
- Soil quality to identify soils best used to grow food, not cover with the urban core
- Historic and archaeological study to identify and protect any sites of significance
- Visual amenity and landscape values to identify places needing protection
- Existing neighbors to identify greenbelt buffers to prevent cross-boundary conflicts
- Transport access to identify roads, rail, wharfs and/or airfields that may require upgrade

Implementation

The findings of the site survey will govern land use. Wetlands, areas of important flora and fauna, historic/archeology locations and other significant features of value will be protected, and where possible made a part of the Greenbelt not the urban core. Where streams run through the urban core, they will be enhanced, not enclosed in concrete raceways. If historic or archeological sites must be in the urban core, they will be enhanced and protected to serve an educational function.

Prevent air, water & soil pollution

Principle of Prevention – Unnecessary pollutants shall not be brought into or used in the VillageTown construction or ongoing operation.

Timber – chemically treated timbers used only where absolutely necessary. Cutting of treated wood shall be in enclosed areas where all sawdust can be collected and properly disposed, with appropriate safety precautions.

Motor Vehicles – No internal-combustion engines vehicles or combustible fuels within the VillageTown walls. For motorpool cars and trucks and for farm vehicles requiring liquid fuels, the VillageTown shall seek to produce biofuel from sewage and solid waste.

Chemicals used in farming and gardens shall be limited to only that which is absolutely necessary. Organic methods shall be encouraged. Where chemicals are used, handling shall follow the strictest procedures to avoid runoff into water courses, release into the air or contaminating land. Spray drift prohibited.

Heating shall seek to use sources that do not require burning of fossil fuels – solar water heating, solar electric with heat pumps, wind, water and other technologies.

Prevent noise pollution

Principle of Prevention – Unwanted noise shall be kept out of the VillageTown and its surrounds and design shall contain noise within the VillageTown.

Vehicles – By designing everything within a 10-minute walk, conventional public (and private) transport is not needed within the VillageTown. Permitted Low Speed Vehicles to use electricity or compressed air.

Motors – Stationary internal-combustion motors shall not be used in the VillageTown except where essential; where they are used, stationary motors shall be housed so as to not be heard. In addition to noise, fuel for these motors adds a combustible hazard.

Construction Equipment – In construction zones a higher level of noise shall be permitted, but only if the zone's noise does not spill over into inhabited zones. If ongoing cutting or drilling is required, sound-absorbing temporary buffers shall be used to minimize noise pollution. Compressors shall be muffled.

Fans, air conditioners, heat pumps – Placement of exhaust- and climate-control systems shall be designed so they are not heard by neighbors or on the street. Such systems shall be built into buildings so their noise is absorbed and not heard.

Amplified music and sound – Private music and sound shall not be heard outside the residence. Residential walls shall absorb sound and use windows that block sound transmission. Different residential zones shall have different sound tolerances (quiet zones, young people's party zone) with different design standards. Public music and sound shall be permitted in specified noise zones including café music and outdoor concerts and film showing, with appropriate standards set by VillageTown or the particular village.

Natural noise (loud voices and pets) – The architectural code shall provide standards in design to contain natural sound, through the use of thick walls between buildings. Individual villages in the VillageTown have the right to prohibit some or all pets.

Energy efficiency and carbon neutral

Principle of Prevention – VillageTown buildings shall be designed to maintain comfortable micro-climates within the structures using the minimum amount of electricity or other non-passive fuel sources. Buildings shall be constructed using advanced sustainable methods. Standby appliances that use electricity when not operating shall be discouraged.

Maximum use of solar gain shall be incorporated into all buildings. Very high insulation shall be used in floors, walls, ceilings and fenestration where solar gain is not a factor.

Lighting shall use natural lighting where possible, and low-energy lights after darkness. Electric motors shall be of a high-efficiency design to consume less electricity. Integrated systems shall be used where appropriate (example, HVAC with hot water and refrigeration).

Solid-waste reduction and management

Principle of Prevention – The VillageTown local economy shall be structured in a way that reduces the need for packaging and waste products.

Waste shall be separated at the source with multiple collection systems for food, paper, glass, metals, plastics and other waste products. Advanced systems shall be adopted as they become commercially viable, including systems that convert waste into energy or fuels.

Sewage – treatment or use as an asset;

Kitchen sinks shall use a garbage disposal unit for vegetable waste. It shall run into a separate pipe system that only collects such composting vegetable waste for reprocessing. This is deemed more efficient than collecting compost buckets from 4,000 homes twice a week.

Grey water and black water may be treated separately and locally. Black water shall be viewed as a valuable resource and advanced systems should be implemented as they become commercially available. This may include systems in which algae converts black water sewage into biofuel or using blackwater to grow biofuel plants or feed certain types of fish.

This greenhouse processes 7,000 gallons of sewage per day producing purified, cleaned water

Water Management

Principle of Prevention – Water is a limited resource and given uncertain concerns about climate change, the VillageTown shall be designed to use water in the most efficient manner.

Separation – Drinking water shall be purified to a higher-than-generally-accepted municipal standard. Buildings shall have multiple pipe systems, one supplying pure drinking water, a second supplying a high quality of utility water for cleaning and bathing, and a third for toilets (grey water). Where applicable, rain water shall be captured on roofs and stored within the VillageTown (under streets, behind buildings, under commercial establishments, in visible ponds and lakes).

Reuse – Clothes washing uses a significant amount of water. Where technology is available, the VillageTown will provide neighborhood launderettes that continually refilter the washing water, thus never requiring disposal of dirty water to be replaced by new water. Clothing may line-dried instead of using electricity.

Street cleansing and maintenance

Principle of Prevention – VillageTown streets shall not have oil-dripping cars. Trees and plants shall be selected and placed with species that tend not to drop leaves that clog storm drains. The VillageTown governance shall enforce rules governing fouling of the streets.

Streets shall be made of materials that do not naturally look dirty or shabby. Asphalt shall not be used as a street material or patch material. Streets shall be designed so utility providers do not need to cut into the streets to access pipes or cables. Streets shall be designed so they are easy to clean with brooms or other dry systems, not requiring substantial water. Care shall be taken not to foster mold on shaded, damp streets and lanes.

Protection of flora and fauna

The VillageTown shall be designed with high perimeter walls and gates to keep domestic pets inside the VillageTown, and to preserve wildlife outside. If possible, secure more land for the VillageTown, allowing 30% of land for the urban settlement and 60% for a Greenbelt with 10% for Industrial Park, Transport Center and Freight Depot. Outside the walls set out some land as wildlife habitat and seek professional expertise to assure appropriate plants and wildlife corridors exist to make the habitats functional.

Through neglect and monoculture farming, earth is losing its genetic stock of domesticated plants and animals. The VillageTown shall encourage large community-owned gardens outside the VillageTown walls to grow heritage plants and support seed-bank farming.

Environmental education and protection

Principle – All human beings require a healthy physical environment in order to maintain a sense of wellbeing. Environmental awareness comes through calling attention to the physical and natural environment, and through policies that demonstrate respect for it.

The VillageTown shall be the campus for primary, secondary and tertiary education, thus becoming a laboratory for environmental (and the broader standard of quality of life) education.

Healthy, low impact building design and materials.

Principle – With greenhouse gasses becoming a major global concern, the VillageTown shall design and choose building systems that overall reduce greenhouse gas emissions through a change in human lifestyle. This includes eliminating unnecessary transport and freight, requiring buildings that use less energy and make use of solar gain, weaning its citizens off a disposable consumer lifestyle.

During construction:

- Provide living space for builders so they do not commute on the public roads
- Provide silos and batch-mixing plants for cement, aggregate, etc. so deliveries are in bulk; controlled to reduce access-road wear, noise and congestion.
- Build on-site manufacturing facilities for joinery, building materials, etc.

In design:

- Avoid chemically treated timber and other toxic materials that require special handling when being installed, when burned (including uncontrolled fires that produce hazardous toxic smoke) and when disposed either as trash during construction or at the end-of-life of the building.

- Use a single bulk-building system that promotes energy efficiency. Recommended: lightweight concrete, also known as Variable Density Aggregate, a cement-foaming-system technology that produces a concrete in which heavy aggregate is replaced by closed-cell air bubbles. Design thick walls, floors and ceilings to produce a high insulation factor.

- Choose bulk materials with a short distance from raw material to useful material on the job site. Choose materials with low-energy components in manufacturing.

- Design winter rooms. Face thermal heat-sink walls toward the winter sun. Use glass windows to allow the low sun to passively warm heat-sink floors. Design internal rooms so passive heat naturally flows to areas where warmth is desired.

- Design walls that naturally "breathe" to create a lower-humidity interior climate. If this is not possible in specific places, use thick gypsum (25 mm) on interior walls and apply only breathable coatings (not paints that form a vapor barrier). This is an ancient technique known to produce warmer, more comfortable rooms.

- Choose materials that do not produce toxic gasses during their useful life in the building. The oldest materials are often the safest. New materials, especially those which are petroleum based (plastics) or use toxic glues, may have unanticipated negative side effects not yet documented.

- Design buildings to take advantage of natural lighting and not need artificial lighting during daylight hours. Where lighting is required select low-energy-consumption systems, but avoid bulbs containing toxic materials that require special handling for safe disposal at end of useful life.

- Design whole-building systems, so refrigeration, heat pumps and other energy exchange systems work as a single system. Use high-efficiency electric motors.

- Install food boxes at every house, so local foods may be delivered from nearby farms directly to the customer's home. The energy component of food is related to delivery costs. Food boxes enable the shortest distance between the farm and the table, because one delivery vehicle services a whole street.

- Install a high speed, high-capacity telecommunications system for all buildings in the VillageTown, capable of real-time video conferences so people need not travel by vehicle in order to meet and to work cooperatively. Assure the system is easily upgradable.

PRINCIPLES AND RULES FOR DESIGN

VillageTown Layout:

- **Town of Villages:** The fundamental principle of the VillageTown layout is multiple villages built around public plazas in the center of each village. Accessed by many pedestrian streets, the public life is defined by these mixed-use villages.

- **10-minute walk:** Where geography permits, primary destinations (homes, shops, workplaces, services, etc.) to be within a 10-minute walk, roughly 3000-foot (1000 m) diameter with 25-30 units per acre. (70-75/h)

- **Contour:** Land defines the VillageTown. Work with the natural lay of the land and avoid major reshaping of the earth. Build homes and even shops on slopes, and provide for steep walks except in infirmity overlay zones. (Note: for ease of construction, choose relatively flat land to allow rapid build using large mobile factories).

- **Urban Open Space:** Within the urban core, allow 25-35% of the land for plazas, streets, footpaths, gardens, courtyards, etc.

- **Wall:** The VillageTown will benefit by a roughly 8-foot (2.4 m) high perimeter wall enclosing the whole of the VillageTown, punctuated with doors, access gates, gateways and one main VillageTown gate. The wall may be soft adobe-type design or in places living hedgerow. This wall sets the boundary – once built there will be no future expansion. The walls keep pets, toddlers and elders suffering dementia inside the villages.

- **Greenbelt:** Beyond the urban core, where land is available a Greenbelt is an important component, and it is desirable that its width be equal to the radius of the urban core. Place large parks, sports and equestrian fields, major food and flower gardens, festival fields and cemetery outside VillageTown walls in what is called a greenbelt.

- **Industrial Park:** Also, outside the urban core, a walk-to Industrial Park is essential to the economic well-being of the VillageTown. It is recommended that the industrial park be about 50 acres (20 h) in site coverage. If feasible, the roof of the Industrial Park should be made of turf that can be used for sports fields which lowers heating costs while providing additional Greenbelt land for recreation.

- **Village Plazas:** The heart of each village is its plaza, around which cafés, shops, services and workplaces are set. With residences set behind or over the workplaces. Plazas can be round, square, rectangular or irregular. Allow 11 plazas for a 5,000-population VillageTown, 21 for 10,000 people. This works out to an average of 500 persons per village, plus the town center's larger plaza.

- **Café:** Each plaza should have at least one café for gathering. The VillageTown shall provide rent-free, publicly owned sitting and dining space for plaza cafés. For a proprietor to serve the rent-free space, the tables must be regularly cleared and cleaned, but not ask people to vacate if they are not buying. Optionally, a village may elect to add the cost of a café or two to the price of their homes, and then provide the space at a nominal rent to a café operator. The terms would then require the price of food and drink sold reflect the lower overhead, and the quality meet the village's expectations.

- **Labyrinth Walk:** Multiple pedestrian streets and at least one boulevard shall connect each plaza. Plazas should be set out so a person can walk from one plaza to another for 1-2 hours as if in a labyrinth without having to retrace steps. This is to enable multiple village walks for residents and visitors that can be enjoyed frequently without becoming boring. Mark walks with subtle signs, distinctive patterns or marker stones, so visitors do not get lost or disoriented.

- **Attached housing:** Circular plazas will result in radial streets with tighter density closer to the plazas. Buildings along the plazas and on the pedestrian streets should share common walls (row houses). Some buildings may stand alone, including small cottages and grand homes (in the town-center zone with its higher four story height limit) that would be located away from the plazas and recessed from pedestrian streets.

- **Scale:** In determining the level of public prominence of particular plazas (the extent to which they are frequented by visitors), the surrounding buildings shall be higher and the plaza larger. Identify plazas as *center, primary, secondary and other*:

  Commercial Town Center: The town center will have the tallest buildings in the VillageTown including four-story office buildings and higher a clock/bell tower, bell or similar that is the highest building in the VillageTown (accessible by citizens and visitors as a lookout). Grand homes may be built in this district that may be three or four story, some of which may stand alone with grounds for gardens and courtyards.

  Primary plazas: three-story buildings with artist guild hall, non-denominational church, primary school classrooms. Non-uniform height encouraged.

  Secondary plazas: two- and three-story buildings, with artist guild hall, non-denominational church, primary school classrooms. Non-uniform height encouraged.

- **Town Center:** The VillageTown shall have one Central Town Plaza located in the center of the VillageTown, with the VillageTown Parade leading to it from the Main Gate. The VillageTown Hall shall be prominently located on this plaza; secondary and tertiary schools shall be on this plaza. The non-denominational cathedral for marriages, funerals as well as regular religious services shall be prominently located on this plaza. Capital and maintenance costs on these buildings are paid by the VillageTown.

  Note on Terminology: The terms *chapel, church* and *cathedral* do not imply a particular religion (or lack thereof). They do imply scale and ornamentation of buildings designed according to principles of sacred architecture. They are intended for sacred uses including rites of passage, such as birth, coming of age, marriage, and death – a place of peace, contemplation, meditation and prayer. Any religious group may arrange use of such buildings at no additional cost. In the case of a village founded around a common religion, the villagers may request their church be designed as a house of worship according to their needs. A religion that requires consecrated space to use the cathedral may pay for the construction of a small wing for which they would have exclusive use.

- **Size:** The town-center plaza shall be large enough to hold the whole population. Both the town hall and cathedral should have a balcony visible and audible by all in the plaza.

- **Location of public buildings:** The VillageTown libraries, museums, school rooms, artist guilds, sacred halls, municipal services and other prominent public buildings should be carefully distributed among the primary and secondary plazas to create a tapestry of interest throughout the VillageTown.

- **Overlays:** Provide for sensorial overlays (zone maps), including:

  Noise overlay identifying quiet and loud VillageTown areas

  Pleasant smells overlay: bakeries, spice grinders, roses

  Micro-climate overlay: warmer and colder places

  Visual interest overlay: framing natural and built places pleasant to view and for visitors/ media to photograph

  Infirmity overlay: identify parts of the VillageTown easier or harder to access by a person needing a cane to walk

  Activity Overlay: identify busy streets, less busy streets and lanes where residents go

- **Curved Streets**: VillageTown streets should avoid straight lines, except where sunlight is to be captured. Careful attention should be given to wind patterns to avoid creating cold wind tunnels but at the same time, supporting cooling breezes in summer. Buildings used to make turns (trapezoidal shaped) can be subsidized buildings (artist housing, parallel-market housing, elder housing, youth housing).

- **Links:** Most streets, lanes and alleys should connect. The exception would be small closes (enclosures) surrounded by attached homes and hotels – intimate public courtyards.

- **External Linkage:** Public service buildings, such as a primary medical center, that may be used by citizens of the region, shall be placed near the transport linkage center which is set outside the VillageTown walls near the primary road that connects with the world.

- **Food Boxes:** Food delivery boxes (a door in the wall) and recycling boxes (a door in the wall) required for every residence; designed to blend in with the streetscape.

Nature within the Village Town

Principle:

The VillageTown is medium density, attached housing. This typically means a high level of artificial surfaces: roofs, streets, plazas. Outside the urban core, the Greenbelt is intended to provide a high level of natural surfaces: fields, forest, gardens, green. However, people need plants, birds, butterflies and insects within the urban core, where the flora will be planned and planted. Often these plantings are most pleasing when they are done with love by a resident who lives nearby. Plantings tend to look artificial and passion-less when designed by the typical municipal consultant and put in by municipal maintenance staff.

Recommendations for village plans

Front of Homes: Each village will develop its own planting scheme based on its values and available land. The street in front of most homes should be considered as more formal and efficient. It is where people walk past and delivery vehicles bring mail, goods and food, and pick up empty food boxes and solid waste for recycling (food waste goes via a special pipe). As such, front streets should have a "fast" feeling to them; more formal.

Rear of Homes: In contrast, the alley behind most homes can have a slow feeling, less formal and designed to encourage a closely knit neighborhood. The alley should not be a thoroughfare, but almost private, for the people who live along both sides of that block. Thus, it should not be a typical city alley with fences, trash cans and stray cats fighting, but something more intimate. In some cases, a street may decide to put a neighborhood swimming pool in, or a shared playground or a barbecue ground with picnic tables.

- Most buildings should open directly onto the front street. Deliveries use the front. Front setbacks should be avoided, never at street corners. Avoid front gardens, but encourage plants and vines in pots or in window boxes. Arcades may provide cover over part of the street, and the adjacent house may use the living space above for raised gardens. Roof gardens are recommended on flat, partially shaded roofs.

- Consider green-streets instead of rear alleys. A green-street is planted, with a footpath in the middle, and plants flowers, dwarf trees (avoid trees that grow too tall over time), decorative shrubs, herbs and vegetables planted by adjacent neighbors. The VillageTown should own the street, but grant permission for the residents to tend their part. Some villages may encourage back porches along green-streets that can have potted plants. In cold climates, some may elect to glass-cover their green-streets.

- Flowered green-streets and intimate footpaths should provide many shortcuts between streets and lanes. Design these so their use does not annoy residents inhabiting homes adjacent (e.g. people walking home at 2 a.m. from a nearby pub).

- Plazas should have comprehensive planning for trees, flowering plants, even herbs for the restaurants and cafés. Trees that will grow big should be given prominence and space.

Transport and Roads

Plazas, Streets and Lanes

Definitions

Road types

- A **plaza** is open space in the center of a village with the highest level of daily activity
- A **street** includes mixed-use activity with parking for LSV's (low speed vehicles)
- A **lane** has only residential frontage and no on-street LSV parking
- A **road** is outside the VillageTown walls
- A **boulevard** is a wide street, typically the primary street connecting villages
- The **parade** is the widest street running from the main gate to the town center
- An **alley** runs behind homes and may provide access for collection and delivery
- A **green-street** is an alley with a footpath in the middle, and community-owned but neighbor-tended greenery along the sides – flowers, trees, grass, ornamentals
- A **winter-walk** is an alley that is weather enclosed and may be a green-street
- A **roadway** is any of the above
- A **footpath** is a narrow access way only for foot traffic, not suitable for wheels
- **Pedestrian streets/roads** may be as narrow as several yards/meters in width. Actual width will be based on projected traffic as well as on sunlight angles and aesthetics.
- **Connector footpaths** join pedestrian lanes/streets, may include steps and gates
- **Access roadway** – Each building must have direct access to a roadway of sufficient width to deliver goods and services. Each building must have at least one handicap access in accordance with law. The access width must provide for:
  1. Safe parking of a standard LSV
  2. Safe, slow passing room for a second LSV
  3. Pedestrians walking on the access street.
- **Pedestrian boulevards** connecting the main plazas may be substantially wider, but shall not be wider than the average adjacent building height unless for good reason.
- The **VillageTown Parade** is a single street wide enough to host a festival parade with all residents present. It connects the main gate to the central town plaza.

Road Surfaces, standards and details

Principle: Roads should be attractive, easily repaired and well engineered for the climate.

Surfaces: Asphalt is suitable for highways but is ugly and inappropriate for a human-scaled VillageTown. Better alternatives exist. When VillageTown streets must be dug up and reset, it is unacceptable to leave an obvious patch as with asphalt or slab concrete.

Flood Channel: While the VillageTown should have underground stormwater pipes, roads should be designed and maintained to carry overflow rainwater from five-hundred year storms without flooding buildings. This rule recognizes that storms that were once calculated to occur infrequently seem to be happening more frequently in recent years.

Permeability: Semi-permeable surfaces for some footpaths are recommended, including decorative rock and pavers with openings for topsoil that grows grass or moss. This enables rainfall to penetrate the earth and slow stormwater flow. Select easy-to-walk-on materials that do not require mowing. Where mowing is required, design for sheep and shepherds.

Rules

Durability: VillageTown streets shall be designed to a lighter standard than roads made to bear heavy trucks. During construction, access streets/roads shall be left unpaved with only gravel so as to not be damaged by the heavier vehicles required during construction.

Surface Materials: Street/road surfaces shall not use asphalt and slab cement as the exposed surface. Both have an adverse effect on the physical environment, and are bland at best and can be distinctly unattractive. Cobblestone or slab stone pavers shall be used for streets, and some lanes may use permeable grass-block in the centers (green streets).

Quiet strips: Streets and lanes may have narrow smooth separated lanes for pulling shopping carts, baby carriages (prams), and wheeled suitcases (quieter than dragging on cobblestone) and separate semi-smooth lanes for cycles and LSV's.

Curbs: VillageTown curbs may be provided on busier access streets, pedestrian boulevards and the VillageTown Parade to separate bicycles and low speed vehicles from pedestrians. Curbs generally shall be made of natural stone, not poured concrete because it tends to last for centuries and not take on a shabby appearance when worn.

Vehicle width: All roadways are owned by and subject to rules and regulations made by VillageTown authority. The VillageTown shall establish a maximum width of service vehicles and design lanes and streets accordingly. Example: width of a golf cart (1.2 m/48").

Motorpool: Outside the VillageTown walls, in a transport center, a motorpool shall provide covered parking for conventional cars and trucks, including visitors' vehicles and rental vehicles for residents. The transport center shall include storage of combustible fuels, vehicle-repair facilities and parts storage.

Freight Depot: A freight depot shall provide a place for goods to be off-loaded from delivery trucks and carried within the VillageTown by LSV's.

Pass Through: Regional roads shall connect with VillageTown streets at the Motorpool and Freight Depot. Regional roads shall not pass through the VillageTown. However, if a right of way is required or there by prior right, it shall either be placed below grade (or in a tunnel), or be walled in so it shall not interfere with VillageTown life. If a seaport is present, a connector road may need to go through the VillageTown – consideration may be given to placing it below grade to not impose on the pedestrian primacy of the VillageTown.

Vehicles: Village Town self-propelled and human-propelled vehicles

Definitions

LSV is a small Low Speed Vehicle for deliveries or passengers. It is propelled by an electric motor or compressed air, but not combustible fuels. It has two or more wheels. It has a speed governor that limits speed to a fast walking pace; speed limit set by the VillageTown.

Cycle is a human-powered bicycle, tricycle or quadracycle.

Trolley is any wheeled vehicle propelled by human or animal power, including a shopping cart, baby carriage (pram), wheeled suitcase, vendor cart or horse-drawn carriage.

Permitted Vehicle includes all of the above.

Principle

Cars and trucks are too big for human-scaled, medium-density villages. Their primary virtues, high-speed transport, are inappropriate within the limited distance of the VillageTown. Therefore, they are prohibited (except by special permit) within the VillageTown walls, where instead people will walk or use permitted vehicles. Delivery vehicles will be of a similar LSV size. All vehicles restricted to a fast walking pace except for emergency. This is a fundamental, non-negotiable characteristic of a VillageTown.

Rules

The VillageTown shall be enclosed by walls with gates, and no automobiles or trucks shall be permitted within the VillageTown walls except by special permit issued by the VillageTown, for a specific purpose and a specific time. Internal-combustion-propelled motorcycles and mopeds are not permitted on VillageTown streets because of their speed, noise and the need to store combustible fuels at fueling stations.

The VillageTown shall set speed limits for all permitted vehicles. This shall apply to all vehicles except emergency-service vehicles when on-call with activated emergency signals. LSV's shall have a speed governor to prevent speeding.

In Florence Italy, this electric garbage truck is small, slow and secondary to pedestrians. Contrast this to the typical big-city garbage truck that dominates and also is excessively loud. Note the sign that designates central Florence as a pedestrian and bicycle area.

Public service vehicles

Public service vehicles shall be owned by the VillageTown for the purposes of delivery of mail, goods and food, for trash collection, maintenance and other typical municipal services. These vehicles shall have VillageTown-standard speed governors on them.

Emergency fire service and vehicles

The VillageTown shall provide its own emergency services for building fires. Instead of designing the roads to suit large, conventional fire trucks, the VillageTown shall be designed for alternative and superior methods to deal with fire. All buildings will be made of non-combustible materials and have domestic or commercial sprinkler systems. Fire-suppression apparatus including hoses, ladders and extinguishers shall be permanently located in rapidly accessible places throughout the VillageTown to preclude to the need for fire-protection services transporting their own hoses, ladders or water on fire trucks.

Emergency-services vehicles will have a speed governor override that may be activated provided the emergency signals (lights and perhaps horn) are switched on.

Ambulance

Ambulance: Medical clinics in the VillageTown shall be equipped with machines and medicines found on a rural ambulance, where the role of emergency medical technicians is to provide on-site intervention and transport the patient to a clinic no more than two minutes from any house, or to the VillageTown helicopter pad for medical evacuation.

Low speed vehicle access

Principle

LSV's require access and parking. They may not be used on footpaths.

Pedestrians hold primacy, wheeled vehicles are secondary – the faster the vehicle can go, the lower its priority (in other words a bicycle is lower priority than a slower mobility scooter).

Rules

Off-street parking and garage access for privately owned LSV's shall not be paved with a driveway made of asphalt or slab cement. Where smooth surfaces are required for trolleys, narrow strips of paving or hard rubber may be used to suppress wheel noise.

In higher-traffic streets and roads in the VillageTown, wheeled traffic may be separated from pedestrian by a curb and elevation.

Because of narrowness, presence of stairs and to provide walks with no vehicles, VillageTown-permitted vehicles may not use or block footpaths.

The VillageTown may elect to provide on-street, community-owned LSV's that may be used by pre-qualified residents activated by swipe cards. Such vehicles parked at on-street charging stations.

Low-speed electric four-wheeled car and two-wheeled electric scooter at a public charging station. Note that both should have speed governors to keep to a walking pace for use in the urban core.

Public utilities including cables, wires and pipes

Avoid wireless systems using radio frequencies (RF). The cumulative effects of RF are unknown. Use cables and provide connection points everywhere. Overhead or surface-mounted wires or cables are not permitted in the VillageTown. Avoid wireless networks in every home, and if wireless transmitters are required in public spaces, use low-power, short-range systems that only connect to a designed part of the space. While cell phones have become almost universal, they tend to have adverse effects on human interaction, especially children. Avoid a cell-phone culture, encourage face-to-face contact.

All services shall be installed in trenches (or walls) covered with removable panels to provide access without requiring the breaking of any surface (no jack-hammers). Pipes shall be placed in the same trenches except where engineering or safety requires separation. The trenches shall be owned by the VillageTown, which shall license any private services who require use of them. Where wireless is essential, design transmission to be short distance, such as part of a café set aside for wireless reception.

Utility provision shall include sufficient room and access for changes in technology, so installation of new cables or pipes is a simple matter of removing lockable or heavy (if stone/concrete) panels and installing the new cables or pipes.

Utility access grids, grills, covers and other access;

Grills, grids, inspection covers and all visible components of service providers shall comply with a prescribed VillageTown standard, which it may from time to time update. Note that different villages within the VillageTown may choose different standards. The exposed components shall comply with an artistic standard set by the VillageTown. For example, iron grates shall be made with decorative visible design, not just a utilitarian finish.

Earthworks including reshaping, landscape and plantings

Principle

Work with nature, do not dominate it. Let buildings and access follow the contour of the land. Land contouring and earthworks shall be part of the original design brief and once completed, no further work done unless there is a compelling reason that was not anticipated during the original project. Work with the land where feasible. Design buildings that cascade down hills rather than flatten the hills. Except to provide for infirmity, build exterior stairs: give people exercise; reduce escalator and elevator energy consumption.

Rules

In the original design brief, the VillageTown shall identify all landscape features with clear and precise language governing their preservation or removal. Any future changes to landscape features shall be subject to permission by the VillageTown and any appropriate approving agencies, in accordance with law.

Within the VillageTown walls, plants in the ground shall be subject to a comprehensive pre-planting regulatory plan to prevent them from growing into nuisances due to size, shadow, maintenance, pollen or debris. The plan shall encourage easy-to-manage plants in moveable pots and also encourage household gardens but not on street frontages.

Consistency in landscape features

The VillageTown seeks to have a particular character that makes it distinctive from everywhere else. This is attained by a clear statement identifying the distinctive character and then assuring the landscape features are planned to be consistent with that statement. Consistency does not mean sameness. VillageTown character can include diversity, village by village, but within in this diversity, a measure of harmony.

The houses in this often photographed street in Poundbury England are attached, the street is narrow and it curves, adding visual interest.

Architectural Harmony and Integration Rules

The Design Code created by the VillageTown founders in the Dynamic Engagement process shall set the architectural style and set out the distinctive character of each village. Different villages may have radically different architecture – one with historic references such as the Poundbury example above, and the next cutting edge architecture. However, within a particular village it is important that one building does not clash with the next. This is accomplished through a village-wide dialogue at time of Dynamic Engagement.

Reference: As a general reference manual, this Design Code incorporates *A Pattern Language* by Christopher Alexander (1977© ISBN 0-19-501919-9). The patterns found therein provide guidance in determining what will work, and add to the quality of life of the VillageTown.

Building materials, shape of buildings and of roofs.

Principle

A general theme shall be established for the VillageTown, but within that theme, individual villages shall establish a distinctive architectural style in accordance with the character planned for the particular village. The VillageTown plan sets out the level of prescriptive rules, village by village.

Unless a village's character is set otherwise, a timeless vernacular appearance is encouraged as the overall character of the village and a classical formal appearance for prominent public buildings. The VillageTown design seeks to remain standing and useful for at least seven generations (175 years) and perhaps much longer. Thus, it becomes important to design for timeless beauty that is durable and functional.

> ### Recommendation
>
> It is recommended to use *variable density aggregate* (VDA) as a single bulk material for almost all buildings in the VillageTown. This material combines cement, sand and water with a foaming additive that reduces density to increase thermal and acoustical insulation qualities and substantially increase its fire rating, to four-hour or greater. By pouring a 12 inch (300 mm) thick wall, exceptionally high insulation qualities can be achieved requiring to make the wall a complete package - no additional insulation, cladding on inside or outside, and doors, windows, utility conduit and other building services are installed and locked in by the VDA. If carved molds are used inside the forms, a completely finished wall, complete with ornament and functional features (such as window sills) can be poured in a single day. The same system can be used for floors and the roof, using pre or post tensioning to create sound-proof floors that have four-hour fire ratings. Sprinkler systems can be installed before pouring, using a conduit/pipe system that is encased in the solid ceiling. VDA was invented in Germany in the 1920's. It is in its second generation, and is a proven product. Its construction technique is standard slab wall and floor.
>
> On interior, non-load-bearing walls, the same material can be used in what is called a key-block, where the VDA is poured into a mold that makes a Lego® type locking block that also is non-combustible, but can be altered when interior space requirements demand it. Typically this block is plastered, and can be painted or whitewashed.

Rules

All foundations, walls, floors and roofs shall be predominantly made of non combustible, high fire-rated mineral materials. Under almost all circumstances, cavity wall construction using timber or metal studs shall be prohibited. In some jurisdictions the International Building Code - Class II-a (non-combustible masonry) standards may be applicable.

Combustible or toxic materials, such as polystyrene insulation or vinyl cladding shall not be permitted. Timber shall be permitted for exterior and interior ornamentation, for doors and windows, floor and wall surfaces and solid lintels if left exposed, but in all cases it shall be used in a way that makes conflagration impossible. (Example: a solid timber floor is laid over VDA with a 1" (25 mm) raised gap).

Comment: Architects and owners are asked to consider the overall feeling, harmony and integrity of the design of each village, and not propose to build a design intending to fly in the face of the overall design and integrity of that village.

Thick walls shall be encouraged, for aesthetic purposes and for thermal and noise insulation. No site coverage penalty shall be incurred by the use of thick walls up to 600 mm thick.

Principle
Human-scaled buildings appear timeless when their surfaces are not completely regular, and when they have a softer feeling to them. This is best achieved by hand finishing using natural materials.

Rules
Synthetic materials (such as vinyl cladding) prohibited.

Angled roofs shall be made of natural, long lasting materials that hold in highest winds. No iron or color steel (but copper can work), no asphalt shingles or synthetic roofing. Clay or concrete tile and slate are permitted. A color standard shall be set for villages. Shed-style low-angled roofs (3 to 19 degree pitch) shall require a village architectural review, as they tend not to work in medium-density buildings.

Flat roofs with roof gardens and outdoor living shall be encouraged. Such designs require careful installation to avoid leaks over time.

Building shapes to be variable but in harmony. Trendy styles that may soon become obsolete shall not be permitted unless a whole village is done in such a style. Simple styles are variations on angular basic forms, with set back for walls, courtyards and attached buildings. Encourage ornament and detail to break up flat surfaces. Most buildings not to exceed two or three stories, some with gables permitted in livable attics above.

Open Fire and Chimneys
The fireplace harks back to an ancient sense of home. It plays an important archetypal role and can serve as a backup in the event of catastrophic loss of public power. However, it should not be used as a primary heat source in a VillageTown due to the density and the logistics related to firewood. Residential chimneys should be built of the same VDA and may require smoke scrubbers to prevent air pollution. If metal chimneys are required for earthquake safety or to control capital building costs, they shall be clad in a rectangular

metal frame and mineral sheeting, plastered with a render that matches the rest of the building. Depending on local circumstances it may be necessary to restrict such open fires to public gathering places and to require smoke scrubbers to remove pollutants.

Exterior Visible Doors and Windows

Principle

Fenestration: windows and doors form the faces of the community – its eyes and mouths. When they are beautiful, the village is more beautiful; when they are not – the village looks less loved. Beautiful fenestration often comes from local artisans, and for this reason, the action plan for this part of the code may include fostering such local crafts. If beautiful doors and windows are easy to purchase, and come with little overhead since the maker is the vendor, one can expect these to be the solution selected by owners, designers and builders. Beyond this economic action plan, however, the Code should set out rules for fenestration.

The art of fenestration is both demanding and too often neglected, yet it has the greatest impact on the presentation of the community – its public face. Considerable care is needed in defining the terms for fenestration, especially as recent history showed us maverick architects who rose to the challenge of producing a very controversial design that technically met the design code but upset people who had to live next to it.

Rules

The plazas shall be surrounded with work places – offices, shops and cafés, workshops. These workplaces shall have large windows so children get to observe role models, and the workers get to keep an eye on the children.

Large windows shall be required on all ground-floor buildings facing the plazas. Decorative windows with small panes shall be encouraged. Wood-frame windows, especially with multiple panes provide a desirable detail and are encouraged. Each village shall establish its own code for the windows and doors to be used on buildings facing the plaza.

Plate-glass window shall be discouraged, especially at corners, unless the village intent is for a trendy look that will eventually become a historic period piece. Windows should frame rather than spread too wide or high.

Doors and surrounds – Public entry doors are a major definer of the community. Encourage entry doors to be of carved or joined wood. Antique, recycled doors of distinctive character recommended where weatherproofing can be addressed. Secondary screen/storm doors to be of equal quality or installed so they are invisible from the street or plaza.

If 2% for art is applied to commercial buildings consider allowances for carved fenestration.

Recommendation
Establish joinery (window/door making) shops on site during construction to minimize deliveries and provide high-quality products for local conditions. Note that in a 10,000-population VillageTown with 4,000 buildings, one may reasonably project the need for over 100,000 doors and windows. Such doors and windows will require a special boxing system if they are installed using a poured-wall system. By using such a system the cost of installation is significantly less since there is no final fitting after the wall is up.

Doors and windows in private homes

Principle
The front doors of a private home, when in public view, make a significant contribution to the character of the village. The VillageTown should encourage owners to make them beautiful and substantial.

Rules
Front doors shall be hinged not open outward except where they open onto a porch. They shall be made of solid core wood, and carved or panelled wood is recommended. In private homes, glass is not recommended in the bottom half of the door. If storm doors are required, they must be of the same thickness, beauty and build standard as the front door. Surrounds and lintels shall be encouraged, especially carved and/or ornamental.

Windows

Windows shall be harmonious both with the building design and with the streetscape. Large plate-glass slabs shall be discouraged and where used, need to be handled with great care so as to not be overwhelming in appearance and create environmental problems in terms of overheating in summer, and heat loss in winter.

Placed with care, larger glass windows and doors facing the sun can be most effective in collecting solar heat in winter on heat-sink floors and walls (thick stone or aggregate) and being blocked out by carefully calculated overhangs.

Window flower boxes may be encouraged on facing designated streets, and if they are so designated, the construction specifications shall include permanent, pre-installed (in wall slab) grey-watering tubes direct to the window base, to enable automatic watering of the flower boxes so they remain alive and attractive.

Window shutters are recommended, both for their practical application in shading and cooling, and for the manner in which they dress the building.

Security Bars

If required, make security bars decorative as well as functional. Fine wrought iron sends not the message of fear and crime, but rather one of elegance. Consider such doors and windows as qualifying for the 2% for art standard, which means they are done to a higher standard.

Recommendation

Encourage the art of the blacksmith to produce works of art, not merely the utility of passive protection. Support a local blacksmith industry early in the construction phase to provide an economic opportunity for artisans in metalwork to move in and get established at the time of highest demand for services.

Factories and Industrial Zone Buildings

Principle

While most VillageTowns are expected to have a separate Industrial Park near the Freight Depot, not all larger work places, factories and industrial buildings need to be located there. They may be within the VillageTown, provided they blend in and do not emit noxious dust, offensive smells or loud noise, nor have too many deliveries coming and going. As larger buildings, the necessity to blend them into their village sets an expectation for design, especially door and window design that fits the neighborhood. Code language might be general, as below, or prescriptive:

Rule

Industrial buildings in villages shall follow a building design consistent with the VillageTown master plan, and shall use doors and windows that fit harmoniously with the neighboring non-industrial buildings. This may include attractively designed false windows and doors in cases where the utility needs of the industry conflict with the aesthetic needs of the village.

2% for art in all public buildings and plazas.

Principle – Art is the mark of a community that values more than just the practical, the functional and the efficient.

Comment

Art often speaks to the state of humanity. If that state is confused, angry, detached from love of land, place and community, such art may undermine the sense of village.

Thus, the founders are advised to enter into a deep discussion about what art, before selecting it – and in doing so yield not to the experts, pundits or tastemakers – remember it's your village not theirs, and it will stand for generations.

Recommend language

2% of the construction budget for all public buildings and plazas shall be set aside for works of artistic merit. Mandatory funds for art shall be deposited in an escrow account at the beginning of the project to assure it remains available for art. Art may include ornament, but shall be subject to architectural harmony standards.

It is recommended that the artist guilds be invited to participate (but not dominate) the dialogue on public art. The guild members should be encouraged to bid on contracts to provide public art, understanding that as with any vendor the VillageTown decision makers must hold the artist at arms length prior to awarding the contract.

It is recommended that specifications for public art include either a durability clause, assuring the work will last, or be a time limited lease, at the end of which the artist understand their obligation to remove the artwork at their expense. Without such clauses, the VillageTown can find they are saddled with a deteriorating work that involves unanticipated expense for the public.

The VillageTown may want to classify public art as timeless or time limited. Prior to purchase or lease, set a specific length of time when the art will be reviewed to determine if it should remain in place or be removed.

In addition to public art placed in plazas and public buildings, the VillageTown may consider sponsoring or seeking sponsorship for sculpture gardens, halls for performance art, experiential labyrinths and other creative physical environments intended to enhance the experience of contemporary art.

Note: Some of the 2% may be used for ornament and carving on the buildings.

Walls and fences between properties

Principle – Walls and fences can be an important part of medium-density housing, as they balance the private and public spaces. In some cases walls may be a full story or even two stories in height, functioning more as outdoor rooms than walled-in grass or garden. This may include rooftop open space where the side wall adjoining the next house becomes important. If there is a mansion district (probably in the Town Center with its higher, larger buildings) with custom-designed detached homes that pay for extra land, iron fences balance security with the ability to see architecture that deserves to be seen.

In approving fences and walls, the VillageTown must give consideration to sunlight, not depriving a neighbor of sun due to extreme height. As each village sets out its own wall and fence code, consider the extent that it should be prescriptive. Walls are easy to get wrong, and can have an adverse impact.

Rules: Walls shall be built of solid wall materials of a vernacular form, not ugly materials such as exposed cinder block. The irregular, hand-made appearance marks the difference between a lovely garden wall and a prison. Adobe or whitewashed finishes provide a low-cost, easily maintained surface. In some cases, consider the living hedgerow instead of a wall. This especially may apply for walls marking the end of one village.

The VillageTown shall be surrounded in most places by the VillageTown wall, both to establish a clear boundary between it and the rural aspect beyond the VillageTown, and to keep domestic pets from becoming predators for wildlife outside the VillageTown. Some parts of that wall may form part of a privately owned building, but VillageTown controlled. In some parts, the wall may be made of hedgerow, meaning it is made of living, woody plants that maintain their form over thousands of years if properly cared for.

Fences shall not be purely utilitarian. Chain-link fences and fences made of roof iron or other sheet materials shall not be permitted in the VillageTown except perhaps for chain link used to enclose tennis courts. Wrought-iron fences are recommended. Wooden fencing is prohibited in the VillageTown due to the risk of fire and the problem of rot.

Exterior paint, coatings and render.

Principle

A long-standing tenet of architecture says that large and flat wall surfaces need to be broken up if they are to be attractive. In recent times, pressure to cut costs and standardize finishing pushed architecture into large flat painted surfaces, with the unfortunate result that the buildings add nothing to the character of the community. Too often the result is boring – practical but ugly. The problem is not paint alone, but the sheet material used underneath. It lacks texture, or if it has texture it is machine applied, and the eye can immediately spot the artificiality of it. In contrast, renders that are applied with an irregular color and texture can break up the surface especially as they weather over time.

Paint can be cheap to first apply, but repainting can be expensive and produce noxious noise and dust as surfaces are prepared. Render (whitewash, clay-based slurry, distemper and other mineral-based traditional coverings, can be exceedingly inexpensive, forgiving, easy to clean up and easy to re-apply.

Exterior fenestration and building detail may be painted provided it covers less than 10% of the building exterior's surface, and it is able to be maintained without significant noxious noise, odor or dust when it must be removed and repainted.

Rules

Exterior walls: All exterior wall coatings to be mineral: Stone tile or native-clay slurries (with sand, cement or lime) No paint.

All wall coatings to be maintained without requiring extensive scraping, sanding, blasting (other than water) or other labor-intensive preparation. Recommended coatings include natural clay tints, optional supplements with oxide tints of earth tones. In areas where the visual effect of white buildings is deemed attractive, permit pure white, limewashed coatings.

Verticality – External Staircases, Bridges & Catwalks

Principle – In higher-density developments such as a VillageTown, careful use of verticality – exterior stairways, bridges over footpaths and narrow elevated walkways (often known as catwalks) both add texture to the character of the community, and provide more efficient, lower-cost land use than enclosed stairways and hallways.

Design with external staircases to homes, with upper-level bridges and walkways.

A Place to Sit or Rest

The VillageTown shall provide many benches, wide public steps, low walls, buildings with places to sit as part of their structure and other comfortable places to sit and to lie down. Care shall be taken to design them for variable weather conditions, some wind protected, some shaded in hot summer, others sunny for cooler days.

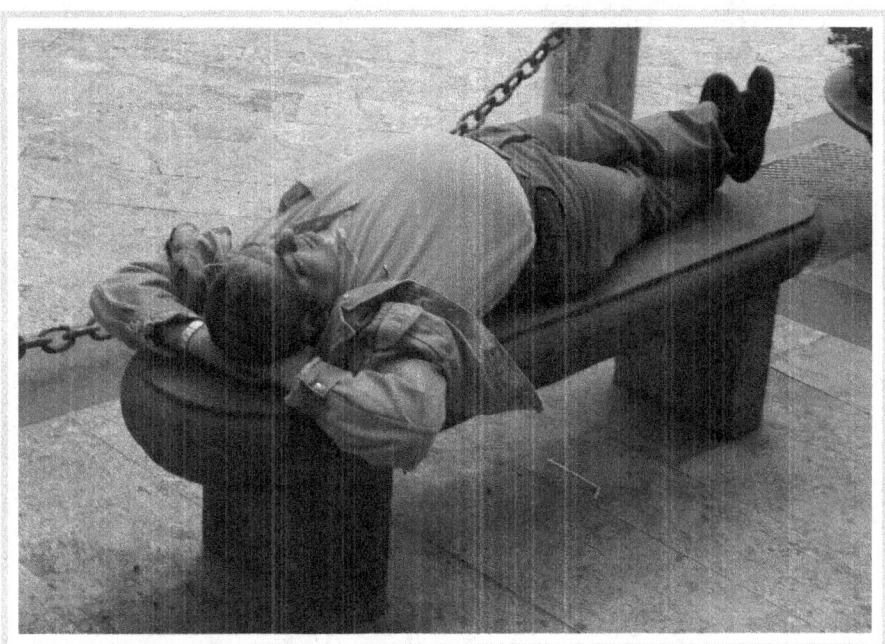

In setting out both formal seating and casual seating designed for other purposes, such as steps, consider the informal communities that will gather there. Some will become places for teenagers, others for workers eating their lunch. Some will provide views, others for rest or passing the time of day. Avoid placing seating near rubbish bins. Place seating near stone or concrete walls that absorb sunlight and create a warm micro-climate in the evening.

Public Spaces Design and Ornament

Principle – The functionality and visual appearance of the ornament and furniture that graces the public outdoor spaces become an important part of the quality and identity of each village. Decisions on their design and appearance should not be left to purchasing agents or engineers.

- Signs shall have a consistent and attractive form of design and lettering. Each village shall decide if it wishes to use posts with mounted signs, or street

signs permanently mounted on corner buildings, carved in stone or formed concrete. Use intuitive design to avoid dependency on signs with many rules or directions. Favor smart design not words. Where words are essential the VillageTown shall establish a prescriptive sign ordinance requiring beautiful lettering and prohibiting signs with logos larger than one hand in size.

- Street lighting shall be selected that it does not spill light (where it is not needed, such as upward into the sky which means the night time is never dark) or waste energy. Street lights shall be ornamental, not strictly utilitarian.

- Bollards (traffic posts) and other traffic-control devices shall be of a handsome appearance, not easily damaged or bent.

- Street furniture, including seats and benches, shall be attractive, comfortable and placed appropriately for sun and wind.

- Public gardens and plantings shall be carefully selected in location and plants to enhance the VillageTown ambiance. Low fencing should clearly delineate flower and fruit plants that should not be touched in contrast to those which may freely be picked by residents. The VillageTown should plant many fruit-tree varieties to encourage residents, especially children, to pick and eat. Select location carefully so leaves and peels do not become litter.

MODEL VILLAGE PATTERNS

Each village will be different. However, each village will establish its own design code based on what is called *Pattern Cards*. Patterns, as defined by Christopher Alexander in *A Pattern Language* give the future villagers a language within which to identify what is important for them. The VillageTown Design Code sets out the basic framework – for example, no ten story buildings or quarter acre house sites. Within that code, each village then sets out its own framework to achieve a harmony of streetscape and architecture.

This framework is completed by the founding villagers in the Dynamic Engagement process. It then guides the design of individual buildings to be built by private buyers using the assistance of VillageTown architects in some cases, and privately retained architects in others.

In this section, we select a sample theme, the Italian Village and then include alternatives to stimulate thought.

Name

Italian Village.

Tutorial:

The name should refer to its primary theme so people understand it in a word or two. The name can be humorous or clever within limits, noting that generations to come have to live with it. For example, in the book *Life Liberty Happiness*, where the VillageTown idea is told in story form, one village is called Suvieville, where SUV stands for Single Unencumbered Villager – a village for single people who wish to enjoy the freedoms and conviviality that comes from living alone without the constant pressure from friends and family to get into a long-term relationship. In this village, the village coordinator was second generation of Italian ancestry who loved the warmth and family nature of her childhood in the new world, and the experiences when going back to visit her extended family's village in Italy. In proposing to use this as the archetype, she found interest in Italians living in Italy who find while visitors love it, the present day reality is very different – to the point where they wish to emigrate.

Theme

The theme of this village is taken from the archetypes found in present day Italian towns, embracing the warm and artistic architectural style, slow food conviviality, alfresco life, and hosting a significant number of Italian migrants. The Italian Village is based on nationality or ethnicity, but will expect that many of its residents may not be Italian or of Italian descent – that instead they choose the Italian Village because they love going to Italy, and would love to live there except for the challenges of learning a new language, the insularity of doing business or finding a professional job and the inefficiency and insider nature of its politics and economy.

Tutorial -The character of each plaza and surrounding neighborhood is hopes to be unique, and to reflect the common character of the people who cluster together to design it. A few ideas about clustering commonality: nationality or ethnicity, social networks (big families, solo trendies or the youth zone), occupational clusters, food & beverage, film making or music or theater or all three, sculptors, painters, carvers and furniture makers, cultural and intellectual - the university connection, scholarly - think tanks, high-tech and venture capital, religious (but tolerant), blue-collar, architectural, the town central plaza - uptown larger homes

Architectural Guidelines

These first few items are the highlights of what makes the theme of the village. These highlights are then supported by a list of the relevant patterns as developed in the Pattern Language portion of the Dynamic Engagement design process.

Vernacular and Classical

Italian vernacular architecture is characterized by warm, welcoming softness. Its classical architecture is formal, geometrical, detailed, ornamental, balanced and harmonious. At its best, the vernacular reflects the owner, such as flower boxes and potted plants growing up the wall, the colors chosen for each building and the choice of half hidden gardens, courtyard or rooftop living.

Windows are both for light and for viewing, with outside balconies to sit and watch life go by or read the paper in the early warming sun. Shutters are actively used and are traditional, with real shutters, not from plastic molds. Paints are made from lime and chalk based slurries so they wear out beautifully, not looking worn and chipped like modern paints. Some buildings will be coated with different colors from time to time, and over the years, the older colors will show through to become a favorite subject of travel photographers.

The important buildings in the Italian Village will be based on classical design principles, formal and ornamented. Colors will be whites and sometimes contrasting blacks. Balance and harmony are paramount. It should be noted that modern Italian design follows different principles, which this Italian village does not embrace. The street-front visual design of important buildings will be approved by the village design panel (elected by the future villagers) on a case-by-case basis.

Color and textures

Colors include warm earth tones with brown, warm yellows, soft oranges and deep reds or lighter maroon pinks. Warm means the color of a peach not the color of a fire-truck. Base tones tend to match those found in nature: goldenrod, rich clays, rusts, soft sunsets, straw, although with care they can also include the occasional cooler colors of with tints of light greens, blues and purples. Details may be contrasting. Shutters may be dark green, for example. An arch over a door may be maroon. Color may be used to break up surfaces with a wall face having a main color of deep orange and beltlines and corner blocks of ocher yellow. Natural unpolished stone imbedded as tiles or stones can add a wonderful feel to the streetscape, and has the advantage of lasting for centuries.

Texture goes from the microscopic to large carved ornament. At the microscopic level, the wall surfaces are not shiny; they have a softness that comes from mineral finishes, not paint. Surface ornament breaks up flat slab surfaces, and walls can have a surface irregularity that traditionally came from hand applied plaster, but which can be replaced in 3d molds.

Windows and Doors

Upper floor windows tend to open onto balconies if they are floor length or flower boxes if they are waist height. Most have active real shutters that are in regular use, both for privacy and to control sunlight. Upper floor windows tend not to be wider than one yard or meter, never plate glass, and taller than wide. Often they are hinged on both sides, opening in or out rather than single or double hung that slide up in the track. Some have divided panes, and detail is important.

Front doors tend to be wood, custom made with fine detail and hardware to make a major statement about the home and occupant.

Guild Hall

The Designers Guild – Italian design is world renowned. In deciding what guild hall to hose, the Italian village was divided between several of the arts. Opera was strongly advocated, however, advice from one of opera's superstars suggested this would always prove a disappointment as success in opera is limited to a few parts of the world. Finally, the broad term of design was selected, to enable the guild to attract top designers in many fields who would thrive given the strong new venture and entrepreneur character of the wider VillageTown.

Sample: Patterns for Village with an Italianate Theme

The following is a sample of the work done using the Pattern Cards. Pattern Cards are business card sized magnetic-backed cards printed on an inkjet printer that contain a summary of a timeless piece of wisdom that forms the language of architecture, design and construction. Inspired by Christopher Alexander's *A Pattern Language* the founding villagers examine all the patterns on a magnetic whiteboard, and select cards that are applicable to their work. Obviously Pattern 2 *The Distribution of Towns* for example, is not relevant to planning a village within the framework of the VillageTown so it is discarded.

In addition to the patterns selected (which are numbered to correspond with *A Pattern Language*) the workshop participants will create their own patterns. For simplicity, below only the book patterns are used. For the most part, the patterns as drafted do not repeat the pattern card, or the supporting material in the book, as the book is available and anyone having gotten this far is well advised to order a copy from patternlanguage.com or through normal book buying channels (although to support Christopher Alexander, it is kinder to order direct from www.patternlanguage.com/leveltwo/books.htm as his team earns more than if the order goes through the distribution system).

These annotated patterns form the design code from which the 100:1 scale model will be developed and the design code set out for the design of individual homes.

Patterns

14 - **Identifiable Neighborhood**: The primary identity of the Italian Village is Italy. This is brought about by its founders who include first generation immigrants whose native tongue is Italian, as well as children and grandchildren of migrants who wish to honor their ancestry. The identity is established by architecture, especially building face ornament, style and colors. It is made living by foods, the character of conviviality and by its Artist Guild Hall.

15: **Neighborhood Boundary** - The village boundary will be defined by a surrounding loop bike and pony path on three sides and the VillageTown wall on the fourth. Horses and ponies are important for the young, and for the most part are kept in the Greenbelt. However, they are permitted to be ridden on special paths within. The loop path has a low decorative sitting wall (see pattern 243) running down its middle, whose purposes include separating ponies and bikes into two proximate but safe paths, preventing young children from wandering beyond their village and a place for the young to hang out at the edge of their neighborhood, to meet with young from other neighborhoods. At the primary street's boundary, the village gate (Pattern 53) will ceremonially mark the transition into and out of the village.

18 - Network of Learning: By removing cars from the villages, natural learning occurs through the public life of the village. Children, working adults and elders are all in proximity to each other, which creates the environment where the older teach the young. This occurs informally, through the classrooms set among the village, through part time jobs, internships and apprenticeships.

21 - Story Limit: Homes in the Italian village will be two or three stories with height limits governed by sunlight orientation. The top floor can have a split roof where above it some is a flat space for outdoor living covered by a raised roof, meaning the sides are open (no glass or dark screens) but the flat area is protected from sun and rain.

24 - Sacred Sites: The village will have a single-floor, high-ceiling chapel and behind it an open garden for mediation.

26 - Life Cycle: The seven stages of life are incorporated in the village's design

Infant – Homes are soundproof and private, streets are for promenade designed for comfortable wheeling of baby carriages or buggies. The cafés and public spaces are designed for parents with babies.

Young Child – The plaza offers play areas. Older children look after younger. Elders are available to baby-sit. Parents establish play groups and share the load. The greenbelt can provide a place for a petting zoo with domestic animals such as goats who can visited.

Child – The streets are safe so a child may walk into the plaza unsupervised. The neighborhood boundaries and greenbelt wall establish limits to wandering. The home intranet system will enable parents to buzz each other to keep track of children easily. The village decided to offer an early Montessori learning center for children beginning at age 2 to 6.

Youngster – The school classrooms to be on the plaza. Because the village is along the perimeter wall, the proximate part of the greenbelt will include a wooded play area with trees for building forts, holes for children's caves and other places of child-built fantasy. Several of the boundary homes will overlook the greenbelt with their workplaces facing outward. The plaza playground will offer several stages so that older, more active children will not overwhelm younger.

Youth – For teens, the plaza will have hang-out places, niches where intimacy can occur without going too far. In the greenbelt access to the climbing wall and skateboard / bike park and the equestrian fields will be within a ten minute walk. The village will have a policy of supporting youth jobs, seeking to create both opportunity and to teach good work habits. For high-school graduates, opportunities include internships, apprenticeships and the ability to buy homes in the youth zone. While in another village there will be a university abroad program, those youth going on to tertiary education are expected to leave the village for a time, as they experience the wide world. Those who wish to remain, may do so by moving directly to the youth zone, and those who graduate from university will find they can return if they so choose.

Young Adults — Small homes will provide the next stage of housing; homes for couples; some of whom will have met in the youth zone and sold two youth homes to buy their first home together. Rites of passage marked in the village chapel for marriage and birth of children. The many job and career opportunities enable the young to begin to build wealth and establish themselves.

Adult — The wide range of work and industry provides opportunities to establish one's career and thrive. Larger homes provide for growing families, and the plaza and VillageTown life provide a wide range of artistic and intellectual opportunities, conviviality and the invitation to be involved in the citizenship role of managing one's community. The sports fields provide access to local sport, the guild halls to enriched culture.

Elder — Downsizing into elder housing, small single floor homes especially built for (and restricted to) individuals and couples where the eldest is over age 64. When infirm, the nursing care facilities allow the elder to remain in the village, all the way to death with hospice care. Settled work places enable elders to remain active, some working alone, others in groups. Elders encouraged to volunteer with the schools and establish mentor relationships with the young.

29 - Density Rings: The village uses density rings, or micro-zoning as it is called. The central plaza provides for the highest level of activity and general background noise. The shops and offices with the highest level of foot traffic are set on the plaza, and on upper floors, either more offices with less foot traffic, visitor accommodations or apartment style residences for people who enjoy overlooking the bustle of the plaza. Radiating out, the primary village street provides for more shops, quieter restaurants and offices that have lower, but still significant foot traffic. Finally, two grades of secondary streets: quieter and very quiet, where the latter are dead-end so the only foot traffic are people delivering to or walking to home.

31 - Promenade: Going from the village gate to the village plaza will be one primary street that serves as the promenade. It will be the widest street in the village, wide enough that the whole village can be out walking and not feel crowded, even as they stop to greet each other. It will have two-way strips for bikes and LSV's, as well as separate smooth strips for baby carriages and people walking with shopping carts and wheeled suitcases. The promenade will have seating along its edges where people may sit and rest, and will provide widened space so cafés may have outdoor tables and umbrellas along its edges. The promenade will have brighter down-lighting so people can see each other's faces after dark. This lighting will switch to low-lumen motion activated LED lighting after 11 p.m. The promenade is connected to the network of primary streets, so a parade from one village to another has proper linkage.

32 - Shopping Street Promenade: The main pedestrian street leading into the Italian Village will be lined with ground floor commercial establishments that have regular foot traffic.

33 - Night Life: Active night life is intended to occur on the main village plaza to contain noise. The access streets are designed so the noise should not bother those in the quiet areas.

34 - Household Mix: Families, extended families, solo homes, elder housing all mixed. Upper floor living over the plaza commercial establishments.

35 - Degree of Publicness: Upper floor residences and hotel rooms over the plaza and along the primary pedestrian street are intended for people who enjoy high levels of activity. Secondary streets that connect will provide quieter living but still people passing by. Off the secondary streets, small clusters with dead-end streets will provide the least public places where typically the only pedestrians are residents and visitors to those residents.

36 - Housing Clusters: Groups of homes may share a common, semi-private courtyard.

38 - Row Houses: Almost all homes will be attached, but few will be narrower than deep. Most will be wide and in some cases, the alley in the back will be wider than the pedestrian street in the front.

40 - Old People Everywhere: Elder Housing will be ground floor with most built close to the plaza with easy to transverse roads. The plaza shall house an 8 bed nursing facility with windows that open onto the plaza so even the bedridden may feel a part of daily life if they choose to open the curtains and windows. Numerous warm sitting areas to be provided on the plaza and on the streets, designed to be usable by elders.

41 -Work Community: Because the Guild Hall is about design, it can support surrounding businesses that benefit from design. Some of these businesses will be on the plaza, and others will be in a cluster adjacent to the Guild Hall.

43 - University as a Marketplace: The Guild Hall will offer classes in design for all the villages and for visitors. The small visitors' inn and the tavern on the ground floor will provide a place for interaction between locals and visitors, that provides for informal education.

46 - Market of Many Shops: The Italian Plaza is a Slow Food Plaza. While much food will be direct from farm to food boxes, the main plaza in the Italian village will sponsor a weekly farmer's market, and will have many individual food shops. Fresh fruit, vegetable and flower shops; the butcher, fish monger, baker and specialty food stores are the kinds of stores intended to have a presence on the plaza. In addition, the presence of the Design Guild is hoped to provide support for design businesses that market through the Internet, but also have public shops on the plaza and the village's primary pedestrian street. Support for

Settled Work (Pattern 156) by elders (Pattern 40) is incorporated in the many shops plan.

47 - Health Center: The village will not have its own health center, but will use the medical clinic in the Town Center and the wellness clinic in the Suvie Village.

53 - Main Gateway: The village has secured the right to obtain a digital model of a 2,000 year old carved Roman gateway that will be carved in mold form and poured at the entrance to the village along the primary pedestrian street. This gateway will provide shelter from the weather and serve a ceremonial function when welcoming visitors and new residents to the village. The gateway will be made in cast white concrete with a 3-D digitally scanned surface replicating the original.

56 - Bike Paths and Racks: In the center of the streets, two smooth strips of paving will provide comfortable bike and LSV* riding separate from the pedestrian strips and the cobblestone stopping parts of the streets. Generally, everyday bikes are restricted to one-speed, to keep bikes and LSV's to a fast walking pace.

57 - Children in the City: The village is designed to enable children to roam free without the necessity for constant adult supervision. The plaza shall contain play areas where children can be seen, sufficiently separate to not disturb adults also enjoying the plaza.

58 - Carnival: The village plaza shall be designed to accommodate Italian festivals and carnivals.

59 - Quiet Backs: The village has selected an outer location in the VillageTown so one side faces the greenbelt near the public food gardens. The village is in the quieter (but not the quietest) part of the VillageTown noise overlay.

60 - Accessible Green: See Pattern 59, above

61 - Small Public Squares: The Italian Village Square or Piazza is a secondary plaza, meaning it is neither the large size of the town center nor the smallest size of VillageTown plazas. It forms the core of the public life of the village.

69 - Public Outdoor Room: The village plaza provides the needs addressed in this pattern, with separate places for young children wanting to play, teens wanting to enjoy their own company, adults relaxing and old people enjoying sitting in the sun.

74. Adventure Playground: On the village plaza, an area set aside for children includes a low-walled playground divided into parts for different aged and different level of activity children. The low walls stop balls from flying where they should not, but allow adults in the cafés and surrounding workplaces to see what is going on.

74-79 Housing Options: While these are discussed as separate patterns, in the Italian

---

*   LSV - Low Speed Vehicle. A small sized, slow speed vehicle, similar in scale to a golf cart. Most expected to be powered by electricity, but some may use compressed air. LSV's also include longer custom vehicles for delivery, trash collection, emergency services and other non-passenger utility functions.

village the founding buyers determine housing needs. These include conventional large homes as well as small family homes that cost less, smaller couple's homes designed for two people, and elder housing for elders wanting a simple home. Young people buying their own first home opted to live in the Youth Zone.

80 - Self-governing workshops and offices: Most of the business establishments in the Italian village are SME's (Small to Medium Enterprises) or they are remote Telepresence-linked offices where the worker is part of a larger organization, but works independently in the VillageTown.

83 - Master and Apprentices: The businesses and workshops operating in the village are intended to provide for apprenticeships and internships.

84 - Teenage Society: The village plaza includes several cafés where seating is in part owned by the VillageTown rather than the proprietors. This allows teens and adults to sit and socialize as long as they want without the pressure to buy. Some of these tables include board games. In addition, the plaza has seating steps on the side of the Guild Hall that are partially covered so people can sit and hang out. These are intended for use by teens as well as others.

85 - Shopfront Schools: The village supports four primary school classrooms on the plaza, all clustered in one area with sliding internal walls so the classes can be taught separately or teachers can open the walls for various configurations of team-teaching or class sharing. In addition to the formal learning, the students take their free time on the plaza – including dining among adults– where they see many role models of adults and teens going about their daily lives.

86 - Children's Home: The founding villagers discussed the idea of a children's home as described in this pattern, and determined that the open-home nature of the village achieves the same intent.

87 - Individually Owned Shops: This is deemed a very important pattern for both the village and the wider VillageTown, and it is understood that the terms of sale and use within the VillageTown make it very difficult to occupy under other terms.

88 - Street Café: This too is deemed very important, and the plaza provides for several cafés that serve alfresco weather permitting. Indoors next to the café additional room is provided that is owned by the VillageTown both to provide overflow and to allow villagers and visitors to sit without feeling the pressure to buy.

91 - Traveller's Inn: The village will have a small inn, but the large one will be in the Town Center.

94 - Sleeping in Public: Some of the benches in the plaza, those facing the winter sun and sheltered from the high summer sun are designed for people to lie down and take a snooze.

96 - Number of Stories: In the Italian Village, most buildings will be two or three stories, except for the town center which will be four.

100 - Pedestrian Street: All streets are pedestrian, with a primary street connecting directly to the rest of the VillageTown.

106 - Positive Outdoor Space: The village intends to have a romantic rose garden, dedicated to roses and companion planting. The garden will be walled (see pattern 173), designed for sunlight, and have walking and sitting places, some sheltered so they can be enjoyed even in rain. The garden will be cared for by a committee of volunteers, but is fully open to the public.

107, 135, 159, 161, 162 Patterns on Sunlight: Numerous patterns speak to the importance of positioning to take advantage of natural light and the warmth of the sun. These patterns should be incorporated into the village, including decisions on street width in relationship to building height shading, shape of buildings to receive beneficial sunlight but avoid the baking or bleaching sun, and placement of seats where warming sun can be enjoyed, both indoors and out. The village calls for a sunlight analysis of all placements.

108 - Connected Buildings: All relevant buildings in the village shall be connected. In part this is to provide human scale by not separating destinations further than they need to be. It also provides for more energy efficiency as shared walls do not lose heat.

110 - Main Entrance: All homes will have their main entrance on the street. Some may have "set-fronts" (arcade with open living space above) but none will have set-backs. Where buildings provide flats, the access stairways seek to be external, so it is clear how to approach the front of the building. Not all entrances will be the front door however; some

111 - Half-Hidden Garden: Italian homes and workplaces often have a half-hidden garden that can be glimpsed from the street, but private enough to require an invitation to enter. These add texture to the streetscape, breaking it up so it is not a monolith of walls. The extra land does add to the price of the home, but many will deem it worth the money.

112 - Entrance Transition: The entrance transition provides an archway through which visitors transit before coming to the doorway of the building. In larger buildings these provide a transition and give the street more variety.

115 - Courtyards which live: Like the entrance transition, larger buildings and several buildings built around a shared courtyard provide outdoor living with privacy.

118 - Roof Garden: Homes and workplaces in the village are encouraged to use roof space for living, for gardens and a more private outdoor experience. In many cases this will serve as an alternative to back yards.

119 - Arcades: An archetypal part of the Italian village, the vaulted arcade provides weather-sheltered walking space with beauty. These will be used on part of the plaza.

120 - Paths and Goals: The village is part of the VillageTown labyrinth, a way to take hours to explore all the villages without backtracking. The paths are the narrowest of tracks, essentially provided for the pleasure of walking and also to allow walking with more privacy.

121 - Path Shape: The village shuns grids; the streets and paths will wind and curve. Some turns will come from staggering the buildings, and others from the trapezoidal shaped connector homes provided to the artists and perhaps as parallel market homes.

122 - Building Fronts: No setbacks unless there is a convincing specific case.

123 - Pedestrian Density: Given the 24 hour nature of the plaza, with workplaces and classrooms, it is expected density will be higher than projections in this pattern.

124 - Activity Pockets: The edges of the plaza will contain high activity. The cafés with seating extending into the plaza bring people out. People walk the edges to shop, and the students come in and out of their classrooms – noting however that their play area will be halfway between the edge and the center.

125 - Stair Seats: In Florence, Italy's Piazza Della Signoria under the high arcade sheltering sculptures, what appear to be very high steps provides a perfect place for people to sit. This same design will be used in the central plaza of the village, without the Renaissance sculptures.

126 - Something Roughly in the Middle: The Italian plaza is grateful to a benefactor who donated a large classical style water fountain with seating around it, that promises to be an attraction year round, but especially in warm weather.

151- Small Meeting Rooms: The village classrooms will be designed to be used for public meeting space outside the school day. At the end of class, school work on the walls will slide into a wall pocket and school equipment put into locking closets.

153 - Rooms to Rent: Home design should include sufficient exterior entrances to allow parts of the home to be locked off and rented as separate domiciles as face-to-face rentals. For upper floors, such space should use exterior stairways.

154 - Teenager's Cottage: In the village, the provisions of the above pattern 153 will be used to provide comparable living space for teens.

155 - Old Age Cottage: The village will not have many separate detached buildings, but instead offer elder housing. These are ground floor apartments facing the street with no thresholds or other barriers to impaired mobility. They will include safety features such as panic buttons and stoves that shut off when excess smoke or flames are detected. They may be in separate title, or attached to a larger family home, and the title easily converted from separate or attached.

156 - Settled Work: At the onset of the village development plan, work-space planning shall include provision for settled work. This may include workshops attached to elder housing as well as spaces on the plaza and primary street for settled work. Some will be for individuals, and some for groups of elders. Given the uncertain future of national retirement plans, settled work opportunities may become essential to assure a comfortable old age.

157 - Home Workshop: Village microzoning will permit modest, quiet work operations in all homes except those in the quietest secondary streets (and even there, home offices are permitted). Activity is judged on noise, dust, lights, visual amenity and visitor activity including deliveries.

158 Open Stairs: As much as possible, open stairs should be used for both access within a home and where several apartments share a building. They can be provided with roof shelter for bad weather. Open stairs should be designed as an art form to add to the streetscape.

160 - Building Edge: As row houses are built, provide irregular edges, including shifting wall placement so the buildings do not form a continuous flat wall. Provide crenels, indentations and buttresses to break up the flat surfaces and provide space for benches, potted plants, even sculptures and art, as well as access doors for food delivery and hidden solid waste collection.

163 - Outdoor Room: Outdoor rooms are permitted within private residences, noting that some may be provided as rooftop (pattern 118). In order to provide for ground floor outdoor rooms, additional land may be required. Alternatively, an outdoor room can be on an upper floor, but not the rooftop, in essence creating a cut down part of the building. This may especially work facing the front or back street, and if an arcade is built (Pattern 119), the top can serve as an outdoor room, provided it is somewhat but not fully enclosed.

164 Street Windows: Very important for the village. Provide them with seats, and some with balconies, comfortable enough to use and to put out potted flowers and vines. On the plaza design the ground floor windows large enough and low enough that workers can see the plaza life (including working parents seeing their children independently playing outside) and children can look in to observe adults working without disturbing their work.

165 - Opening to the Street: Essential element of work-place design. There are three levels of workplace ranked by their level of visitor & delivery access, and environmental liveliness. The more active the workplace the more it should allow not only visual access – glass windows, but also open access, meaning that when the weather is good, the wall can actually open so people can look in and the workers can breath fresh air.

166 - Gallery Surround: Provide for dimensionality with porches, balconies, verandahs, stairs and elevated walkways as well as arcades, retractable awnings and terraces.

167 - Six foot balconies: Narrow balconies are for hanging out bed linen to air on the rail or for potted plants. Wide balconies are for life, for sitting and living. Balconies may extend out into the village street up to six feet provided they are higher than 10 feet above the ground.

168 - Connection to the Earth: Because all buildings are of mineral aggregate, they shall feel naturally anchored to the earth and then surrounded by paving stones that sheet water away into the streets and gutters. Plants shall be in planters; although they can be permanent with open bottoms to the earth. Gradual connection can be provided especially in the rear if the home faces onto a green-street

171 - Tree Places: "When trees are planed without regard for the special places they can create, they are as good as dead for the people who need them.*" For the most part, trees belong in Nature, in the greenbelt. Very careful selection of any trees within the village is necessary to allow them to work well. The village notes than an ancient oak tree that predated the development shall have its own section of unbuilt land large enough to give it the necessary space for it to live and to be appreciated. The nearby buildings shall be designed to not increase wind speed on the tree, but instead to provide shelter from damaging storms.

173 - Garden Wall: The wall that divides the village from the greenbelt shall be made like an Italian garden wall: about 8 feet tall and designed for growing ivy, with an irregular track. The village will also provide a rose garden with its own garden wall (see pattern 106)

174 - Trellised Walk: Restaurants, art galleries and shops as well as private homes are encouraged to use trellised walks to provide access to rear spaces. Such walks can also be used where the streets turn to provide the trapezoidal angles as open space between the buildings not parallel or at right angles to each other.

175 - Greenhouse: Given the medium density of the village, designers are encouraged to put greenhouses on roofs or as part of a cascading building design where the greenhouse faces the winter sun and brings warm air into the building. In such cases, design heat sink collectors.

181 - The Fire: Due to the pollution challenges of medium density housing, homes may have wood fires without restriction if they install scrubber chimneys that eliminate the soot and toxins that otherwise will foul the air and dirty buildings over time. In the plaza several traditional fireplaces will be permitted including an open pizza oven and a large hearth in the tavern.

190 - Ceiling Height Variety: While ceiling height is a personal decision for each home owner, the village strongly encourages that these be varied, not uniform so that from the streetscape view, window height varies, as does belt lines and other ornamental detail.

191 - The Shape of Indoor Space: The village strongly encourages home owners to use

---

* Ibid *A Pattern Language* Page 798

imagination in indoor space, rather than build a village solely made of large shoe boxes. Take advantage of the capabilities of thick walls. Consider special forms that are bent, that curve, that form living spaces more varied that just the rectangular, straight lined room.

192, 222, 223, 236, 239: Windows - Overlooking Life, Low Sills, Deep Reveals and Small Panes - The window defines the architecture, and in the village they need to be more than just light openings - they need to connect inside life with outdoor. Italian windows tend to be casement, meaning they open fully and are hinged on both sides rather sliding up or to the side. Bifold does work as well, especially given the intended thick walls where the bifold can fold flat on the wall. Some use divided light panes. The thick walls create opportunity for dual sets of windows for the ultimate in soundproofing. The inner set opens inward, the outer side either slides into a pocket in the wall, or folds flat using bifold hinges.

Windows tend to be longer than wider, in a 3:2 ratio or larger, as much as 4:1. Many have working shutters (not plastic imitations) that are used for privacy, to control excess sun and for storm protection. Ornamental surrounds include various shapes of arches, hanging flowers and flower window boxes (build in passive watering lines). Some homes hang clothes out to dry between windows, and this is permitted on specifically designated streets.

197, 206, 207 - Thick Walls, Efficient Structures and Good Materials: Much of the research in this area will be VillageTown wide, using thick walls poured with variable density concrete to achieve high thermal and acoustical insulation at low cost with rapid build and almost infinite variety of surface treatment. The surface treatment is where the architecture defines itself as Italian. Traditionally, hand applied plaster or stone mark the Italian surface. The plaster shows the irregularity of hand application, which becomes more valued, as construction move more and more to a perfectly flat machine-scaled society. In pouring variable density concrete, the art comes in the shaping of the soft plastic mold that is inserted in the form that shapes the exterior wall. The village strongly encourages using this mold to provide ornamental detail. Irregularity can be cast into the wall surfaces; window detail such as arches and sills can be preformed. Oxide based color can be painted on the mold so it blends with the concrete saturating to provide instant finished color. If stone is to be used, including stone tile, these can be affixed to the mold using a binder that is weaker than locking concrete, so the wall becomes tiled instantly.

203 - Child Caves: During the design phase for the village, some of the children participating found the pattern on Children's Caves and too ownership. Inspired by Tolkien, they transformed the pattern into Hobbit Holes, and asked that some be built. The village elected to fund the construction of hobbit holes, some basic and others finished. All scaled for children under 3 feet in height. Some will be on the plaza, others in neighborhood streets, some for young children others for older.

205 - Structure Follows Social Space: This pattern is of the utmost importance when designing buildings and clusters of buildings within the village.

209 - Roof Layout: In the Italian Village, roofs will tend to follow traditional lines which tend to involved flat planes in various shallow angles that were originally driven by clay tiles keeping out water. Some round roofs are based on the dome. As discussed in Pattern 118 and 163 some homes may chose to have a roof garden, which means the open part has a flat, recessed roof with a building-code height wall around it. Some homes, as mentioned in Pattern 21, may choose to have a raised roof, meaning the top floor is built as a flat living roof, and then above it a traditional multi-angled, flat plane roof provides sun and rain protection for outdoor living. Roof height and layout will also be governed by sunlight angle to assure it does not block important sunlight in neighboring buildings. The traditional clay tile finish will be encouraged, although tiles may be made in the industrial park using tinted concrete rather than fired clay imported from Italy.

213, 216, 226, 227 - Columns, Layout, Box Columns, Column Place, Column Connection - Columns are an archetypal part of Italian Architecture, and the industrial park shall host a column factory that manufactures traditionally shaped columns and ornament out of durable aggregates that resemble the traditional carved stone columns. Such columns will be used for arcades and other architectural detail, both structurally and for ornament.

219, 220 - Vaults: Vaulted ceilings and vaulted roofs form part of the tradition of Italian buildings and add an exceptional beauty. The construction tooling will include various preformed vault molds to allow rapid pouring of these complex angled shapes merely by setting the mold in place and installing the required internal reinforcing and any cable conduits. Home owners are strongly encouraged to take advantage of the vault technology in their designs.

229 - Duct Space: While this pattern refers to ducts within buildings, duct planning in the village is a major design challenge. Ducts need to be placed so they can easily be accessed to upgrade utilities as technology changes. In the streets, it is best if they are formed from smooth caps that can be lifted by crane to expose pipes, wires, conduit and channels. Similar caps with trenches should connect to each home, and then accessible ducts provided. Some conduit will be entombed in the thick walls where wires can be drawn in and out easily. Other utilities should follow the service duct recommendations of Pattern 229 showing the wall-ceiling triangle.

241 - Seat Spots: Essential in the design of the Italian village are the right seat spots to encourage the good life pursuits of conviviality, citizenship, artistic, intellectual and spiritual expression. These different activities require different types of seats. Citizenship involves talk, seats and standing room where people look at each other. Conviviality can involve company - comfortably sitting side-by-side in the warm sun. Artistic expression is a seat placed opposite a place worth capturing, especially for sketches, paintings or people

-watching. Seating for intellectual expression may involve the café, or even a table with a built in chess set or backgammon board, as often the convivial aspect of the game provides the setting for the intellectual exchange. Spiritual experience is akin to the artistic – a place of solitude and contemplation.

242 - Front Door Bench: As discussed in Pattern 160, the irregularity of building walls facing the street provides the opportunity for front door benches. These should be encouraged.

243 - Sitting Wall: Sitting walls will be placed in the plaza, especially around the children's play area where parents can sit while their children play. It also serves the function of keeping balls within. In addition, at the neighborhood boundary (Pattern 15), the village plans to provide a bike and pony path that has a sitting wall running down its middle.

244 - Canvas Roofs: The village encourages canvas awnings.

245, 246 - Raised flowers and Climbing Plants: Flowers and climbing plants are defining aspects of the Italian village. Generally, in the urban area they are not in gardens but either in large clay or fired pots, or in raised permanent forms that have an earthen bottom. Climbing plants require careful wall design to assure the plant roots do not start breaking up the wall or getting out of control. While there may be a desire to select fast growing plants to get the mature effect rapidly, note this involves considerably higher long-term maintenance to keep the plants under control.

247 - Paving with Cracks Between the Stones: Some of the most beautiful paving in the world is found on Greek Islands, where they have a grade of marble not adequate for art or slabs but which gives a special irregular sheen as paving. The village intends to seek out paving like this for its streets, preferably locally sourced. If it is unavailable, it will use pavers made in the industrial park. See Pattern 229 for details on how the streets will provide for baby buggies and other wheeled carts.

249 - Ornament: A fundamental design principle in the Italian village is the breaking up of flat wall surfaces to achieve a variety that is more pleasing to the eye. In some cases, this may involve significant ornament, both cast and affixed. Ornament is strongly encouraged, but use of artists and masters of the crafts is advised, as bad ornament can look awful.

250 - Warm Colors: In the Italian village warm colors is the presumption. Yellows, reds, peach, pinks, oranges, and browns tend to cover the spectrum of the Mediterranean surface colors. On occasion, light greens can work, as can pastel blues, but handled with great care. Contrasting colors can be bold - dark green shutters, bold Italian or Spode blue.

Appendix 4: The New Zealand Project

Given the state of the world in 2011, (when this book is being written), the VillageTown Stewards determined that perhaps New Zealand is the best candidate for the first VillageTown project. In a time of economic turmoil, social unrest and uncertainty, New Zealand's distance, climate, low population, and relatively stable economy make it attractive. It is considered one of the safest, most peaceful, beautiful, and stable counties in the world. It also is where several of the key Stewards live.

Global Attraction - Identifying Overseas Buyers

Expatriate New Zealanders: Approximately one in five New Zealanders live overseas. Many of them left to secure opportunities not available in their home country. Often when they have done well in their profession, and are ready to start a family, they come home. The VillageTown will make it much easier for some of those New Zealanders to repatriate. A New Zealand VillageTown campaign would focus attention on this target group. With its Legacy Fund to help businesses make the move and become profitable, it offers economic support that would otherwise be difficult to find. With its investment in a sophisticated infrastructure to support conviviality and culturally-enriched social pursuits, it offers a social environment that can compete with what is on offer overseas.

Talent Search for Immigrants: With New Zealand's open immigration policy, we have the opportunity to search the world for exceptional people and exceptional businesses, and to invite them to move to New Zealand. The most effective way to do this would be to focus on a nationality and create a whole village for that nationality. In this way, families are able to move overseas, but in their village, they will not feel that they are foreigners. This offers a strong form of security. In today's world of global transport and communication, this can be done provisionally – try it for a few years, and if it does not meet expectations, one can return home. We believe those who do try it, will love it and stay.

Local Attraction – Buyers already living in New Zealand

Looking for something better: Much of New Zealand's recent development has been in suburban sprawl. Few are pretty; most follow a formula to maximize profits. As fuel prices rise and congestion grows, the prospect of jumping out of the rat race and into a socially and culturally enriched community appeals. This is especially the case if it offers a strong local economy and provides local protection in the event the State finds it can no longer deliver the level of services it does today. In the local market, focus would be placed on existing and emerging businesses looking for new commercial or industrial offices – find the businesses and their workers will follow. In addition, telepresence would be showcased. Many people in New Zealand find that much of their work is transportable – they work on the phone or on the computer. Their employers would be encouraged to support their move to the VillageTown, understanding that in the long term their costs may be lower, especially in office space and overhead. Unlike working at home, the VillageTown offers the same sort of social stimulation that one finds in the office, thus avoiding the isolation that tends to make telework from home problematic.

Already a Community: One of our VillageTown Stewards trained in Seminary and is active in his local Catholic church. He explains that in addition to the teachings of his faith, for him it is about family. He seeks a community where his neighbors share his values on children – safe, kind, caring, protected from the destructive trends of drug abuse, alcohol, violence, foul-mouthed peer-posturing and alienation found among so many children today. He has seven children of his own, and through his church has a strong social network. He and his wife have done well raising their children: they all have been high achievers in school and the oldest are moving toward promising careers. This Steward commented that through his connections with others in his faith, he believes he could attract enough families to form a whole village. Many of those who may join in are already friends and acquaintances. In that village, the church would be consecrated in his faith, but we would not be surprised if the village also attracted non-Catholics – parents seeking a wholesome family atmosphere for their young children.

We shall strive to identify pre-formed groups such as this one. In addition to this group, there are several other likely ready-to-go candidates. There is a strong environmental movement in New Zealand with people who want to live in ecovillages. They would be likely to find the VillageTown as an appealing place for them to form their village as an an ecovillage. Similarly, the arts community – both the creative artists and their appreciative audience – has a prominent presence in New Zealand. The investment in the Guild Halls to make it unique in the country, and may make the VillageTown the most culturally-concentrated locality in the nation. This will appeal to the arts community. A third area of focus would be the economic-development community. New Zealand works hard to support its locally-emerging industries, with various *hothouse* programs involving mentors, investors and sponsorship. A village devoted to this may find support as it would provide the sort of stimulation (and capital) found in places like Silicon Valley in California.

ALIGNMENT WITH NEW ZEALAND LAW

New Zealand has a remarkable zoning law that governs land use – the Resource Management Act (RMA). While its principles are exceptional, in practice it has tended toward professionalization. Instead of enabling people and communities, it tends to rely on expert planners and lawyers to argue that whatever plan the developer proposes will have only minor adverse effects on the environment. We seek to change that.

The RMA states that its purpose is to promote the sustainable management of natural and physical resources. It defines sustainable management as managing the use, development, and protection of natural and physical resources in a way, or at a rate, which enables people and communities to provide for their social, economic, and cultural well-being and for their health and safety while sustaining the potential of natural and physical resources to meet the reasonably foreseeable needs of future generations; and safeguarding the life-supporting capacity of air, water, soil, and ecosystems; and avoiding, remedying, or mitigating any adverse effects of activities on the environment.

While this is a mouthful of words, from the onset the VillageTown Stewards sought to take the words seriously, and ask how one enables people and communities to provide for their well-being while protecting the environment. Thus, when the organizing company approaches the Council for consent or rule changes to build a VillageTown, they will do so with the highest alignment of intent to law.

The organizing company will enable the people (future villagers) and communities (each of the villages) in a way unprecedented in New Zealand and perhaps in the world. Typically, while the law speaks of enabling people and communities to provide for their wellbeing, it usually is a developer with retained expert consultants who pronounce *the adverse effects will be minor* so the developer gets what he wants. Not so with a VillageTown where it is the people and communities who ask the approving Council to enable them.

The VillageTown plan will propose how it intends to attain and sustain economic well-being for its people and the surrounding region, with a comprehensive, self-supporting local economy that begins with a strong financial foundation. Socially, it will invest in structures and systems that support strong communities – complete communities, not solely the privileged and well off. Culturally, it will make a huge investment in a very broad definition of culture. This includes culture as the arts, the culture of the different village themes, and culture as the knowledge and lore passed from one generation to the next.

In health and safety, the VillageTown plan goes to the heart of modern afflictions. Removing cars instantly has a positive impact: from cleaner air and safer streets, to enabling a more cohesive community that staves off alienation and depression. With better foods and a local medical system focused on making people healthier, not just treating the sick, it intends to set a higher standard of health than that of the nation.

In matters of environmental protection, the VillageTown will have a large development budget and brings a commitment to identify and implement the most proven, sustainable technologies to be found in the world today. It can become a national, or perhaps global, showcase. The walking home range is an excellent example of avoiding, rather than mitigating adverse environmental impact. Removing the need for cars, buses or trains on a daily basis will set the pattern for a whole new form of development and have a greater positive environmental impact than shifting from petroleum to electric cars or trains.

Consider this section to be an essay that proposes to explore new legal territory that happens to be aligned with some of the VillageTown principles. In essence, it looks at a Victorian-era treaty, written in haste, that introduced non-Western concepts into British common law. It introduced a set of legal principles based on an ancient way of life – a way of living locally, before the concept of the nation-state or empire emerged. It set out values that are essentially local. In the past several decades, it has given effect to those values as a national tribunal seeks to right historic wrongdoing. What makes it interesting is a single phrase that exists in the signatories' Maori-language version of the treaty, but not the English version. The key words are *all the people of New Zealand* (see underlined words below) where the document refers to whom the treaty's protections will extend to. Whether all the people of New Zealand can legally claim protection under the Treaty of Waitangi is outside the scope of this essay. That's not the point. It's about the alignment of values.

In 1840, the British representative of Queen Victoria assembled native chiefs to sign a treaty that would enable the Crown to claim sovereignty over lands already populated and governed by the indigenous peoples. In exchange, the Crown promised certain rights or principles that it would guarantee. In doing so, the effect of translation produced two very different documents, both of which are regarded to have legal effect as the founding contract upon which the legal status of New Zealand as a Crown Colony and now a sovereign nation stands. The English version is not particularly relevant to the VillageTowns:

Her Majesty the Queen of England confirms and guarantees to the Chiefs and Tribes of New Zealand <u>and to the respective families and individuals</u> thereof the full exclusive and undisturbed possession of their Lands and Estates Forests Fisheries and other properties which they may collectively or individually possess so long as it is their wish and desire to retain the same in their possession

It reads as a contract between the Maori and the Crown regarding property. However, the Maori version extends these guarantees to *all the people of New Zealand* and it covers a wider range of principles. While these rights have not been tested by other than people of Maori descent, it happens that they have a high level of alignment with the purpose and intent of VillageTowns. They are natural principles of social organization which, in Western Society, were disrupted by the Industrial Revolution. The VillageTown is a post-industrial model that seeks to restore a quality of life that better fits people – a model made possible by new technology to enable people to have priority over large-scale machinery. Thus, we find it useful to introduce a lesson in the Maori language. The Maori version of the English paragraph quoted above, reads as follows:

Ko (now, therefore) te Kuini o Ingarani (the Queen of England) ka wakarite (will fulfill/perform) ka wakaae (will guarantee) ki nga Rangatira (to the leaders) ki nga hapu (to the tribes) --<u>ki (to) nga (the) tangata (people) katoa (all) o (of) Nu Tirani (New Zealand)</u> te tino (the paramount/sacred) rangatiratanga (principle of leadership) o ratou (their) wenua (principle of land) o ratou kainga *(principle of common locality) me o ratou taonga (principle of all that is of value/treasures) katoa (all).*

A literal translation by the Sir Hugh Kawharu as found on the New Zealand government web site reads: *The Queen of England agrees to protect the chiefs, the subtribes <u>and all the people of New Zealand</u> in the unqualified exercise of their chieftainship over their lands, villages and all their treasures.*   (www.waitangi-tribunal.govt.nz/treaty/kawharutranslation.asp)

What are these principles of rangatiratanga, wenua (whenua), kainga and taonga katoa, and why would they be relevant to the VillageTown? Let us explore them:

Kainga: Common Locality: The Village

One of the fundamental bases on which any society is organised is that of locality, since certain spatial relationships are inherent in the very nature of every group, whether settled or migratory. And the great importance of association in a common locality is that it represents not merely a physical fact, but also leads to the formation of a whole body of psychological bonds, due to the common interest of the members and their contact in everyday life. Among the Maori the local group, patent to the eye of every observer, is the village.   p.91 <u>Economics of the New Zealand Maori</u>, 1929 Dr. Raymond Firth – R. E. Owen - Government Printer, Wellington NZ

One of the qualities of the village is that it becomes more than a place to stay. For many living in the modern world, especially in suburbs or high-rise apartments, there is little connection to what Firth calls the common locality. Not so in the VillageTown where one intentionally builds a place that can be loved for many generations.

Thus, it fits wonderfully to build villages in a country that is founded upon the principle of the Crown guaranteeing the unqualified chieftainship over such villages. Rather than make this a challenge to the legal system, make it a showcase. Demonstrate what happens when a community is formed around villages; where people have a say – not merely in the somewhat toothless process of consultation, but the deep experience of being a participant. To better understand this, we next should examine the principle of *rangatiratanga*, which was translated by Sir Hugh Kawharu as *chieftainship*. While literally accurate, use of the word *chieftainship* provides no explanation: a chief can be a tyrant, dictator, autocrat, steward or figurehead, and chieftainship also can mean a process rather than refer to an individual.

Rangatiratanga: The Maori principle of leadership has been a point of contention between Maori activists and the Crown; an issue the VillageTown will avoid. However, we were grateful to Bishop Whakahuihui Vercoe who explained to us that *ranga* comes from the word *to weave*, *tira* is a word for *choir*, and *tanga* is an organized group of people. In other words, the Maori principle of paramount leadership may be understood as *to weave an organized group of people into the harmony of a choir*. In traditional Maori society, leaders are not elected, but acknowledged based on a complex mixture of ancestry, character, conduct, stature and extent of influence. If a leader *blows it*, there is no recall election, they simply are ignored; they lose all status and respect. Thus a good leader listens carefully.

They let everyone have their say and then seek to divine and articulate the wisdom of the group. They weave the people into the harmony of a choir.

This is a very different leadership principle than *life-liberty-property* in which civil order is maintained through what is at the core a *fear-based* system. Do what we say or we will take your property (fines/confiscation), your liberty (imprisonment) or your life (execution).

Local communities do not hold the rights to fine, imprison or execute offenders; that is reserved to the state. At one time, local communities had sufficient moral influence to define acceptable behavior, and as a result, they had a low incidence of crime. Today, modern communities suffer because they lack such a leadership structure. The state steps in only when serious offences occur, with the unfortunate outcome that quality of life declines, and ordinary citizens live in fear for their property and sometimes for their safety.

The VillageTown does not propose to emulate the governance system of Maori, which is deeply rooted in family ties and a particular cultural tradition. But the broader pan-human principles, that happily are guaranteed by the Crown in its founding document, do apply to VillageTown life. In essence, at the village level, the identity of the common locality is structured in a way that on an informal basis, the village will look after its own affairs. Further, on the larger scale of the 20 villages and the Town Center, the VillageTown operates a formal system to enable the people and communities to manage their own affairs, to work toward conflict resolution – to enable people to get along with each other.

The next question one then should ask is *what exactly does the VillageTown concern itself with?* In this, we are reminded of advice from investment banker C.A. Fitts: *Know your farmer, know your banker.* The Maori food sources were their surrounding land and waters. They did not use money (currency), but did use barter and gifting. Let us explore these two principles of *whenua* and *taonga* to see if they too have relevance for the VillageTown.

Whenua: In Maori, a single word will have several meanings, and *whenua* means both *land* and *placenta*. These two meanings have a closer relationship than one may think. Because Maori ate local food, they depended on the surrounding land for their survival. In the modern world, most Maori, like other New Zealanders, eat mostly of food bought in stores or restaurants – global food. Ill health of Maori ranks high in national statistics. Yet in 1929 Raymond Firth wrote: *The Maori may be said to have had a cult of fitness... The Maori was fit because of his mode of life... From dental caries he was remarkably free...*ibid Firth page 53-4

From this we can deduce something obvious: food that is local and not laden with sugars, fats and chemicals is probably better for our health than most foods sold in the supermarkets. Thus as we examine this right to whenua – the land that protects and feeds us, we return to the obvious point that it is better for the VillageTown if it control the lands that will feed it. In addition to the health aspects of this, the 21st century faces a growing global population where *demand* rather than *cost-plus-reasonable-profit* will set the price of food. Under such conditions, it makes sense to decouple VillageTown food from the global market. Secure the unqualified chieftainship over food-producing land (either through outright ownership, or binding contracts and ownership of development rights [that cannot be exercised]). Know your farmer, or perhaps the VillageTown should be its own farmer.

Taonga: In New Zealand, the concept of *taonga* is broad in its meaning. While it is usually translated as treasure, it means more than a pirate's chest of gold, silver and jewels. Language, culture, and intellectual property all are considered taonga. In Maori culture, many aspects of what we call property were collectively owned by the family, not the individual. The wealth of a tribe was measured in the beauty of its communal buildings, the carvings on its *waka* (both inland and ocean-going boats), as well as the eloquence of its speakers, and its knowledge of its indigenous arts and sciences. It is that which is passed down through the generations as well as that of value which is created now and later passed down.

The VillageTown is anchored in the more individualist culture of the West. It encourages and supports private enterprise where individuals and families own the fruits of their labor. Having said that, the VillageTown begins with a substantial profit base set aside to enable those individuals and families maximize their success. It does this because successful individuals and families collectively create what is known as the *commonwealth*. The commonwealth is more than the funds or assets owned by the VillageTown corporation. It is the overall well-being of the community. It is measured by the spirit of the people; how they meet not only their needs, but their aspirations.

In today's global economy, it is important that a community is able to secure its treasures. It is especially important to protect them from predatory practices of large industries which lobby governments and international organizations to write rules and regulations that favor the pecuniary interest of those industries over the commonwealth of the people.

The purpose of this section is not to declare the VillageTown claiming rights under the Waitangi Tribunal or some other official body, but merely to observe the close alignment between its values and that of the Treaty. This is not coincidental. It is the natural outcome of designing a human-based, human-focused framework for community living.

People are inherently social. Most enjoy each other's company. People are more effective when they master skills and work cooperatively – when they specialize. The Industrial Revolution changed the social order, pitting one group against another, such as capitalist versus worker or, in Marxist countries, the elite versus the proletariat. In the post-industrial era, where technology is becoming the new slave class – not a class of humans or animals, but of machines – the principles of a human-scaled society, such as that addressed in New Zealand's Treaty of Waitangi, once again become relevant. We do not propose that a VillageTown emulate the 18th-century Maori model, but merely to extract from New Zealand's founding document relevant principles for today.

Appendix 5: About the Author and the Idea

Claude Lewenz, historian, entrepreneur, classical scholar, philanthropist, is the visionary behind the VillageTown concept. He started his first company at 16, employing three schoolmates to repair defective new Levittown roofs on weekends. After earning his degrees (B.A. History, M.Ed. Administration), Claude worked in public service until age 30, when he entered the emerging field of computer software. He started, built, and ran several profitable companies in business partnership with IBM, while earning a reputation for honesty and ethical conduct. As his career and material well-being flourished in the elite town of Greenwich, Connecticut in the United States – Claude found that something vital was missing: community. When he began to search for community, first throughout America and then the world, he could not find that sense of community that he could see in his imagination. He began to discuss what he imagined, and word got back to Libby Rouse, who with her husband Jim, built some of the most innovative developments in America. She heard his vision and was the first to ask him to promise he would do more than talk about it.

So, in 1995, he negotiated funding for a think tank to explore what eventually became the VillageTown concept. Two years later, at the conclusion of that research, he moved with his family to pristine Waiheke Island, New Zealand, where he continued to develop and refine his ideas into the comprehensive plan you now hold in your hands.

VillageTowns: The Next Step, is Claude's third book on this subject, following 2008's *How To Build a Village* (revised as *How To Build a VillageTown*), and 2010's *Life Liberty Happiness*.

Bio written by James Welcome, Larchmont NY USA

January 23, 2010 Claude's last meeting with VillageTown Stewards Chairman Emeritus Stewart Udall, two months before Stewart passed away in Santa Fe, NM on the Vernal Equinox 2010. Like Libby Rouse, Stewart was another prominent elder who said to Claude "*this work is very important. You must do it. You are young enough to see it through. Do it.*"

Printed in July 2019
by Rotomail Italia S.p.A., Vignate (MI) - Italy